STUDIES IN IMPERIALISM

General editor: Andrew S. Thompson
Founding editor: John M. MacKenzie

When the 'Studies in Imperialism' series was founded by Professor John M. MacKenzie more than thirty years ago, emphasis was laid upon the conviction that 'imperialism as a cultural phenomenon had as significant an effect on the dominant as on the subordinate societies'. With well over a hundred titles now published, this remains the prime concern of the series. Cross-disciplinary work has indeed appeared covering the full spectrum of cultural phenomena, as well as examining aspects of gender and sex, frontiers and law, science and the environment, language and literature, migration and patriotic societies, and much else. Moreover, the series has always wished to present comparative work on European and American imperialism, and particularly welcomes the submission of books in these areas. The fascination with imperialism, in all its aspects, shows no sign of abating, and this series will continue to lead the way in encouraging the widest possible range of studies in the field. 'Studies in Imperialism' is fully organic in its development, always seeking to be at the cutting edge, responding to the latest interests of scholars and the needs of this ever-expanding area of scholarship.

Cultures of decolonisation

Manchester University Press

SELECTED TITLES AVAILABLE IN THE SERIES

WRITING IMPERIAL HISTORIES
ed. Andrew S. Thompson

MUSEUMS AND EMPIRE
Natural history, human cultures and colonial identities
John M. MacKenzie

MISSIONARY FAMILIES
Race, gender and generation on the spiritual frontier
Emily J. Manktelow

THE COLONISATION OF TIME
Ritual, routine and resistance in the British Empire
Giordano Nanni

BRITISH CULTURE AND THE END OF EMPIRE
ed. Stuart Ward

SCIENCE, RACE RELATIONS AND RESISTANCE
Britain, 1870–1914
Douglas A. Lorimer

GENTEEL WOMEN
Empire and domestic material culture, 1840–1910
Dianne Lawrence

EUROPEAN EMPIRES AND THE PEOPLE
Popular responses to imperialism in France, Britain, the Netherlands, Belgium, Germany and Italy
ed. John M. MacKenzie

SCIENCE AND SOCIETY IN SOUTHERN AFRICA
ed. Saul Dubow

Cultures of decolonisation

TRANSNATIONAL PRODUCTIONS
AND PRACTICES, 1945–70

Edited by
Ruth Craggs and Claire Wintle

MANCHESTER UNIVERSITY PRESS

Copyright © Manchester University Press 2016

While copyright in the volume as a whole is vested in Manchester University Press, copyright in individual chapters belongs to their respective authors, and no chapter may be reproduced wholly or in part without the express permission in writing of both author and publisher.

Published by Manchester University Press
Oxford Road, Manchester M13 9PL
www.manchesteruniversitypress.co.uk

British Library Cataloguing-in-Publication Data
A catalogue record for this book is available from the British Library

ISBN 978 1 5261 3430 1 paperback

First published by Manchester University Press in hardback 2016

The publisher has no responsibility for the persistence or accuracy of URLs for any external or third-party internet websites referred to in this book, and does not guarantee that any content on such websites is, or will remain, accurate or appropriate.

Typeset
by JCS Publishing Services Ltd, www.jcs-publishing.co.uk

CONTENTS

List of illustrations—vii
List of contributors—ix
Acknowledgements—xi

Introduction: Reframing cultures of decolonisation
Ruth Craggs and Claire Wintle — 1

PART I – Decolonising metropolitan cultures?

1 Black America and the overthrow of the European colonial order: The tragic voice of Richard Wright *Bill Schwarz* — 29

2 Humanist modernism: Ralph Hotere and 'New Commonwealth Internationalism' *Damian Skinner* — 51

3 Henry Swanzy, Sartre's zombie? Black Power and the transformation of the Caribbean Artists Movement *Rob Waters* — 67

4 Anxiety abroad: Austerity, abundance and race in post-war visual culture *David C. Wall* — 86

PART II – Performing decolonisation

5 The peasant armed: Bengal, Vietnam and transnational solidarities in Utpal Dutt's *Invincible Vietnam* *Abin Chakraborty* — 109

6 Cultural heritage as performance: Re-enacting Angkorian grandeur in postcolonial Cambodia (1953–70) *Michael Falser* — 126

7 'I still don't have a country': The southern African settler diaspora after decolonisation *Jean Smith* — 156

PART III – Decolonising expertise

8 Managing the cultural past in the newly independent states of Mali and Ghana *Sophie Mew* — 177

CONTENTS

9 More than tropical? Modern housing, expatriate practitioners and the Volta River Project in decolonising Ghana *Viviana d'Auria* — 196

10 Designing change: Coins and the creation of new national identities *Catherine Eagleton* — 222

11 What colonial legacy? The Dewan Bahasa dan Pustaka (House of Language) and Malaysia's cultural decolonisation *Rachel Leow* — 245

Index—265

ILLUSTRATIONS

		page
2.1	Ralph Hotere, *Polaris*, 1962, acrylic on hardboard, 610 x 510 mm (Private collection, by permission of the Hotere Foundation Trust)	57
2.2	Ralph Hotere, *Algérie*, 1962, oil on hardboard, 1210 x 740 mm (Private collection, by permission of the Hotere Foundation Trust)	59
2.3	Ralph Hotere, *Black Painting*, 1964, acrylic on wood, 1207 x 1207 mm (Auckland Art Gallery Toi o Tāmaki, purchased 1965, by permission of the Hotere Foundation Trust)	60
4.1	John Bratby, *Jean and Still Life in Front of Window*, 1954, oil on canvas, 1220 x 1080 mm (Southampton City Art Gallery, Hampshire, John Bratby Estate by courtesy of Julian Hartnol/Bridgeman Images)	95
4.2	Richard Hamilton, *Just What Is It That Makes Today's Homes So Different, So Appealing?* 1956, collage, 260 x 248 mm (Kunsthalle Tübingen, Tübingen, by permission of the Kunsthalle Tübingen, Collection Zundel)	98
6.1	The 'Ploughing of the Sacred Furrow', performed by Norodom Sihanouk on 27 April 1967 on Angkor Thom's Royal Square inside the Archaeological Park of Angkor (*Kambuja*, 26 (15 May 1967), 60–1)	132
6.2	Norodom Sihanouk and the Independence Monument during the sixteenth anniversary of Cambodia's National Independence, 9 November 1969 (*Kambuja*, 57 (December 1969): 22–3)	135
6.3a	The Royal Khmer Ballet performing in San Francisco's Sheraton Hotel on 16 October 1958 (Private archive Charles Meyer/Paris)	137
6.3b	Princess Bopha Devi as dancing Apsara in front of the bas-reliefs of Angkor Wat (*Cambodge d'Aujourd'hui* (July/August 1962), 46–7 and 22)	137
6.4	The *son et lumière* show at Angkor Wat during the visit of Charles de Gaulle, 1 September 1969 (*Photo-Souvenirs du Cambodge: Sangkum Reastr Niyum, 1955–1969, vol. 7* (Phnom Penh: Ramat Print, 1993), pp. 166–7)	144
6.5	Phnom Penh's National Stadium during the celebrations of Cambodia's fifteenth anniversary of National Independence	

on 9 November 1968 (*Photo-Souvenirs du Cambodge: Sangkum Reastr Niyum, 1955–1969*, Vol. 3 (Phnom Penh: Ramat Print, 1993), pp. 349–50) 146
9.1 Map of the Volta River Project, 1966 (Drawing by author) 199
9.2 Maxwell Fry and Jane Drew, drawing for 'Fry Drew Flat' (four-storey flat for high-income 'cosmopolitan' residents), 1954–59 (Tema Development Corporation Archives, courtesy of Tema Development Corporation Archives) 204
9.3 Women and men at work in the resettlement town of Ajena, c. 1962 (Charles Abrams, *Man's Struggle for Shelter in an Urbanising World* (Cambridge: MIT Press, 1964), unpaginated image section. © Massachusetts Institute of Technology, by permission of The MIT Press) 208
9.4 Mayer & Whittlesey, master plan for aluminium smelter township, Volta River Project, for Aluminium Laboratories Limited, 1955–56 (Preparatory Commission, *The Volta River Project, Vol. 2: Appendices to the Report of the Preparatory Commission* (London: HMSO, 1956), unpaginated) 211
9.5 Doxiadis Associates, density studies of verandah-equipped row-housing and multistorey blocks in Tema's Community Class Sector, 1964 (Constantinos A. Doxiadis Archives, Doxiadis Associates, DOX GHA A-88, Low-income Housing in Tema, Athens, 1964, pp. 23, 25, 33. © Constantinos and Emma Doxiadis Foundation) 216
10.1 Shilling coin, Uganda, 1966 (British Museum, 1970,0401.141. © Trustees of the British Museum) 226
10.2 Christopher Ironside, design options for the Tanzanian coinage, 1965, as shown to the Royal Mint Advisory Committee (British Museum, Christopher Ironside Archive, 2006,0601.428. © Trustees of the British Museum/Crown Copyright) 230
10.3 Final version of the one-shilingi coin, Tanzania, 1966 (British Museum, Christopher Ironside Collection, 2006,0601.59. © Trustees of the British Museum) 232
10.4 One-shilling coin, Kenya, 1966 (British Museum, 1970,0401.83. © Trustees of the British Museum) 234
10.5 Gold coins celebrating Jomo Kenyatta's seventy-fifth birthday, 1966 (British Museum, 1966,1106.1-3. © Trustees of the British Museum) 236

CONTRIBUTORS

Viviana d'Auria is Assistant Professor in International Urbanism at the Department of Architecture, KU Leuven (Belgium), and Rubicon Research Fellow at the Department of Geography, Planning and International Development Studies, University of Amsterdam (The Netherlands). Exploring 'practised' architecture is an integral part of her research within a more general interest in the trans-cultural construction of cities and their contested spaces.

Abin Chakraborty is currently teaching as Assistant Professor in the Department of English in Chandernagore College. His articles have been published in several national and international journals and he is the co-editor of *Uneven Terrains: Critical Perspectives in Postcolonialism*.

Ruth Craggs is a Lecturer in Human Geography at King's College London. Her research focuses on decolonisation, the Commonwealth and modern architecture and planning. She is on the editorial board of the *London Journal* and *Round Table: The Commonwealth Journal of International Affairs*.

Catherine Eagleton is Head of Asian and African Collections at the British Library and was previously Curator of Modern Money at the British Museum, where she led the Money in Africa research project.

Michael Falser (MA, MSc, PhD) is an architect and art historian by formation and senior researcher and project leader at the Chair of Global Art History at the 'Cluster of Excellence "Asia and Europe in a Global Context: The Dynamics of Transculturality"' at Heidelberg University, Germany. From 2009 onwards his 'Habilitation' project investigated the formation of the modern concept of cultural heritage by charting its colonial, postcolonial/nationalist and global trajectories through a case study of Angkor Wat.

Rachel Leow is Lecturer in Modern East Asian History at Cambridge University and a Fellow of Murray Edwards College.

Sophie Mew (MA, PhD) is an independent researcher specialising in the formation of cultural institutions and the display of cultural heritage

CONTRIBUTORS

in the UK and West Africa. In addition to publishing on this subject, she has worked with the musée national du Mali and the British Museum since 2000 and founded a series of collaborative photography exhibitions (*Bamako&London*) between Mali and the UK.

Bill Schwarz teaches in the School of English and Drama at Queen Mary, University of London. He is an editor of *History Workshop Journal*.

Damian Skinner is an art historian and Curator of Applied Art and Design at the Auckland War Memorial Museum Tāmaki Paenga Hira. He is part of the Multiple Modernisms research project (www.multiplemodernisms.org).

Jean Smith holds a Leverhulme Trust Early Career Fellowship at King's College London. Her research focuses on migration, settler colonialism and decolonisation. Her work has appeared in *Twentieth Century British History* and *Women's History Review*.

David Wall is Assistant Professor of Visual and Media Studies in the Department of Art at Utah State University. He is currently working on a book project entitled *Space, Place, and Empire: Art, Culture, and Crisis* in post-war Britain.

Rob Waters teaches in the Department of English at Queen Mary University of London.

Claire Wintle is a Senior Lecturer in the History of Art and Design at the University of Brighton. Her research focuses on museums, material culture, empire and decolonisation. Her book, *Colonial Collecting and Display: Encounters with Material Culture from the Andaman and Nicobar Islands*, was published by Berghahn in 2013.

ACKNOWLEDGEMENTS

This edited collection arose from the conference 'Cultures of Decolonisation' which took place in May 2012 at the Institute of Commonwealth Studies, School of Advanced Studies, University of London. We would like to thank all those who presented at and attended the conference and made it such a success. Thanks in particular go to Liz Buettner, Felix Driver, Philip Murphy and Bill Schwarz for their enthusiastic support of the conference and the wider project. Thanks also to the Institute of Commonwealth Studies, the University of Brighton and St Mary's University College for supporting the event.

We would like to thank the series editors, John MacKenzie and Andrew Thompson, managing editor, Emma Brennan, and the team at Manchester University Press for their support throughout the production of this book. We are grateful to the reviewers of the book proposal and manuscript for their useful input on the volume as a whole. Finally, thanks go to the chapter authors for their fascinating contributions and for their encouragement with the overall project.

INTRODUCTION

Reframing cultures of decolonisation
Ruth Craggs and Claire Wintle

In London, in 1962, as the sun continued to set on the British Empire, the Commonwealth Institute opened the doors of its new exhibition complex. Designed by Robert Matthew, Johnson-Marshall and Partners, the purpose-built modernist building outwardly eschewed an imperial past; it represented an optimistic vision for a Commonwealth successfully transformed by recent global constitutional shifts from a pre-war 'white' club into an egalitarian multiracial family. The institute's architects had opted for innovation and change, utilising a futuristic, curving, tent-like roof and slender concrete beams to provide unobstructed views across the exhibition hall inside. The fabric of the building itself was intended to represent collaboration and equality in a decolonised world, with the copper of the roof gifted by the Northern Rhodesia Chamber of Mines, the hardwood floors of the galleries donated by the governments of Nigeria and Ghana, and decorative timbers sent as gifts from various other independent countries of the Commonwealth.[1] For Kenneth Bradley, the director of the institute, the inauguration of this new complex was a crucial opportunity for those involved to 'throw away our old imperial spectacles'.[2] Indeed, seen through the lens of the institute's publicity material, the story of this cultural site provides a useful, applied example of the established narrative of twentieth-century decolonisation as a neat, amicable and graceful retreat from power.

But if the annual reports and the visitor guides of the Commonwealth Institute provide insight into the official line of decolonisation as viewed from the metropole, further investigations also reveal the 'end of empire' at the institute (and beyond) as a more complex phenomenon. Some of the institute's exhibits were directly transferred from its predecessor, the Imperial Institute, and much of their content reflected a view of the colonial past as unproblematic.[3] The arrangement of the space continued to privilege an Anglo-

[1]

centric view of the world, and in many ways the Commonwealth was positioned as the fulfilment of a teleological British imperial narrative.[4] For R.S. Hudson, the British chairman of the institute's Board of Governors, the value of the institution was in 'preserving *our* cultural leadership of the Commonwealth'.[5] Yet these (neo-)colonial aspects of the institute were also countered by the diversity of its management, curatorial practices and audiences. Whilst the building was sited in London, it was managed by a board of governors dominated by Commonwealth high commissioners who had a substantial role and vested interest in shaping the exhibits concerning their respective countries. Dioramas for the Indian exhibit, for example, were made by the institute's artist, but funded by an Indian businessman to a design approved by the Indian High Commission. In turn, the institute's staff actively courted the perspectives of those they hoped to represent.[6] Moreover, the institute opened in a city that was also rapidly changing. Growing numbers of migrants had begun to arrive in London from the Commonwealth from the late 1940s onwards, reaching a peak before immigration controls were tightened from 1962. Many Commonwealth immigrants settled in Bayswater, Kensal Rise and Notting Hill – neighbourhoods close to the institute in Holland Park – and their children formed some of the numerous school groups trooping through its doors. Against a backdrop of the racist tropes of threat, miscegenation and national decline that often accompanied discussions of Commonwealth immigration, the institute was one of the only spaces for the valorisation of the Commonwealth and its member states in the city.[7]

The institute, then, functioned on multiple levels: through the approaches of its staff, governors and visitors, and through its architecture and displays, it was in turn a neo-colonial and liberal arena founded on British self-interest, collaboration *and* influence from the 'periphery'. Sites such as the Commonwealth Institute provide us with valuable insight into the mechanics of decolonisation beyond constitutional change. In the production and consumption of the institute's displays, we see decolonisation as a nuanced process which retained imperial characteristics but was also influenced by the multiple and ambivalent agendas of both the formerly colonised and former colonisers.[8] Yet, just as cultural forms can provide today's students of the demise of empire with a crucial historical tool, for those involved at the time, objects, images and literary texts were also valued as important instruments of decolonisation. In the case of the Commonwealth Institute, for example, officials from the Canadian Government's Information Division had considered redirecting funds to other causes but ultimately maintained their support for the institute, in part as a way to encourage emigration to Canada, but also because they feared 'Canadian unwillingness would ... be taken as a sign of disinterest in or dissatisfaction with the Commonwealth.'[9] More specifically, officials worried that 'failure to [remain involved] would set Canada against the other senior members of the Commonwealth (which are more friendly towards the activities of the Institute)'.[10] This brief example hints at the efficacy of utilising cultural forms to explore the political shifts of the middle years of the twentieth century. It emphasises their active role in diplomacy and their perceived importance in fostering the international connections that inflected political change during this period. Architecture and exhibition design, artistry and spatial arrangement, cultural diplomacy, institutional structure, the economics of cultural production, and audiences for culture are all integrated into the mechanics of decolonisation.

Yet the Commonwealth Institute is not unique in its utility. *Cultures of Decolonisation* draws on visual, literary and material cultures in order to evidence the complex role of cultural forms in decolonisation. We argue that the examination of a broad range of cultural productions and practices reveals the diverse ways in which cultures were active in wider political, economic and social change, working as crucial gauges, microcosms and agents of decolonisation. In this opening chapter, we begin by exploring the existing historiography of decolonisation, before explaining the interdisciplinary and transnational approach of the volume. We then delineate our approach to reframing the role of culture in decolonisation, highlighting three main arguments and strands of investigation. First, a claim is made for the agency of culture in a process more often understood through a political-economic lens; second, the value of focusing on the role of cultural institutions in decolonisation is emphasised; and third, we contend that it is crucial to recognise the transnational and comparative character of cultures of decolonisation (and of decolonisation itself). Finally, the structure of the book and the contributions of individual authors are introduced in detail.

Here, and in the following chapters, we contribute to the theoretical, methodological and empirical diversification of the historiography of decolonisation, arguing for the need to engage with the complexities of decolonisation as enacted and experienced by a broad range of actors beyond 'flag independence' and the realm of high politics. We consider 'decolonisation' to include formal acts of withdrawal from the colonies, but also anti-colonial struggles and neo-colonial models of 'freedom' and the social acts of reimagining and practising European and colonial lives after empire. Although decolonisation as a process is evidently ongoing, and it is clear that many acts of decolonisation find their roots in the nineteenth and early twentieth centuries, we argue that the mid-twentieth-century period provides an important focus for research, and thus the volume focuses on the years between 1945 and 1970. Differentiated from earlier and later periods by the intensity and geographical reach of constitutional decolonisation, these years were also understood by many contemporary actors as defined by these transformations. Rather than see the moment of constitutional handover as a date after which decolonisation is complete and scholarship begins or ends, we conceptualise this particular period as a global 'decolonising moment' from which to spin out temporally and geographically, highlighting the diverse but often interconnected cultures through which decolonisation was practised, experienced, represented and wrought.

A series of questions is posed throughout the volume: what were the distinctive cultures of decolonisation that emerged in the years between 1945 and 1970, and what can they uncover about the complexities of the 'end of empire' as a process? How did these cultures reflect, but also influence, the processes of dramatic geopolitical change wrought by the dismantling of European empires? How were cultures of decolonisation produced through transnational connections between people, institutions, ideas and things? And how does comparison – between places, and between different creative outputs – help to reveal the complex processes of decolonisation?

These questions build on what has now become a rich field of academic interest, yet the study of decolonisation has taken time to mature. Curiously, for some time at least, the historiographical silos of the twentieth century prevented a thorough engagement with the period and processes of decolonisation. In many studies of the post-1945 world, decolonisation remained demoted to a subplot feeding into the more prominent narratives of European post-war reconstruction, the Cold War and the ascendancy of the United States.[11] Still today, histories of empire often finish before decolonisation, or examine it only cursorily, while even research influenced by postcolonial theory has shown a remarkable inattention to this period of formal political decolonisation. Thus, while scholars in history, geography, art and design history, literature and other disciplines – often drawing on the ground-breaking work of Edward Said and his subsequent critics – have now produced careful, highly textured accounts of the relationships between culture and imperialism in a range of contexts, their work has generally stopped short of the mid-century era of decolonisation.[12] Instead, this body of material has focused on the nineteenth- and early twentieth-century period of high imperialism, or jumped forward to the present day, utilising postcolonial theory to address current injustices.[13] In the process, in some arenas, decolonisation has been quietly underestimated, imagined as a containable and peaceful moment of constitutional change, left, in the main, to specialists in constitutional history.[14] Yet this investigation into high politics by way of a heavily edited imperial archive promulgates the myth that decolonisation was effected, in John Darwin's words, 'over tea in an atmosphere of sweetness and light'.[15] Moreover, by focusing overwhelmingly on understanding why decolonisation happened, traditional accounts have foregrounded political impulses and underlying economic motivations, rather than exploring how culture was interwoven with imperial collapse.[16]

However, as is now clear, the process of decolonisation was one of the most important and protracted shifts in the geopolitical landscape of the twentieth century. The historiographical and imaginative divides that once promoted a sense that 'independence' constituted a point at which colonial history ended and the 'postcolonial' period began are now being rewritten to acknowledge decolonisation as a long-term, as yet incomplete, political and economic shift.[17] Building on the influence of feminist and postcolonial theory and their advocates across the humanities and the social sciences, and on the momentum of the 'new' imperial history, there have also been calls for a more comprehensive social and cultural history of decolonisation.[18] Increasingly, this challenge is being met.

Over the last twenty years, for example, there has been a proliferation of writings on the pervasive impact of decolonisation on British society. Contributions to Manchester University Press's Studies in Imperialism series, and the pioneering work of the founding editor of the series, John MacKenzie, provided some of the first investigations on this theme, whilst the various reflections of Bill Schwarz on the racialisation of England in the middle years of the twentieth century have also directed the field.[19] Stuart Ward's 2001 edited volume on *British Culture and the End of Empire* provided the first book-length project dedicated to investigating decolonisation in Britain as a cultural phenomenon. The contributors set out to critique the contention that decolonisation failed to register in the British consciousness, contesting what Ward termed the 'minimal impact thesis' by drawing careful attention to the ambivalence and anxiety experienced in Britain during this time.[20] In the years since the publication of Ward's collection, a steady stream of important contributions further nuancing these assertions has emerged. For example, the first of Schwarz's three-volume series on the making of Britain's post-war racial politics places party politics and political heavyweights, from Jan Smuts to Enoch Powell, at the heart of its analysis. Yet, unlike more traditional politically focused accounts of decolonisation, these figures are used to unpack the idea of the 'white man' and his creation during and after empire through myth and memory.[21] Jordanna Bailkin's research on personal experiences of the welfare system in Britain and Elizabeth Buettner's writings on the lives of empire employees, families, settlers and repatriates have both demonstrated the value of progressing beyond considerations of constitutional wrangling, the transfer of power and the 'official mind' to examine the lived experiences of decolonisation of a wide range of subjects.[22] Notably, Buettner's more recent work investigates decolonisation as experienced across other European metropolitan centres, comparing the domestic impact of decolonisation, postcolonial migration and the emergence of contemporary multicultural societies in Britain, France, the Netherlands, Belgium and Portugal.[23]

Increasingly, scholars have also drawn upon images, objects, texts and cultural institutions to investigate the composition of decolonisation and its impact on metropolitan societies. Exploring the 'end of empire' through the lens of visual culture, Simon Faulkner and Anandi Ramamurthy have argued that the fracturing of imperial culture during decolonisation created a particular milieu that allowed new cultural forms and identities to emerge.[24] Wendy Webster's work on mainstream British media, Simon Potter's study of the British Broadcasting Corporation (BBC), and a recent spate of important edited volumes investigating documentary and non-fiction film and the novel have all provided rich detail on the contested, pervasive nature of decolonisation in Britain.[25] While writing on Dutch metropolitan cultures of decolonisation has tended to prioritise the identity politics of contemporary 'postcolonial migrants' in the Netherlands today rather than engage with mid-twentieth-century cultures directly, the literature on the impact of decolonisation in the French cultural sphere between 1945 and 1970 is increasingly rich, with contributions by Robert Aldrich on the role of monuments and museums as sites of memory and Daniel J. Sherman on the adaptability of museums, fine art and tourist practices leading the field.[26]

Much of this material is firmly grounded in a postcolonial framework that recognises the 'metropole' and the 'colony' as mutually constitutive, yet there is a focus here on decolonising cultures within metropolitan arenas. In part, of course, this is because 'decolonisation' is a term most commonly employed by colonising nations; in discussions about the perspectives of those in the colonies and former colonies, 'liberation', 'independence' or 'nationalism' continue to be more regularly used as active terms which intentionally remove the 'colonial' from the process entirely.[27] Highly significant studies have, however, engaged with 'decolonisation' beyond this metropolitan focus and prioritised the perspectives and agency of those located beyond Europe. Key contributions in the 'decentred' cultural history of decolonisation and anti-colonialism include Frederick Cooper's work on labour relations in Africa, Philippa Levine's writing on 'gendering decolonisation', and a series of recent edited volumes: James D. Le Sueur's *Decolonization Reader*, for example, gathers together seminal contributions on the subject, grouping them under subtitles such as 'Economy and labor', 'Race and ethnicity' and 'Gender and sexuality', while Els Bogaerts and Remco Raben have assembled new material on the social dimensions of decolonisation and its impact on public security, the urban environment and the reorientation of economies in Africa and Asia.[28] There is also an emerging literature on the ways in which literary, cinematic and visual texts, as well as material cultures and institutions, have provided a voice for and insight into those experiencing the 'end of empire' in the colonies: scholarship concerned with these themes in Africa, the Caribbean and India, especially, has enlivened the field.[29]

Many of these accounts focus on one nation's experience of decolonisation. Yet there is a danger that a focus on the cultures of individual nations fragments what is actually a global history, and severs the interconnections and networks uniting different empires, anti- and post-colonial movements, geographical regions and individual countries.[30] Susan Legêne and Martijn Eickhoff have argued that in post-Second World War Europe, histories were often constructed to commemorate national (rather than pan-European) stories of empire or to support the nation-building process of the (singular) independent state.[31] The value of comparative work on the end of empire is increasingly being acknowledged, but the wider historiographical trend of placing the bounded nation at the heart of decolonisation studies persists and is particularly noticeable in studies of cultural forms.[32] Many accounts of culture in decolonisation also focus on a single genre of cultural production, such as visual culture, film or museum displays, leaving the important commonalities and connections between creative genres unexamined.[33] There is therefore opportunity to bring together analyses of different productions and practices across wide-ranging geographical contexts in order to investigate the full complexities of decolonisation.

Cultures of Decolonisation addresses this lacuna. Interdisciplinary and international perspectives are utilised to develop a case for understanding decolonisation through the lens of culture. Both 'high' and 'popular' material in visual and literary forms are embraced in this volume, with chapters considering novels, non-fiction, fine art, film, poetry, theatre, architecture, heritage sites, museums, festivals, coin design, language, interior design, dress and leisure activities. There is an emphasis on objects, images and words as texts and tangible entities, but the authors also engage with the processes and practices that were involved in the production and consumption of specific media as well as the sites, institutions and discursive frameworks through which they operated. In the following chapters, therefore, we find not only objects and texts but also the perceptions, opinions and actions of artists, poets, playwrights, authors, designers, museum professionals, architects, linguists and their multiple publics.

The volume brings together studies from across the disciplines of architecture, English literature, geography, history of art and design, history, and museum studies. Adopting this interdisciplinary perspective highlights the value of analysing diverse cultural forms alongside one another: through these juxtapositions, common political, economic and aesthetic concerns become clear, as do the specificities of local cultural responses. The contributions exemplify the variety of methods and sources – from oral history interviews to the analysis of theatrical performances, from the examination of the built environment to the analysis of domestic material culture – through which to study decolonisation.

Bringing together diverse geographical case studies provides similar insights by uncovering the commonalities and connections between different decolonising locations, as well as highlighting the multiple influences of individual and institutional actors, including colonial officials, nationalist leaders, architects and writers, located in a wide range of places. In particular, through this interdisciplinary approach, an understanding of the pivotal but also highly cosmopolitan and transnational nature of metropolitan cultures in decolonisation is progressed, the impact of performance on individual, national and transnational decolonising identities can be considered in novel ways, and the role of experts in the political and cultural shifts of the middle years of the twentieth century is evaluated anew. These ideas are examined, in turn, in the three parts of this volume. However, before outlining the structure of *Cultures of Decolonisation*, the following pages will highlight three important themes which run throughout the book – themes which promise to reframe our understanding of the middle years of the twentieth century. It is to these we now turn.

INTRODUCTION

The agency of cultural forms in decolonisation

The chapters in *Cultures of Decolonisation* each stress the active role that visual, material and literary cultures and creative arenas played on the process of decolonisation. Throughout the volume, cultural forms emerge as crucial sites for the commentary, reflection, activation and articulation of agendas that promoted constitutional and wider shifts. Here, in line with recent scholarship which has argued for the 'agency' of objects and shown that almost all social relations are mediated by way of material things, we examine the world of decolonisation beyond only human actors to see the impact of the visual, material and literary on the political and economic spheres.[34] People construct their identities and points of view through the production and consumption of the material and visual world;[35] as (former) colonisers and the (formerly) colonised constructed new positions and affiliations across a rapidly changing globe, visual and material culture and the written word acted as powerful tools with which to generate, acknowledge and celebrate these identities.[36] The creative processes of reflection, selection and experimentation enacted by authors, designers and artists, amongst others, forced active consideration of, and engagement with, this changed world.[37] In articulating his thoughts on the end of empire through the writing of texts such as *Black Power* or *The Color Curtain*, Richard Wright, the African-American intellectual discussed by Bill Schwarz in Chapter 1, negotiated, managed and cemented his ideas on the subject; for the architects involved in the development of housing projects for a newly independent Ghana considered by Viviana d'Auria in Chapter 9, navigating the practicalities of a decolonising economy and society through building design transformed their own architectural and political understandings.

The production and reception of cultural forms also helped to create the communal as well as personal identities upon which decolonisation was built: for the Bengali audiences that came together to watch the anti-colonial plays analysed by Abin Chakraborty in Chapter 5, the ritual of going to the theatre and their mutual spectatorship would have worked to forge solidarity and a communal perspective – here in support of freedom in both India and Vietnam.[38] Similar processes would perhaps have been experienced by those who came together to participate in the cultural festivals held to celebrate Malian independence as discussed by Sophie Mew in Chapter 8.

In these chapters we also get a sense of the discursive power of literary, visual and material cultures in influencing audiences and promoting change. For those whose economic and political power was

[9]

limited, objects, images and texts that could be cheaply replicated and disseminated held great value, while the mobility and accessibility of the visual had a particular significance for those who wished to communicate across boundaries of language. Creative outputs ranging from anthropological texts and paintings to advertisements and museums have long been recognised as constituting some of the 'apparatuses' that Michel Foucault identified as regulating the social body.[39] The visual and textual shaped audience attitudes and approaches to decolonisation and the nationalism, anti-imperialism and neo-colonialism therein.[40] Understanding this, the politicians in East Africa described by Catherine Eagleton in Chapter 10 had a vested interest in how their leaders and nations were represented in the coin design produced for their newly independent states; for the government of an independent Malaysia, as Rachel Leow argues in Chapter 11, postcolonial language policy was a rich ground for rejecting the identity of the former oppressors and distributing a homogeneous Malay replacement. Notably, cultural productions were not always used to promote the new, forward-facing, identities forged during the middle years of the twentieth century: while in Chapter 4 David C. Wall argues that both art and film registered the changing dynamics of nationhood and ethnicity in British society in the 1940s and 1950s, for some of the British South Africans and Rhodesians described by Jean Smith in Chapter 7, retaining material culture from a period before the end of empire functioned as an important method of displacing and disavowing unwelcome political change. Moreover, cultural items did not need to be new to support independence: as Michael Falser shows in Chapter 6, the temple site of Angkor, constructed between the ninth and the thirteenth centuries CE, became a central part of the staging of new Cambodian nationalist regimes.

Cultural forms also provided important frameworks for enacting and subverting traditional gender roles during decolonisation. Many of the chapters in *Cultures of Decolonisation* focus on male actors, perhaps reflecting yet another hierarchy of power that was present during the middle years of the twentieth century (and which might still be present in the retelling of decolonisation).[41] Indeed, the artistic productions of this period often cemented a long convention of presenting women as subject to the 'male gaze': the majority of the artists and film-makers discussed by Wall in Chapter 4, for example, frame women as possessions and subjects, rather than as agents in their own right. As Philippa Levine has argued, independence struggles often led to the suppression of women's rights within a nationalist framework.[42] However, in some of the chapters there is select evidence that the cultural outputs and institutions of decolonisation provided a platform for women to articulate their disparate decolonising agendas, and to destabilise traditional gender hierarchies. As Chakraborty notes in Chapter 5, female characters in the plays of Bengali playwright Utpal Dutt were often framed as 'independent and active agents of rebellion and struggle'. In Chapter 6 Falser demonstrates how Princess Kossamak, the mother of Norodom Sihanouk, took a central role in producing the visual symbols that fed Cambodian anti-colonial nationalism. The example of British architect Jane Drew, whose professional success in West Africa, South Asia, Europe and the Middle East is highlighted in a number of the chapters, demonstrates that, particularly for white women, visual, material and literary activities in late colonialism and decolonisation often provided opportunities for mobility, freedom and expert recognition. Focusing on the romantic partnerships of Constance Webb and C.L.R. James, Ellen and Richard Wright, and Dorothy Pizer and George Padmore, in Chapter 1, Schwarz notes not only the key roles of these women in the construction and maintenance of informal intellectual and social networks of anti-colonial thought and action, but also their writerly contributions to decolonisation. Cultural productions and practices thus forged new understandings, opinions and possibilities within broader processes of decolonisation.

Institutions of decolonisation: expertise, development, disavowal

There is a strong focus in *Cultures of Decolonisation* on the role of cultural institutions such as museums, artists' groups and architectural practices. This emphasis illuminates the role of these organisations as important platforms for the new artworks, displays and styles that promoted decolonisation. Yet, examining such sites allows us to explore the ways in which decolonisation was a complex, multifaceted process in which culture, politics and economics were inseparable. Eagleton's study of the Royal Mint (Chapter 10), for example, examines an institution directly involved in the economy of decolonisation through the minting of coins for Britain and many of its former colonies after independence. The Mint's designers had to adapt to new aesthetics of coin design for independent countries, and also to a changing economic landscape in which their employer had moved from holding a colonial monopoly to competing in a global marketplace for the business of newly independent countries.

The chapters in this volume highlight the value of exploring institutions like mints or architects' firms – often viewed as technical rather than cultural establishments – alongside sites of fine art, popular culture and performance such as museums and theatres. Across these apparently diverse institutions we see evidence of the role of the expert in decolonisation, as well as of how the value and location of 'expertise' was debated in the middle years of the twentieth century. While much of the academic discussion of expertise in late colonialism and decolonisation to date has focused on science and infrastructure,[43] in a broader investigation of institutions of decolonisation we also see the influence of experts in law and social science, as well as design, art, education, language and history. In this era, in which 'the expert' claimed particular authority,[44] experts in art history were drawn upon to inform the public image of new nations' leaders (as with Cambodia's Norodom Sihanouk, discussed by Falser in Chapter 6), and anthropologists and planners were asked to respond to problems of urbanisation through the planning of new towns (as d'Auria demonstrates was the case in Ghana, in Chapter 9).[45]

Indeed, there were shared impulses and assumptions employed by these diverse individuals, and they ran across the intertwined cultural, technical, political and economic worlds of decolonisation. Suppositions as to the relative value of 'local', Western and hybrid knowledges, as well as opinions about the benefits of modernist aesthetics, modernisation and development emerge again and again in various sites across the decolonising globe. For example, architects from the firm Fry, Drew, Drake & Lasdun, brandishing their conflation of (assumed) indigenous requirements and modernist paradigms, appear as expert consultants in the building of the Institute of Contemporary Arts in London (as noted by Wall in Chapter 4), the National Museum of Ghana (considered by Mew in Chapter 8) as well as townships in the Volta River Project, again in Ghana (discussed by d'Auria in Chapter 9). Notably, these recurring, common visions were often promoted through transnational professional associations.[46]

Cultural institutions were an important part of the project of 'development' which emerged in late colonialism and remained as the central policy of many nations after independence. After the Second World War, huge investment was poured into many colonial territories as development became central to bolstering the legitimacy of empire (and informal imperial influence) in an era when both were increasingly being questioned.[47] Development in this period was understood, by Western experts and some modernising nationalists alike, in terms of Euro-American ideals of modernisation and was rooted in the assumption that states should progress towards a stable, democratic and capitalist society and economy.[48] Experts in agriculture, health, housing, planning, resource extraction and administration were seen as crucial to securing rapid development along these lines.[49] Yet development was to be materialised not only through grand infrastructural schemes but also through the construction of more modest cultural forms such as educational and cultural institutions.[50] These too were crucial to legitimating continued colonial rule, and, later, to securing national prestige and domestic support for the leaders of newly independent states.

Development, the figure of 'the expert' charged with delivering change, and the new cultural institutions emerging in this era have often served the purpose of consolidating a technocratic unilinear notion of modernisation as progress towards a 'Western' developed state.[51] Dams, such as that which formed part of the Volta River Project (the focus of d'Auria's Chapter 9), have often been understood in precisely these terms.[52] However, the infrastructure of the developmental state produced in this era – including cultural institutions – could also be adapted to produce (or indeed, be produced through) local, non-Western modernities that challenged the hegemony of the former coloniser.[53] The cultural festivals in Mali held during the 1960s discussed by Mew in Chapter 8 provided opportunity for the products of nationalised factories to be presented to the newly independent Malian people, while the demonstration of mechanical tractors was incorporated into pageants organised at the heritage site Angkor Wat in order to promote the status of independent Cambodia's King Sihanouk to the international community (including the former French rulers).

An attention to cultural institutions also highlights the explicit rejection of imperial arbiters of cultural value in decolonisation.[54] In this volume we see British linguistic, professional and cultural institutions rejected in favour of other standards, located elsewhere. In Chapter 11, Rachel Leow examines how Malay national elites pushed for linguistic purity by embedding Malay as the national language through the Dewan Bahasa dan Pustaka (House of Language and Literature), a state-sponsored agency. Rejecting both English and a multilingual/multi-ethnic model for the new nation, language was utilised to produce a powerful but exclusive Malay nationalism. In Chapter 3, Rob Waters explores the rejection of another British institution, the BBC, by the members of the Caribbean Artists Movement. Waters demonstrates that the BBC offered an increasingly problematic institutional affiliation and arbiter of cultural worth for a group aiming to decolonise their means of cultural production and dissemination. The Caribbean Artists Movement increasingly looked not to Britain, but across the Atlantic to the Black Power politics of the United States as a guide for their practices. As Mew's account of the national museums of Ghana and Mali in Chapter 8 shows, institutional rejection could also be more subtle and prosaic, through the gradual withdrawal of funding in favour of other forms of cultural expression, and a diminishing number of visitors.

Transnational geographies at the end of empire

Bringing cultures of decolonisation to the fore also highlights new transnational geographies of decolonisation. As suggested above, in early writings on the history of decolonisation, the 'end of empire' was drawn as a phenomenon led by those in the metropole. However, with the gradual (if controversial) filtering of postcolonial theory into imperial history, and insights from historians working in Africa and India particularly, an 'excentric' view of decolonisation has increasingly been highlighted.[55] The undifferentiated and hierarchical 'core and periphery' model of former imperial and post-imperial histories has been redrawn, while the agency of the colonised in the process of decolonisation has been recognised. Notably, it has often been in the realm of culture and the quotidian that 'histories from below' have been constructed and the agency of the colonised acknowledged.[56] Much of this is to do with the fact that the ability to leave a material mark on the cultural world is not subject to the same restrictions of class, gender and ethnicity which often dictate opportunities to contribute to government archives or published documents.[57]

In *Cultures of Decolonisation*, European powers are present (and seen as highly significant), but they are understood as shaped through flows of people, ideas and objects from across (and beyond) the decolonising world. Similarly, Cold War battles between the Superpowers appear, yet we also see that many in the global South framed their postcolonial agendas beyond this twofold international system.[58] Indeed, a focus on culture highlights the priorities, actions and agency of the majority colonised world, and in doing so dislodges prevailing historiographical readings of this period as dominated solely by the Cold War. In a series of case studies which dedicate significant attention to places, peoples and approaches in the (former) colonial spaces of Cambodia, Ghana, India, Jamaica, Kenya, Malaysia, Mali, Aotearoa/New Zealand, Rhodesia (now Zimbabwe), South Africa, Tanzania, Trinidad, Uganda, the United States and Vietnam, alongside Britain and France, decolonisation is shown as experienced in and driven from the 'margins'.

Moreover, through the analyses presented in the book, these places are shown not to be marginal at all; instead, many of the nations, communities and individuals discussed are conceptualised as tied together in the transnational politics of decolonisation. A focus on cultural forms elucidates these crucial connections that existed between geographically distant places in this period. It also shows that many of the transnational connections in decolonisation often circumvented the metropole altogether. Thus the chapters in this book highlight the need to redress the historiography of empire and decolonisation not only by placing the so-called 'metropole' and 'colony' in the same 'analytic field', but also by focusing more carefully on the connections between (former) colonial territories often understood only in relation to imperial powers.[59]

Our approach draws on the work of a number of authors who have explored the transnational networks of empire and postcolonial migration in recent years.[60] The ties and interactions connecting people and institutions beyond the nation-state and the staple metropole–colony binary in the nineteenth and early twentieth centuries have been considered most effectively by Kevin Grant, Philippa Levine and Frank Trentmann, and by Alan Lester and David Lambert.[61] In the context of empire, Lester and Lambert argue that 'ideas, practices and identities developed *trans-imperially*' rather than being formed in one place and exported, unchanged, to another.[62] Similarly, in the middle years of the twentieth century, as decolonisation unfolded, artists, authors and architects, among others, journeyed the world, inspired in their critiques of colonialism and support for nationalism by the multiple sites, things and peoples they encountered during their travels. As Damian Skinner explains in Chapter 2, the Māori artist Ralph Hotere travelled to Britain and France, where his engagement with European decolonisation – particularly in Algeria – melded with his own experiences of imperialism and indigenous rights in Aotearoa New Zealand to create his transnational art of decolonisation. As described in the chapters by Schwarz (Chapter 1) and Waters (Chapter 3), as African-American and West Indian authors travelled across Europe and its (former) colonies, their outputs were variously informed by the anti-imperialisms of US Black Power and Civil Rights, the struggle for independence in the West Indies, the broader collapse of European empires, Pan-Africanism and Communism. While Utpal Dutt, the playwright discussed by Abin Chakraborty in Chapter 5, remained in his native Bengal, his vision of decolonisation was international, as he drew on the parallel independence struggles of Vietnam and India for his artistic inspiration.

Transnational associations were identified and emphasised through cultural forms: artists' colonies and collectives provided sites for the dissemination of global experiences; listening to, reading and viewing the work of their contemporaries around the globe allowed individuals and collectives to forge transnational imaginaries where personal connections were not always possible.[63] Indeed, the powerful ways in which the conditions of oppression and liberation were articulated in creative forms meant that they had an important role beyond direct encounters: as Schwarz describes, a whole host of geographically disparate authors and intellectuals, including C.L.R James and Frantz Fanon, saw evidence of their common experiences in Richard Wright's creative outputs, even before they met him in person. The written word provided the catalyst for their subsequent friendships, interactions and solidarities. Notably, while the nation-state retained great importance in forming and articulating their global gaze, the sympathies and affiliations of creative individuals traversed the boundaries of (former) European empires. Dutt saw parallels between those colonised under British and French rule, while for artists and authors working in in France and Britain, the influence of those struggling for freedom in North America was also paramount.

This period was also one in which many international organisations were formed, not least of which were the modern Commonwealth, the Organisation of African Unity, the Non-Aligned Movement and the United Nations (UN) and its numerous agencies. These organisations were of course crucial in decolonisation, as central arenas for ideological debate and the claiming of rights.[64] Ideas filtered through these channels: as Catherine Eagleton explains, it was through the involvement of Kwame Nkrumah and Julius Nyerere in the Organisation of African Unity that the former was able to influence the latter's decision to break up the East African Currency Board, claim a unique national currency for Tanzania and begin the process of articulating new symbols of the independent nation-state through coinage. Organisations also fostered the melding of ideas drawn from disparate geographical sources. The UN made available housing experts who provided crucial input into Ghana's Volta Dam, as d'Auria notes in Chapter 9. These international experts drew on a whole gamut of architectural references sourced from around the world and worked in practices that had been forged in countries beyond their own, constructing housing designs for a project ostensibly intended as a symbol of Ghanaian independence. Of course the UN was by no means apolitical, and the dominant role of global capital in shaping and funding the project provides an even clearer reminder that the transnational was not always simply aligned with anti-colonial change and freedom.[65] Contemporary criticisms of the Commonwealth also support this point.[66]

One consequence of this transnational flow of people, ideas and images across the middle years of the twentieth century was the comparative impulse that spurred many into action. Policymakers, professionals and publics consistently compared their own situations to those elsewhere in the world and crafted their own practices and visions for the future as a result. As in the case of Dutt, who assessed the state of his own nation in relation to the plight in Vietnam, and the Caribbean Artists Movement, who re-evaluated their fight against racism in the UK in relation to the actions of African Americans, such comparisons provided campaigning tools, constructed solidarity, and developed creative practice.[67] Notably, however, comparison also led to processes of differentiation. Lines of demarcation were most often drawn between ex-colony and ex-colonial power, but as Eagleton's chapter demonstrates, regional comparisons were part of decolonisation too: coin designs for an independent Uganda were chosen on the strength of their power to represent the nation's separation from neighbouring Kenya and Tanzania.

Recent work on contemporary transnationalism has emphasised how 'distinct multilocal sets of identities and memories' can be formed across national boundaries through 'fluid and hybrid forms of cultural production'.[68] In their focus on electronic media in the contemporary epoch, Arjun Appadurai, and Ella Shohat and Robert Stam, have pointed to the 'communities of sentiment' that have been fuelled by transnational forms of culture.[69] The chapters in *Cultures of Decolonisation* demonstrate that, in an earlier period, many other forms of cultural products facilitated the development of similar transnational communities of affiliation and experience.

If the content of *Cultures of Decolonisation* offers a means to explore connections, transmutations and comparisons across national boundaries, it also allows us to make our own comparisons between different places and a variety of cultural forms as they were experienced and operated in the processes of decolonisation. Scholars of decolonisation can better understand the driving concerns of creative practitioners and the meanings and diverse impacts of their outputs in these broader transformations if they expand their gaze across art, design, architecture, language and performance, and across the globe. Thus the volume contributes to a growing field of comparative research into decolonisation that has now begun to emerge and counter the traditional historiographical fragmentation of transnational processes into colonial or national histories severing extra and inter-colonial connections.[70] Jenny Robinson has noted that the 'universalising ambitions of comparative methods' have led to suspicions from postcolonial scholars concerned with the colonial roots of the comparative impulse and the potential of comparison to promote generalisation within a Eurocentric framework. Yet she remains convinced that such comparative approaches remain powerful when they stay attentive to geographically and temporally specific circumstances and perspectives.[71] Here we follow Robinson's argument that, deployed carefully, comparison offers an effective way of bringing into conversation places often 'kept apart' in research, and through this, of internationalising research into the processes of decolonisation.[72]

Structure

Cultures of Decolonisation is divided into three parts. Part I, 'Decolonising metropolitan cultures?', brings together chapters that explore the experiences of artists and film-makers, poets, writers and philosophers in London and Paris, in this period of decolonisation. These cities provided the sites of engagement for colonial and ex-colonial subjects, for visitors from other nations speaking back to colonialism, and for a British and French public experiencing the end of empire. In Chapter 1, Bill Schwarz explores the connections between British decolonisation and the American Civil Rights movement, through the life and writings of Richard Wright, and in particular his experiences in post-war Paris. Chapter 2, by Damian Skinner, explores the art and experiences of the Māori modernist artist Ralph Hotere in Europe. In Chapter 3, Rob Waters examines the Caribbean Artists Movement in London and demonstrates its progression away from British establishment sponsors such as the BBC, and towards a more radical politics of Black Power emerging in North America. David C. Wall's contribution in Chapter 4 draws attention to the dual themes of plenty and privation in British fine art and film in order to explore the anxieties of decolonisation.

Demonstrating the continuing importance of metropolitan locations for cultivating cultures and networks of anti- and postcolonial thought, even in the midst of decolonisation, these chapters nevertheless collapse the hierarchies of core and periphery by showing how metropolitan culture was inspired (and often contested) by the cultures of (former) colonies. These contributions clearly demonstrate the movement of people and ideas between European imperial capitals, as well as within and beyond imperial systems. For individuals in Britain and France, the Caribbean and North Africa loomed large, but so did places outside (recent) colonial experience, particularly the United States. Taken together, the chapters in this section highlight, first, the value of studying the experience of

INTRODUCTION

decolonisation in Europe comparatively, and, second, the need to emphasise the transnational connections within and beyond Europe, and beyond the former colonies, in these processes of decolonisation.

Part II, 'Performing decolonisation', considers 'performance' across a number of different sites and practices, from the spectacular to the everyday. Exploring theatre, architectural sites, community conventions and the family home, the chapters stress the role of performance in constructing inclusive and exclusive national identities during decolonisation. In Chapter 5, Abin Chakraborty explores Utpal Dutt's play *Invincible Vietnam*. His account demonstrates not only the value of analysing theatre as cultural product, but also of considering the role of performance in producing and reflecting transnational solidarities, in this case between those in Bengal and Vietnam. Chapter 6, by Michael Falser, focuses on performances at Angkor in Cambodia. Situating these in the context of French colonial performances, the chapter shows how places, sites and architectural monuments of 'real and/ or restaged' Angkorian antiquity were utilised to visualise the newly born Cambodian nation-state. Chapter 7, by Jean Smith, focuses on the personal performances of settlers in Rhodesia/Zimbabwe and South Africa through an examination of accents, life stories and interior design, and demonstrates the role of culture in contesting decolonisation. Bringing together contributions from the disciplines of English, history and art history, this part of the book illustrates the ways in which diverse performances and performance sites were utilised alongside one another to construct and contest identities in decolonisation, and it again demonstrates the value of the interdisciplinary study of this period.

Part III, 'Decolonising expertise', focuses particularly on the role of experts – in architecture, the design of currency, the designation of language and museum practice – within the process of decolonisation. In Sophie Mew's Chapter 8, the role of museum professionals is explored in Mali and Ghana. Focusing on the construction and curation of buildings and exhibitions, she shows that as funding and policy priorities shifted during decolonisation, the museum became a site for the cultural expertise that had been informed by colonial legacies to be challenged. Chapter 9, by Viviana d'Auria, examines the Volta River Project, Ghana's flagship development project during decolonisation. D'Auria demonstrates the contribution of multiple colonial, national and international housing experts in shaping the project's plans, and in doing so highlights competing claims for, and designs on independent Ghana. In Chapter 10, Catherine Eagleton attends to the coins produced for newly independent Kenya,

Tanzania and Uganda by London's Royal Mint. She demonstrates the intertwining of aesthetic and economic considerations driving the decisions of both the Mint and its partners, and the ways in which regional relationships and rivalries in Africa shaped money produced in the UK. Chapter 11, by Rachel Leow, focuses on the Malay Dewan Bahasa dan Pustaka (House of Language and Literature), a state-sponsored agency established in order to transform Malay into a modern national language. Leow's study elucidates the processes through which linguistic experts contributed to the reproduction of the colonial past in the postcolonial era. The interdisciplinary perspectives brought together in this section facilitate a tracing of the shared aesthetic, technical and political concerns that animated a range of experts and their policies, designs and practices in this period.

The lens of culture thus provides unique insights into the processes of decolonisation. Taken together, the chapters in *Cultures of Decolonisation* illustrate the value of interdisciplinary research into this period. In the single example of the Commonwealth Institute – the exhibition complex introduced at the start of this chapter – it was possible to isolate plural perspectives on decolonisation ranging from the neo-colonial to the nationalist to the liberal and forward-facing; the importance of cultural forms and the international affiliations that they fostered throughout the mid-twentieth century began to drift into view. The following contributions to this volume move far beyond this single institution at the heart of the British Empire to provide highly geographically and materially diverse evidence of how productions and processes in the cultural and social sphere were active in decolonisation as well as mirrors of this political shift. The impact of cultural forms and institutions are emphasised and the transnational nature of decolonisation unpacked. We hope that, for the reader, these contributions suggest exciting new avenues for further interdisciplinary research into the complex processes of decolonisation.

Notes

We are grateful to Paul Ashmore, Katherine Brickell, Tim Livsey and Bill Schwarz for their helpful comments on this introduction, and Rob Waters, Darcie Fontaine, Vincent Kuitenbrouwer and Jen L. Foray for their bibliographic suggestions.

1 Commonwealth Institute, *Commonwealth Institute: A Guide Describing the Work of the Institute and the Exhibitions in the Galleries* (London: Commonwealth Institute, 1966), p. 19.
2 Commonwealth Institute, *Annual Report* (London: Commonwealth Institute, 1963), p. 10.

INTRODUCTION

3   C. Wintle, 'Decolonising the Museum: The Case of the Imperial and Commonwealth Institutes', *Museum & Society*, 11:2 (2013), 188–90.
4   R. Craggs, 'The Commonwealth Institute and the Commonwealth Arts Festival: Architecture, Performance and Multiculturalism in Late-Imperial London', *London Journal*, 36 (2011), 256; M. Crinson, 'Imperial Story-Lands: Architecture and Display at the Imperial and Commonwealth Institutes', *Art History*, 22 (1999), 119–21.
5   The National Archives, UK, ED121/808, 'The Future of the Imperial Institute' [Draft], April 1956. Emphasis added.
6   Wintle, 'Decolonising the Museum', 191.
7   Craggs, 'The Commonwealth Institute and the Commonwealth Arts Festival', 255–7. For these tropes see B. Schwarz, '"The Only White Man in There": The Re-Racialisation of England, 1956–1968', *Race and Class*, 38:1 (1996), 65–78; F. Mort, 'Scandalous Events: Metropolitan Culture and Moral Change in Post-Second World War London', *Representations*, 93 (2006), 106–37.
8   Wintle, 'Decolonising the Museum', 185–201.
9   Library and Archives, Canada, RG25 Volume 15112 File no. 55-4-CWLTH INST Part 2, memorandum from Commonwealth Division to Information Division, 14 December 1966.
10 Library and Archives, Canada, RG25 Volume 5336 File no. 10033-40 Part 4, memorandum on 'Canada's Relations with the Commonwealth Institute', 20 June 1963.
11 Stuart Ward and Mohammed Ayoob make this point in relation to history and international relations respectively. See S. Ward, 'Introduction', in S. Ward (ed.), *British Culture and the End of Empire* (Manchester: Manchester University Press, 2001), p. 4; M. Ayoob, 'Inequality and Theorizing in International Relations: The Case for Subaltern Realism', *International Studies Review*, 4:3 (2002), 27–48. See also K. Fedorowich and M. Thomas (eds), *International Diplomacy and Colonial Retreat* (London: Frank Cass, 2001).
12 E.W. Said, *Orientalism* (London: Routledge, 1978); E.W. Said, *Culture and Imperialism* (London: Chatto & Windus, 1992). On the early, problematic, relationship between imperial history and postcolonial theory, see D. Kennedy, 'Imperial History and Post-Colonial Theory', *Journal of Imperial and Commonwealth History*, 24:3 (1996), 345–63.
13 For this argument in relation to the discipline of geography, see R. Craggs, 'Postcolonial Geographies, Decolonization, and the Performance of Geopolitics at Commonwealth Conferences', *Singapore Journal of Tropical Geography*, 35 (2014), 39–55; for this argument in relation to museum studies and art history, see C. Wintle, 'Decolonising the Museum', 185–6.
14 J. Darwin, 'Decolonisation and the End of Empire', in R.W. Winks (ed.), *The Oxford History of the British Empire, Vol. 5: Historiography* (Oxford: Oxford University Press, 1999), p. 554.
15 J. Darwin, 'Diplomacy and Decolonization', *Journal of Imperial and Commonwealth History*, 28:3 (2000), 6.
16 See for example, on a weakening British appetite for colonialism, R. Holland, *European Decolonization, 1918–81: An Introductory Survey* (London: Macmillan, 1985); on British anti-imperial feeling, J. Strachey, *The End of Empire* (New York: Random House, 1959) and C. Easton, *The Twilight of European Colonialism: A Political Analysis* (London: Methuen, 1961); on the impact of American anti-colonial feeling, see W.R. Louis, *Imperialism at Bay: The United States and the Decolonization of the British Empire, 1941–1945* (Oxford: Oxford University Press, 1978); on the role of colonial peoples in rejecting colonialism, see D.A. Low, 'The Asian Mirror to Tropical Africa's Independence', in P. Gifford and W.R. Louis (eds), *The Transfer of Power in Africa: Decolonization, 1940–1960* (New Haven: Yale University Press, 1982). For a good summary of this historiographical debate see Darwin, 'Decolonisation and the End of Empire'.

17 Darwin, 'Decolonisation and the End of Empire'; J. Darwin, *The End of the British Empire: The Historical Debate* (Oxford: Blackwell, 2001); D. Rothermund, *The Routledge Companion to Decolonization* (Abingdon: Routledge, 2006), pp. 21–31.
18 P. Levine, 'Gendering Decolonisation', *Histoire@Politique: Histoire, Politique, Société*, 11 (2010), 1–15; Rothermund, *The Routledge Companion to Decolonization*, p. 30.
19 See, for example, elements of J.M. MacKenzie, *Propaganda and Empire: The Manipulation of British Public Opinion, 1880–1960* (Manchester: Manchester University Press, 1984); J.M. MacKenzie (ed.), *Imperialism and Popular Culture* (Manchester: Manchester University Press, 1986); B. Schwarz, '"The Only White Man in There"', 65–78. For a fuller bibliography, see W. Webster, *Englishness and Empire, 1939–1965* (Oxford: Oxford University Press, 2005), pp. 1–3. On the impact of the series see A. Thompson (ed.), *Writing Imperial Histories* (Manchester: Manchester University Press, 2013).
20 Ward, 'Introduction', p. 4.
21 B. Schwarz, *Memories of Empire, Vol. 1: The White Man's World* (Oxford: Oxford University Press, 2011).
22 J. Bailkin, *The Afterlife of Empire* (Berkeley: University of California Press, 2012); E. Buettner, *Empire Families: Britons and Late Imperial India* (Oxford: Oxford University Press, 2004). See also E. Buettner, '"We Don't Grow Coffee and Bananas in Clapham Junction You Know!": Imperial Britons Back Home', in R. Bickers (ed.), *Settlers and Expatriates: Britons Over the Seas*, Oxford History of the British Empire Companion Series (Oxford: Oxford University Press, 2010), and other contributors to this volume.
23 E. Buettner, *Europe After Empire: Decolonization, Society and Culture* (Cambridge, Cambridge University Press, forthcoming). See also J. House and A. Thompson, 'Decolonisation, Space and Power: Immigration, Welfare and Housing in Britain and France, 1945–74', in Thompson, *Writing Imperial Histories*.
24 S. Faulkner and A. Ramamurthy, 'Introduction', in S. Faulkner and A. Ramamurthy, *Visual Culture and Decolonisation in Britain: British Art and Visual Culture since 1750, New Readings* (Aldershot: Ashgate, 2006), p. 5.
25 Webster, *Englishness and Empire*; S. Potter, *Broadcasting Empire: The BBC and the British World, 1922–1970* (Oxford: Oxford University Press, 2012); R. Gilmour and B. Schwarz (eds), *End of Empire and the English Novel Since 1945* (Manchester: Manchester University Press, 2011); L. Grieveson and C. MacCabe (eds), *Film and the End of Empire* (London: Palgrave Macmillan/ British Film Institute, 2011). See also chapters in A. Thompson (ed.), *Britain's Experience of Empire in the Twentieth Century*, The Oxford History of the British Empire (Oxford: Oxford University Press, 2011): W. Webster, 'The Empire Comes Home: Commonwealth Migration to Britain' and A. Thompson with M. Kowalsky, 'Social Life and Cultural Representation: Empire in the Public Imagination'.
26 R. Aldrich, *Vestiges of the Colonial Empire in France: Monuments, Museums, and Colonial Memories* (London: Palgrave Macmillan, 2004) and D.J. Sherman, *French Primitivism and the Ends of Empire, 1945–1975* (Chicago: University of Chicago Press, 2011). See also H. Feldman, *From a Nation Torn: Decolonizing Art and Representation in France 1945–1962* (Durham: Duke University Press, 2014) and K. Ross, *Fast Cars, Clean Bodies: Decolonization and the Reordering of French Culture* (London: MIT Press, 1996). For recent work on 'postcolonial migrants' in the Netherlands, see J. Cote and L. Westerbeek (eds), *Recalling the Indies: Colonial Culture and Postcolonial Identities* (Amsterdam: Aksant, 2005) and G. Oostindie, *Postcolonial Netherlands: Sixty-Five Years of Forgetting, Commemorating, Silencing* (Amsterdam: Amsterdam University Press, 2011). Notably, the Tropenmuseum as a site of decolonisation in the Dutch metropole has been the subject of some useful critique: see C. Kreps, 'Changing the Rules of the Road: Post-Colonialism and the New Ethics of Museum Anthropology', in J. Marstine (ed.), *The Routledge Companion to Museum Ethics: Redefining*

INTRODUCTION

  Ethics for the Twentieth-Century Museum (London: Routledge, 2011) and J. van Dijk and S. Legêne (eds), *The Netherlands East Indies at the Tropenmuseum* (Amsterdam: KIT Publishers, 2011).

27 P. Levine, *The British Empire: Sunrise to Sunset* (Harlow: Pearson Education, 2007), p. 191.

28 F. Cooper, *Decolonization and African Society: The Labor Question in French and British Africa* (Cambridge: Cambridge University Press, 1996); Levine, 'Gendering Decolonisation'; E. Bogaerts and R. Raben (eds), *Beyond Empire and Nation: Decolonizing Societies in Africa and Asia, 1930s–1970s* (Leiden: KITLV Press, 2012); J.D. Le Sueur (ed.), *The Decolonization Reader* (New York: Routledge, 2003). See also M. Chamberlain, *Empire and Nation Building in the Caribbean: Barbados, 1937–66* (Manchester: Manchester University Press, 2010); A. Spry Rush, *Bonds of Empire: West Indians and Britishness from Victoria to Decolonization* (Oxford: Oxford University Press, 2011).

29 E.g. Ngũgĩ wa Thiong'o, *Decolonising the Mind: The Politics of Language in African Literature* (Portsmouth: Heinemann Educational, 1986); O. Enwezor, 'The Short Century: Independence and Liberation Movements in Africa, 1945–1994, An Introduction', in O. Enwezor (ed.), *The Short Century: Independence and Liberation Movements in Africa, 1945–1994* (Munich: Prestel, 2001); B. Schwarz (ed.), *Caribbean Literature After Independence: The Case of Earl Lovelace* (London: Institute for the Study of the Americas, 2008); B. Ashcroft, G. Griffiths and H. Tiffin (eds), *The Empire Writes Back: Theory and Practice in Post-Colonial Literatures* (London: Routledge, 2nd edn, 2002); J. Genova, *Cinema and Development in West Africa* (Bloomington: Indiana University Press, 2013); R. Armes, *Postcolonial Images: Studies in North African Cinema* (Bloomington: Indiana University Press, 2005); R.M. Brown, *Art for a Modern India, 1947–1980* (London: Duke University Press, 2009); T. Guha-Thakurta, *Monuments, Objects, Histories: Institutions of Art in Colonial and Postcolonial India* (New York: Columbia University Press, 2004); P. Greenough, 'Nation, Economy, Tradition Displayed: The Indian Crafts Museum, New Delhi', in C. Breckenridge (ed.), *Consuming Modernity: Public Culture in a South Asian World* (Minneapolis: University of Minnesota Press, 1995). A recent volume edited by M. Knol, R. Raben and K. Zijlmans entitled *Beyond the Dutch: Indonesia, the Netherlands and the Visual Arts, from 1900 until Now* (Utrecht: KIT Publishers, 2009) dedicates a substantial section of its analysis to the fine art produced in Indonesia between 1950 and 1970 that responds to decolonisation.

30 T. Shepard, 'Making French and European Coincide: Decolonization and the Politics of Comparative and Transnational Histories', *Ab Imperio*, 2 (2007), 339–60.

31 S. Legêne and M. Eickhoff, 'Postwar Europe and the Colonial Past in Photographs: The NIOD Visual Archive in Amsterdam as a Site of European Memory-Construction', in A. Rigney and C. de Cesari (eds), *Transnational-Memory: Beyond Methodological Nationalism* (Berlin: De Gruyter, 2014).

32 Frederick Cooper has long been doing comparative work between British and French colonial Africa; see Cooper, *Decolonization and African Society*. See also the range of texts discussed in Ashcroft, Griffiths and Tiffin, *The Empire Writes Back*. Further comparative work is now emerging: see, for example, M. Shipway, *Decolonization and its Impacts: A Comparative Approach to the End of the Colonial Empires* (Oxford: Wiley-Blackwell, 2008); M. Thomas, *Fight or Flight: Britain, France, and their Roads from Empire* (Oxford: Oxford University Press, 2014); Buettner, *Europe After Empire*. An important exception to the trend of focusing on one country in research on culture and decolonisation is Mark Crinson's *Modern Architecture at the End of Empire* (Aldershot: Ashgate, 2003), which ranges across nations and empires as well as 'periphery' and 'metropole' in its consideration of the built form. Similarly, a special edition of the *Round Table* journal considers independence day ceremonies across the globe and their role in masking the tensions and conflicts of decolonisation ('Special Issue: Freedoms at

Midnight', *Round Table: The Commonwealth Journal of International Affairs*, 97 (2008)). See also the three chapters in the 'Culture and Contests' section of Le Sueur, *The Decolonization Reader*.
33 For example, Faulkner and Ramamurthy, *Visual Culture and Decolonisation in Britain* and Webster, *Englishness and Empire*. The benefits of assessing different cultural forms alongside one another in one volume is demonstrated in Ward, *British Culture at the End of Empire*.
34 On material agency see A. Gell, *Art and Agency: An Anthropological Theory* (Oxford: Clarendon Press, 1998); on actor network theory, see B. Latour, *Reassembling the Social: An Introduction to Actor-Network Theory* (Oxford: Oxford University Press, 2005). For a useful discussion of both, see S. Byrne, A. Clarke, R. Harrison and R. Torrence, 'Networks, Agents and Objects: Frameworks for Unpacking Museum Collections', in S. Byrne, A. Clarke, R. Harrison and R. Torrence (eds), *Unpacking the Collection: Networks of Material and Social Agency in the Museum* (New York: Springer, 2011). On the ways in which material and visual culture can enable the negotiation of decolonisation as a broader process, see Wintle, 'Decolonising the Museum' and Faulkner and Ramamurthy, 'Introduction'.
35 D. Gauntlett, *Making Is Connecting: The Social Meaning of Creativity, from DIY and Knitting to Youtube and Web 2.0* (Cambridge: Polity, 2011); C. Tilley, 'Objectification', in C. Tilley, W. Keane, S. Kuchler, P. Spyer and M. Rowlands (eds), *Handbook of Material Culture* (London: Sage, 2006); R. Sennett, *The Craftsman* (London: Allen Lane, 2008).
36 Faulkner and Ramamurthy, 'Introduction', p. 9.
37 Wintle, 'Decolonising the Museum', 196.
38 Ella Shohat and Robert Stam make a similar point in relation to imperial cinema in their *Unthinking Eurocentrism: Multiculturalism and the Media* (London: Routledge, 1994), p. 103.
39 M. Foucault, *Power/Knowledge* (Brighton: Harvester, 1980), p. 194; S. Hall, 'The Work of Representation', in S. Hall (ed.), *Representation: Cultural Representations and Signifying Practices* (London: Sage, 1997), p. 47. Significant examples include Said, *Orientalism*; T. Bennett, *The Birth of the Museum: History, Theory, Politics* (London: Routledge, 1995); W.J.T. Mitchell, 'Imperial Landscape', in W.J.T. Mitchell (ed.), *Landscape and Power* (Chicago: University of Chicago Press, 1994).
40 Grieveson and MacCabe, *Film and the End of Empire*; Faulkner and Ramamurthy, 'Introduction', pp. 7 and 9.
41 Levine, 'Gendering Decolonisation', 13.
42 Levine, 'Gendering Decolonisation', 13.
43 J. Tischler, *Light and Power for a Multiracial Nation: The Kariba Dam Scheme in the Central African Federation* (New York: Palgrave Macmillan, 2013); B.M. Bennett and J.M. Hodge (eds), *Science and Empire: Knowledge and Networks of Science Across the British Empire, 1800–1970* (Basingstoke: Palgrave Macmillan, 2011).
44 J. Hodge, *Triumph of the Expert: Agrarian Doctrines of Development and the Legacies of British Colonialism* (Athens, OH: Ohio University Press, 2007).
45 See also, for example, on anthropologists: J. Ferguson, *Expectations of Modernity: Myth and Meanings of Urban Life on the Zambian Copperbelt* (Berkeley: University of California Press, 1999), pp. 24–37 and Bailkin, *Afterlife of Empire*; on constitutional law advisers: H. Kumarasingham (ed.), *Constitution Maker: Selected Writings of Sir Ivor Jennings* (Cambridge: Cambridge University Press/Royal Historical Society Camden Series, 2016); H. Kumarasingham (ed.), *Constitution Making in Asia: Decolonisation and State-Building in the Aftermath of the British Empire* (London: Routledge, 2015); R.K. Home, 'Town Planning and Garden Cities in the British Colonial Empire, 1910–1940', *Planning Perspectives*, 5 (1990), 23–37.

INTRODUCTION

46 C. Andersen, 'Internationalism, and Engineering in UNESCO during the End Game of Empire, 1940–68', *Technology and Culture* (forthcoming).
47 D.A. Low and J.M. Lonsdale, 'Introduction: Towards the New Order, 1945–1963', in D.A. Low and A. Smith (eds), *History of East Africa, Vol. 3* (Oxford: Clarendon Press, 1976).
48 On modernisation theory, see M. Latham, *Modernization as Ideology: American Social Science and 'Nation Building' in the Kennedy Era* (Chapel Hill: University of North Carolina Press, 2000) and D. Ekbladh, *The Great American Mission: Modernization and the Construction of an American World Order* (Princeton: Princeton University Press, 2011).
49 See chapters in 'Part III: Knowledge and Networks at the End of Empire' of Bennett and Hodge, *Science and Empire*; H. Tilley, *Africa as Living Laboratory: Empire, Development, and the Problem of Scientific Knowledge, 1870–1950* (Chicago: Chicago University Press, 2011); J. Hodge, 'British Colonial Expertise, Postcolonial Careering and the Early History of International Development', *Journal of Modern European History*, 'Special Issue: Modernizing Missions: Approaches to "Developing" the Non-Western World After 1945', 8 (2010), 24–46; Crinson, *Modern Architecture*.
50 Wintle, 'Decolonizing the Museum', 194–5; T. Livsey, '"Suitable Lodgings for Students": Modern Space, Colonial Development and Decolonization in Nigeria', *Urban History*, 41:4 (2014), 1–22; A. Apter, 'The Pan-African Nation: Oil-Money and the Spectacle of Culture in Nigeria', *Public Culture*, 8 (1996), 441–66; A. Apter, *The Pan-African Nation: Oil Money and the Spectacle of Culture in Nigeria* (London: University of Chicago Press, 2005).
51 J. Scott, *Seeing Like a State: How Certain Schemes to Improve the Human Condition Have Failed* (New Haven: Yale University Press, 1998); G.K. Bhambra, *Rethinking Modernity: Postcolonialism and the Sociological Imagination* (Basingstoke: Palgrave Macmillan, 2007), pp. 56–82.
52 See the panel convened by Birte Förster and Julia Tischler: 'Large-scale Infrastructure Projects in Sub-Saharan Africa: Spatial Inscriptions of Imperialism and Globalisation?', at the conference Embattled Spaces, Contested Orders, Cologne University, 30 May–2 June 2012.
53 T. Livsey, 'The University Age: Decolonisation and Development in Nigeria, 1930–1966' (PhD dissertation, Birkbeck, University of London, 2014); G. Prakash, *Another Reason: Science and the Imagination of Modern India* (Princeton: Princeton University Press, 1999); Brown, *Art for a Modern India*, pp. 103–30.
54 See also Faulkner and Ramamurthy, 'Introduction', p. 4.
55 Rothermund, *The Routledge Companion to Decolonization*, pp. 23–8. See, for example, Cooper, *Decolonization and African Society*; Ranajit Guha, *Elementary Aspects of Peasant Insurgency in Colonial India* (Delhi: Oxford University Press, 1983).
56 See, for example, D. Haynes and G. Prakash (eds), *Contesting Power: Resistance and Everyday Social Relations in South Asia* (Delhi: Oxford University Press, 1991); C. Hall, and S.O. Rose (eds), *At Home with the Empire: Metropolitan Culture and the Imperial World* (Cambridge: Cambridge University Press, 2006); J.F. Codell and D. Sachko Macleod (eds), *Orientalism Transposed: The Impact of Colonies on British Culture* (Aldershot: Ashgate, 1998); N. Thomas, *Entangled Objects: Exchange, Material Culture and Colonialism in the Pacific* (Cambridge: Harvard University Press, 1991).
57 C. Wintle, *Colonial Collecting and Display: Encounters with Material Culture from the Andaman and Nicobar Islands* (Oxford: Berghahn, 2013), p. 3; P. van Dommelen, 'Colonial Matters: Material Culture and Postcolonial Theory in Colonial Situations', in C. Tilley (ed.), *Handbook of Material Culture* (London: Sage, 2005), p. 113.
58 M. Bradley, 'Decolonization, the Global South, and the Cold War, 1919–1962', in M.P. Leffler and O.A. Westad (eds), *The Cambridge History of the Cold War, Vol.*

1: *Origins, 1945–1962* (Cambridge: Cambridge University Press, 2010), p. 465, makes a similar point.
59 The call to place metropole and colony in one analytical field has been most prominently made by Anne Laura Stoler and Frederick Cooper: A.L. Stoler and F. Cooper, 'Between Metropole and Colony: Rethinking a Research Agenda', in A.L. Stoler and F. Cooper (eds), *Tensions of Empire: Colonial Cultures in a Bourgeois World* (Berkeley: University of California Press, 1997), p. 4.
60 S. Vertovec, *Migration, Diasporas and Transnationalism* (Aldershot: Edward Elgar, 1999); S. Vertovec, *Transnationalism* (London: Routledge, 2008); P. Levine, K. Grant and F. Trentmann, *Beyond Sovereignty: Britain, Empire, and Transnationalism, c. 1860–1950* (Basingstoke: Palgrave Macmillan, 2007); D. Lambert and A. Lester (eds), *Colonial Lives Across the British Empire: Imperial Careering in the Long Nineteenth Century* (Cambridge: Cambridge University Press, 2006); D. Lambert and A. Lester, 'Geographies of Colonial Philanthropy', *Progress in Human Geography*, 28 (2004), 320–41.
61 Levine, Grant and Trentmann, *Beyond Sovereignty*; Lambert and Lester, *Colonial Lives Across the British Empire*.
62 D. Lambert and A. Lester, 'Introduction: Imperial Subjects, Imperial Spaces', in Lambert and Lester, *Colonial Lives Across the British Empire*, p. 2. Emphasis in the original.
63 See chapters by Bill Schwarz (Chapter 1), Damian Skinner (Chapter 2), Rob Waters (Chapter 3) and Abin Chakraborty (Chapter 5), this volume.
64 G. Sluga, 'Editorial: The Transnational History of International Institutions', *Journal of Global History*, 6 (2011), 219–22; V. Prashad, *The Darker Nations: A People's History of the Third World* (New York, New Press, 2007).
65 On the argument that transnationalism is not always a force of cultural creativity progressive in its political consequences, see P. Jackson, P. Crang and C. Dwyer, 'Introduction: The Spaces of Transnationality', in P. Crang, C. Dwyer and P. Jackson (eds.), *Transnational Spaces* (London: Routledge, 2004), p. 9.
66 M. Power, 'The Commonwealth, "Development" and Post-Colonial Responsibility', *Geoforum*, 40 (2009), 14–24.
67 See also G. Brown and H. Yaffe, 'Non-Stop Against Apartheid: Practicing Solidarity Outside the South African Embassy', *Social Movement Studies: Journal of Social, Cultural and Political Protest*, 12 (2013), 227–34; P.M. von Eschen, *Race Against Empire: Black Americans and Anticolonialism, 1937–1957* (Ithaca: Cornell University Press, 1997).
68 Levine, Grant and Trentmann, *Beyond Sovereignty*, pp. 1–2.
69 A. Appadurai, *Modernity at Large: Cultural Dimensions of Globalization* (Minneapolis: University of Minnesota Press, 1996), p. 8; E. Shohat and R. Stam, 'Introduction', in E. Shohat and R. Stam (eds), *Multiculturalism, Postcoloniality, and Transnational Media* (New Brunswick: Rutgers University Press, 2003).
70 E.g. Thomas, *Fight or Flight*; Buettner, *Europe After Empire*.
71 J. Robinson, 'Comparisons: Colonial or Cosmopolitan?', *Singapore Journal of Tropical Geography*, 32 (2011), 125 and 137.
72 Robinson, 'Comparisons', 138.

PART I

Decolonising metropolitan cultures?

CHAPTER ONE

Black America and the overthrow of the European colonial order: The tragic voice of Richard Wright
Bill Schwarz

At the end of the 1990s, when Britain's jurisdiction of Hong Kong was coming to an end, Wm Roger Louis turned his considerable scholarly energies to the history of the final years of the British Empire in Pacific Asia. In 2001, for his presidential address to the American Historical Association, he chose to speak on 'The Dissolution of the British Empire in the Era of Vietnam', later published in the *American Historical Review*. This is a fine essay. It focuses on the diplomatic connections between the US and Britain which resulted, on the one hand, from the American military involvement in Vietnam and, on the other, from that of the British intervention in Malaysia between 1963 and 1965 – that is (in the latter case), from the moment of the formal independence of Malaya up until the massacres of the Indonesian Communists which presaged the downfall of President Sukarno. The purpose of the essay was to consider the very different outcomes of Western intervention in Vietnam and Malaysia. One element in this story which Louis highlighted was the strategic gravity of domestic opposition to the Vietnam War in the United States and the degree to which anti-war mobilisation paralleled the race politics of Civil Rights and Black Power. In an intriguing closing passage, referring to 'the interaction between the American Civil Rights movement and British decolonization', he observed that 'the comparison is fundamental for an understanding of the era. Even though the currents were parallel and not directly connected, the rivers of decolonization and Civil Rights flowed in the same direction.'[1]

Not long after, there came from the same locale – Austin, Texas – a similar perspective, in this case from A.G. Hopkins. Hopkins sought to rethink the general question of decolonisation. In doing so, he argued that there existed a historical homology between the racial policies of the white settler colonies in the British Empire and those in the United States, suggesting the need to grasp the underlying connections between the destruction of the social systems in each of these two spheres. He concluded by highlighting Martin Luther King's regard for Gandhi and Nkrumah, and cited King's belief that the Vietnam War 'seeks to turn the clock of history back and perpetuate white colonialism'. He closed his argument with these words:

> King recognized that the movement for full emancipation in the United States was part of a broader struggle to eliminate discrimination and oppression elsewhere. It is a perception that should encourage historians to think of the transfer of power after the Second World War as being a global (and globalizing) process that overrode rather than underwrote conventional political and historical boundaries.[2]

Both Louis and Hopkins raise the question of the connections between US black politics and the end of the British Empire.[3] It is this theme I explore here. In doing so I touch on the heroic vision of those who understood themselves to be poised on the threshold of the postcolonial age. But in the case of the author Richard Wright – the focus of this chapter – we are also required to appreciate the sense of impending tragedy by which the postcolonial future entered his imagination.

To follow this argument I will be making certain detours and working with a measure of indirection.[4] In order to understand Wright it is important to bring into the field of vision the role of the West Indian intellectuals, who often acted as a bridgehead between black militants from North America, such as Wright, and the forces in metropolitan Britain pressing for decolonisation. The chapter begins by exploring these connections. Next, we need to add a further link in the chain: that of the francophone black Atlantic and, more particularly, the significance of Paris as an organising centre for anti-colonial activity, the focus of the second section. The chapter concludes with a discussion of Wright's visit to the Gold Coast on the eve of independence. Through these diverse spaces, and the people, ideas and political impulses that connected them, the transnational nature of decolonisation becomes clear.

I have been impressed for a long time by the intellectual politics of New World writers who found themselves in Europe during the collapse of the colonial order. Part of their influence turned on their critiques of colonialism, and part on their conception of race, particularly their endeavours to uncover the mysteries of racial whiteness. These endeavours included a series of interventions which appeared in the 1950s and which inaugurated a challenge to the imperatives of racialised thought. I am thinking of Frantz Fanon's *Black Skin, White Masks*, which appeared in 1952; the essays and fiction of James Baldwin, most particularly his essay 'Stranger in the Village' (1953) and his novel *Giovanni's Room* (1956); and Richard Wright's polemical *White Man, Listen!*, published in 1957.[5] In this chapter, however, I am taking a narrower perspective, principally exploring Wright's encounters with British colonialism.

The differences between these various texts are conspicuous: in generic form, tenor and philosophical affiliation, they are distinct. No-one could confuse the writings of Fanon, Baldwin and Wright. Even so, there are significant common properties. First, each author sought to bring into the open the fact of whiteness, insisting that racial whiteness – for all its invisibilities – carries with it inescapable political consequences. Second, the shared Parisian location of these writings is significant. This is so, both in terms of intellectual life (the presence of existentialism), and in terms of politics (the relative proximity of decolonisation to the metropole). And third, they were all New World intellectuals. They had all determined to cross the Atlantic: Fanon from Fort-de-France in Martinique; Wright from Chicago, Brooklyn and Harlem; and Baldwin from Harlem and Greenwich Village. They were well versed in the practices of Western civilisation and knew no other. Until the time when his political allegiances took him to the cause of Algeria, Fanon's identifications with France were absolute; Wright wrote passionately about his commitment to the ideals of the European and American Enlightenment, in which he was schooled; while Baldwin reiterated throughout his life the conviction that he was first and foremost an American – 'as American as any Texas G.I.'[6] None had ever imagined himself to have been a 'native', cut adrift from the pulse of Western life.

Fanon, due to his colonial background, may have been perceived by others as a native. This misrecognition dominated his early writing, but he had never imagined himself as such. Or he had not until there occurred the encounter which has come to stand as the primal moment in postcolonial history, when he was confronted on a cold Lyon street by the exclamation of the young white child: '*Mama, tiens un nègre!*'[7] It was precisely at that point that Fanon's white mask – his cultivation in the ways of French civilisation – collapsed, leaving him to contend as best he could in the metropole with his Antillean self and his abused black body. Although for Wright and Baldwin the particulars differed, Fanon's predicament was one which they recognised.[8] The experience of entering life as black but 'of the West', and thence crossing the seas and travelling to Paris, generated a particular mentality. It allowed new ways of thinking to emerge, constituting a powerful strand in the intellectual life of European – including British – decolonisation.

Although my concern here is with Wright, we should appreciate the degree to which his story was part of a larger history. Although the lingua franca of black radicals in the United States and of those fighting to bring about the end of British colonial rule was largely English, the francophone element proves important. So too does the connection between West Indians working for the independence of their region and those struggling for racial emancipation in the United States.[9] Penny von Eschen's path-breaking *Race Against Empire* revealed the extent of anti-colonial agitation in the US. Yet it is strange that its predominating domestic frame works, analytically, to marginalise the role of expatriates, of whom Wright is the most noticeable, and amongst whom Baldwin should also be counted.[10] Wright's absence from his native land serves to exclude him from von Eschen's discussion. Yet as Paul Gilroy deftly demonstrates, Wright's exile was neither destructive of his work nor inconsequential for black America.[11]

Wright was born in poverty in rural Mississippi in 1908. Like many blacks of his generation, as a young man he made the journey northwards to Chicago's South Side, where his first political sympathies were for Marcus Garvey's United Negro Improvement Association – an allegiance which resurfaced later in his life, during the desegregation crisis of Little Rock in the autumn of 1957.[12] In 1934 he joined the Communist Party, to which he remained affiliated for some ten years until he made his break public, describing in his article, 'I Tried to be a Communist', the unscrupulousness of his erstwhile comrades.[13] In 1940 he published his novel, *Native Son*. Its depiction of Bigger Thomas marked a sensational challenge to the ideals of white America and, notwithstanding its provocation, established Wright not only as the leading black author in the United States but also as a writer who could rightfully claim his place in the American literary canon, *tout court*. Shortly after, he was officially invited by Claude Lévi-Strauss – at this point cultural attaché in the French embassy in Washington – to visit France. He went first in May 1946, returning to the US some months later. In July 1947 he and his family set sail from New York to Paris, taking with them their Oldsmobile sedan, with radio and automatic gears.

As Gilroy notes, there occurred 'a gradual change in his thinking whereby a sense of the urgency of anti-colonial political struggle displaced an earlier exclusive interest in the liberation of African-Americans from their particular economic exploitation and political oppression'.[14] What, though, of the impulses for this transformation?

In order to approach this question I will explore Wright's links to a network of prominent Caribbean anti-colonial thinkers, in New York, in London and in Paris.

The Caribbean diaspora

In the summer of 1944, in New York, Wright first met C.L.R. James, the most luminous intellectual of the twentieth-century anglophone Caribbean. James, Trinidadian born, had spent much of the 1930s as part of an influential cadre of Pan-Africanists in London, before travelling to the United States in 1938 to continue his political work which, at this stage, was dominated by the imperatives of the Trotskyist Fourth International.[15] In May 1940 James had written an ecstatic review of Wright's *Native Son*, welcoming it 'not only as a literary but also a political event'.[16] He was fired with enthusiasm after meeting with Wright. In a series of letters to Constance Webb, his lover and future wife, James explained that Wright was the person he had most wanted to talk with in the entire United States, a desire driven principally by his conviction that Wright – almost alone, he inferred – truly understood the Negro question. On reading the proofs of *Black Boy*, James deduced that Wright, in the field of letters, and he, in the field of history, in his own *The Black Jacobins*, had arrived at the same conclusion, albeit by different means.[17] Both, claimed James, apprehended the degree to which the US Negro represented the decisive social force of the future. Or, as Wright was to articulate this later, 'The Negro is America's metaphor'.[18] 'Our conclusions are identical,' James declared.[19] This enthusiasm was contagious, for not long afterwards Webb herself determined to write a full-scale study of Wright, prompted in part by James, and in the early days coming under his tutelage.[20] In turn, Wright himself was sufficiently impressed by his new friend that soon after they planned to co-author, with Ralph Ellison (soon to be renowned as the author of *Invisible Man*), a study of black America.

When Wright left for France, with both James and Ellison at the quay to see him off, relations between Wright and James became less close, the geographical distance between them inhibiting the intimacy which had prevailed in New York. However, James passed Wright on to his contacts in Europe, particularly to his old friend and political co-worker, George Padmore. Padmore had grown up with James in Trinidad. He had left Trinidad to study in the United States, was drawn to the Communist Party and thence moved to the Soviet Union, where he became a prominent functionary in the Communist International. Through the late 1920s and early 1930s he was an indefatigable, resourceful agitator throughout continental Europe, seeking to mobilise the colonised under the banner of Communism. In 1933-34 he broke with the Communist Party (just when Wright was joining) due to the change in line which, he feared, relegated the colonial issue to a matter of secondary, or minor, importance. Padmore moved to London, met up again with James after many years and worked as the active inspiration in the network of Pan-Africanists, composed mostly of West Indians.[21]

After he left England for the US, James had maintained contact with Padmore. When James met Kwame Nkrumah in Harlem, for example, and discovered that Nkrumah was planning to travel to London, James alerted Padmore. When Nkrumah arrived by the boat-train at Euston station, Padmore was there to welcome him, and to orient him towards those in the anti-colonial movement whom James and Padmore trusted. I suspect the same occurred when Wright arrived in Paris. After initial contact was made, Wright and Padmore remained in close contact, either in London or Paris, and corresponded regularly until Padmore's death in 1959, when Wright attended his funeral in London.

Wright, James and Padmore, the one American, the others West Indian, constituted a network in their own right, each with a distinct political investment in the anti-colonial struggle, and each able to claim a myriad of further political contacts whose collective influence radiated throughout the black Atlantic. Friendship and politics were indistinguishable – although, as one might expect, incessant political argument stretched the bonds of friendship. Notwithstanding the triumphs, and the sense that history was moving their way, the demands made by their public lives caused a deal of frustration, grief and mutual recrimination. Private letters and recorded conversations provide evidence of hurt feelings and exasperation. Padmore, for example, thought James's new investments in the politics of popular life in the United States bewildering, and on occasion – when James was incarcerated on Ellis Island by the immigration authorities, and later in 1958 when he hoped to return to the Caribbean for the inauguration of the Federation – there occurred a fraught correspondence about money. James was hurt by the suspicion that Wright had never taken the trouble to read his *Black Jacobins*.[22] And so on. It is difficult to know how deep such differences ran, but they do not detract from the significance of the intellectual-political nucleus which Wright, James and Padmore represented.

These masculine relations were mediated by their female partners, all of whom were white. Wright was married to Ellen Poplar, the daughter of Polish-Jewish migrants. When they first met in 1939 she had been organising the Fulton Street Communist Party cell in Brooklyn. Their initial encounter was not propitious. 'At the time', she recalled, 'I was all Party, no room for romance or anything.'[23] At the same time James encountered Constance Webb at a meeting on 'The Negro Question' at a black church in Los Angeles. She was then, as James subsequently learned, eighteen years old and unhappily married to a young Trotskyist from Fresno. Despite her youth she had long been a political activist, active in fighting for black rights and – displaying considerable courage – in organising aid and medical care for migrant workers on the industrialised agricultural estates in southern California. She was to try her hand at poetry, dancing and acting (appropriately, for one of her avant-garde sensibilities, apprenticing herself in the techniques of the 'Method'), and, as we have seen, went on to write a serious appreciation of Richard Wright. She modelled for Salvador Dalí, with disastrous results, and was employed by a chic modelling agency in New York. As James was to concede, meeting Webb was decisive for him intellectually. He was enraptured by her and by the day-to-day freedoms which, as a modern woman, she assumed to be hers, as a matter of right. She became his American muse. 'Nello', she wrote many years later, referring to James, 'believed that any idea I had, almost the breath that I drew, was vital and significant politically.'[24] Less is known about Dorothy Pizer, Padmore's partner. She too was a Marxist, coming from an impoverished London East End Jewish family; as she explained to Nancy Cunard, she had grown up accustomed to the 'racial animosities' which surrounded her.[25] Through their partnership she worked closely with Padmore, entertaining the stream of political contacts who made their way to Cranleigh Street, cooking for them, but leaving the washing-up for Padmore. She was, according to James, a decidedly modern woman, 'a Londoner and sophisticated to the last degree'; she earned their income by working, on her own terms, as a secretary for a wealthy businessman.[26] Her desire, however, was to be a writer. Her contributions to Padmore's books and journalism were significant, or perhaps more than significant, although little appeared under her own name.[27] Later she proved instrumental in planning Nkrumah's autobiography, *Ghana*, published in the year of his nation's independence, in 1957.[28]

The dynamic which underwrote the relations between these white women – two of whom were Jewish – and these black men is intriguing. Ras Makonnen, one of Padmore's group in London in the 1930s, commenting on the number of 'white girls' who worked alongside them, believed that 'One way of rejecting the oppression of men was to associate with blacks', an idea echoed by James when he recounted his observations of London after he had first arrived in 1932.[29] The emphasis which Ellen Wright, Constance Webb and Dorothy Pizer placed on their roles as modern women, though, is revealing. They all imagined themselves, through their relationships with their non-white lovers, through their politics and through their writing, to be active participants in the modern world, moving across different public domains and making them their own. Although they received, and sought, less public recognition than their men (for a time Webb was probably an exception), their independence of thought remained unassailable. Their claims on the modern world – contingent and perpetually in need of reassertion – mirrored those of their black male partners.[30] The realisation of these aspirations did not come easily, for either the white women or for the black men. Who, subjectively, was compelled to pay the greater cost remains an open matter.

Neither Ellen Wright, Constance Webb nor Dorothy Pizer was West Indian. But they were active in the political lives of James and Padmore, in the axis which they created, and for the relations between them – on the one hand – and Richard Wright – on the other. Ellen and Richard Wright were intimates of James and Webb when all four were in the US, and of George Padmore and Dorothy Pizer in Europe. It was the women who maintained the personal and political relations of the group, keeping Wright in contact with the dominating elements of Caribbean radicalism. It was Pizer, moreover, who directly suggested to Wright that he should travel to the Gold Coast, which enabled him first to contend with the realities of British colonial rule.

Paris

Michel Fabre once published an essay with the wonderful title, 'Paris as a Moment in African-American Consciousness'.[31] For the Wright years this seems exactly right. It is a complex story, with many competing strands. But the salient points take us far.

The literary sensibility in which Paris was twinned in the American imagination with Greenwich Village has a long history in twentieth-century letters.[32] To travel to Paris was a very American, very writerly, thing to do. And, given the centralisation of the French Empire, there also gravitated to Paris, from the 1920s and 1930s, a galaxy of young black colonial intellectuals hoping to seek out modernity at its most vital.[33] As the German forces were to discover when they occupied Paris in 1940, the city possessed, amongst other expressions of a modernist aesthetic, a vibrant black jazz scene.[34] During the Occupation many of these new urban forms, and the aspirations which gave rise to them, were forced underground but never entirely obliterated. Indeed, in the immediate post-war years, the French capital came to function as an orbit not only of Greenwich Village, but of Harlem too, as black US writers, musicians and artists endeavoured to cross the Atlantic in search of new freedoms.[35] Recalling his time in Paris in the 1950s, the English poet Christopher Logue observed that it was 'the black voices that rise up and speak to me'.[36] And, as Fabre and others have concluded, in this moment Paris generated a plurality of home-grown, syncretic 'Afromodernisms'.[37]

The experience of the Occupation and of Liberation created the history for the intellectual dominance of existentialism in post-war France. Yet the continuing rejuvenation of existentialism, and its hold over popular mentalities, can also be explained by the presence of *Paris noir*, in which the overriding imperative of the constitution of black subjectivity – after colonialism, after slavery – recast the traditions of classical philosophy.[38] Phenomenology in the technical nomenclature and existentialism in the popular idiom represented, in David Macey's words, 'philosophy in the first person'.[39] It moved to the centre of philosophical life in France, propelled by the urgency of a revivified black politics. The contrast to the intellectual culture of post-war England could not be more striking: in England, the question of blackness – 'race' – barely impinged; in France, it signalled an urgent, live matter.

The degree to which anti-colonial, anti-race commitments entered the categories of French philosophy can be tracked in the writings of the nation's dean of existentialism, Jean-Paul Sartre. In contemporary anglophone cultures Sartre is best known, in this respect, for his blistering 1961 preface to Fanon's *The Wretched of the Earth*, but there is a deeper history at work. An early issue of Sartre's journal *Les Temps Modernes*, founded on the morrow of Liberation, published an extract from his own *Anti-Semite and Jew* (1946), which proved conceptually an immediate inspiration for Fanon's *Black Skin, White Masks*. Shortly afterwards the journal carried many instalments of Sartre's *What is Literature?* (1947), in which Wright was lauded as the exemplar of the 'committed writer', and which ran alongside extracts from Wright's *Black Boy* (1945).[40] Simone de Beauvoir pressed for the journal to carry George Lamming's *In the Castle of my Skin* (1953), a Barbadian *Bildungsroman* closely modelled on Wright's *Black Boy*. Sartre's influential essay 'Black Orpheus' was published in 1948 as an introduction to a collection of black writing, with extracts previewed in both *Les Temps Modernes* and *Présence Africaine*. Early issues of *Présence Africaine* had promised future articles by Sartre, including a philosophical consideration of slavery, and at the time he was contemplating writing a study of the Martiniquan poet, Aimé Césaire.[41] Through the 1950s the Algerian crisis impressed itself ever more deeply in Sartre's thought, and questions of colonialism were always present, even in his most abstract works.[42] In the mainstream anglophone world of the time, such interventions, when not regarded as gratuitously abstruse, were commonly perceived as strident, or vulgar, inappropriate matters for philosophical reflection.

The overlaps between *Les Temps Modernes* and *Présence Africaine* are revealing; for all their distinct intellectual and political trajectories, they inhabited a common epistemological world in which the phenomenological traditions were immediate. Both Wright and Sartre appeared in the opening issue of *Présence Africaine*. The founding precepts of the négritudeians – of Aimé Césaire, Leopold Senghor, Léon Damas – sought to discover a means of overcoming the irresolution of the black self, from which could evolve a more profoundly effective anti-colonial politics.[43] Despite his own theoretical predilections, Sartre was right when he proclaimed that 'To use Heidegger's language, negritude is the Negro's being-in-the-world', and that it represented a means of 'becoming'.[44] Although the route from *négritude* to *Présence Africaine* was far from direct, the continuities were pronounced. And just as *Les Temps Modernes* could fuse together high philosophy with everyday political strategy, so too could its black counterparts, as the subsequent public careers of Césaire, Senghor and Damas all demonstrate.[45] In this regard, the divide between the francophone commitment to the poetics of *négritude* and the espousal of an anglophone, Marxisant Pan-Africanism was no divide at all, notwithstanding the contending philosophical approaches in play.[46]

In the person of Richard Wright these varied currents conjoin, and the 'moment in Afro-American consciousness' described by Fabre as 'Paris' was, pre-eminently, articulated by Wright. Wright had first met Sartre in New York early in 1947, and when he arrived in Paris there developed a degree of intimacy between the two, which also drew in Simone de Beauvoir.[47] For the intellectual-political cadres of *Les Temps Modernes*, Wright, the black writer-celebrity who had taken America by storm, was a figure to be prized, as the pages of the journal testify. He was published in the second issue. In the early days he had a hand in shaping the American material included in the review, especially the 1946 double issue devoted to the US. In turn, his own commitments to phenomenology became more explicit, especially at the start of 1948 when he determined to tackle Heidegger and Husserl. This foray into existentialism culminated in his novel, which became *The Outsider*, and in which the figure of the Negro evolved into a metaphor, not only for America, but for the modern world itself. (The manuscript was completed in 1952 in Catford in south-east London, not known at the time – nor since – as a locale of Afromodernism). Two things are clear. First, Wright's overtures to the world represented by *Les Temps Modernes*, both to its personnel and to its ideas, were for the early years concerted and significant. They did not make him an existentialist, in the card-carrying sense, although he – like many others of the time – absorbed the recurrent categories. The language of the existentialists entered his being. Second, in terms of how Wright imagined his own practice as a writer, his conviction that black America lived – and that *he* had lived – what the philosophers were theorising is persuasive. To read high existentialism through *Native Son* and *Black Boy*, in other words, makes sense. This does not transform Wright into a Parisian existentialist but it does highlight one dimension of the structure of feeling of black America on the eve of Civil Rights. To borrow from Macey's reading of Fanon, this may have resulted in 'bad' phenomenology, but politically it was no worse for that.[48]

Wright's relation to *Présence Africaine* and to its tyros was, if not more straightforward, probably less charged than his relations with *Les Temps Modernes*. He was present at the founding meeting of the journal at Brasserie Lip, thanks, it seems, to an initial invitation from Albert Camus.[49] Wright was close to Césaire and Senghor, curating an important exhibition with the former in the early 1950s. At the beginning of 1953 Fanon wrote to Wright in order to alert him to the publication of *Black Skin, White Masks*, indicating that the book bears 'on the human breadth of your work'. Perhaps this was no more than a plug, the young, nameless Fanon – 'My name must be unknown to you' – seeking the imprimatur of the distinguished public intellectual,[50] but other transactions were also at work. The connection to *Présence Africaine* not only allowed Wright access to Africa and to Africans, but also deepened his ties to the Caribbean diaspora. So James and Padmore entered his life, as well as Césaire and – intellectually if not personally – Fanon (who, we know, was a close reader of Wright).

In 1949 Wright sailed to Argentina, where – owing to difficulties in the US – *Native Son* was being filmed. On the way, he stopped off in Trinidad. The following year, on his return trip, he visited Trinidad again, and went with Eric Williams, the future prime minister of Trinidad and Tobago, to listen to steel pan.[51] From there he travelled to Haiti, which – as for so many others of his generation – proved a revelation. (A few years earlier, according to legend, Césaire's stammer had been cured as result of this first encounter with Haiti.) He was so inspired by the blackness of the nation that he urgently embarked on a film script about Toussaint L'Ouverture, the leader of the slave revolt out of which the independent nation of Haiti emerged in 1804. By this stage it is probable that he had not read James's *Black Jacobins* and almost certain that he would not have ever come across James's own play about Toussaint. Even so, Wright's was a very *Caribbean* response to Haiti.

These varied collective efforts embraced the shared francophone and anglophone investments in the idea of *Africa*, and also in the idea of blackness *as a means of becoming*. The dramatic, public culmination of these emergent mentalities occurred at the First Negro Writers' and Artists' Congress, organised by *Présence Africaine*.[52] This took place over three days at the Sorbonne in September 1956 – just as France, Israel and Britain were beginning, behind a wall of secrecy, to initiate a joint military invasion against Nasser's Egypt. Although the congress was fronted by Alioune Diop, Wright, in conjunction with Padmore, was a presiding spirit: a dynamic, behind-the-scenes organiser, and the closing speaker.[53] Césaire and Senghor represented the older, *négritude* generation, although neither could have been called elderly, while Fanon and Lamming were the youngest of the participants.[54] James Baldwin was present, not as a speaker but as a journalist, contributing an incisive account.[55] For my purposes here, there they all were: Wright; Fanon; Baldwin.

There was, predictably, much dissension, particularly on the question of Africa, and one could witness the legacies of *négritude* unravelling. But for all the controversies, the participants themselves were aware that history was on the move and that the old colonial order was on the point of breaking up. The intensity of this historical consciousness provided the predominating leitmotif of the congress. As Wright declared as the conference closed, that such a meeting could have taken place, in the heart of metropolitan Paris, was itself testament to 'the beginning of the end of European domination'.[56]

There is, however, a darker story to tell. The maestro Pan-Africanist, W.E.B. DuBois had been invited to the congress, but was unable to attend because of the US government's refusal to grant him a passport. It transpires that this decision was based on – or could have been based on – information supplied by Wright. James Campbell is persuaded that Wright approached the US authorities in Paris in order to inform on his political allies, and that he did so on his own initiative.[57]

This is a brutal Cold War story, as many aspects of the history of decolonisation turn out to be, and although much remains murky, one thing is clear. Like his contemporary champion of black emancipation – Paul Robeson – Wright can be perceived as a Cold War casualty.

As we have seen, Wright had been a member of the Communist Party in the 1930s and early 1940s. When he left the Party he explained himself in his widely published article 'I Tried to be a Communist', where he condemned as sickening the incessant practice of betrayal which had possessed his one-time comrades. Yet his act of public atonement did little to quell the suspicions – about Wright – of the anti-Communist militants in the US. To choose exile could be construed as un-American. Sidney Hook thought that Wright's reasons for abandoning Communism were personal, not political.[58] With varying degrees of dedication, the CIA and the FBI continued to monitor him for the rest of his life. When he first travelled to Paris, James advised him always to have a return ticket ready and warned him that, were the USSR to invade, he would be executed.[59] Wright lived in constant fear of having his passport withdrawn – and that if he were forced to return to the US he would be called before the House of Un-American Activities Committee. 'France', he wrote in August 1957 with Algeria in mind, 'is sinking each day, each hour.'[60] In an attempt to escape the pressure, he attempted – unsuccessfully – to move his family to London. The malevolent, menacing figure of David Schine, close to the apparatuses of US military intelligence, had Wright in his sights, and came knocking on his door.[61] Fear dominated his life. Towards the end, as Dorothy Pizer recorded, he was sure that the French security services, the FBI and various ex-Trotskyists were all – in a phantasmagoric, heretical alliance – plotting against him. When he died, a number of his friends believed he had been assassinated.[62]

Having indicted Communism as corrupted by the reflexes of betrayal, Wright found his own friendships and political alliances a source of anxiety and – as the existentialist part of him must have recognised – he capitulated to bad faith and set about betraying those closest to him. The growing rapprochement, from July 1952, between *Les Temps Modernes* and official Communism could not have heartened him. After the 1956 Congress, he distanced himself from *Présence Africaine*.[63] The US had failed him, as had France and (as we shall see) as Africa would too.[64] In 1954, when he was hoping to renew his passport, he chose to pass names of alleged Communists to the US authorities. He did so again in 1956, when he was immersed in organising the congress. He kept the State Department informed about Padmore's relations with Nkrumah, and about Communist sympathisers in Ghana's Convention People's Party.[65] His foreword to a 1956 publication of Padmore's opened with the unequivocal statement, 'Concerning George Padmore I am biased, for he is my friend,' and to his dying days his friendship with Padmore's partner,

[41]

Dorothy Pizer, remained – so far as she knew – trusting and intimate.[66] Such dissociation indicates the degree to which the unforgiving realities of the Cold War were internalised.[67]

In his closing speech to the 1956 Congress Wright took for his theme 'Tradition and Industrialization: The Plight of the Tragic Elite in Africa'. The tragedy, however, was not confined to African elites.

The Gold Coast on the eve of independence

Through the 1950s, Wright authored three books which engaged with the collapse of the European colonial order, and they instantly became part of the larger history that they were describing, such that we can view them now as classic texts of decolonisation. *Black Power*, published in 1954, told of Nkrumah's Gold Coast (soon to be Ghana) in the dying days of British rule. *The Colour Curtain*, which came out in 1956, reported on the historic Bandung Conference of Asian and African states that took place in April 1955. And the last – *White Man, Listen!*, dedicated to Eric Williams – appeared in 1957, composed of speeches he had delivered across Europe in the previous years, including his address to the Paris Congress. Together they testify to Wright's conception of the end of the epoch of the white man. They indicate that the parallel histories which Roger Louis had identified – European decolonisation and US Civil Rights – never existed only in 'parallel'.[68] In this volcanic historical conjuncture these distinct historical times intersected, the one imbricated in the other, and as they did so the matter of race came to be overdetermined.

To track this, I will highlight only one or two of the principal issues raised by Wright's account of the Gold Coast and, in so doing, I will return to the question of his apprehensions of the postcolonial as inaugurating a new time of tragedy. The year before Wright published *Black Power* he wrote the introduction to the US edition of Lamming's *In the Castle of my Skin*, in which he commented:

> almost all of human life today can be described as moving away from traditional, agrarian, single handicraft ways of living toward modern industrialization. [*In the Castle of my Skin* is] a symbolic repetition of the story of millions of simple folk who, spread over half the earth's surface and involving more than half the human race, are today being catapulted out of their peaceful, indigenously earthly lives and into the turbulence and anxiety of the twentieth century ... We have to lift our eyes and look into the streets and we can see countless young, dark-skinned Lammings of the soil marching in picket lines, attending political rallies, impulsively, frantically seeking a new identity.[69]

This idea of the non-white masses entering history animated the Paris Congress of 1956, and through the decade it also provided the founding precept for Wright's view of the world. It coexisted with his fierce indictment of 'white, Western, Christian civilization' and looked forward to the 'de-Occidentalization of mankind'.[70] This telescopic perspective offers a heroic reading of decolonisation in which the black masses take charge of their own destinies and, in this vein, Wright's writing transparently serves as the medium through which an epic history of decolonisation is articulated.

But, up close, as he travelled through the Gold Coast from June to August of 1953 – his first encounter with Africa – a more troubled persona revealed itself. During a lunch in Paris with Dorothy Pizer, who had been close to Nkrumah when he had lived in London, Pizer suggested to Wright that he should make the journey to the Gold Coast. When Wright recounted this story in the opening pages of *Black Power* he was at pains to emphasise his disorientation, discovering himself to be 'on the defensive, feeling poised on the verge of the unknown', 'as something strange and disturbing stirred slowly in the depths of me'.[71] Troubling for Wright was the prospect that *he* should be in *Africa*. This presentiment stayed with him: he travelled to London (where he listened to the coronation of Elizabeth II on the wireless) and thence to Liverpool for the boat to Accra. On the journey he read James's *Black Jacobins* and Williams's *Capitalism and Slavery*. When he arrived in the Gold Coast, and throughout his stay, he was conscious of his own predicament: on the one hand he was the committed anti-colonial, receptive to all that Africa symbolised; on the other, he inhabited ever more deeply his enlightened, American self, disturbed by the everyday lives he encountered. 'As detached and resistant as I try to be, I find myself sometimes falling heir to the reaction pattern which lingers on here as a kind of legacy of British imperialism.'[72] He portrays himself on his hotel balcony surveying the strangeness, disorder and unknowability which swirl below him.[73] And as his disorientation deepens so he resorts to hazardous generalisations about the personality of the African: 'he' inhabits space not time; 'he' suffers from a lack of a developed ego; 'he' cannot distinguish between good and evil.[74] Contending with an anxiogenic world of this magnitude, Wright finds himself 'immobilized'.[75] Notwithstanding the critical self-consciousness with which he depicts his own psychic unease, such sentiments make the book awkward to read. DuBois disliked it, and it continues to remain controversial.[76]

However, deep in his bones Wright was convinced that for the majority of the world's population the colonial system represented the harshest impediment to general emancipation. His allegiance to what C.L.R. James later defined as the 'Ghana Revolution' was uncompromising.[77] He closed *Black Power* with a long, heartfelt letter to Nkrumah, coolly assessing the prospects for the independence movement. Yet, as the reader will by this stage have anticipated, Wright's psychic 'immobilization' did not encourage him to present the forthcoming struggle as – in any way – heroic.

He often defined his 'Westernness' by way of his commitment to *thought*, and to the freedoms which this enabled, and he expressed his ideals in a peculiarly American idiom: 'I believe that man, for good or ill, is his own ruler, his own sovereign, his own keeper.'[78] This was not a reified conception in which reason is elevated to Reason. He knew all too well that much of the thought he most valued represented a possibility for the future rather than a given, established, fact and that it was necessary for inherited intellectual paradigms to be 'purged of racism and profits'.[79] The philosophical truths which he took to be self-evident were, in his own imagination, indistinguishable from his indictment of colonialism.

His journey to the Gold Coast proved, as he himself demonstrates, a mighty test. What most regularly crossed his field of vision were what he identified as superstition, tribalism and primitivism, none of which he was persuaded could act as a vehicle for human emancipation. In this he and Padmore were one. 'I hate primitivism,' Padmore informed Wright on one occasion; he (Padmore) remained unrepentant that he had advised Nkrumah to launch an African OGPU (Soviet Union secret police), harking back to his own memories of Stalin's intelligence services. He – this veteran, principled anti-Stalinist – shared with Wright his private reverie that only Stalinism possessed the power to break the hold of tribalism, and that when the job was done its speedy dismantling would, of course, be required.[80] For his part, in his open letter to Nkrumah, Wright announced that the 'one honourable course', indeed the only possible course, was to ensure that 'AFRICAN LIFE MUST BE MILITARIZED!' – in the expectation that 'a militarized social structure' could replace 'the political', at least 'for a time'.[81] These are unnerving words to read. They suggest that when this generation of anti-colonialists – or when some of them – were confronted by a strategic choice between tradition or modernity, they concluded that the only political solution lay with the latter. As Wright explained to Nkrumah, 'Our people must be made to walk, forced draft, into the twentieth century!'[82] Underwriting the tragic properties of this dilemma was the fact that – as they knew from other domains of their political lives – modernity, in its capitalist or Stalinist incarnations, could not deliver the freedoms for which they lived. Either way, it seemed, they were doomed.

As the anti-colonial struggles of the 1950s came closer to their realisation, Wright's commitments, while never weakening, became more oblique. When he was present at the Bandung Conference he felt unable to share many of the collective sentiments expressed. This was particularly so when he witnessed Sukarno address the delegates:

> Sukarno was appealing to race and religion; they were the only realities in the lives of the men before him that he could appeal to. And, as I sat listening, I began to sense a deep and organic relation here in Bandung between race and religion, *two of the most powerful and irrational forces in human nature.* Sukarno was not invoking these twin demons; he was not trying to create them; he was trying to organize them ... The reality of race and religion was there, swollen, sensitive, turbulent ...[83]

What Wright believed was beginning to coalesce as the public voice of the Third World was, in other words, advocating not the destruction of militant unreason, but its mobilisation. This, for Wright, represented a perilous political manoeuvre. But it was not uncontested, for, as he saw things, the educated, Westernised elites of Asia and Africa acted as a potential counterpoint and offered the greatest hope for human salvation. These men, 'stripped of the past and free for the future', although 'tragic and lonely', constituted 'the FREEST MEN IN ALL THE WORLD TODAY'.

> They stand poised, nervous, straining at the leash, ready to go, with no weight of the dead past clouding their minds, no fears of foolish customs benumbing their consciousness, eager to build industrial civilizations. What does this mean? It means that the spirit of the Enlightenment, of the Reformation, which made Europe great, now has a chance to be extended to all mankind![84]

After the plethora of interventions in postcolonial theory these are not fashionable sentiments. For sure, Wright's dilemma need not be ours. We need not be constrained, in the way that Wright believed that he was, by the polarised contrarieties of tradition and modernity. Yet at the same time we have to be watchful of the condescension which posterity bestows. In the succession of terrors and emergencies which have punctuated the postcolonial world since Wright's time, there is too much evidence of pathological thought and of the perpetual imbrication of violence in the workings of the imagination. Wright, in a prescient moment in 1957, identified what he called 'Post-Mortem Terror'. This he defined as 'a state of mind of newly freed colonial peoples who feel that they will be resubjugated; that they are abandoned, that no new house of the heart is as yet made for them to enter'.[85] To fight for the sovereignty of thought in such circumstances can be no bad thing.

Where, finally, is the tragic voice of Richard Wright to be located?[86] In his own being? In the impossible political choices with which he and his generation were confronted? Or in the postcolonial condition itself?

Notes

This is for James. It entered life as a presentation to the Imperial and Global Seminar at the Institute of Historical Research, London in February 2010. Thanks to Richard Drayton for the invitation and to those who responded. And big thanks, also, to Ruth Craggs and Claire Wintle for their editorial acumen.

1. W.R. Louis, 'The Dissolution of the British Empire in the Era of Vietnam', *American Historical Review*, 107:1 (2002), 25; P. Lashmar and J. Oliver, 'How we Destroyed Sukarno', *Independent* (1 December 1998).
2. A.G. Hopkins, 'Rethinking Decolonization', *Past and Present*, 200 (2008), 247.
3. The literature includes J. Carew, *Ghosts in our Blood: With Malcolm X in Africa, England, and the Caribbean* (Chicago: Lawrence Hill, 1994); J. Carew, 'Paul Robeson and W.E.B. DuBois in London', *Race and Class*, 46:2 (2004), 39–48; M. Sewell, 'British Responses to Martin Luther King Jnr and the Civil Rights Movement, 1954–1968', in B. Ward and T. Badger (eds), *The Making of Martin Luther King and the Civil Rights Movement* (Basingstoke: Macmillan, 1996); J. Street, 'Malcolm X, Smethwick, and the Influence of the African American Freedom Struggles on British Race Relations', *Journal of Black Studies*, 38:6 (2008), 932–50; K.H. Perry, '"Little Rock" in Britain: Jim Crow's Transatlantic Topographies', *Journal of British Studies*, 51:1 (2012), 155–77; S. Tuck, 'Malcolm X's Visit to Oxford University: U.S. Civil Rights, Black Britain, and the Special Relationship on Race', *American Historical Review*, 118:1 (2013), 76–103; A. Angelo, 'The Black Panthers in London, 1967–1972: A Diasporic Struggle Navigates the Black Atlantic', *Radical History Review*, 103 (2009), 17–35; G. Abernethy, '"Not Just an American Problem": Malcolm X in Britain', *Atlantic Studies*, 7:3 (2010), 285–307; M. Sherwood, *Malcolm X: Visits Abroad* (Los Angeles: Tsehai, 2011); S. Ambar, *Malcolm X at Oxford Union* (New York: Oxford University Press, 2014); and R. Waters, 'Imagining Britain Through Radical Blackness: Race, America and the End of Empire' (PhD dissertation, Queen Mary, University of London, 2014).
4. More directly, G. Horne, *End of Empire: African-Americans and India* (Philadelphia: Temple University Press, 2008).
5. B. Schwarz, *Memories of Empire, Vol. 1: The White Man's World* (Oxford: Oxford University Press, 2011), ch. 3, 'Remembering Race'. Wright was unsure if the US could still be regarded as constituting a 'New World': R. Wright, 'America is Not the New World', in K. Kinnamon and M. Fabre (eds), *Conversations with Richard Wright* (Jackson: University of Mississippi Press, 1993).
6. J. Baldwin, 'The Discovery of What it Means to be an American', in J. Baldwin, *Nobody Knows my Name: More Notes of a Native Son* (New York: Dell, 1961), p. 17.
7. F. Fanon, *Black Skin, White Masks* (London: Pluto Press, 1986), p. 112; D. Macey, *Fanon: A Life* (London: Granta, 2002).
8. For the anglophone counterparts to Fanon, see B. Schwarz (ed.), *West Indian Intellectuals in Britain* (Manchester: Manchester University Press, 2004); and for James Baldwin's response to European decolonisation, C. Kaplan and B. Schwarz, 'America and Beyond', in C. Kaplan and B. Schwarz (eds), *James Baldwin: America and Beyond* (Ann Arbor: University of Michigan Press, 2011).
9. W. James, *Holding Aloft the Banner of Ethiopia: Caribbean Radicalism in Early Twentieth-Century America* (London: Verso, 1998); on the Caribbean-

Harlem-Paris connection, J.M. Turner, with W.B. Turner, *Caribbean Crusaders and the Harlem Renaissance* (Urbana: University of Illinois Press, 2005); S.D. Pennybacker, *From Scottsboro to Munich: Race and Political Culture in 1930s Britain* (Princeton: Princeton University Press, 2009).

10 P. von Eschen, *Race Against Empire: Black Americans and Anticolonialism* (Ithaca: Cornell University Press, 1997).
11 P. Gilroy, *The Black Atlantic: Modernity and Double Consciousness* (London: Verso, 1993); this point was also made by Constance Webb (of whom more below) about Wright at the time of his death: 'A Few Words about Richard Wright', *Correspondence* (24 December 1960). It is curious that the West Indian connections to Wright do not touch Gilroy.
12 M. Fabre, *The Unfinished Quest of Richard Wright* (Urbana: University of Illinois Press, 1993), pp. 80–1 and 458. On Little Rock, Wright declared, cited by Fabre, that 'The Negro in the United States may very well suffer the fate of the Jew in Germany', a view with which Baldwin concurred.
13 This was republished in R.H.S Crossman (ed.), *The God that Failed* (London: Hamish Hamilton, 1950), a palpitating Cold War text. It had previously appeared in *Les Temps Modernes*, 45 (July 1949), 1–45.
14 Gilroy, *Black Atlantic*, p. 148. For the similar trajectory of Baldwin, Kaplan and Schwarz, 'America and Beyond'.
15 B. Schwarz, 'C.L.R. James's *American Civilization*', *Atlantic Studies*, 2:1 (2005), 15–43.
16 C.L.R. James, 'Native Son and Revolution: Review of *Native Son*', republished in S. McLemee and P. Le Blanc (eds), *C.L.R. James and Revolutionary Marxism: Selected Writings of C.L.R. James, 1939–1949* (Atlantic Highlands: Humanities Press, 1994), pp. 88–91.
17 C.L.R. James, *Special Delivery: The Letters of C.L.R. James to Constance Webb* (Oxford: Blackwell, 1995), p. 190.
18 R. Wright, *White Man, Listen!* in his *Black Power: Three Books from Exile: Black Power; The Color Curtain; and White Man, Listen!* (New York: HarperPerennial, 2008), p. 734.
19 James, *Special Delivery*, p. 190, and the letters through the summer and autumn of 1944.
20 James expected the book to be written quickly, for in October 1948 he was instructing Webb to send copies to Jean-Paul Sartre, Simone de Beauvoir and Albert Camus: *Special Delivery*, p. 361. A while later she published a brief consideration, 'What Next for Richard Wright?', *Phylon* (2nd quarter 1949): 161–6, which bears James's imprint. The final text eventually appeared as *Richard Wright: A Biography* (New York: Putnam, 1968). By then Webb and James had been separated for many years, and there is no indication in the book of the part James played in its genesis.
21 B. Schwarz, 'George Padmore', in Schwarz, *West Indian Intellectuals*.
22 A. Bogues, 'C.L.R. James and George Padmore: The Ties that Bind: Black Radicalism and Political Friendship', in F. Baptise and R. Lewis (eds), *George Padmore: Pan-African Revolutionary* (Kingston: Ian Randle, 2009); C. Polsgrove, *Ending British Rule in Africa: Writers in a Common Cause* (Manchester: Manchester University Press, 2009), p. 130. Both Bogues and Polsgrove understand these differences to have been more consequent politically than I do.
23 Cited in H. Rowley, *Richard Wright: The Life and Times* (Chicago: University of Chicago Press, 2001), p. 166.
24 Schwarz, 'James's *American Civilization*'; James, *Special Delivery*; and C. Webb, *Not Without Love: A Memoir* (Lebanon: University Press of New England, 2003), p. 72.
25 Cited in Polsgrove, *Ending British Rule*, p. 84.
26 C.L.R. James, 'Notes on the Life of Padmore', *Nation* (15 January 1960), n.p.
27 She, rather than Padmore, reviewed James's *Black Jacobins*, in *Controversy*, 28 (1939), n.p. and she was named as collaborator on Padmore's *How Russia*

Transformed her Colonial Empire: A Challenge to the Imperial Powers (London: Dennis Dobson, 1946).
28 Polsgrove, *Ending British Rule*, pp. 151–2.
29 R. Makonnen, *Pan-Africanism from Within* (Nairobi: Oxford University Press, 1973), pp. 146–7; and C.L.R. James, *Letters from London* (Oxford: Signal Books, 2003). For the later period, P. Gilroy, *There Ain't No Black in the Union Jack: The Cultural Politics of Race and Nation* (London: Hutchinson, 1987); M. Nava, *Visceral Cosmopolitanism: Gender, Culture and the Normalisation of Difference* (Oxford: Berg, 2007).
30 For Padmore and others of his generation, see B. Schwarz, '"Shivering in the Noonday Sun": The British World and the Dynamics of "Nativisation"', in K. Darian-Smith, P. Grimshaw and S. MacIntyre (eds), *Britishness Abroad: Transnational Movements and Imperial Cultures* (Melbourne: Melbourne University Press, 2007), pp. 23–6; and Belinda Edmondson's reading of the Victorian sentiments of the James-Padmore generation of Caribbean men, *Making Men: Gender, Literary Authority and Women's Writing in the Caribbean* (Durham: Duke University Press, 1999).
31 M. Fabre, 'Paris as a Moment in African-American Consciousness', in W. Sollors and M. Diedrich (eds), *Black Columbiad: Defining Moments in African American Literature and Culture* (Cambridge: Harvard University Press, 1994).
32 M. Cowley, *Exile's Return: A Literary Odyssey of the 1920s* (New York: Viking, 1974; first published 1934).
33 B.H. Edwards, *The Practice of Diaspora: Literature, Translation and the Rise of Black Internationalism* (Cambridge: Harvard University Press, 2003).
34 J.H. Jackson, *Making Jazz French: Music and Modern Life in Interwar Paris* (Durham: Duke University Press, 2003); F. Newton, *The Jazz Scene* (Harmondsworth: Penguin, 1961).
35 T. Stovall, *Paris Noir: African Americans in the City of Light* (Boston: Mariner, 1996); B. Jules-Rosette, *Black Paris: The African Writers' Landscape* (Urbana: University of Illinois Press, 1998); T. Danielle Keaton, T.D. Sharpley-Whiting and T. Stovall (eds), *Black France/France Noir: The History and Politics of Blackness* (Durham: Duke University Press, 2012).
36 Cited in James Campbell, *Exiled in Paris: Richard Wright, James Baldwin, Samuel Beckett and Others on the Left Bank* (New York: Scribner, 1995), p. 89.
37 F. Sweeney and K. Marsh, 'Afromodernisms: Modernity, Paris and the Atlantic World', *International Journal of Francophone Studies*, 14:1 & 2 (2011), 11–24.
38 S. Gikandi, 'Response to Bill Schwarz', "George Lamming and the Measure of Historical Time"', paper presented at the Center for Afro-American and African Studies, University of Michigan, October 2002.
39 D. Macey, 'Fanon, Phenomenology, Race', in P. Osborne and S. Stanford (eds), *Philosophies of Race and Ethnicity* (London: Continuum, 2002), p. 35. It was due to this centring of subjectivity that Lévi-Strauss pronounced phenomenology to be illegitimate, dispatching it as 'shop-girl metaphysics': *Tristes Tropiques* (New York: Penguin, 1992; first published 1955), p. 58.
40 J.-P. Sartre, *What is Literature?* (New York: Philosophical Library, 1949), pp. 77–80.
41 M. Contat and M. Rybalka, *The Writings of Jean-Paul Sartre, Vol. 1: A Bibliographical Life* (Evanston: Northwestern University Press, 1985), p. 267.
42 J.-P. Sartre, *Colonialism and Neocolonialism* (London: Routledge, 2006; first published 1964); P. Arthur, *Unfinished Projects: Decolonization and the Philosophy of Jean-Paul Sartre* (London: Verso, 2010). The opening volume of his *Critique of Dialectical Reason* (London: Verso, 1991; first published 1960) includes the chapter 'Racism and Colonialism as *Praxis* and Process'.
43 Edwards, *The Practice of Diaspora* offers an indispensable pre-history; V.Y. Mudimbe, *The Surreptitious Speech: Présence Africaine and the Politics of Otherness, 1947–1987* (Chicago: University of Chicago Press, 1992).

44 J.-P. Sartre, 'Black Orpheus', in J.-P. Sartre, *What is Literature?' and Other Essays* (Cambridge: Harvard University Press, 1988), pp. 314 and 325, which largely stands as his appreciation of Césaire.
45 Especially Aimé Césaire's *Discourse on Imperialism* (New York: Monthly Review Press, 2000; first published by *Présence Africaine* in 1955).
46 Given the preponderance of West Indians in both movements it may be tempting to recruit Paget Henry's distinction between the 'poetic' traditions of Caribbean thought and the 'historicist'. But this does a disservice both to these intellectual currents and to Henry's original argument: P. Henry, *Caliban's Reason: Introducing Afro-Caribbean Philosophy* (New York: Routledge, 2000). Through the postwar period *Présence Africaine* published, amongst others, Basil Davidson, Ronald Segal, Kwame Nkrumah, Julius Nyere, Eric Williams, George Padmore, Richard Pankhurst and Fenner Brockway.
47 Simone de Beauvoir's *America Day by Day* (London: Gollancz, 1998; first published in English in 1954) was dedicated to Richard and Ellen Wright; the latter became de Beauvoir's literary agent in the US.
48 Macey, 'Fanon, Phenomenology, Race'.
49 Fabre, 'Wright and the Existentialists', p. 40.
50 M. Fabre, 'Wright's Exile', in D. Ray and R.N. Farnsworth (eds), *Richard Wright: Impressions and Perspectives* (Ann Arbor: University of Michigan Press, 1973), p. 150; E. Julien, 'Terrains de Recontre: Césaire, Fanon, and Wright on Culture and Decolonization', *Yale French Studies*, 98 (2000), 149–66.
51 Fabre, *Unfinished Quest*, p. 352.
52 The proceedings are collated in *Présence Africaine* 8–10 (1956), available online at www.freedomarchives.org/Documents/Finder/Black%20Liberation%20Disk/Black%20Power!/SugahData/Journals/Presence.S.pdf (accessed 21 April 2015).
53 M. Fabre, *The World of Richard Wright* (Jackson: University of Mississippi Press, 1985), p. 197; Polsgrove, *Ending British Rule*, p. 150.
54 B.H. Edwards, 'Césaire in 1956', *Social Text*, 28:2 (2010), 115-25.
55 J. Baldwin, 'Princes and Powers', in Baldwin, *Nobody Knows my Name*.
56 Cited in Baldwin, 'Princes and Powers', p. 54.
57 Campbell, *Exiled in Paris*, pp. 191–3.
58 F.S. Saunders, *Who Paid the Piper? The CIA and the Cultural Cold War* (London: Granta, 1999), p. 69.
59 Webb, *Richard Wright*, p. 283.
60 Quoted in Rowley, *Richard Wright*, p. 489.
61 For Schine, see N. von Hoffman, *Citizen Cohn* (London: Harrap, 1988).
62 Campbell, *Exiled in Paris*, p. 243.
63 Fabre, *Unfinished Quest*, p. 441.
64 This was Baldwin's view: R.H. King, *Race, Culture, and the Intellectuals, 1940–1970* (Baltimore: Johns Hopkins University Press, 2004), p. 199.
65 Campbell, *Exiled in Paris*, pp. 97–103; Polsgrove, *Ending British Rule*, pp. xiv and 124–5.
66 R. Wright, 'Foreword', in G. Padmore, *Pan-Africanism or Communism? The Coming Struggle for Africa* (London: Denis Dobson, 1956), p. 11.
67 How this situation entered the fiction can be gauged from J. Campbell, 'The Island Affair', *Guardian* (7 January 2006); R. Gibson, 'Richard Wright's *Island of Hallucination* and the "Gibson Affair"', *Modern Fiction Studies*, 51:4 (2005), 896–920.
68 See also essays published in M.L. Krenn (ed.), *The African American Voice in US Foreign Policy Since World War II* (New York: Garland Publishing, 1998).
69 R. Wright, 'Introduction', in G. Lamming, *In the Castle of my Skin* (New York: Collier Books, 1953), p. vii.
70 All quotes are from the edition of *Black Power* cited above, containing not only *Black Power* but also *The Colour Curtain* and *White Man, Listen!* To clarify in which book the quote originates I will signal with one of the following abbreviations: *BP; CC; WML*. Hence here *WML*, p. 651 and *CC*, p. 594.

71 *BP*, p. 18.
72 *BP*, p. 216.
73 *BP*, p. 106.
74 *BP*, pp. 317, 410 and 400.
75 *BP*, p. 172.
76 A response which dwells on the 'Conradian' features of *Black Power* is K.A. Appiah, 'A Long Way from Home: Wright in the Gold Coast', in H. Bloom (ed.), *Richard Wright* (New York: Chelsea House, 1987); for a contrary view, see M. Diawara, 'Richard Wright and Modern Africa', in M. Diawara, *In Search of Africa* (Cambridge: Harvard University Press, 1998).
77 C.L.R. James, *Nkrumah and the Ghana Revolution* (London: Allison and Busby, 1977).
78 *WML*, pp. 708–9.
79 *WML*, p. 723.
80 Polsgrove, *Ending British Rule*, p. 134; R. Lewis, 'George Padmore: Towards a Political Assessment', in Baptise and Lewis, *George Padmore*, p. 167; Polsgrove, *Ending British Rule*, p. 159.
81 *BP*, pp. 415 and 417.
82 *BP*, p. 413.
83 *CC*, p. 541, emphasis and ellipses in original. It seems that the quotes Wright took from Sukarno's speech differ in important respects from the official record. Whether this was Wright's doing, inadvertently or not, or whether the Cold War sensibilities of his publishers intervened, remains unclear: Y. Yoshida, 'Bandung and the Literatures of Decolonization: Richard Wright, George Lamming and Ngũgĩ wa Thiong'o' (MA dissertation, Queen Mary, University of London, 2010), pp. 11–13. I follow closely D. Chakrabarty, 'The Legacies of Bandung: Decolonization and the Politics of Culture', in C.J. Lee (ed.), *Making a World After Empire: The Bandung Moment and its Political Afterlives* (Athens: Ohio University Center for International Studies, 2010).
84 *WML*, p. 722.
85 *WML*, p. 683.
86 Inevitably I have in mind D. Scott, *Conscripts of Modernity: The Tragedy of Postcolonial Enlightenment* (Durham: Duke University Press, 2004).

CHAPTER TWO

Humanist modernism: Ralph Hotere and 'New Commonwealth Internationalism'
Damian Skinner

The second half of the twentieth century was an era of decolonisation, with the formal withdrawal of colonial powers taking place around the globe, and colonised populations everywhere turning their attention to the great project of the 'decolonisation of the imagination'.[1] Settler colonial societies, identified by mass European settlement that displaces indigenous populations, offer a specific challenge to theories of decolonisation, primarily because the colonisers never leave, but also because the settlers occupy dual identities as colonisers (in relation to the indigenous peoples) and colonised (in relation to the imperial metropolitan centre).[2] In settler societies such as Aotearoa New Zealand, decolonisation cannot unfold as it does in Third World contexts.[3] As Lorenzo Veracini suggests, if decolonisation is understood to be a process whereby a colonial state is transformed into a self-governing territorial successor polity, then the settler state is already this polity, and the process has already happened. Furthermore, if decolonisation is understood to involve sovereignty negotiated between polities (the metropolitan centre and the colony), then this is quite different to the settler colonial situation, where sovereignty has to be negotiated within a single polity.[4]

As a result, decolonisation in settler contexts is not a process of withdrawal and seceding of control by the colonial power to the indigenous populations, but rather a strategic play for political power, the restoration of resources, and the recognition of indigenous peoples within the settler state. Indigenous peoples have to assert their indigeneity in the face of settler claims for the same status. This perennial struggle between native and settler indigeneity is what Chadwick Allen calls the 'Fourth World condition', and at stake are not just rights to tangible resources such as land, minerals or fisheries, but symbolic resources like authenticity and legitimacy. In Aotearoa New Zealand, as in other settler contexts, decolonisation followed two trajectories: one driven by a settler culture need to 'reinvent' itself as independent of Britain and Britishness, the other driven by Māori aspirations to assert their cultural claims on the national future.[5]

As a symbolic practice that creates images and objects that operate in the sphere of representation (including the prestigious space of high culture), art has been highly visible within processes of decolonisation. Indigenous peoples all over the world have been quick to realise the potential of art to assert new ideals of nation, cultural practice and identity. In the paradigmatic instances of political decolonisation, art asserts new identities for newly decolonised nations, replacing prior representations once shaped by the agendas of the colonisers. Within settler societies, however, indigenous peoples use art as a counter to the ongoing colonialism of settler culture, operating at the level of the national imaginary to assert indigenous political and cultural claims. This has often been a process intended to disrupt settler self-fashioning and to challenge the settler cultural nationalisms that replace indigenous cultures on the national stage, even while depending on references to these cultures' identities to fashion their own.[6] In Aotearoa New Zealand, 'decolonisation' is a term more widely applied to educational and academic discourses than to visual arts practice, even though Māori artists and art history have been deeply engaged with the task of identifying and challenging the historical and ongoing impact of settler colonialism on indigenous art practices.[7]

In this chapter I want to propose that applying the term 'decolonisation' to the work of indigenous Māori artists is productive. Through a focus on the work and travel of artist Ralph Hotere, the chapter illustrates the possibilities of indigenous modernism – and of creativity more broadly – as a decolonising process within settler societies. It also highlights the need to understand decolonisation through a transnational lens. First, an approach that moves beyond the decolonising state in isolation is required in order to understand the work and references of an artist such as Hotere, formed through and responding to the global processes of decolonisation. Second, and more broadly, the focus on the relationship between art and decolonisation in Aotearoa New Zealand demonstrates the need to understand the settler dominion experience of decolonisation alongside that of the dependent colonies. A.G. Hopkins has suggested that the self-governing status of the dominions of Aotearoa New Zealand, Australia, Canada and South Africa, achieved between 1867 and 1910, obscures the connections between processes of decolonisation in these 'empire-Commonwealth' sites and the colonies of Asia, Africa and the Caribbean that achieved independence after the Second World War. He argues that the achievement of formal self-government did not result in total cultural independence for settler colonies, and that it was only after 1945, when the colonies also began to achieve their independence, that settler societies also gained true freedom.[8] In line with Hopkins, and in its examination of the transnational artistic vision of Ralph Hotere, this chapter argues that we need to bring the trajectories of decolonisation in the dominions and in the colonies into the same temporal frame in order to enrich our understanding of the 'end of empire' in both.

Modernism and decolonisation

Indigenous modernism is not simply a question of modernist styles turning up in indigenous artworks, but rather involves a shift in the status of artworks and their relationship to communities and histories. Indigenous modernist artworks can be defined as those that function as autonomous entities, operating outside community values or ceremonial contexts.[9] Modernism gave Māori artists such as Ralph Hotere access to a discourse of universalism and a means to challenge the binaries of indigenous/modern and tradition/modernity. Modernism's reframing of historical forms of culture presented a set of tools with which to negotiate the new subjectivities that were emerging as a result of the rapid changes in indigenous societies in the post-war period.[10]

Modernist Māori art was a political practice, most obviously in its explicit challenge to cultural hierarchies and to the idea that Māori did not have an active and authentic relationship to modernity and modernism. It contravened the assertion that Māori belonged to a culture that was, like their art, traditional and outside of time and thus in opposition to modernity. Māori modernism reframed Māori art as contemporary, and created objects that were designed to circulate in the spaces of high art. The gallery, rather than the museum, emerged as a new home for Māori cultural production, which was now redefined as 'fine art' rather than 'ethnography'.[11]

If the image and the wider realm of visual culture constitute a key site for the contest between coloniser and colonised, then it is worth noting that fine art brings with it specific possibilities for decolonisation, precisely because it is the most valued and highly ranked form of creative activity, and aesthetic sensibility has often been seen as a crucial signifier of 'civilisation'. It has long been a field in which European dominance has been asserted and affirmed, and from which the colonised has been denied access.[12] As Kobena Mercer writes, 'the dynamics of inter-cultural exchange went through significant shifts during the 1940s and 1950s when formerly colonial subjects engaged in acts of artistic borrowing in their own right.'[13]

Other modernisms were created in this process as part of 'a broader international dialogue in which the artistic quest for expressive freedom was joined by non-western and minority modernists who made their stylistic choices on the social terrain of the anti-colonial quest for national liberation.'[14] According to Iftikhar Dadi, the era of decolonisation involved

> a profound and intensive search for new artistic languages ... that would seek to recover 'native' expressivity that had been repressed under colonialism, and that would actively *produce* a new modern national culture. This growing awareness of national independence and sovereignty created a demand for a new aesthetic of decolonisation, one that would remain in dialogue with metropolitan developments, but which also accounted for regional and nationalist specificities.[15]

This 'new aesthetic of decolonisation' was also an issue for modernist Māori artists in Aotearoa New Zealand. They struggled with the same paradox that Rebecca M. Brown identifies in relation to modern art in post-independence India: how to be native/indigenous *and* modern, if being modern involved 'catching up' with metropolitan artistic developments and participating in a universal paradigm, albeit also recuperating elements of the past that could form the foundation of new national identities.[16]

London and the New Commonwealth Internationalism

The post-war period saw a generation of artists such as Uzo Egonu (Nigeria), Francis Newton Souza (Goa) and Aubrey Williams (Guyana) move from the United Kingdom's colonies to London to pursue their artistic practices as modernists.[17] Alongside a number of New Zealand settler artists, Hotere did the same, moving to England in search of greater artistic opportunities. Many of these former colonial artists introduced specific references to the political and cultural processes of decolonisation in their work. The human condition, or what Olu Oguibe calls 'a humanist sensibility ... that sought meaning not in pure abstractions or the formal sources of the period, but in beliefs, knowledge, and forms from older cultures', was reinserted into formalist modernism, fed by anti-colonial awareness and an alliance to the processes of decolonisation happening internationally.[18] The modern consciousness that accompanied modernist art and aspired to change, progress and individual freedom was also fundamental to anti-colonial struggles. As Rasheed Araeen suggests, 'It was perhaps the anticolonial position held by many artists that helped them "appropriate" the ideas of rebellion and revolt inherent in the avant-garde.'[19]

Kobena Mercer calls this moment of postcolonial internationalism in the British art scene of the 1950s and 1960s the 'New Commonwealth Internationalism'. It was fostered by institutions such as the Commonwealth Institute, which evolved from the Imperial Institute in 1958 and opened in 1962 in a new architecturally designed building in London's High Street Kensington and included a spacious and modern art gallery dedicated to exhibiting art from Commonwealth countries.[20] While artists from Africa, South Asia and the Caribbean were central to this moment rather than marginal, and while New Commonwealth Internationalism did foster a politically engaged form of modernism, it was also clearly indebted to a continuing sense of empire. As Mercer argues, this was a form of 'internationalism-from-above' that tried to manage the end of empire by modernising Britain's relationship with the newly independent countries, rather than breaking ties completely.[21]

The prevalence of settler artists from Australia, Aotearoa New Zealand and Canada in London during the moment of New Commonwealth Internationalism is a further sign that artistic decolonisation during this period was a mixed affair, not always aligned with anti-colonial forces, and that this moment was experienced differently depending on the varying allegiances and opportunities of settler and native/indigenous artists. The differences between Hotere and settler artists from Aotearoa New Zealand, who do not make reference to political or cultural processes of decolonisation in their work, reveal that more than one kind of artistic decolonisation was in play among artists from settler colonies. Further, understanding New Commonwealth Internationalism through the native modernism of artists from Africa, Asia and the Caribbean without reference to settler colonial modernism produces an even more partial perspective about this movement. This chapter provides evidence of the ways in which settler colonialism might challenge our understanding of modernism, decolonisation and New Commonwealth Internationalism in this period.

Ralph Hotere and New Commonwealth Internationalism

In September 1961, Ralph Hotere moved to London, courtesy of an Association of New Zealand Art Societies Travelling Fellowship, which provided £500 per annum 'for either one or two years to a practising artist or craftsman to enable him to undertake an approved project or course of study, either in New Zealand or overseas'.[22] This award, funded by the New Zealand government, was responsible for taking a large number of New Zealand artists to London (and then Europe). It represented the ongoing ties between the dominion and the metropole, which had made London the authorised destination for New Zealand artists from the nineteenth century onwards. Hotere spent a period at the Central School of Art, where his contact with British artist William Turnbull proved critical: not just in terms of artistic possibilities and new languages of art, but in terms of politics. It was Turnbull who introduced Hotere to Countess Catherine Karolyi, who had established the Michael Karolyi Memorial Foundation near Vence in southern France in 1959. The Foundation provided residencies for artists and writers with sympathetic attitudes to left-wing politics. Hotere was awarded a three-month residency there in 1962 and ended up staying for much longer, working as a caretaker over the winter.[23]

This period in Hotere's art is marked by an explicit painted engagement with politics of different kinds. There are, for example, the *Polaris* paintings of 1962 (e.g. Figure 2.1), which are anti-nuclear and specifically refer, in their titles, to the deployment of an American Polaris nuclear submarine in Holy Loch, Scotland – something that Hotere personally protested against by taking part in the 1961 Easter anti-nuclear march from Aldermaston to London.[24] The year 1962 was also when Hotere painted the *Algérie* series (e.g. Figure 2.2), in which he makes explicit reference to decolonisation via the long Algerian struggle to gain independence from France, which finally happened that year. Another series, the *Sangro* paintings of 1962–64, take their name from the Sangro River in Italy, where Hotere's brother Jack was killed during the Second World War in a protracted battle that claimed the lives of 1,634 New Zealand soldiers in two months.[25] These three series were shown at an exhibition at the Middlesbrough Art Gallery in 1964, where their messages of protest were obvious to those who visited. In a review for the *Guardian* newspaper, W.E. Johnson wrote:

> In their own quiet, occasionally hard-edged way, many of these are undemonstratively anti-war, as are other pockets of resistance, set up in gallery 5, where Hotere shows his ten-strong tachiste "white writing" Polaris series, painted at the height of the Cuban crisis and stencilled this time with the letters ICBM; and again in gallery 8, where there are five blood-red bullet-shattered works again stencilled this time OAS and FLN, in an Algeria series painted in Vence, the home of both the colonial opposition and of Matisse's famous Chapel for the Dominican Convent.[26]

Hotere's story is, for the most part, very similar to that of the other settler artists from Aotearoa New Zealand who spent time in Britain in the 1950s and 1960s seeking to become modernists. For example,

Figure 2.1 Ralph Hotere, *Polaris*, 1962, acrylic on hardboard, 610 x 510 mm.

Pat Hanly, Edward Bullmore and Michael Illingworth, who were all based in London in the early 1960s, each produced paintings that grapple with the anxieties and heightened political protest of a Britain convulsed by the threat of nuclear annihilation and all of which in different ways experiment with the impact of modernist styles that were available in Britain and Europe at first hand.[27] Yet what stands out in Hotere's work is the explicit interest in the struggle for decolonisation in Algeria, a connection to what Mercer calls the anti-colonial quest for national liberation. Vincent O'Sullivan suggests that Hotere's connection to the issue of French colonisation in Algeria was, at least in one sense, personal:

> Before he left England, he was advised to sport a New Zealand flag on his luggage. Had he done so, the police who took him in for questioning in Menton may not have insisted he was Algerian, nor brought home to him the level of prejudice and right-wing nationalism in the south. The Sixties were a bad time for French colonialism, and the issue was a hot one in Vence.[28]

Kriselle Baker also suggests that Hotere came into contact with Algerian students at the Karolyi Memorial Foundation and it was because of 'their first hand accounts of Algeria's war of independence that Hotere began the *Algérie* series.'[29]

Using materials and methods that have a certain tactility and literal physical weight, the surfaces of the *Algérie* series are equated with surfaces from the world beyond the paintings themselves. In examining the paintings (e.g. Figure 2.2), it is as though we are looking at the walls of the Casbar in Algiers where Algerian nationals were confined under curfew and the site of extreme violence during the war of resistance which began in 1954.[30] Hotere seems to favour two basic methods of manufacture: in three of the paintings, precise holes drilled into the hardboard are joined by smeared and gestural passages of red paint – suggestive of bullet holes and human blood; in two other paintings the surfaces are inscribed with marks that read as graffiti, including the acronyms FLN (Front de Libération Nationale) and OAS (Organisation de l'Armée Secrète, which was fighting to keep Algeria under French control).[31]

Discussing *Algérie* (Figure 2.2), Baker suggests that the nine holes are precise and aligned, creating the 'impression of an organised and clinically precise execution', while an X, 'drawn by dragging a dry brush across the wet surface of paint in a single slashing stroke', itself erased by a patch of red brushstrokes, indicates 'a cancelling out of life'.[32] The strokes of the X contain a 'sense of anger and violence', the rest of the brushwork is 'hasty and irregular', while the word 'fall' has been crossed out with a thick black line at the bottom of the painting.[33] Baker's description is relevant to the effect of the painting on its audience, demonstrating how suggestive these marks and compositional devices are to being interpreted as signs of struggle and violence. The politically engaged work that Hotere produced in the early 1960s after moving to Europe follows the codes of European art such as taschism, both in terms of the formal devices of gestural and

Figure 2.2 Ralph Hotere, *Algérie*, 1962, oil on hardboard, 1210 x 740 mm.

impasto paint surfaces, and in terms of the emotional potential of this kind of abstraction to reveal the tragedy and inhumanity of war and other forms of injustice and oppression.[34]

Following the shifts in the British art world (which in the 1960s started orienting itself towards the United States), Hotere also began to absorb lessons from American artists like Ad Reinhardt.[35] Politically engaged but not linked through titles to any specific instances of injustice, Hotere's *Human Rights* paintings from 1964 replaced the gestural abstraction of his earlier work with a hard-edged geometric abstraction that is based on the repetition of elements presented in different combinations (e.g. Figure 2.3). The *Human Rights* series is constructed from wooden packing crates that originally held the

Figure 2.3 Ralph Hotere, *Black Painting*, 1964, acrylic on wood, 1207 x 1207 mm.

cathode tubes for televisions.[36] These empty-centred squares have been arranged in a variety of geometric forms, and Hotere painted them using a restricted palette of matt and gloss black, with red and blue applied only within the holes at the centre of each square.

The artworks in the *Human Rights* series feature careful paint surfaces that mostly erase the trace of the artist's hand, thus refusing the audience's ability to identify emotion or a point of view in the formal qualities of the works themselves. Hotere aligns his work with the post-painterly geometric abstraction of the American Reinhardt, rather than the post-war angst and emotion of European art informel. As Francis Pound points out, Hotere's paintings use the matt black and 'dark grey' of Reinhardt's work – the two colours or 'colourlessnesses' that Reinhardt suggests can attain immateriality – while the shift from a highly textured paint surface is in line with Reinhardt's assertion that 'Painterly painting is ugly' and his opposition to the common modernist emphasis on brushwork and the materiality of paint.[37] While Hotere did not attend Reinhardt's lecture 'Art-as-art-dogma' at the ICA in London in 1964, he did quote from the text of this lecture in the catalogue for his 1967 exhibition at the Barry Lett Galleries in Auckland, as well as using one of Reinhardt's statements as a wall text and in a leaflet for another exhibition of his paintings in 1968.[38]

The relationship between the politics of the *Human Rights* series and the way these paintings engage with the various challenges and formal investigations of modernism cannot be easily settled, although the timing of the series, and the title, suggests a connection to the Civil Rights movement in the United States.[39] In Hotere's work of this time, as with a number of artists from former colonies of the British Empire who settled in London in the 1940s and 1950s, formalist modernism is infused with anti-colonial awareness. As Baker puts it, 'It is this struggle to represent the real world while at the same time pushing the boundaries of what is considered acceptable as high modernist art that drives the work and keeps it relevant to its time.'[40] The New Zealand dealer Rodney Kirk Smith, who knew Hotere when he returned to Aotearoa New Zealand in 1965, captures the dynamics of this process perfectly when he says that 'Ralph was not political in a self-conscious sense but he certainly was in the sense that he recognised that certain things – to do with Cuba or Algeria, for example – were happening and he had to respond. These things were integrated into the art.'[41] It is notable not so much that Hotere was responding to his environment, but that his attention was captured by specific political struggles that were closely tied to the end of empire, as well as the desire of native and indigenous peoples to achieve independence.

While attempts have been made to align Hotere's love of black, for example, with aspects of Māori symbolism, cosmology and mythology, O'Brien suggests that 'the artist would prefer to see the works as essaying a *universal* myth – a priority he would have assimilated in England in the early 1960s when he became interested in Ad Reinhardt and the art that grew out of that myth-obsessed movement, Abstract Expressionism.'[42] This is no doubt true, but the moment of New Commonwealth Internationalism provides us with another way to understand this dynamic, and to make sense of the ongoing political commitment in Hotere's work, his ranging across regions and languages, and his willingness to make gestures to anti-colonial struggles, be it decolonisation in Algeria and the Civil Rights movement in the United States in the 1960s, the fight against apartheid in South Africa – which is the subject of the *Black Union Jack* series (1983) – or the first Gulf War in the *Song of Solomon* series from 1991.[43] Hotere, like many other native artists who spent time in Britain and who can be considered part of New Commonwealth Internationalism, made 'the discourse of global politics, and especially of the postcolonial condition, part of the humanist imperative of late modernism'.[44]

Paintings from the *Human Rights* series were first exhibited in the Young Commonwealth Artists exhibition at the Whitechapel Art Gallery in 1964.[45] Here, they were part of the New Commonwealth Internationalism, which was, by the late 1960s, an institutional discourse as well as an aesthetic imperative (the politicisation of late modernism). This institutionalisation was first manifested in the independent gallery sector, through establishments like the New Vision Group, formed by South African artist Denis Bowen and dedicated to promoting abstract artists from Commonwealth countries alongside European tachism, constructivism and kinetic art, and Victor Musgrave's Gallery One, which profiled artists like Francis Newton Souza as well as European modernists like Yves Klein. Eventually these developments were incorporated into the official activities of the government-funded Commonwealth Institute, which supported initiatives like Denis Bowen's First Commonwealth Biennial of Abstract Art in 1963, as well as hosting numerous solo shows by artists from colonies and dominions who were now part of the Commonwealth.[46]

As part of the Commonwealth, New Zealand artists had an immediate entré into the myriad exhibitions that were organised under that rubric: Pat Hanly was included in the 1962 Young Commonwealth Artists exhibition at the RBA Galleries in London; James Boswell, William Culbert and John Drawbridge took part in the First Commonwealth Biennial of Abstract Art in 1963; Edward Bullmore joined Hotere in the 1964 Young Commonwealth Artists exhibition at the Whitechapel and was also included in the Second Commonwealth Biennial of Abstract Art at the Commonwealth Institute in 1965, alongside Michael Browne, Melvin Day and Edgar Mansfield; and so on.[47]

Hotere exists on the edges of this moment in British art history, and, as this chapter argues, placing him in this context makes sense of dimensions of his practice that otherwise remain invisible and inexplicable if he is defined only as a New Zealand artist. And yet, the presence of other settler New Zealand artists in this milieu enable us to see something distinctive about Hotere's perspective, and what he made of his contact with New Commonwealth Internationalism. The task of constructing a discourse of Commonwealth art in the 1960s involved pulling together disparate practices, and especially involved negotiating the differences between the ex-colonies and the dominions. The example of the Commonwealth Institute and the activities of in-house curator Donald Bowen illustrate this clearly. In Bowen's texts, and in the exhibitions hosted by the Commonwealth Institute, there is a notable split between settler and non-settler countries. In exhibitions on Australia, Canada and Aotearoa New Zealand, indigenous art practices were overlooked in favour of settler nationalism; the focus was on the ways in which (white) artists in the dominions had managed to establish their independence from British and European art movements. In contrast, when it came to Africa, India or the Caribbean, for example, the emphasis was on native artists and the ways in which they had grappled with the encounter of modernity, modernism and tradition. In this curatorial moment, then, settler artistic decolonisation – which is often antithetical to indigenous aspirations for independence, and always problematic in its relationship to indigenous peoples and cultural practices – was set alongside native artistic decolonisation, and the tensions between them were massaged away through the device of the Commonwealth itself. Indigenous peoples, who unlike settlers tended not to move to London in the post-war period, were effectively invisible in this moment.

Conclusion

The decision of Māori artists like Ralph Hotere to be modernists is a challenge to the art historical structures that equate indigeneity and otherness. For non-Western artists, an interest in modernist art leads to a displaced identity, as neither fully indigenous nor fully modern, and thus as always 'late' and 'outdated'. Because colonial discourse denies that modern or contemporary art can be embedded in indigenous cultures, artists are faced with two choices: to be exactly the same as international modernist art (and thus uninteresting), or to be exotically different (and thus a kind of folk art located outside modernist art).

Indigenous artists such as Hotere sought to locate themselves in the geo-cultural territory of white modernism, as modern artists with modern subject positions. To do so was to pursue a kind of artistic decolonisation because, as Leon Wainwright argues, 'being "modern" was an inaccessible status since they were aiming to insinuate themselves in a "place" or "position" predicated on their exclusion.'[48] This chapter therefore presents Hotere as another case study in the growing art history of alternative modernisms that challenge reductive formulations of modernism unable to properly identify indigenous appropriations of modernist artistic strategies as tactics of liberation.

Bringing Hotere into contact with various modes of decolonisation also opens up productive ways to understand his artistic achievement. Divorced from the European artistic milieu he encountered in the 1960s in England and France, Hotere's art becomes inscrutable, as his politics become isolated from the broader decolonising struggle that was central to this art world.

Placing Hotere's experience within a broader movement of artists from the ex-colonies who travelled to London in order to become modern artists also suggests differences between his perspective and that of settler artists who followed the same trajectory. This insight illustrates the different modes of artistic decolonisation at play in this moment: not only the claims to sovereignty of former colonial states, but also the connected, but different (and conflicting) claims to independence of settler and indigenous peoples in countries such as Aotearoa New Zealand. Highlighting these diverse experiences also highlights the different projects of decolonisation that were caught up in New Commonwealth Internationalism.

Notes

This research was funded by a Newton International Fellowship from the British Academy, and with support from the Museum of Archaeology and Anthropology, University of Cambridge.

1 See S. Faulkner and A. Ramamurthy, 'Introduction', in S. Faulkner and A. Ramamurthy (eds), *Visual Culture and Decolonisation in Britain* (Aldershot: Ashgate, 2006), pp. 1–2.

2 For a discussion of these issues, see A. Johnston and A. Lawson, 'Settler Colonies', in H. Schwarz and S. Roy (eds), *A Companion to Postcolonial Studies* (London: Blackwell Publishers, 2000), pp. 362–3.
3 Aotearoa is the Māori name for New Zealand.
4 L. Veracini, *Settler Colonialism: A Theoretical Overview* (London: Palgrave Macmillan, 2010), p. 105.
5 P. Brunt, 'Decolonization, Independence and Cultural Revival, 1945–89', in P. Brunt, N. Thomas, S. Mallon, L. Bolton, D. Brown, D. Skinner, S. Küchler, *Art in Oceania: A New History* (London: Thames and Hudson, 2012), p. 371.
6 Nicholas Thomas describes this as the problem of the 'native and/or national' identity: N. Thomas, *Possessions: Indigenous Art/Colonial Culture* (London: Thames and Hudson, 1999), p. 12.
7 For example, there is no art historical equivalent to the use of the term 'decolonisation' in Linda Tuhiwai Smith's *Decolonizing Methodologies: Research and Indigenous Peoples* (London and Otago: Zed Books and Otago University Press, 1999).
8 A.G. Hopkins, 'Rethinking Decolonization', *Past and Present*, 200 (2008), 215.
9 J.C. Berlo and R. Phillips, *Native North American Art* (Oxford: Oxford University Press, 1998), p. 210.
10 See D. Skinner, 'Indigenous Primitivists: The Challenge of Māori Modernism', *World Art*, 4:1 (2014), 67–87.
11 For a detailed discussion, see D. Skinner, *The Carver and the Artist: Māori Art in the Twentieth Century* (Auckland: Auckland University Press, 2008).
12 O. Oguibe, 'Nationalism, Modernity, Modernism', in O. Oguibe, *The Culture Game* (Minneapolis: University of Minnesota Press, 2004), pp. 47–8.
13 K. Mercer, 'Introduction', in K. Mercer (ed.), *Discrepant Abstraction* (London and Cambridge: Institute of International Visual Arts and MIT Press, 2006), p. 8.
14 Mercer, 'Introduction', p. 8.
15 I. Dadi, 'Rethinking Calligraphic Modernism', in Mercer, *Discrepant Abstraction*, pp. 96 and 98.
16 R.M. Brown, *Art for a Modern India, 1947–1980* (Durham: Duke University Press, 2009), pp. 1–2.
17 See O. Oguibe, '"Footprints of a Mountaineer": Uzo Egonu and Black Redefinition of Modernism', in Oguibe, *The Culture Game*, pp. 60–72; and L. Wainwright, 'Francis Newton Souza and Aubrey Williams: Entwined Art Histories at the End of Empire', in Faulkner and Ramamurthy, *Visual Culture and Decolonisation in Britain*, pp. 101–26.
18 Oguibe, '"Footprints of a Mountaineer"', p. 68.
19 R. Araeen, *The Other Story: Afro-Asian Artists in Post-war Britain* (London: Hayward Gallery, 1989), p. 12.
20 For more information about the Commonwealth Institute, see R. Craggs, 'The Commonwealth Institute and the Commonwealth Arts Festival: Architecture, Performance and Multiculturalism in Late-Imperial London', *London Journal*, 36:3 (2011), 247–68.
21 K. Mercer, 'Black Atlantic Abstraction: Aubrey Williams and Frank Bowling', in Mercer, *Discrepant Abstraction*, p. 186.
22 'ART AWARDS', in A.H. McLintock (ed), *An Encyclopaedia of New Zealand* (Te Ara: Encyclopedia of New Zealand, updated 22 April 2009, www.TeAra.govt.nz/en/1966/art-awards/1 (accessed 21 April 2015) (first published 1966).
23 K. Baker, *The Desire of the Line: Ralph Hotere Figurative Works* (Auckland: Auckland University Press, 2005), p. 4.
24 Baker, *The Desire of the Line*, p. 18.
25 K. Baker, 'Ralph Hotere: The Vence Paintings – Sangro, Polaris, Algerie' (MA dissertation, University of Auckland, 2002), p. 19.
26 W.E. Johnson, in *Guardian* (28 March 1964), quoted in G. O'Brien, *Hotere: Out the Black Window* (Auckland: Godwit Publishing, 1997), p. 25.

27 See G. O'Brien (ed.), *Pat Hanly* (Auckland: Ron Sang Publications, 2012); P. Jackson, *Edward Bullmore: A Surrealist Odyssey* (Tauranga: Tauranga Art Gallery, 2008); A. Lister, '"A New Lord Demanding Much Attention": Unpacking Michael Illingworth' (MA dissertation, Victoria University of Wellington, 2003).
28 V. O'Sullivan, 'Sketching the Artist', in K. Baker and V. O'Sullivan, *Ralph Hotere* (Auckland: Ron Sang Publications, 2008), p. 311.
29 Baker, 'The Vence Paintings', p. 86.
30 Baker, 'The Vence Paintings', p. 87.
31 For an overview of these organisations, and the anti-colonial struggle in Algeria, see D. Rothermund, *The Routledge Companion to Decolonization* (London: Routledge, 2006), pp. 178–184.
32 Baker, 'The Vence Paintings', p. 88.
33 Baker, 'The Vence Paintings', p. 88.
34 K. Baker, 'Ralph Hotere, 1968–1977: A Decade of Black and Light' (PhD dissertation, University of Auckland, 2009), p. 21.
35 Interestingly, Hotere's engagement with American modernism through the work of Ad Reinhardt (an important part of his encounter with New Commonwealth Internationalism) comes at the same time that the growing American focus of the British art world was effectively marking the end of the metropolitan interest in modernists from the colonies. As Rasheed Araeen notes, London's marginal status as an international art centre was a major driver in the acceptance and celebration of artists from the former colonies, fed by the hope that London would develop into an international cultural centre within the newly independent Commonwealth. The turn to the United States basically brought to an end the viability of Commonwealth artists in London. The artists who made such an impact on British art as part of New Commonwealth Internationalism effectively became invisible from the late 1960s (Araeen, *The Other Story*, p. 15).
36 Baker, 'Ralph Hotere, 1968–1977', p. 23.
37 See F. Pound, 'Tiger Country: Hotere, Reinhardt and the US Masters', in I. Wedde (ed.), *Ralph Hotere: Black Light* (Wellington and Dunedin: Te Papa Press and Dunedin Public Art Gallery, 2000), pp. 10–25.
38 Pound, 'Tiger Country', p.15.
39 Baker has a very interesting discussion about these paintings and their relationship to the Civil Rights movement. See 'Chapter 1: Hotere's Modernism', in Baker, 'Ralph Hotere, 1968–1977', pp. 23–37.
40 Baker, 'The Vence Paintings', p. 16.
41 Rodney Kirk Smith, quoted in O'Brien, *Hotere*, p. 23.
42 O'Brien, *Hotere*, pp. 76–7.
43 Nicholas Thomas has also pointed out that Hotere's artistic practice is notable for its ongoing refusal of a notion of identity that is modelled on nationality: a unitary selfhood (as Māori) that defines his artistic expression (as Māori art). Instead, as Thomas suggests, Hotere's art conveys 'a sense of location and engagement that is neither as particular nor as general as the nation. ... His work acknowledges moods and sentiments that afflict us all, and to that extent is humanist, implicitly rejecting national or cultural specification' (Thomas, *Possessions*, p. 183).
44 Oguibe, '"Footprints of a Mountaineer"', pp. 68–9.
45 Baker, 'Ralph Hotere, 1968–1977', p. 25.
46 Mercer, 'Black Atlantic Abstraction', pp. 186–7.
47 For more information on these artists and the kind of practices they had in London, see G. O'Brien (ed.), *John Drawbridge: Wide Open Interior* (Wellington: City Gallery Wellington, 2002); and Jackson, *Edward Bullmore*.
48 Wainwright, 'Francis Newton Souza and Aubrey Williams', p. 105.

CHAPTER THREE

Henry Swanzy, Sartre's zombie? Black Power and the transformation of the Caribbean Artists Movement
Rob Waters

In the summer of 1968, the Caribbean Artists Movement, a literary-artistic collective of Caribbean writers, artists and critics in Britain dedicated to defining a Caribbean aesthetic, fell into crisis. The moment itself is significant. In Britain, the rise of a new popular politics of race had broken apart traditional political affiliations and practices as thousands marched in support of Enoch Powell's anti-immigration speeches. In the US, Martin Luther King's recent assassination marked how far the struggle for Civil Rights still had to go, while a politics of Black Power, and particularly of the Black Panther Party, moved into an international arena. Growing discontent with the post-independence governments of many Caribbean states, meanwhile, was fostering a new black radical politics in the region. Many of those at the heart of the Caribbean Artists Movement (CAM) had long been concerned with how to define, discover or create decolonised Caribbean literary and artistic practices in which the ethics and aesthetics of the colonial period were challenged, abandoned or remade. In the summer of 1968, however, it was the sociology of cultural production and consumption which came to the forefront of discussions in CAM, as the movement's members were challenged to restage their artwork in new, communal, 'blacker' spaces, subverting the cultural authority of the traditional institutions of the British arts establishment. This was a demand for new cultural practice informed by a politics of Black Power.

In the transformation of CAM, we can see a late politics of decolonisation, or what Richard Drayton has recently termed 'secondary decolonisation', playing out in Britain and the Caribbean.[1] Occurring some years after the formal acquisition of constitutional sovereignty in the former colonies, and questioning the limits of that event for overturning the previous colonial order, this second decolonisation was of a different historical moment, in which transactions with North American black radicalism were paramount. This is a moment worth returning to for our understanding of cultural decolonisation, for it is in the protracted debates over the proper modes of black cultural expression reaching their height in the late 1960s and early 1970s that we can see many of those positions which moved to the heart of British black cultural studies in the following decades first emerge. Much changed in this short period. The literary cultures of Caribbean writing in the 1950s were, as Gail Low has recently observed, closely bound up with the literary cultures of post-war Britain. Published primarily by British publishers, reviewed often in British literary periodicals, printed and sold in Britain, or shipped from there to the West Indies, Caribbean writing was determined by a metropole–colony relationship. The 'communication circuit' of this writing – as Low, borrowing from Roger Darnton, terms these networks in the production and consumption of literary cultural artefacts that generate symbolic social value – was tied to end-of-empire liberal-imperial designs to foster new Commonwealth literary cultures modelled along metropolitan lines.[2] It was precisely the structuring of this 'communication circuit' that came under attack in the late 1960s, as the relations of production and consumption of cultural artefacts for a decolonising culture were rethought.

This chapter explores how the communication circuits that structure the production and consumption of cultural artefacts were rethought and reordered through ideas of radical blackness in the black Atlantic world of the late 1960s. This was a transnational process which played out beyond just the former colonies and the declining metropole and included a shift in the attribution of social value to cultural artefacts, effecting what could be seen as 'authentic' and effective sites of decolonising cultures. In Britain, the transformation of CAM played a central part in this transition.

This story begins with an eerie feeling. At the Caribbean Artists Movement's conference at the University of Kent, on 1 September 1968, Henry Swanzy, former editor and producer (from 1946 to 1954) of BBC radio's *Caribbean Voices*, a man who had contributed immeasurably to the development of West Indian literature and to the destabilisation of 'correct forms' of English as the proper artistic medium in metropole and colony,[3] chose to deliver his address in a green, grey and black tie. 'I've put on a zombie tie, really, or at least what I think is a zombie tie, with a lot of green and grey and black, to indicate what I feel my position is,' announced Swanzy. 'And it is a very eerie ... feeling, to come back as a sort of zombie ... after so many years, and after so many things have happened in the world, and particularly in the Third World, since the year 1954.'[4]

Swanzy's description of himself as a zombie, a being removed from the life it observes, formed an indirect reference to Jean-Paul Sartre's preface to Frantz Fanon's *The Wretched of the Earth*, a text which Swanzy alluded to in his following speech.[5] Invoking the zombie, Sartre had described the movement of the white European, in the period of decolonisation, from centre to periphery, and from actor to acted upon:

> For the fathers [of the colonised], we alone were the speakers; the sons no longer even consider us as valid intermediaries: we are the objects of their speeches. ... This indifference strikes home: their fathers, shadowy creatures, *your* creatures, were but dead souls; you it was who allowed them glimpses of light, to you only did they dare speak, and you did not bother to reply to such zombies. Their sons ignore you; a fire warms them and sheds light around them, and you have not lit it. Now, at a respectful distance, it is you who will feel furtive, nightbound and perished with cold. Turn and turn about; in these shadows from whence a new dawn will break, it is you who are the zombies.[6]

Becoming a zombie, for Sartre, divests the white European of agency – note the passivity of the subject in his claim that 'we in Europe are *being decolonised*: that is to say that the settler which is in every one of us is being savagely rooted out'.[7] And yet, in such bleak prognosis, was Henry Swanzy Sartre's zombie? Born at Glanmire rectory, near Cork, just a year before the Easter Rising, Swanzy was from the other side of the colonial encounter to Sartre's zombies. *Caribbean Voices*, moreover, was a programme at the heart of the development of post-war West Indian literature. Of Swanzy's work with the programme, the Barbadian author George Lamming had suggested that 'No comprehensive account of writing in the British Caribbean during the last decade could be written without considering his whole achievement and his role in the emergence of the West Indian novel.'[8] If, just eight years after Lamming wrote this accolade, Swanzy could experience himself only as a haunting presence, this marked how far relations in the struggle for political and cultural decolonisation in Britain and the Caribbean had changed since the heyday of *Caribbean Voices*: it points us to a profound historical rupture.

The West Indian novel, the pre-eminent form in the nation-building efforts of Caribbean anti-colonial cultural production from the 1930s to the 1960s, was a site in which the popular life of the Caribbean was centred. As Lamming wrote in 1960,

[T]he West Indian novelist did not look out across the sea to another source. He looked in and down at what had traditionally been ignored. For the first time the West Indian peasant became other than a cheap source of labour. He became, through the novelist's eye, a living existence.... It is the West Indian novel that has restored the West Indian peasant to his true and original status of personality.[9]

And yet, as the Trinidadian literary critic Kenneth Ramchand, recently returned from his own long sojourn as a student and academic in Britain, lamented in 1970, 'Since 1950, most West Indian novels have been first published in the English capital, and nearly every West Indian novelist has established himself while living there.'[10] The content of the West Indian novel may have centred on the life of the Caribbean peasantry, but its 'raw material',[11] like that of the peasant's labour, was processed, transformed to commodity and consumed in, and sent back to the colonies from, the metropole. London, Ramchand concluded, was 'indisputably the West Indian literary capital'.[12]

Caribbean Voices defined the early moment of West Indian nation-building that Ramchand, by 1970, was impatient to move beyond. A radio programme on the BBC Colonial Service founded under the editorship of the Jamaican poet and broadcaster Una Marson in 1943, *Caribbean Voices* solicited submissions of Caribbean poetry and prose to be read on air and discussed the following week on the programme. Providing a platform for aspiring writers from Sam Selvon to George Lamming, V.S. Naipaul, Edgar Mittelholzer, Michael Anthony, Jan Carew, Edward Brathwaite and Andrew Salkey, and even broadcasting the work of the young Stuart Hall, just then beginning his academic career at Oxford, *Caribbean Voices* was formative in the careers of a generation of Caribbean writers coming of age in the 1950s. As editor from 1946 to 1954, Henry Swanzy fostered a growing community of contributors and readers on the programme, and in so doing sustained, materially and intellectually, the development of a new Caribbean literary tradition.[13] Although the programme had been developed by the BBC in part as a tactic to solicit West Indian support for the war effort in the wake of anti-colonial and labour unrest across many Caribbean colonies in the late 1930s, in a pleasing historical irony it became, too, a major site in the formation of new nationalist sentiments in the post-war years.[14] However, in this irony lay a paradox: the development of Caribbean nationalism, and of a Caribbean diasporic identity in Britain, was here dependent on and channelled through the major institutional networks of cultural authority that sustained imperial hegemony. 'Every what you call major writer of the region', as Lamming recalled, 'came through these particular channels of writing in the islands, almost paying to get published in local literary magazines, and then being taken up by the BBC *Caribbean Voices* programme and channelled back to the islands.'[15]

Caribbean Voices was, in this respect, embedded within the wider networks that placed London at the centre of Caribbean literary production. V.S. Naipaul, reflecting on his early years as a struggling writer, claimed he 'couldn't have become a writer without London'. This necessity reflected a material consequence of empire: London was where 'the whole physical apparatus of publishing, of magazines, the BBC, [the] apparatus [that] enables a man to make a living', was located. However, the need for London was more than just material and, especially for a writer like Naipaul, revealingly demonstrated the symbolic power of the colonial myth of the metropole as the origins, and the only real centre, of 'culture'. '[W]ithout London,' wrote Naipaul, 'without the ... critics and editors, one would be trying to write in a wilderness, without any sort of tradition behind oneself.'[16] In the moves made here from the absence of an accredited and institutionalised literary-critical culture to the perception of the Caribbean as a cultural wilderness, devoid of 'tradition', are the processes by which material relations of colonialism assumed symbolic importance. Among the generation of West Indian writers in the British metropole of the 1950s, Naipaul is far from representative in his readiness to ascribe the colonial space from which he came as an absence, but what his comments reveal about the symbolic power of the institutions he describes extends beyond just Naipaul himself. As David Dabydeen has suggested, *Caribbean Voices* was not only the main platform for West Indian writers to get their work heard: being on the programme 'signified that the writer had arrived'. Dabydeen recalls Sam Selvon's account of receiving his first payment from the BBC for *Caribbean Voices*. The cheque was 'printed on thick textured paper which gave it imperial authority'. This was an attribute which gave the cheque more than just monetary value. Selvon 'confesses being dead broke, but carrying his cheque around for days before cashing it, so as to experience the privilege of being a writer, one so designated and anointed by the BBC'.[17]

Caribbean Voices ceased broadcasting in 1958, marking, it seemed, the end of the high period for West Indian literature that the programme had done so much to support. In 1966, the Barbadian poet and historian Edward Brathwaite, a former contributor to the programme, wrote to a fellow contributor, the Jamaican novelist and broadcaster Andrew Salkey, expressing his sense of the passing of this moment. 'It doesn't seem', as he told Salkey, 'that West Indian writers are being noticed any more. The fifties, yes, they were noticed. We don't hear from them [anymore], they are not in the book shops, I don't see anybody giving talks in London, and so on.'[18] As a solution, Brathwaite would propose a 'W[est] I[ndian] artists and writers' group concerned with discussing W[est] I[ndian] art and literature' that could 'link-up with C[ommon]wealth and British writers and artists, ... meet and discuss the work of French and Spanish-speaking West Indians', and engage with 'publishers, BBC types and British critics'.[19]

It was thus that the Caribbean Artists Movement was established. A London-based collective for Caribbean artists and intellectuals that drew together in its short six-year history the luminaries of contemporary Caribbean art and literature, CAM acted as a central nexus in the intellectual and political currents of 1960s black British life, a meeting place for Caribbean, North American and British black politics from which new practices of cultural decolonisation emerged or were anticipated. CAM was formed on 19 December 1966 in Brathwaite's basement flat at a University of London hall of residence near King's Cross. Brathwaite, who proposed CAM to its co-founders, Andrew Salkey and the Trinidadian poet and publisher John La Rose, aimed to create a Caribbean writers' and artists' collective in which new directions in Caribbean arts could be explored. From early private meetings in Brathwaite's flat and the flat of the Jamaican sociologist and novelist Orlando Patterson, CAM branched out to regular public meetings at the West Indian Students' Centre in Earls Court in March 1967, also producing a bimonthly newsletter publishing the papers and recording the critical discussions from these meetings.

In its early form from its founding in December 1966 to its second conference in September 1968 at which Swanzy delivered his zombie address, CAM held many similarities to *Caribbean Voices*, the last major nexus to bring together Caribbean artists with a British and Caribbean audience. Beyond fostering links between diasporic Caribbean artists and critics living in Britain, and providing public spaces for critical discussion, CAM also sought to build links between its members and the publishing and arts industries in Britain. Brathwaite wrote to British publishers providing an outline of CAM's aims and activities, and when CAM held the first of its annual conferences at the University of Kent in September 1967, invitations were extended to the editors the *Observer*, the *Sunday Times*, the *London Magazine* and the *New Statesman*, and to the Arts Council and the British Council.[20] In these appeals to the BBC and the British arts establishment, the project was firmly embedded in relationships with the established institutions of cultural authority in Britain, and these connections were echoed not only in the institutional networks within which CAM attempted to embed itself, but in its symbolic practices, too. The first conference in 1967, advertised as 'a chance for detailed and continuous discussion on several aspects of West Indian artistic expression in comfortable, attractive surroundings', complete with buffet suppers on the lawn and sherry parties, repeated in its execution the cultural codes of a formal, colonial Englishness.[21]

Given these similarities between CAM and *Caribbean Voices*, whence Swanzy's 'eerie feeling'? By late 1967, a year into CAM's existence, Brathwaite had begun to reframe its activities in an opposition between community and authority, now suggesting that CAM was constituted by 'an anti-authoritarianism, a distrust of people who hold power and who like to use power ... You've got to be able to break it down, to hand it over, to share it, and this is connected with a sense of community.'[22] Tensions were developing in CAM's relationships with those institutional bodies that had traditionally sustained Caribbean arts in Britain. A few months before the 1968 conference, anger had been directed at the Jamaican artist Karl 'Jerry' Craig for inviting the Jamaican High Commissioner to open an exhibition of CAM artists at the West Indian Students' Centre. Shortly after this, there was also a breakdown in relations between CAM and the Institute of Contemporary Arts following a proposed exhibition there in June – John La Rose complained that 'Those cats don't have respect for black people. I hope they learn from this reaction of ours.'[23] This growing sense of unease with CAM's existing affiliations was a sign of the times: as racial discrimination and violence became an entrenched feature of British society, and postcolonial governments in the Caribbean appeared to be reneging on the liberatory promise of their new political independence, a growing sense of dissatisfaction demanded new ways of conceptualising decolonisation in former metropole and former colony alike.

CAM's transformation occurred at its second conference, in 1968. As one report on the conference noted, 'why C.A.M. exists, what it should be doing, where it should be meeting, and above all, with whom it should be communicating' became the key questions of the weekend.[24] At this conference, the very same at which he donned his zombie tie, Swanzy noted Black Power supporters in the audience fixing the white academics present 'with a penetrating stare'.[25] Calls for Black Power repeatedly surfaced. One conference member demanded that CAM move its activities to the 'ghettos' of Brixton and Ladbroke Grove, areas of London with historically high levels of working-class Caribbean settlement, while another, recalling the recent developments of the Black Arts Movement in the United States, called for CAM to follow this lead and make 'artistic expression run ... parallel with political struggle'.[26] In the conference discussions, Stokely Carmichael, the leading voice of American Black Power, Le Roi Jones (Amiri Baraka), the most prominent figure of the US Black Arts Movement, and James Baldwin, an African-American writer whose critiques of race in America were becoming increasingly uncompromising in tone, formed frequent points of reference.[27] By the end of the weekend, under a last-minute vote, a resolution was passed to send a cable from CAM to the Jamaican government in protest at its recent banning of the literature of Malcolm X, the Nation of Islam's Elijah Muhammad and US Black Power leader Stokely Carmichael.[28]

The objections to CAM's existing structure and affiliations turned on new modes of radical blackness that were gaining hold across the black Atlantic world. The late 1960s – and, most cataclysmically, 1968 – were host to global political and cultural ruptures. These were, as the great Trinidadian intellectual C.L.R. James observed in an address to a London audience in August 1967, years in which 'history moves very fast ... and can quickly leave the dull behind'.[29] James was speaking in the aftermath of one event that was quick to transform radical black politics in Britain. On 15 July 1967 Stokely Carmichael had arrived in Britain for a ten-day tour of London. Carmichael, a leader in the US Civil Rights body the Student Non-Violent Co-ordinating Committee, had changed the tide of the Civil Rights movement when he called for 'Black Power' at a march in Mississippi in June 1966. Following his rallying cry, political organisations and protean popular movements for Black Power sprang up across the United States and further afield, held together through the international availability of an emergent Black Power literature and coverage of events in the US, and through the movement of Black Power leaders on an international stage.[30] In Britain, Carmichael's presence was explosive. In addition to two high-profile speeches in Camden, he spoke to Caribbean, African and black British audiences at the West Indian Students' Centre and Africa House as well as community centres in Brixton and Dalston, and at a soapbox platform in Hyde Park's famous Speakers' Corner.[31] At CAM's 1968 conference, La Rose remembered Carmichael's visit as 'a catalyst in a way that nothing before had been', while Brathwaite would later describe how, in London, Carmichael 'magnetized a whole set of splintered feelings that had for a long time been seeking a node'.[32] In the wake of his departure, Black Power groups were established across the country.[33]

The US held a central place in the development of cultures of radical blackness in the late 1960s – the Black Panther Party, in particular, articulating a politics of 'the brothers on the block', provided a model of radical blackness that changed the face of black politics, while inner-city uprisings across the country expressed the levels of black discontent[34] – but the political crises wrought by this politics played out across the black Atlantic. In Jamaica, where Rastafarian and Garveyite politics were beginning to be joined together through the influence of the young Guyanese intellectual Walter Rodney, the government's decision to banish Rodney from the island led to days of protests and riots and the consolidation of a new oppositional alliance of Black Power, labour and Rastafarian politics.[35] In Montreal, the Congress of Black Writers had brought together US and diasporic Caribbean black radicals in October 1968, and over the following four months a dispute between a newly radicalised faction of black students and staff at Montreal's Sir George Williams University escalated into a stand-off that ended with ninety-seven arrested and many hospitalised in confrontations with the police. The Sir George Williams affair sparked protests across the Caribbean and a Black Power rebellion in Trinidad, with mass demonstrations and an army revolt bringing Eric Williams's government close to collapse in early 1970.[36]

These events were not just simultaneous; they were mutually reinforcing and intimately interconnected with each other. The West Indian Students' Centre (WISC), where C.L.R. James had delivered his speech reflecting on the impact of Carmichael's visit to Britain in 1967, was a space that would prove central to the development of Black Power cultures in London, and to the transformation of CAM. The base of CAM's regular meetings, the WISC also acted as a political hub of West Indian life in Britain in the 1960s. At a time when 'it was very difficult to get meeting halls', as one regular WISC attendee recalls, 'the Students Centre became the centre of activity where full-time students and working class people could meet. ... And a lot of people who might not have been involved in politics locally, where they live, did participate in activities there'.[37] From the mid-1960s, under the influence of Richard Small, a Jamaican solicitor and race-relations activist, and Locksley Comrie, an engineering student from a poor neighbourhood of Kingston, the WISC came to provide a forum in which Caribbean culture, British racism and, most prominently, Black Power – especially in its North American manifestations – were readily engaged with. Talks on the relevance of Black Power to Britain drew on the literature emerging from the US, some brought over from WISC members' own visits there, and the WISC provided a space in which films on the US Civil Rights struggle and black American culture were screened and visiting political leaders spoke.[38] Events at the WISC were often attended by the local Black Panthers and other Black Power groups, and lists of those present at meetings provide a roll-call of London's black political classes of the era. In August 1968, one such event, a weekend 'Seminar on the Realities of Black Power', was run at the WISC by Small and Comrie, and it was from the success of this endeavour that they were encouraged to launch critiques of CAM at its conference two weeks later.[39]

Something of the new mood at the Students' Centre was captured in an event on 3 February 1968 at which James Baldwin spoke, along with a fellow American, the comedian Dick Gregory.[40] Baldwin was hosted by Salkey, and spoke to an audience that brought together West Indian students and local working-class black Londoners, with the odd white face scattered among the crowd. An extraordinary film of the encounter provides a rare insight into shifting black politics in Britain at this moment.[41] Baldwin, in a dark suit and tie, delivering his address, as always, with humour and a pace and cadence that stood, in its careful articulation and rising crescendos, somewhere between the political rally and the energies of a Harlem store-front pulpit, was received with warmth by the audience. At the end of his speech, he fielded responses from the audience. From an objection to his terminology – using 'negro' when 'black' was the order of the day – to a request that he predict 'the black man's' fate, 'say within 50 years ... throughout the world', and an invitation to pitch 'Black Power' against 'integration', it was a politics of blackness that dominated the audience's questions to Baldwin. His replies also placed considerations of blackness at their core. Invoking 'the black experience', Baldwin suggested a historical experience that has placed a premium on the sovereignty of the body. Emerging from a dominating 'white Christian' American culture that has defined itself, Baldwin suggested, through the mortification of black flesh, the 'vigour, ... vitality and ... sense of life' of 'the black personality' was forged through the realisation that 'the flesh is all you have'.

Baldwin was far from alone in finding in the experiences of black oppression a source for future cultural and political redemption. For Richard Small, one intellectual was particularly prominent in forming this new Black Power politics: Walter Rodney. Rodney was a recent addition to the History Department at the University of the West Indies' Mona campus who had publicly advocated a Black Power politics for Jamaica. His ideas proved influential in British black radical circles, with the publishing house Bogle L'Ouverture reprinting his essays and speeches in 1969. Rodney refused to understand Jamaica's achievement of political independence in 1962 as marking any real victory for Jamaican decolonisation, condemning the ruling class as 'merely acting as representatives of metropolitan-imperialist interests'.[42] Investing the possibilities for a truly *post*colonial future in the radical politics of the 'black masses', he, like Baldwin, demanded that real independence required that the Caribbean 'think black', reorganising its society according to a politics organised by a black historical experience in which 'White property was of a greater value than black humanity'. This history, and the insights derived from it, Rodney found among the 'black masses' at the lowest socio-economic stratum of Jamaican society. 'They can tell you and I about Black Power,' he wrote. 'You can learn from them what Black Power really means. You do not have to teach them anything. You just have to say it and they add something to what you are saying.'[43]

Rodney's conviction that 'the black intellectual, the black academic must attach himself to the activity of the black masses',[44] centring the experiences of black dispossession as a new driving force in history capable of remaking the social and political world, was typical of its moment. Moving beyond the lecture halls and seminars of the university, Rodney spoke in the 'less respectable groupings' in Kingston and the surrounding villages, discussing African history and culture, Jamaican politics and Black Power with 'anybody who wanted to hear him'.[45] Incorporating the Rastafarians and the Jamaican poor, this was a direct challenge to the existing networks of political and intellectual cultures on the island.[46] It provided a model for the reorganisation of cultural production and consumption, focused on routing these practices through the black poor who were conceived as the source of a radical black politics.

Thinking black, then, required reorganised social relations. At the Students' Centre in February 1968, echoing Baldwin, Dick Gregory had also demanded a new political formation in which 'cats ... think black'. This was the centring of a politics that Baldwin claimed had 'been submerged so long' but was now the necessary redemptive force for that moment. When a self-confessed 'white liberal' stood to put his question to Baldwin and Gregory – 'Do you think that there is any place for the white liberal in the Black Power movement?' – he was met with jeers and protestations from the audience. There was a clear sense that, whatever the current political project, it would be black-organised. 'Life is a game, and you know, you played baseball as a kid and you say, "ok, let me hit a couple". And you know, like black folks that have gone to wars in what I call white man's armies, without black folks being at the top echelons', answered Gregory. 'And now we saying, "ok, white folks, it's your turn. I'm gonna be the general, and you gonna be the private. And this is the way you gonna march."'[47]

This was a period in which new institutions in the cultural, social and political lives of black Britons were being founded with unprecedented speed. As well as the plethora of new Black Power groups established in Britain between 1967 and 1972, new community arts centres, bookstores, publishing ventures and supplementary schools were founded throughout the major cities. London, the largest but by no means the only city host to such ventures,[48] provides a useful case study. In London, the Black House, a black community space and free lodging house for homeless black teenagers, was established in 1969,[49] while two similar projects, Harambee and Dashiki, were founded soon after. Arts centres such as the Mkutano Project, the Melting Pot and the Keskidee, where CAM would later base its operations, were established as venues for black youth theatre and performance. Black bookstores – the Black People's Information Centre, Grassroots, Unity Bookshop, Back-a-Yard – also sprang up across London in these years. One of these bookshops, New Beacon Books, an early venture by John La Rose that sold its wares at CAM and WISC events, doubled up as a publishing house specialising in Caribbean and black literature, while Bogle L'Ouverture, a black radical publishing house established by Jessica and Eric Huntley in 1969, also traded as a bookstore from 1973. Supplementary schools, aimed at countering the discrimination that black youth faced in the education system, were established across the city: the Kwame Nkrumah School, the Malcolm X Montessori Programme, the George Padmore School, the South-East London Summer School, Headstart, the Marcus Garvey School and even the Free University for Black Studies.[50] These were ventures with which CAM and WISC members were closely involved. In 1969 La Rose (with the Black Parents Movement) had been a driving force behind the George Padmore School, while Salkey was closely involved with the WISC's establishment of the Black Arts Workshop. Both, too, helped in the establishment of the WISC's C.L.R. James School for Black People that same year.[51]

In this political atmosphere, it was no longer possible for CAM to continue in its existing form. From Jamaica, a former secretary of CAM, Marina Maxwell, offered one solution. In 1968, Maxwell established the Yard Theatre, 'an attempt to find West Indian theatre and to find it in the yards where people live and are'. Staging outdoor plays in Kingston backyards, Maxwell's project aimed to bring together trained and untrained actors and writers in a space with 'no company, no committee, no show'.⁵² This was a re-envisioning of artistic production and consumption as something more dialogic and, it was hoped, communal. It was an explicit rejection of existing theatrical forms, a new architecture and spatiality for theatre in which, as Maxwell proposed, 'the medium is the message':

> We have been tied to metropolitan forms and formats for a century. Moving out of the theatre building, away from the proscenium, away from the £20 a night fees and the expensive battery of lights. ... The deepest hope is that ... people freed of what 'theatah' has been will meet to find, to synthesize, to produce their own thing.⁵³

Maxwell's project was well received by CAM members in Britain, and Brathwaite, moving to Jamaica shortly after CAM's second conference, soon joined Maxwell's Yard Theatre too. In post-Rodney Riots Jamaica, the Yard Theatre was part of a wider radical cultural politics, with new publications, most notably the journal *Abeng*, equally aiming to share artistic and editorial control with those previously excluded from such platforms.⁵⁴ But this reorientation of cultural institutions was also demanded in Britain, and CAM was pressed to respond to the black working class there. The Students' Centre, Locksley Comrie demanded, must be 'open to the bus conductor, the bus driver'.⁵⁵

It was at the Students' Centre, and no longer at the University of Kent, that CAM held its third and final conference in August 1969. A joint symposium with the West Indian Students' Union, at the forefront of this conference was the question of how to reform CAM's activities in line with radical blackness. 'Black awareness', as Salkey declared in his address to the conference, 'is the beginning of our search and definition of revolution.' This required a reorientation of the artist to the community:

> Our own Caribbean communities must become the new centres of which we first seek approval of the fruits of our imagination. Only then may we move from within our society outward with assurance. I really mean this. Because this is not the way I began. I began by seeking metropolitan approval. We must first seek approval of the fruits of our imagination within our society.⁵⁶

Salkey was here explicitly refusing the earlier links to the British arts establishment that CAM and its associated artists had held. But this demand for a revolution *defined* by blackness also required that CAM's new organisation must be understood as itself a form of 'thinking black'.

'The need for the programme arose', Gary Burton, president of the West Indian Students' Union and the chair at the conference, announced, 'out of the West Indian students' realisation as students, we're about to shed the illusion of a middle class sort of white identity and go straight back, straight back to our brothers and sisters, those who catch hell in this community'. The project was described as a 'black sort of initiative', part of a wider drive to 'found a teaching and social service corps which would go to meet the direct, and urgent and desperate needs of that sector of the black community which is not middle class and is not privileged and does not think white and is suffering'.[57] In this rhetoric, 'thinking white' was equated somewhat vaguely with class privilege, but as the converse – thinking black – was deployed, Burton stressed not just new communication circuits, but the jettisoning of those performances of cultural arbitration that had defined the business of criticism and cultural production as something occurring outside the spaces of everyday, popular life. 'I want to structure this meeting to be, not in the usual thing where an audience is intimidated because of the way we are here', Burton continued. 'Let's sort of make it cool, cosy, intimate and black. Black, real black, you know like back home, so that you throw your ideas out.'[58] Emphasising this move to abandon codes of authority and deference, Edward Brathwaite jokingly began his address, 'Brothers and sisters, and to those of you who still prefer it, ladies and gentlemen', and reminded his audience 'not to be intimidated'.[59]

The debates that restructured CAM in the late 1960s are representative of, as well as central to, a broader shift among those black artists, intellectuals and cultural critics in Britain formed through a historical moment defined by the imperatives of radical blackness. If, in the 1950s and early 1960s, there was a sense that not only the publishing industries but also the institutions of cultural criticism necessary for the development of a Caribbean artistic tradition could only be found in the metropole – no such institutions existing in the Caribbean itself – by the late 1960s this position had reversed. Now it was not among the accredited intellectuals and established institutions of cultural authority that Caribbean artists must find the value of their work, but among 'the people'. As Brathwaite demanded of his audience at CAM's third conference, 'it is among the people that we must begin'.[60]

A notable and long-lasting shift that was a direct consequence of this was an emphasis on performance and participation as central to black cultural production. In a 1971 letter to Marina Maxwell congratulating her on the Yard Theatre, Andrew Salkey went so far as to suggest that old, book-based cultures necessarily now required re-staging in communal settings.

Our people are tuned in on the oral presentation of our arts, and this is where the book must get its necessary translation, socially and politically ... Things get locked in and stored away in books, but they live and breathe and have effect in the theatre, in spectacle, in meetings, in parades, in street productions, in the open. That's where our arts are at, and should remain for maximum benefit.[61]

Marina Maxwell's efforts with the Yard Theatre were directed towards the Jamaican situation, and particularly the politics of the post-Rodney Riots era. For Salkey, who remained in Britain until 1976, we can assume that his comments were made with one eye also on Britain. Indeed, ever since the call at CAM's second conference to move proceedings to Notting Hill or Brixton Town Hall, it was the imperative to connect with the 'black sufferers' *within* Britain that drove most critiques of CAM and that reoriented the politics of many CAM members.[62] It is to the legacy of CAM's debates within Britain that I shall reserve my concluding comments, whilst acknowledging that such modes of thought were themselves antagonistic to such strict delimitations of geography.

In accordance with Salkey's emphasis in his letter to Maxwell, the black cultural forms to receive the most critical attention over the coming decades in Britain were indeed those most communal and participatory in their production or in the form of their consumption. Linton Kwesi Johnson's dub poetry of the 1970s and 1980s, as James Procter has observed, has been privileged in its critical reception for its 'immediacy, urgency [and] "nowness"', qualities found both in its placing of the communal space – the street, the dance hall – at the centre of its subject matter, and in its relations of production and consumption, the poems often being originally performed at these same sites, and often as part of a street-level politics.[63]

The founding critics of black British cultural studies in the 1980s similarly focused attention on communal cultural production, often even at the expense of black British literary cultures. Paul Gilroy, in his famous reading of black diasporic music as anti-capitalist critique, discussed dance hall cultures in a language not far removed from that of Maxwell or Salkey almost two decades previously:

> Black performers aim to overcome rather than exploit the structures which separate them from their audiences. The relationship between the performer and the crowd is transformed in dialogic rituals so that spectators acquire the active role of participants in collective processes which are sometimes cathartic and which may symbolize or even create community. ... The whole dialogic process that unites performers and crowds is imported into the culture's forms. It becomes the basis of an authentic public sphere which is

counterposed to the dominant alternative, from which, in any case, blacks have been excluded. The arts which, as slaves, blacks were allowed instead of freedom, have become a means to make their formal freedom tangible.[64]

Gilroy consciously inherits modes of thought that emerged under the various cultures of radical blackness gaining ascendancy across the black Atlantic in the late 1960s. His work often addresses questions of the communication circuits of black cultural production and consumption, questions which are, for him, inherently political.[65] Within the debates and transformations of the Caribbean Artists Movement we can see the early parameters of this mode of thinking first elaborated, a mode of thinking which would prove vital to the reframing of questions of race, politics and culture in post-imperial Britain. These ways of thinking the project of decolonising culture emerged out of particular historical formations and took on determinate historical forms. Their historical specificity should make us wary of any too-generalised theorisations of the formal strategies for or properties of cultural decolonisation. Their continued presence in what have become central tenets of black British postcolonial studies, however, suggests that, as we come to think about the processes of cultural decolonisation in Britain and how these were and are theorised, we would do well to take as a portent Henry Swanzy's eerie feeling at the University of Kent in the summer of 1968. It marks the beginning of a new historical moment, a 'secondary decolonisation' of the Caribbean and of Britain.

Notes

1 R. Drayton, 'Secondary Decolonisation: The Black Power Movement in Barbados, c. 1970', in K. Quinn (ed.), *Black Power in the Caribbean* (Gainesville: University Press of Florida, 2014), pp. 117–35.
2 G. Low, *Publishing the Postcolonial: Anglophone West African and Caribbean Writing in the UK, 1948–1968* (London: Routledge, 2011).
3 G. Griffith, '"This is London Calling the West Indies": The BBC's Caribbean Voices', in B. Schwarz (ed.), *West Indian Intellectuals in London* (Manchester: Manchester University Press, 2003), pp. 204–5. See also P. Nanton, 'What Does Mr. Swanzy Want? Shaping or Reflecting? An Assessment of Henry Swanzy's Contribution to the Development of Caribbean Literature', *Kunapipi*, 20:1 (1998), 11–20.
4 George Padmore Institute, London (hereafter GPI), CAM/4/2/9, paper delivered at the University of Kent by H. Swanzy, 'West Indian Writing – A Proletarian View', 1968.
5 F. Fanon, *The Wretched of the Earth* (Harmondsworth: Penguin, 1967). Discussing their position as an 'internal proletariat', Swanzy described the Christians of the Roman Empire as 'the dispossessed and the wretched of the earth of that period', comparable to the position of West Indians and the white working class in contemporary Britain. See Swanzy, 'West Indian Writing'. Louis James has noted that Fanon's text was 'a strong presence at CAM meetings', and Swanzy had purchased a copy from the New Beacon Books stall at that same conference: L.

James, 'The Caribbean Artists Movement', in Schwarz, *West Indian Intellectuals in London*, p. 219; A. Walmsley, *The Caribbean Artists Movement, 1966 – 1972: A Literary and Cultural History* (London: New Beacon Books, 1992), p. 182.
6   J.-P. Sartre, 'Preface', in Fanon, *Wretched of the Earth*, pp. 9, 11–12.
7   J.-P. Sartre, 'Preface', p. 21. Emphasis added.
8   G. Lamming, *The Pleasures of Exile* (London: Michael Joseph, 1960), p. 67.
9   Lamming, *Pleasures of Exile*, p. 39. On 'nation-building' in the Caribbean, see M. Chamberlain, *Empire and Nation-Building in the Caribbean: Barbados, 1937–66* (Manchester: Manchester University Press, 2010).
10 K. Ramchand, *The West Indian Novel and its Background* (London: Faber, 1970), p. 63.
11 Lamming, *Pleasures of Exile*, p. 27.
12 Ramchand, *West Indian Novel*, p. 63.
13 See Griffith, '"This is London Calling the West Indies"'.
14 Griffith, '"This is London Calling the West Indies"', p. 198. See also D. Newton, 'Calling the West Indies: The BBC World Service and *Caribbean Voices*', *Historical Journal of Film, Radio and Television*, 28:4 (2008), 491–2.
15 G. Lamming, 'The Coldest Spring in Fifty Years: Thoughts on Sam Selvon and London', *Kunapipi*, 20:1 (1998), 9.
16 V.S. Naipaul, 'Without a Place: V.S. Naipaul Interviewed by Ian Hamilton', *Savacou*, 9/10 (1974), 122 and 124.
17 D. Dabydeen, 'West Indian Writers in Britain', in F. Dennis and N. Khan (eds), *Voices of the Crossing: The Impact of Britain on Writers from Asia, the Caribbean, and Africa* (London: Serpent's Tail, 2000), p. 70. See also A.S. Rush, *Bonds of Empire: West Indians and Britishness from Victoria to Decolonization* (Oxford: Oxford University Press, 2011).
18 GPI, CAM/6/64, Brathwaite's words as recalled by Andrew Salkey in an interview with Anne Walmsley, 20 March 1986. See also E. Brathwaite, 'The Caribbean Artists Movement', *Caribbean Quarterly*, 14:1/2 (1968), 57–9.
19 GPI, CAM/3/1, letter from Brathwaite to Bryan King, 30 November 1966.
20 See Walmsley, *Caribbean Artists Movement*.
21 GPI, CAM/2/8, *Caribbean Artists Movement: Weekend Summit Conference*, August 1967; GPI, CAM/2/10, *The Caribbean Arts*, August 1967.
22 Cited in A. Walmsley, 'A Sense of Community: Kamau Brathwaite and the Caribbean Artists Movement', in S. Brown (ed.), *The Art of Kamau Brathwaite* (Bridgend: Seren, 1995), p. 102.
23 La Rose quoted in Walmsley, *Caribbean Artists Movement*, p. 154; on Karl 'Jerry' Craig, see p. 151.
24 A. Walmsley, 'Second C.A.M. Conference', *Bim*, 12:48 (1969), 233.
25 Swanzy cited in Walmsley, *Caribbean Artists Movement*, p. 179.
26 See Walmsley, *Caribbean Artists Movement*, p. 164; GPI, CAM/4/2/11, Richard Small quoted in Anne Walmsley, 'Notes on the Second Caribbean Artists Movement Conference', 2 September 1968. On the Black Arts Movement, see J.E. Smethurst, *The Black Arts Movement: Literary Nationalism in the 1960s and 1970s* (Chapel Hill and London: University of North Carolina Press, 2005).
27 See, for example, GPI, CAM/4/2/2, responses to Stuart Hall's keynote at the conference, 'West Indians in Britain'.
28 Walmsley, *Caribbean Artists Movement*, pp. 187–8.
29 C.L.R. James, *Black Power: Its Past, Today, and the Way Ahead* (London: Frank John, 1968), p. 12.
30 The literature on the international dimensions of Black Power is still in its infancy, but see N. Slate (ed.), *Black Power Beyond Borders: The Global Dimensions of the Black Power Movement* (New York: Palgrave Macmillan, 2012); M.L. Clemons and C.E. Jones, 'Global Solidarity: The Black Panther Party in the International Arena', in K. Cleaver and G. Katsiaficas (eds), *Liberation, Imagination and the Black Panther Party* (New York; London: Routledge, 2001), pp. 20–39.

31 See D. Cooper (ed.), *The Dialectics of Liberation* (London: Penguin, 1968); GPI, JLR/2/5/4, *West Indian Students Centre and Union*, 1967; Walmsley, *Caribbean Artists Movement*, pp. 92–3; 'No Converts for Prophet of Hate', *Sunday Telegraph* (23 July 1967), p. 13; Universal Coloured People's Association, *Black Power in Britain: A Special Statement* (London: UCPA, 1967); S. Carmichael with E.M. Thelwell, *Ready for Revolution: The Life and Struggles of Stokely Carmichael (Kwame Ture)* (New York: Scribner, 2003), pp. 573–6.
32 GPI, CAM/4/2/2, La Rose at CAM's 1968 conference; E. Brathwaite, 'Timehri', *Savacou*, 2 (1970), 40.
33 On Black Power in Britain see G.L. Watson, 'The Sociology of Black Nationalism: Identity, Protest and the Concept of "Black Power" Among West Indian Immigrants in Britain' (PhD dissertation, University of York, 1972); S. Craig, 'Black Power Groups in London, 1967–1969' (MA dissertation, University of Edinburgh, 1970); R.E. Wild, '"Black Was the Colour of Our Fight": Black Power in Britain, 1955–1976' (PhD dissertation, University of Sheffield, 2008).
34 See J. Bloom and W.E. Martin, Jr, *Black Against Empire: The History and Politics of the Black Panther Party* (Berkeley: University of California Press, 2013).
35 See O. Gray, *Radicalism and Social Change in Jamaica, 1960–1972* (Knoxville: University of Tennessee Press, 1991), pp. 144–65.
36 D. Austin, 'All Roads Led to Montreal: Black Power, the Caribbean, the Black Radical Tradition in Canada', *Journal of African American History*, 92:4 (2007), 516–39; R. Pantin, *Black Power Day: The 1970 February Revolution* (Santa Cruz: Hatuey Production, 1990).
37 GPI, CAM/6/31, Eric Huntley interviewed by Anne Walmsley, 28 April 1986.
38 For activity at the Students' Centre, see Andrew Salkey Archive, British Library, 'West Indian Students' Centre: Book One' and 'West Indian Students' Centre: Book Two'.
39 See Walmsley, *Caribbean Artists Movement*, p. 156; GPI, JLR/2/5/4, *Seminar on the Realities of Black Power*, 1968.
40 On Baldwin's presence in Britain, see R. Waters, '"Britain is No Longer White": James Baldwin as a Witness to Postcolonial Britain', *African American Review*, 46:4 (2013), 715–30.
41 Horace Ové, dir., *Baldwin's Nigger* (British Film Institute, 2004; filmed 1969). All subsequent quotations from the event are from this film.
42 W. Rodney, *The Groundings with my Brothers* (London: Bogle-L'Ouverture, 1969), p. 12.
43 Rodney, *The Groundings with my Brothers*, pp. 24, 26, 63.
44 Rodney, *The Groundings with my Brothers*, p. 63.
45 R. Small, 'Introduction', in Rodney, *The Groundings with my Brothers*, pp. 7–11.
46 See Gray, *Radicalism and Social Change*; R.C. Lewis, *Walter Rodney's Intellectual and Political Thought* (Detroit: Wayne State University Press, 1998).
47 Ové, *Baldwin's Nigger*.
48 From the late 1960s, Black Power groups were beginning to appear in Birmingham, Bradford, Cardiff, Coventry, Huddersfield, Leeds, Leicester, Manchester, Nottingham, Reading, Warwick and Wolverhampton. These cities, and others – including Glasgow and Bristol – also saw the establishment of community newsletters and organisations, often connected to black radical political organisation.
49 See Black Cultural Archives, London (hereafter BCA), EPHEMERA 150, *The Black House: A Self Help Community Project in the Making* (London: Sir Joshua Reynolds Press, n.d. [1969]); a similar project was started under the same name in 1973, see C. Jones and M. Phillips, *The Black House* (London: Prestel, 2006).
50 See A. Sivanandan, *A Different Hunger: Writings on Black Resistance* (London: Pluto Press, 1982), pp. 30–1; V. Hines, *How Black People Overcame Fifty Years of Repression in Britain, 1945–1995, Vol. 1: 1945–1975* (London: Zulu Publications, 1998). For New Beacon Books see also B.W. Alleyne, *Radicals Against Race: Black Activism and Cultural Politics* (Oxford: Berg, 2002); for B. L'Ouverture, see

    also H. Goulbourne, *Caribbean Transnational Experience* (London: Pluto Press, 2002).
51 See BCA, WONG/1/1, *Bumbo*, 2 (1969). See also Andrew Salkey Archive, 'Black Community Centre'.
52 GPI, CAM/1/10, M. Maxwell, 'Towards a Revolution in the Arts', *Caribbean Artists Movement Newsletter*, 10 (April/June 1969), 1–13.
53 GPI, CAM/7/1/17, M. Maxwell, 'Yard Theatre: Consciousness I – The Medium is the Message', 1970; Maxwell, 'Towards a Revolution'.
54 See D. Scott, 'The Archaeology of Black Memory: An Interview with Robert A. Hill', *Small Axe*, 5 (1999), 85–94. See also Gray, *Radicalism and Social Change*, pp. 166–82.
55 GPI, CAM/4/2/7, Comrie speaking at the 1968 CAM conference.
56 GPI, CAM/4/3/4, Andrew Salkey, 'The Negritude Movement and Black Awareness', 1969.
57 GPI, CAM/4/3/2, CAM-WISC joint symposium, West Indian Students' Centre.
58 CAM-WISC joint symposium.
59 CAM-WISC joint symposium.
60 GPI, CAM/4/3/2, Edward Brathwaite, 'Africa in the Caribbean', 1969.
61 GPI, CAM/7/1/16, Salkey cited in '"Bongo Man Ah Come!" or Inside Yard Theatre', undated letter from Marina Maxwell to Sebastian Clarke.
62 GPI, CAM/4/3/2, Gary Burton speaking at the CAM-WISC joint symposium.
63 J. Procter, *Dwelling Places: Postwar Black British Writing* (Manchester: Manchester University Press, 2003), p. 103.
64 P. Gilroy, *'There Ain't No Black in the Union Jack': The Cultural Politics of Race and Nation* (London: Hutchinson, 1987), pp. 214–15.
65 See, for example, P. Gilroy, *Small Acts: Thoughts on the Politics of Black Cultures* (London: Serpent's Tail, 1993), pp. 97–114.

CHAPTER FOUR

Anxiety abroad: Austerity, abundance and race in post-war visual culture

David C. Wall

In this chapter, I examine four visual texts of the 1950s: John Bratby's painting *Jean and Still Life in Front of Window* (1954), Richard Hamilton's collage *Just What Is It That Makes Today's Homes So Different, So Appealing?* (1956) and the feature films *Simba* (dir. Brian Desmond Hurst, 1955) and *Sapphire* (dir. Basil Dearden, 1959). Sharing a deep ambivalence over the abundance they depict, Bratby, Hamilton, Hurst and Dearden all employ visual strategies that both contest and contain competing post-war impulses of desire and denial. Their shared visions of abundance offer competing and complementary points of rupture, where the discourses of empire, race, class and nation all meet as images of compelling abundance become images of troubling abandon and excess. Further, each of the four texts locates the body as the critical site for the playing out of these wider anxieties of race, gender and nationhood, speaking to that critical moment when the processes and consequences of decolonisation were increasingly calling those subject categories into question. There may be some weight to John MacKenzie's argument that it was not until the 1960s that popular cultural forms wrestled explicitly with the issues surrounding decolonisation, but the traces of anxiety and ambivalence – what Stuart Ward calls the 'underlying tensions of imperial decline' – are evident long before.[1] It is the principal argument of this essay that those tensions can be identified clearly in representations of abundance and excess throughout the immediate post-war period and on through the 1950s. Indeed, as Anne McClintock has demonstrated, visions of abundance had carried a certain charge ineluctably linked to empire from the nineteenth century onwards.[2] Articulated in the form of advertising, greetings cards, children's games, photography, fine art, film, television and much else besides, visions of the abundance of empire were everywhere and everywhere available for consumption.

But though these discourses of abundance that underpinned the materialism of the British Empire were transcoded successfully across the broad vectors of the domestic arena, the process was by no means seamless. While visions of plenty often presented the possibility of liberation and regeneration, ubiquitously linked as they were to the notion of empire and 'abroad', the deep-seated ambivalences that were attached to the concept of foreignness also codified 'plenty' just as often as something to be mistrusted, if not gravely threatening. This tension became increasingly acute in the 1940s and 1950s as the 'foreign' – in the form of (amongst much else) Italian coffee houses, French fashions, American art and popular culture and, perhaps most significantly as decolonisation began in earnest, the colonial 'other' – established an increasing presence within the metropole.

What Stuart Ward has termed the 'minimum impact' theory of postcolonial history asserts that the decline and dissolution of the British Empire had little (if indeed any) consequence for the lives of the vast majority of the domestic British population.[3] Underpinning my examination of examples of both high and mass culture is the argument that even the most cursory examination of the cultural formations of the post-war period demonstrates the ubiquitous presence of empire within the social imaginary. As Jordanna Bailkin suggests in *The Afterlife of Empire*, it is not that 'Britons were especially knowledgeable about the end of empire. Rather, the consequences of imperial collapse were built into the structures of their world. Decolonization changed how people in Britain lived whether they knew it or not'.[4] Bill Schwarz similarly suggests that 'it would be very curious if, at the very moment of empire's end, all consciousness of the imperial past suddenly vanished'; he then goes further, to argue that we 'are compelled to ask where those traces, or symptoms [of empire], are to be located, and how might we identify them when we see them.'[5] It is precisely those traces and symptoms which this essay sets out to discern.

The chapter begins with a discussion of the Kenya-set film *Simba*, before shifting attention to two key images of post-war British art by John Bratby and Richard Hamilton. It concludes with an investigation of *Sapphire*, a film set in London. In each case, questions of excess are shown to be connected, in a variety of ways, with British anxieties over nation and race in decolonisation. Bringing together a diverse collection of cultural texts, some of which address these issues explicitly and others which leave them unspoken, highlights the ways in which decolonisation was imbricated in British culture in this period, sometimes showing itself in surprising places.

Saving the savages from themselves: Simba (1955)

Individuated as we are through the dynamic intersections of discourses of ideology, economy and culture, the importance of film as a critical element in the experience of decolonisation cannot be overstated. The problematics of post-empire were present in multiple ways across a range of popular cinema, not least in films such as *Pool of London* (dir. Basil Dearden, 1950), *Flame in the Streets* (dir. Roy Ward Baker, 1961) and *Wind of Change* (dir. Vernon Sewell, 1961), which transposed the struggles in the colonies to the streets of Britain's cities. Though ostensibly anxiety-riven responses to post-*Windrush* immigration into the metropole, they are clearly equally resonant with events taking place abroad in the residual colonies such as Malaya, Cyprus and Kenya. In turn, we can read films such as Harry Watt's *Where No Vultures Fly* (1951) and *West of Zanzibar* (1954), which are set in the colonies, as equally resonant commentaries upon tensions existing within the metropole itself. Whether set abroad or at home, not only did British films of the period 'continue to exploit colonial themes', but they were constantly 'modulated to address changing imperial relations'.[6]

Released in 1955 at the height of the Mau Mau rebellion, Brian Desmond Hurst's *Simba* sought to dramatise the conflict through the story of Alan Howard (Dirk Bogarde), who arrives in Kenya to take control of the family farmstead after the murder of his brother by the Mau Mau, and his relationship with the daughter of another family of white settlers, Mary Crawford (Virginia McKenna). Lola Young suggests that this 'late entry into the colonial adventure canon ... may be seen as representing the terror of the imminent end of Empire and the assumption of white supremacy'.[7] In this she is surely correct. *Simba*'s insistent efforts to assert the reasonableness of the British occupation are served by an equal insistence on the native population's propensity for savagery. Indeed, the film employs the full repertoire of racial grotesquerie at precisely that historical moment when the certainty of Britain's grip on colonial power in Kenya seemed to be slipping. It is in this moment that we see, as Wendy Webster puts it, 'witch doctors, superstition, drums and primitivism [taking] on increasingly savage and violent associations'.[8] At the same time, however, post-war empire films such as *Simba* were much less likely to feature the kind of gung-ho, *Boy's Own* approach of the inter-war years. Rather than routinely echoing earlier films which imagined empire as 'a site of heroic masculine adventure', these later films exhibited a deeply 'equivocal' attitude as a direct consequence of the processes of decolonisation.[9] Similarly, Webster argues that the presence in 1950s empire films of powerful yet sensitive female characters, such as Catherine Munro (Phyllis Calvert) in *Men of Two Worlds* (1946) as well as Mary Crawford, gave these films a 'liberal register that softened the image of Britons, gesturing towards a discourse of Commonwealth'.[10] In keeping with this, *Simba* also makes an effort to portray a broad range of white colonial attitudes towards black Kenyans. In doing so, it critiques the kind of overt and vulgar racism that has the main character Alan Howard describing Kenyans as 'a bunch of howling savages'. Indeed, ultimately Howard comes to both understand and reject his prejudice and assumes parental responsibility for an orphaned Kenyan child named Joshua, whose innocent face fills the entire frame for the last few seconds of the film. *Simba* seems to be asserting that, as Empire evolves into Commonwealth, it is this type of relationship, in which the kindly paternalistic hands of white Europeans guide the essentially child-like African, which offers hope for the future. For all of *Simba*'s liberal principles, then, it comes to fundamentally the same conclusion as Mary Crawford's reactionary father who asserts that the Africans have been given 'the wrong kind of toys' and, unable to cope with 'ideas of self-government [and] nationalism', 'the Mau Mau have got hold of them and they've become dangerous'.

There is of course no social or historical context offered for the Mau Mau violence, which is dismissed as largely a result of the Mau Mau chief's – the Simba of the film's title – manipulation of his people. Complex political, racial and cultural registers are reduced to the most simplistic of binaries. For example, shortly before he is butchered by his father's followers, Simba's son Dr Karanja (Earl Cameron), one of the film's primary liberal consciences, provides the mob attacking Alan Howard's homestead with a straightforward choice: 'Will you follow my father and bring more misery and suffering among our people? Or will you follow me and those like me?' It is at this point that Simba appears and declares of Karanja: 'He is not my son, he is a white man.' As Simba goes to strike his son down, Howard shoots and kills him. The mob then descends upon Karanja, their attack stopped only when the police arrive. Dying in Mary Crawford's arms, Karanja says, 'They didn't listen. My father closed their hearts against the truth.' Accordingly, there is no viable narrative or visual space within the logic of the film that allows the white colonial settlers to address, much less try and understand, the motivations of the Mau Mau. Violence by white settlers against blacks can be identified as self-defence, and violence by blacks against white settlers can be casually dismissed as a consequence of savagery rather than the consequence of history. The furious and shocking violence of the Mau Mau is juxtaposed against the tranquil fecundity of the Kenyan landscape in which the plot is set. Indeed, the lush beauty of this landscape serves to further highlight the terrifying horror of their brutality.

In its representation of an abundance that is both spatialised and racialised, *Simba* also draws upon a series of other classificatory tendencies that are typical of the wider imperial project. For example, the film opens with a lengthy credits sequence in which the country of Kenya is laid out before us. We follow the passage of an aircraft, the embodiment of modernity, as it surveys the African countryside, a shot often seen in colonial documentaries of the period. Seen from this perspective, the abundant land is benign, managed and, more importantly, manageable. As it courses across the landscape, the aeroplane's shadow signifies the imprint of control, the hand of whiteness that guides and manages the land. The carefully demarcated spaces of whiteness, from the aeroplane, to the airport, through the city, and onto the farmsteads, police station and internment camp, are all carefully policed. The white body, located across these zones, is always British. It is telling that when Mary Crawford says to Alan Howard, 'I was born here. Africa's my home,' she pointedly does not assert in any sense that she is African.

Such boundaries, however, are not as definite as they may seem: Mary Crawford's place of birth clearly complicates the relationship between empire and 'home'. Although her Britishness and whiteness are apparently immutable, her occupation of a number of different subject positions points to a more troubling ambivalence as both the white and black body function as sites for the playing out of broader anxieties. There is clear sexual tension in the triangulated relationship between Mary Crawford, Alan Howard and Dr Karanja, for example, and Mary Crawford's white body serves as a site of displacement for the struggle over the stewardship of Kenya, which is also clearly gendered. However, ultimately, with Karanja's death, the possibility of any kind of relationship between Mary and Karanja is avoided. In this case, Mary's white body remains safely within the hands of white masculinity.

Yet there are occasions where the black body erupts explosively into the previously inviolate zones and spaces of whiteness, and the terrifying implications of what can happen when a managed abundance is allowed to grow to abandoned excess is revealed. Arguably, excess is a key register of savagery precisely because it reveals the inability to exercise self-control, that key marker of both civilisation and whiteness. Everything about the Mau Mau is excessive: their behaviour, their ceremonies, their demands, their violence and their blind all-consuming hatred of whites. Indeed, it is the control of this excess that provides the crux of the project of empire: the idea is to order both the body and space so that the abundance offered by both (in terms of material resources, land, minerals, crops and labour) is always tightly and carefully controlled. The legitimate black body is ordered to the extent that it is uniformed – we see this, for example, in the military dress of the police or the white lab coat of Dr Karanja – but it is also ordered by the ways in which it is given privileged access to white spaces, such as in the case of the houseboys. In this situation, white space carries with it the ontological legitimacy of whiteness itself. As all social and discursive zones are structured in relation to each other, to allow the transgression and disruption of white space is to accept the collapse of white subjectivity itself.

Though Lola Young is literally correct when she states that *Simba* 'does not engage with the Black presence in England', the film is nevertheless inescapably drawn into the broader discursive vectors of race.[11] Designed as they were for a domestic British audience, films such as *Simba*, *Where No Vultures Fly*, and *West of Zanzibar* allow for the playing-out of a whole set of compelling, and sometimes contradictory, anxieties, tensions and desires. These films assert the normative primacy of whiteness at exactly that moment when, as a consequence of decolonisation abroad and post-*Windrush* immigration at home, those assumptions were being called into question. Part of their significant cultural labour was to assert the stability of a British identity rooted in a sense of nationhood attached fundamentally to that sense of whiteness. As Benedict Anderson persuasively asserts, national identity works as a discursive product made manifest through myriad cultural formations, including, of course, film. This concept of nationalism as what he terms an 'imagined community' is conceived of at its most basic level as a spatial community. In *Simba* the discursive struggles over racial authority are conducted via struggles over space. This becomes no less the case within Britain itself, with obvious notable examples of the period being the Nottingham and Notting Hill so-called race riots of 1958. A nation-state demands that there are continuing struggles and contests as to who should be granted legitimate status within that bounded and determined space. Relying on a rhetoric of seamless purity for its legitimacy, the identity of the nation-state is then always constitutively dependent on that which it is not. In this way, the threat posed by the black body to the racially-determined white spaces of Kenya is all too easily transcoded across the domestic scene. We might argue, indeed, that every empire film is always and inevitably engaged with the black presence in Britain. It is to representations of Britain that we now turn.

The abundant anxiety of John Bratby's Jean and Still Life in Front of Window (1954)

'Race' was critical during this point of historical and cultural crisis, yet its presence in high art was negligible, and mainstream painting and sculpture of the 1940s and 1950s – in terms of both subject matter and practice – remained largely the preserve of an unexamined whiteness. It is in the more fluid arena of mass culture, such as cinema and television, that we see race operating as an overt discursive field. It makes sense, then, that it is with the collapsing of high and low cultural boundaries emerging in the Pop Art movement and its precursor the Independent Group that we can begin to identify the emergence of a self-conscious articulation of race within the arena of fine art.

This most remarkable – and yet largely unremarked – feature of British art of the post-war period needs consideration. First, it needs to be acknowledged that an absence of colour is not an absence of race. The apparent invisibility of whiteness – in that it goes largely ignored as a feature of art of the period – is merely testament to its normativity. Second, it should also be noted that there was no shortage of artists of colour from the Empire and Commonwealth working in Britain in this period. As Stuart Hall explains, Ronald Moody, Avinash Chandra, Aubrey Williams, Ahmed Parvez and Iqbal Geoffrey, among many others, came to the metropole from the broadest reaches of the empire,

> in a spirit not altogether different from that in which Picasso and others went to Paris: to fulfil their artistic ambitions and to participate in the heady atmosphere of the most advanced centres of artistic innovation at that time ... In that sense, they shared, and were clearly part of, the rising optimism of the first 'Windrush' generation of West Indian migrants, who came in the 1950s and 1960s in search of a better life, and whose jaunty self-confidence is so palpable in the images of their arrival produced at the time.[12]

However, the presence of race can be conceptualised and traced, not only through attention to artists of colour working in Britain at this time, but also through an examination of the relationship between colour, nationality, abundance, excess, scarcity and modernism within artworks. Two images serve as a point of departure for this discussion.

One of the critical issues within the post-war art world centred on modernism, itself an arena riven with anxieties over foreignness and efforts to locate and articulate a coherent national British identity within a modernist tradition. An emergent tension between 'realism' and 'abstraction' – which of course was never merely a matter of style – reveals a whole set of broader social and cultural anxieties located around the critical concept of the foreign. In the early 1950s, there developed a clearly defined split between supporters of the traditional realism of painters such as John Minton and Graham Sutherland, and those who turned to the West to embrace not only abstraction but the broad sweep of American culture. Abstraction was to many conservative critics and writers worryingly modern and foreign, with the increasing dominance of the American scene seen as especially troubling. For James Hyman, however, the period is characterised less by the tensions between realism and abstraction and more by what he terms the 'battle for realism' itself. This conflict he frames as one between social realism and what he calls modernist realism and, in gesturing towards the political contexts for reading these distinctive figurative styles, asserts that: 'The battle for realism was fortunate in having two of the twentieth century's greatest art critics at its centre: David Sylvester, a powerful champion of a realism derived from a reading of late Modernism; and John Berger, a persuasive articulator of a personalized Marxist-Leninist reading of culture.'[13] Modernist realism was figurative and yet committed to certain qualities of abstraction and best exemplified by Francis Bacon, Reg Butler and Eduardo Paolozzi. Social realism was more closely associated with the Beaux Arts Quartet, who included John Bratby and came to be known as well as 'the Kitchen Sink School' after a 1954 essay by David Sylvester in *Encounter* identified their principal concerns as being associated with the everyday mundanity of ordinary working-class life. For John Berger, the implicit left-wing critique in the kitchen sink painters made them appear obvious fellow travellers in the fight for art as a deliberate social and political engagement with capitalist and imperialist society. In their apparent critique of the social order Berger saw an implied condemnation of the imperial project as an organising framework for national identity. The artists, however, did not necessarily share his politics or his sense of them as politically engaged painters. They even rejected the notion that they were ever a 'school' in any kind of formal sense, asserting that their only real connection was the fact that they were all represented by Helen Lessore at the Beaux Arts Gallery. For his part, the painter John Bratby rejected these labels altogether and, stating unequivocally in a BBC interview in 1960, 'I am not a social realist painter', he said that he would prefer to call his style 'neo-realism'.[14]

Like much left politics of the period, Berger's socialism was an interesting (and sometimes contradictory) mixture of a fierce (though anti-imperialist) Britishness and an all-encompassing internationalism. Bratby's early career also seemed to embody this apparent dichotomy. As a consequence of his constant and varied iterations of the material culture of everyday life, Bratby is often seen as a peculiarly English artist, yet his style gestures not only towards the early twentieth-century realism of Walter Sickert and the Camden Town Group but also towards a much more cosmopolitan and continental sensibility. Indeed, Garlake situates him quite firmly in the tradition of an expressionism that has an explicitly 'European lineage of modernity'.[15] So, although there may be no immediate or obvious relationship between Bratby's work and the post-imperial moment, he is situated in all sorts of interesting trajectories and conversations around foreignness.

Though the connection between the material abundance of Bratby's so-called tabletop paintings – of which *Jean and Still Life in Front of Window* (Figure 4.1) is a notable example – and the culture of austerity from which they emerged may seem obvious, there are multiple ways in which the relationship between the visual image and its social context may be read. Martin Harrison, for instance, sees Bratby's output not as a cultural critique or 'lament over deprivation' in the way of Berger, but as 'a celebration of the immediate onset of a more materially affluent society'.[16] Bratby, while acknowledging his paintings' social contexts, asserts that they were intended as a deliberate response to 'the aftermath of war, and the climate of the aftermath of war, the austerities. People got used to austerity – the opposite of extravagance. Colour of khaki, restricted foods, ration cards, all contributed to the zeitgeist.'[17]

The 'zeitgeist' to which Bratby refers is also powerfully expressed by the historian David Kynaston, who, in the first volume of his magisterial history of post-war Britain, offers a stark snapshot of the social landscape of the years following 1945:

> Abortion illegal, homosexual relationships illegal, suicide illegal, capital punishment legal. White faces everywhere. Back-to-backs, narrow cobbled streets, Victorian terraces ... Suits and hats, dresses and hats, cloth caps and mufflers, no leisurewear, no 'teenagers'. Heavy coins, heavy shoes, heavy suitcases, heavy tweed coats, heavy leather footballs ... Meat rationed, butter rationed, lard rationed, margarine rationed, sugar rationed, tea rationed, cheese rationed, jam rationed, eggs rationed, sweets rationed, soap rationed, clothes rationed. Make do and mend.[18]

This miscellany of objects and ideas compels us to think not only of what was not available because it had not yet been imagined or realised but also, and perhaps more pertinently, of those quotidian

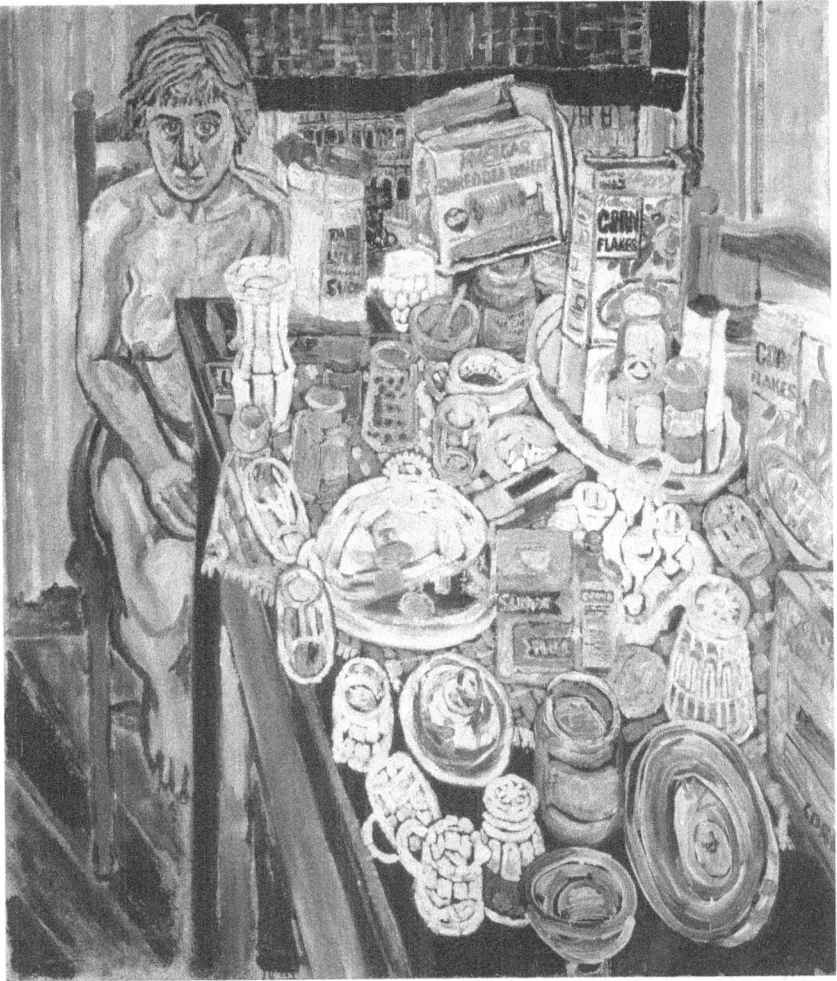

Figure 4.1 John Bratby, *Jean and Still Life in Front of Window*, 1954, oil on canvas, 1220 x 1080 mm.

staples that wartime rationing had morphed into controlled substances. Of course, restrictions did not end with the war: sugar and sweets were still rationed through 1953, and meat did not come 'off the books' until 1954. In acknowledging the oppressive conditions of rationing and austerity, Kynaston's emphasis on heaviness as uniquely symptomatic of the period speaks to not only the material conditions of existence but also a perhaps contradictory sense of literal and figurative over-abundance.

DECOLONISING METROPOLITAN CULTURES?

In his cataloguing of culture, Kynaston could be identifying many of the key concerns of the kitchen sink painters, from the lack of food to the grim realities of cobbled streets and Victorian terraces. And there are other connections: there is a literal heaviness to Bratby's work in the way that he applies his paint that echoes Kynaston's notion of weight. Described by Garlake as 'luxurious impasto that unequivocally signalled Bratby's allegiance to Van Gogh',[19] Bratby described his own work as 'crowded with forms, and colours, and blobs and slabs of paint'.[20] The excessiveness of the form is reflective of the subject matter, with those heavy tabletops overcrowded, laden, stuffed with, and collapsing under, the weight of the things they bear. What they bear is, after all, not only jars of preserves, bottles of oil, tins of beans, loaves of bread, pints of milk, fruit, vegetables and so on, but also the burden of history. Though *Jean and Still Life* seems to offer a fantasy of possession, an explosive and excessive rejoinder to the demands of disavowal that formed official state discourses of denial and restraint, it is absent of any regenerative or cathartic joy. The seductive and liberating abandon promised by the overwhelming mound of stuff, almost literally sliding off the table towards us, is disrupted by Jean's mournful carnality. It is here, at the point of deepest ambivalence, that the crux of the picture resides. It is a difficult image to encounter, not least because of the fearful anxiety betrayed by Jean's pink and blanched skin. She sits, half hidden, behind the table, leaning forwards at an awkward angle, another commodity to be considered. She seems haunted, within and without the frame, present and yet beyond.

'White faces everywhere', writes Kynaston and, in doing so, highlights that no matter how normative its presence, whiteness is also and always an issue of race. Likewise, for the painter John Bratby, race also emerges in such subtle ways. While his art betrayed no explicit racial sensibility beyond the normative ontological condition of an unexamined whiteness as embodied in Jean, interestingly, Bratby himself was haunted by the anxious fear that he was not white. Convinced that he was part Jewish or part black, Bratby saw his work as articulating the unstable and insecure state of his subjectivity via an expressionism that, he asserted, was 'a continental thing'.[21] Bratby centralises race (his anxiety over his supposed blackness and/or Jewishness) as a constituent feature of his art, without ever making it a constituent feature of his subject matter. What we see across the board is work he believes to be 'too strong' for the English; he says: 'I don't think I belong in this country ... compared with English tastes and judgment, I'm a foreigner.'[22] It is in his very excessiveness and abundance, then, that Bratby locates his own foreignness. Here are those lenticular traces of race, ever present yet unremarked.

Race and modernity in Richard Hamilton's Just What Is It That Makes Today's Homes So Different, So Appealing? *(1956)*

Drawing on the world of popular visual culture and addressing the post-imperial moment in a much more self-conscious way than Bratby's offering is Richard Hamilton's *Just What Is It That Makes Today's Homes So Different, So Appealing?* (1956) (Figure 4.2). The image has assumed an iconic status as one of the central visual texts of post-war British art, and the historical context from which it arises offers a fascinating insight into the ways in which high art was riven with anxieties over foreignness and modernity no less than popular culture. *Just What Is It ...?* has its origins in the Independent Group, made up of artists such as Lawrence Alloway, Reyner Banham, Eduardo Paolozzi and Peter and Alison Smithson, all based at the Institute for Contemporary Arts (ICA). In many ways the Independent Group cannot be understood outside of the ICA, which had been formed immediately after the war as a place for the discussion of art, ideas and culture beyond the more strict confines of the Royal Academy. The ICA was avowedly modern (and modernist) and, as well as organising ground-breaking exhibitions by artists such as Pablo Picasso, Georges Braque and Jackson Pollock, it had its Piccadilly premises completely refurbished by the modernist architect and designer Jane Drew.

As Anne Massey explains, pre-war modernism had been characterised as elitist, politically left wing and essentially European in form and origin.[23] Immediately following the war there was an effort to recalibrate a sense of national identity that merged a regressive invocation of British character, rooted in a sense of timeless and unchanging landscape, with utopian visions of a modern future riven from the new world of plastics, telecommunications and 'contemporary' design. The Council of Industrial Design, which had been founded in 1944 by the Board of Trade in an effort to encourage both the domestic and foreign consumption of British manufactured goods, was explicit in its desire to 'unite the best of past British design with a modern design look'.[24] Much of this was intended as a decisive movement away from the austere ethos (and materials) of utility design that had characterised the war years. Nowhere was this more apparent than in the contradictory discourses available at the Festival of Britain of 1951, which articulated a national identity that 'depended largely for its security on traditional values of the past to cope with the future'.[25] This was equally true of the Independent Group, and throughout the emergence of Pop Art we

Figure 4.2 Richard Hamilton, *Just What Is It That Makes Today's Homes So Different, So Appealing?* 1956, collage, 260 x 248 mm.

see deep contradictions that reveal not simply a rejection of the past, but a troubled and anxious effort to both reject it and cling to it simultaneously.

The most celebrated event of the Independent Group's history was the 1956 exhibition, *This Is Tomorrow*. Staged at the Whitechapel Gallery, it was made up of a number of zones or areas, in which different artists, designers, critics and architects produced collaborative visions of the future. Created for the cover of the exhibition catalogue, *Just What Is It ...?* is a deliberately troubling image designed to articulate the ambivalence at the heart of the project of modernity within the context of post-war Britain. As Jonathan Katz puts it: 'Hamilton stands out, even among his proto-pop peers, for his belaboured equilibration of such defining polarities as nature and culture, fine art and commodity, past and future, high culture and popular culture ... male and female, and even gay and straight.'[26] Katz's 'queered' reading of *Just What Is It ...?* is fascinating and compelling and yet, for all its engagement with Hamilton's aggressive 'dissident aesthetic', the issue of race remains, again, unremarked.[27]

On one level, of course, *Just What Is It ...?* offers us a world filled with desirable objects and ideas: furniture, bodies, leisure, space and time. But, as the picture plane is flattened out, so the experience of consciousness – of being – is flattened out. There is little pretence of human agency within this world of material over-abundance. The figures are flattened images reduced to the status of commodities, not only within the logic of our spectatorship, but also within the frame of the image itself. As with Bratby, this world of material abundance offers little comfort or joy. The ambivalence of the image is not inseparable from a relatively widely held anti-Americanism that pervaded much of British culture in the 1950s and which was a significant element of the contemporary arts scene. Dick Hebdige links this attitude quite explicitly to post-imperial anxiety: 'After the war, this covert hostility [to an American presence] persisted and was exacerbated by new factors: by Britain's declining status as a world power, the disintegration of the British Empire coupled with the simultaneous rise in America's international prestige and the first indications of American imperial ambitions.'[28]

It is hard to recognise Francis Spalding's description of *Just What Is It ...?* as 'humorous' and 'playful' in this image of deeply troubling excess.[29] While it embraces the image-saturation of the brave new worlds of glossy magazines and advertising, the collage's bleakness and joylessness seems much more akin to John Bratby's mournful Jean. It is a catalogue of anxiety that, for all its abundance of material goods, offers little in the way of sustenance. Indeed, abundance for Hamilton is excess. As Thomas Crow says, *Just What Is It ...?* 'sneers at the idea that mass-produced possessions and manufactured dreams under the Ford insignia can provide adequate subjective furniture for post-war life'.[30] The obvious focus of *Just What Is It ...?* is the two figures in the forefront of the image. Technologies of leisure and gender have individuated them as entirely consuming beings. Their solipsistic concerns with appearance are the consequence of a world in which their ontological legitimacy is predicated completely on their value as image. They are bodies of excess, not only in terms of their rapacious consumerism but also their physicality and sexuality. The breasts, the muscles, the phallic lollipop, all signal an abundance beyond control. Weighing heavily, suffocating all, is that moon lowering above the open roof.

Though coupled with the assertion that 'this is tomorrow', *Just What Is It ...?* is an image frozen in time. Its vision of tomorrow offers no sense of a future, providing instead only an eternal present in which the figures never age, are never subject to history, and are concerned only with an eternal commitment to narcissistic gazing at the self. However, it is in Crow's further assertion that the image casts light 'onto America's racial hypocrisy in the shape of an advertisement for the blackface mimicry of the singer Al Jolson'[31] that the image reveals something of the broader discourses of race. The whiteness of the image is generally blinding, self-contained and entirely unselfconscious; given that the billboard for Jolson's film *The Jazz Singer* is positioned in the background of the image, beyond the window of the main room, race is 'outside' in every sense. Its visual presence is represented through the complicated layering of the ersatz subjectivity offered by the destabilising possibilities of blackface. While doubtless a gesture towards blackness in the context of the modern American Civil Rights movement, *Just What Is It ...?* is situated more immediately within the visual registers of post-war British culture, in which the black body is consistently represented via the tropes of empire. It is only with the emergence of Pop Art, and its playful collapsing of the traditional boundaries between high and low culture, that the black body begins to make any significant appearance in the arena of fine art. Its early appearance in *Just What Is It ...?* is complicated by the fact that it is a self-conscious representation of an aggressively inauthentic racial subjectivity.

What is to be done with this black body? That we know it to be a representation of a famous white performer, thus providing a further layer of mediation of its racial being, makes it even more complicated. Blackness is simultaneously present and absent and, as a function of white performance, we might see it as another solipsistic fantasy of whiteness that it might be both black and white at the same time. One of Eric Lott's arguments in his extraordinary and ground-breaking analysis of American minstrelsy, *Love and Theft*, is that blackface was never simply an issue of racist denigration.[32] Every blackface performance was striated by multiple and competing discourses of freedom, abasement, denial, liberation and, of course, racism as well. Within the context of post-war Britain Al Jolson's presence points westward towards the United States as well as east and south towards the colonial world. In its inversion of the 'natural' ordering of race, however, blackface poses no significant threat to the strict boundaries of racial hierarchy. For whites, blackface does not trouble the social order because whites are implicitly granted authority and access to all domains and spaces. Rather, it is the black body that must be controlled and spatially restricted. It is for that reason that the boundaries are, then, deeply compromised when blacks pass for white. It means that blacks may be transgressing forbidden zones without the knowledge of whites. This, then, threatens an entire social order in which white supremacy and privilege is predicated on the maintenance of pure zones and spaces of whiteness.

As a vision of post-war modernity, *Just What Is It ...?* embodies those tensions over boundary collapse that were present in broad discussions about the nature of British art and its relationship to both mainland Europe and the United States. As I have demonstrated above, those tensions were themselves redolent of the even broader tensions across the landscape of British culture and society of the period. The transcoding of those anxieties is a useful reminder of the ways in which multiple discursive and cultural domains intersect.

Parsing and passing in Basil Dearden's Sapphire

Sapphire was one of a number of 'social problem' films that Dearden made in the 1940s and 1950s. He also directed a gritty crime drama entitled *The Blue Lamp* (1950), *Violent Playground* (1958), a film concerned with juvenile delinquency and, perhaps most famously, *Victim* (1960), the first serious mainstream treatment of homosexuality in British cinema. An attempt to deal with the issue of racism and prejudice, *Sapphire* is what would be referred to today as a crime procedure narrative and follows the efforts of two London detectives (Nigel Patrick and Michael Craig) to solve the murder of the eponymous Sapphire, whose body is discovered in Hampstead Heath at the very opening of the film. But the deeper mystery to solve is the one of race, for it becomes apparent very quickly that the light-skinned and blonde-haired Sapphire – a student at the Royal College of Music – is black. As they unravel the narrative of events, the police make sense of Sapphire's death by identifying racial prejudice as the killer's motive. But the film wrestles unselfconsciously with deeper ontological issues as it struggles to make sense of the categories of whiteness and blackness themselves. It is, further, no coincidence that the confusions of race should be located within the space of the city. In *Sapphire*, and perhaps post-war Britain more generally, the mystery of race is a mystery of the city.

The city, as cosmopolitan space, possesses an unruliness in its position as a point of conjuncture between empire and home. *Sapphire* spatialises this tense relationship as the colonial body and the domestic body collide. As the murder investigation proceeds and the certainty of Sapphire's blackness emerges, we are taken into the spaces of 'blackness' – initially at Tulip's Jazz Club and then to a boarding-house for young West Indian men, one of whom is initially the prime suspect in the killing. Dead before the narrative begins, Sapphire's body is both present and absent, denied and yet undeniable. Hers is a body of plenty and abundance so that the space of blackness is at once a space of lack (of money, refinement, order, self-control, whiteness) and a space of abundance (of breasts, hair, movement, sexuality, sensuality, otherness, and the over-populating immigrant body).

Tulip's Jazz Club is the determinant low 'other' to the high of the Royal College of Music, the institutional embodiment of the highest evocations of Western culture. The white police officers moving downwards, descending into Tulip's, are rigid, entirely upright figures, self-contained units surrounded by dynamic, moving, black bodies. Space is raced, with black space literally and metaphorically placed below white space. In locating Sapphire's identity in two distinct zones the film racialises the city, and, as the messy meeting between colony and metropole takes place, the key structuring spatial metaphor is that of high and low. As Lefebvre says, 'social space contains a great diversity of objects, both natural and social, including the networks and pathways which facilitate the exchange of material things and information'.[33] As the white police officers traverse these zones, the 'networks and pathways' of exchange are indeed both material and ontological. The key exchanges (marked through information about the murder such as material evidence and witness statements, and the crossing of boundaries of high and low) are those contained within the discourses of race that loop endlessly from the metropole to the colony and back again.

While laying a claim to a progressive politics of racial tolerance and equality, the film actually becomes an assertion of the ontological legitimacy of a whiteness determined via a set of spatial locations naturalised through biological and cultural categorization. Sapphire is simultaneously passing and parsing. As she passes for white she is parsing the grammars of race in ways that unravel the supposed certainties of racial identity and, in so doing, the film inadvertently reveals the essential performativity of race. But it is a performance that must be confined within strictly demarcated boundaries if the privileges and dominance of whiteness are to be maintained. In the context of post-imperial Britain, spatial boundaries are inevitably racial boundaries. Anderson argues that race is linked to nation via its function as a cognate unchosen category into which we are simply born. Naturalised in this way, national identity and racial identity assume what he terms a 'halo of disinterestedness'.[34] This 'halo of disinterestedness' of course then lays an implicit claim to stand outside of politics, ideology, indeed outside history itself. The consequence of this ahistorical naturalisation is that race becomes the post-imperial dilemma from which there is no escape. In her refusal to adhere to the spatial demarcations of race and demonstration of their constantly shifting, and always permeable, boundaries, the consequences of history are no less fatal for Sapphire than they were for the Mau Mau.

Conclusion

In choosing the case studies above I have explored the ways in which those competing discourses of austerity and abundance appear reflected in, and refracted through, a wide range of cultural formations. Though I touch on high and low culture, painting and collage, and film set in both the domestic and foreign arenas, the focus of my study is necessarily relatively narrow. However, the texts – as diverse as they are – clearly reveal shared concerns, anxieties and tensions that were present across the cultural landscape. A study of radio and television programmes of the period such as *Take It From Here*, *Hancock's Half Hour* or *The Goon Show*, newspaper cartoons, children's annuals or travel brochures would reveal similar tensions. I hesitate to call the objects of my analysis 'representative texts' for this assumes that they contain some element of inherent value or that they embody their particular age more deeply than other texts and that it is the job of the critic, then, merely to discern what meaning is hiding within. This is not so straightforwardly the case. The thoughtful critic creates the 'meaningful' text as much as – if not more than – she or he discovers it. In choosing to look at *Simba*, *Jean and Still Life in Front of Window*, *Just What Is It That Makes Today's Homes So Different, So Appealing?* and *Sapphire*, I am asserting that they each have something compelling to say about the period in which they appeared. The tropes of abundance and austerity run through each, as they run through the visual culture of the period and link to those other crucial discourses of race, nationality and space. Images of abundance visible across the vectors of cultural expression through the immediate post-war period and through the 1950s identify something to be desired and yet simultaneously mistrusted. In doing so they seem to suggest that discourses of austerity are always worth examining, not so much for what they say we should do, as for what they say we are.

Notes

1 See J.M. MacKenzie, 'The Persistence of Empire in Metropolitan Culture', in S. Ward (ed.), *British Culture and the End of Empire* (Manchester: Manchester University Press, 2001), pp. 21–36; S. Ward, 'Introduction', in Ward, *British Culture and the End of Empire*, p. 12.
2 A. McClintock, *Imperial Leather: Race, Gender and Sexuality in the Colonial Context* (London: Routledge, 1995), pp. 207–31.
3 Ward, 'Introduction', p. 4.
4 J. Bailkin, *The Afterlife of Empire* (Berkeley: University of California Press, 2012), p. 5.
5 B. Schwarz, 'Introduction: End of Empire and the English Novel', in R. Gilmour and B. Schwarz (eds), *End of Empire and the English Novel* (Manchester: Manchester University Press), p. 6.
6 M. Landy, *British Genres: Cinema and Society, 1930–1960* (Princeton: Princeton University Press, 1991), p. 115.
7 L. Young, *Fear of the Dark: Race, Gender and Sexuality in the Cinema* (London: Routledge, 1996), p. 81.
8 W. Webster, 'Mumbo Jumbo, Magic, and Modernity: Africa in British Cinema, 1946–65', in L. Grieveson and C. MacCabe (eds), *Film and the End of Empire* (Basingstoke: Palgrave Macmillan, 2011), p. 240.
9 J. Chapman and N. Cull, *Projecting Empire: Imperialism and Popular Cinema* (London: I.B. Tauris, 2009), p. xi.
10 Webster, 'Mumbo Jumbo, Magic, and Modernity', p. 241.
11 Young, *Fear of the Dark*, p. 81.
12 S. Hall, 'Black Diaspora Artists in Britain: Three "Moments" in Post-war History', *History Workshop Journal*, 61:1 (2006), 4.
13 J. Hyman, *The Battle for Realism: Figurative Art in Britain During the Cold War, 1945–1960* (New Haven: Yale University Press, 2001), p. 7.
14 M. Yacowar, *The Great Bratby: A Portrait of John Bratby RA* (London: Middlesex University Press, 2008), pp. 31–2.
15 M. Garlake, *New Art, New World: British Art in Postwar Society* (New Haven: Paul Mellon Centre for Studies in British Art, 1998), p. 134.
16 M. Harrison, *Transition: The London Art Scene in the Fifties* (London: Merrell Publishers, 2002), p. 35.
17 Bratby cited in Yacowar, *The Great Bratby*, p. 20.
18 D. Kynaston, *Family Britain, 1951–1957* (New York: Walker & Co., 2009), p. 19.
19 Garlake, *New Art, New World*, p. 133.
20 Bratby cited in Yacowar, *The Great Bratby*, p. 20.
21 Bratby cited in Yacowar, *The Great Bratby*, pp. 15–16.
22 Bratby cited in Yacowar, *The Great Bratby*, pp. 15–16.
23 See A. Massey, *The Independent Group: Modernism and Mass Culture in Britain, 1945–59* (Manchester: Manchester University Press, 1995), pp. 19–32.
24 Massey, *The Independent Group*, p. 7.
25 Massey, *The Independent Group*, p. 17.
26 J.D. Katz, 'Dada's Mama: Richard Hamilton's Queer Pop', in L. Tickner and D. Peters Corbett (eds), *British Art in the Cultural Field, 1939–69* (London: Wiley-Blackwell, 2012), p. 141.
27 Katz, 'Dada's Mama', p. 141.
28 D. Hebdige, *Hiding in the Light: On Images and Things* (London: Routledge, 1988), pp. 53–4.

29 F. Spalding, *British Art Since 1900* (London: Thames and Hudson, 1986), p. 191.
30 T. Crow, *The Rise of the Sixties: American and European Art in the Era of Dissent* (London: Lawrence King Publishing, 1996), p. 44.
31 Crow, *The Rise of the Sixties*, p. 44.
32 E. Lott, *Love and Theft: Blackface Minstrelsy and the American Working Class* (New York: Oxford University Press, 1993).
33 H. Lefebvre, *The Production of Space*, trans. D. Nicholson-Smith (Oxford: Blackwell, 1991), p. 77.
34 B. Anderson, *Imagined Communities: Reflections on the Origin and Spread of Nationalism* (London: Verso, 1991), p. 143.

PART II

Performing decolonisation

CHAPTER FIVE

The peasant armed: Bengal, Vietnam and transnational solidarities in Utpal Dutt's *Invincible Vietnam*

Abin Chakraborty

> A colonized people is not alone. In spite of all that colonialism can do, its frontiers remain open to new ideas and echoes from the world outside ... The great victory of the Vietnamese people in Dien Bien Phu is no longer, strictly speaking, a Vietnamese victory.
> Frantz Fanon, *The Wretched of the Earth*[1]

Fanon's comment not only signifies the bond of solidarity between the Algerian struggle for independence and the Vietnamese success against the same French colonial forces, but also signals that transnational dimension which has been integral to decolonising processes across the world. Whether it is the proliferation of Pan-African discourses on both sides of the Atlantic, the dissemination of Rastafarian culture, Che Guevara's revolutionary struggles in Latin America and Africa, the Gadar Movement of California and its role in the Indian nationalist movement, Subhash Chandra Bose's international networks and the formation of the Indian National Army or the role of various Asian and African diasporic communities in nationalist struggles – all point to a persistently present transnational dimension in decolonising processes.[2] A major aspect of such transnational bonds was the role of Marxist political organisations of one kind or another, especially after Lenin's involvement in the Second World Congress of the Communist International, a conference of all communist or left-wing organisations of the world, in 1920. Lenin stressed the need for developing a network of oppressed nations against oppressor ones, and the Second Congress thus contributed to the proliferation of multilateral lies between communist parties of different colonised countries for the continuation of the liberation struggles. The emergence of Soviet Russia as the world's first communist country in 1917 was obviously of critical significance in this respect and enhanced the transnational networks of diverse nationalist movements, especially by operating as a utopian ideal. This international collaboration between communist organisations and various national liberation movements would further manifest itself through unprecedented events such as the Baku Congress of 1920, in which nearly two thousand people from all across Asia participated, including representatives of those who did not subscribe to revolutionary socialist politics, or the much later Tricontinental Conference of Solidarity of the Peoples of Africa, Asia and Latin America, held in Havana in 1966 and participated in by representatives of many newly independent countries. One of the leading figures of this conference was the international revolutionary Che Guevara. His speeches to the conference clearly illustrated the transnational idiom of postcolonial resistance in which he was so involved. In his message to the Tricontinental he stated:

> What is the role that we, the exploited people of the world, must play? ... The contribution that falls to us, the exploited and backward people of the world, is to eliminate the foundations sustaining imperialism: our oppressed nations from which capital, raw materials and cheap labour (both workers and technicians) are extracted, and to which new capital (tools of domination), arms and all kinds of goods are exported, sinking us into absolute dependence. The fundamental element of that strategic objective will be the real liberation of the peoples.[3]

The Vietnamese struggle against French and American imperialism in search of a socialist ideal played a key role in defining 'the real liberation' to which Guevara referred. Therefore, he went on to add, 'The peoples of the three continents are watching and learning a lesson for themselves in Vietnam ... Attack hard and without letup at every point of confrontation – that must be the general tactic of the people.'[4] Thus, for him and many others like him, Vietnam had already emerged, much like Soviet Russia around fifty years before, as a transnational ideal of postcolonial liberation based on a vision of proletarian internationalism. Unfortunately, apart from a few rare discussions, such as that of Robert Young, drawn upon here, very few postcolonial monographs or anthologies focus on the vibrant international dimension of many anti-colonial struggles. This chapter focuses precisely on this connection by offering a contextual analysis of a Bengali play, translated by the author, Utpal Dutt, as *Invincible Vietnam*. The chapter will first offer a brief introduction to Utpal Dutt and his revolutionary theatre, stressing its pronounced international dimensions. It will then document the political and cultural links between Bengal and Vietnam before offering an analysis of the play which presents Vietnam both as allegory and as ideal for a decolonising India.

Utpal Dutt and his revolutionary theatre

Born in 1929, Utpal Dutt gained maturity during a crucial phase in Indian history which was marked by the struggle for independence, traumatic Hindu–Muslim riots, a devastating famine and an intellectual world shaped by the progression and aftermath of the Second World War and its manifold consequences. Dutt himself confessed how during that time he was thrilled by the stories of the Red Army's sacrifices and heroic victories and that his growing love for socialism was only paralleled by his attraction to theatre, also evident from his performances in St Xavier's College, Kolkata. His subsequent involvements with Geoffrey Kendall's troupe, 'Shakespeareana', as well as the Indian People's Theatre Association (IPTA), a cultural front of the undivided Communist Party of India, testify to not just his deepening attachment to theatre but also his journey towards a distinct domain of political theatre.[5] In fact, as an erudite scholar of Marxism who had an uncanny ability to quote Marx, Lenin, Engels and Mao-Tse-Tung with utmost precision, Dutt's understanding of theatre as a whole, and his own work in particular, was ardently based on his understanding of Marxism. During his brief association with the IPTA and even afterwards, Dutt regularly produced and performed in adaptations or translations of various leftist plays and even participated in street-corner plays which stridently criticised the diverse injustices which were being meted out to the people, especially the subaltern sections of society such as the peasantry and the industrial labourers. All such enterprise was based on the firm conviction that cultural representations could serve to strengthen the radical impulses of the people. For Dutt, theatre could initiate and sustain a process of revolutionary restructuring which he saw as the only panacea to the manifold maladies of India's newly independent nation-state. These beliefs are elaborately discussed in Dutt's *Towards a Revolutionary Theatre*, in which he explicitly announced, 'The revolutionary theatre must, by definition, preach revolution, a radical overthrow of the political power of the bourgeois – feudal forces, a thorough destruction of their state-machine.'[6]

The best way to achieve this end, Dutt believed, was by retelling – through theatre – the numerous heroic struggles of the peasants and labourers against colonial and imperial injustice. Realising with alarm how India's history was being reshaped by its bourgeois leadership and their apparent desire to define the entire nationalist struggle for freedom in terms of Congress-led Gandhian movements, Dutt took up the task of urgently reminding the people about the glorious contribution made by the masses. He aimed to stress how these sectors of society repeatedly launched armed attacks not only against the British themselves but also against those members of the native elite who actively assisted them in vanquishing and exploiting the people. His declaration of this purpose is worth quoting at length:

> We have to set ourselves the task firstly to create plays, songs, ballets to recapture for the people the glorious episodes of their past, when they fought relentless people's wars for freedom, when peasants took up arms against landlords and the British army ... We try to show that the Indian masses have always fought with arms and have always instinctively resorted to guerrilla methods, avoiding direct confrontation, harassing the enemy, ambush and swift retreat ... We are trying to present the approaching revolution not as an isolated phenomenon but as a continuation of a struggle begun two hundred years ago, as the completion of our unfinished freedom struggle.[7]

However, in keeping with the aforementioned tenor of Marxist political internationalism, Dutt's oeuvre was not confined to the exploration of Indian national history. Instead, as an ardent believer of proletarian internationalism, he also staged through his plays the revolutionary struggles carried out by the people in various countries like Russia, Cuba, Vietnam and even countries such as France, Germany and the United States, which he demonstrated as also witnessing several popular uprisings against autocratic and racist regimes that barbarically brutalised the people. Plays like *Krushabiddha Cuba* (*Crucified Cuba*), *Barricade*, *Manusher Adhikarey* (*Rights of Man*) or *Lal, Sada, Neel* (*Red, White and Blue*) aptly illustrate this international range of Utpal Dutt's worldview. Ultimately, he drew on all episodes of revolutionary struggle, anywhere in the world, to ignite the fighting spirit of his own countrymen. Just as Fanon aimed to strengthen revolutionary reconstruction in postcolonial countries by seeking to hear about 'the experiments carried out by the Argentinians or the Burmese against illiteracy or the dictatorial tendencies of their leaders',[8] so Dutt sought to utilise the revolutionary struggles of subaltern groups around the world to fortify the resolve of those struggling against injustice in his own country. Pabitra Sarkar therefore remarks:

> Political struggles for freedom, nationalist liberation movements, workers' struggles for the attainment of financial rights and acknowledgement of human dignity – all were to [Dutt] temporal and spatial explosions of one continuous struggle as he believed that

all valid struggles enrich the traditions of other such struggles as they become part of the unbroken history of oppressed and deprived multitudes'.[9]

Invincible Vietnam[10] operates as another example of this remarkable internationalism.

Vietnam and Bengal

One of the likely reasons as to why the Bengali Dutt chose to write a play on Vietnam was the remarkable long-term political bond that Bengal had shared with Vietnam and its struggle for national liberation. For example, various trade unions and political parties in Bengal observed Indo-China Day on 25 October 1945 in opposition to the British decision to send Indian soldiers to assist Dutch and French colonialists in the region. Furthermore, two years later, the All India Students' Federation decided to observe Vietnam Day on 21 January 1947 in association with other students' organisations. The decision was backed by overwhelming popular involvement by students and this incurred the wrath of the colonial administration. The administration deployed armed police forces against hundreds of student demonstrators and, as the police opened fire in front of the Senate Hall of the University of Calcutta, two students – Sukhendu Bikash Nath and Dheer Ranjan Sen – were killed and several others injured.[11] Such struggles and sacrifices did not go unnoticed. The leaders of the Vietnam Students' Association in France and abroad greeted the leaders of the All India Students' Federation and offered 'Fraternal greetings and warmest thanks for demonstration supporting Vietnam's struggle for freedom with expression of confidence in the final victory of all Asia'.[12] This fraternal bond continued to grow over the next decades, especially as Vietnam was plunged into a terrible and macabre conflict in which the US-backed puppet government of South Vietnam was pitted against the Communist government of North Vietnam and the allied guerrilla units of South Vietnamese peasants. Consequently, protests, especially by students, raged in the 1960s throughout Bengal and attracted the attention of more and more people through ever-widening public outrage against American imperialism. Contemporary newspaper reports suggest that such protests involved thousands of students, who were also joined by workers and employees from different sectors.[13] For example, on 8 April 1965 two student organisations, the Students' Federation and the Democratic Students' Union, observed another Vietnam Day, demanding 'US imperialism quit Vietnam', culminating in a huge procession which went to the

American Commercial Consulate to submit a memorandum. During that same year, students also observed a Vietnam Week, from 7 to 14 July, with a students' strike being organised on 14 July. The strike was accompanied by processions and the burning of effigies of the American leaders, including President Johnson.[14] One of the most striking of these incidents was the massive student demonstration that took place on 20 November 1968 around the then Dum Dum Airport on the occasion of Robert McNamara's visit to Kolkata as the president of the World Bank. Notorious in Bengal as one of the architects of the brutalities in Vietnam, McNamara was identified as a heinous murderer, and the resulting demonstration led to violent clashes between protesters and the police across the city, as a result of which hundreds were beaten or arrested.[15] Such events were not just confined to urban locations but spread to comparatively remote rural regions as well. The following report from a youth conference in Murshidabad, a comparatively traditional northern district of West Bengal, may amply testify to this fact:

> Recently, on the last day of a fortnight of campaigning regarding scientific socialism, a huge gathering was organised in the Grant Law ground by the Murshidabad district committee of the Democratic Youth Federation of India, demanding the recognition of the revolutionary government in South Vietnam ... processions of the youths and fishermen of Lalgola marched in. They came in with red festoons and posters to take a vow. The vow to gather the crops in the house of the peasants – the vow to baptise themselves in the courage of the Vietnamese youths.[16]

Thus, the transnational impact of the Vietnam struggles was culturally and politically disseminated beyond the urban centres, which were generally more open to international influences, and also reached wide-ranging and far-flung rural regions.

All of these events were born out of an ever-growing sense of solidarity which was repeatedly reinforced by an evolving political discourse which highlighted Vietnam as an inspirational ideal of equitable agrarian reform and militant struggle. Vietnam also provided a case study of the grave sacrifices through which that ideal was to be gained. This was of crucial significance within the realm of contemporary politics in Bengal, where leftist organisations were collectively campaigning for the distribution of land to landless villagers by confiscating excess land from landlords and by legally allotting government-owned plots to sharecroppers. Such movements were met with considerable resistance by the landlords and their associates, who also profited from the combination of reluctance and collusion which was exhibited by sections of the administration and the ruling Congress Party.[17] In such a situation the 'Land to the Tillers' project of the Democratic Republic of Vietnam (DRV) and the National Liberation Front (NLF) of South Vietnam captured the imagination of the leftist leaders of Bengal. This bond was bolstered by the fact that Bengal and Vietnam shared rather similar predominantly agricultural economies with large numbers of disempowered peasants. This is why, while one article in *Ganashakti* (the organ of the Communist Party of India (Marxist)) would declare, 'The liberation struggle in Vietnam is an integral part of the revolutionary struggles of all toiling masses of the world,'[18] Kolkata's Mayor Prashanta Shur would, on a different occasion, state, 'May our Ganges and your Mekong unite and may Ho Chi Minh's last wishes be fulfilled through that union.'[19] It is because of such a connection that the world would see the organisation of an exhibition on the Vietnam War in Kolkata, the performance of a play on Vietnam during the Khardah-Titagarh labourers' conference, felicitation of the NLF delegates by workers of Jaya factories and even the acceptance of a proposal to support the Vietnamese struggle against US imperialism at a regional conference of the All India Kisan Sabha in Habra.[20]

What these instances also suggest is that the contemporary leftist political discourse was integrally associated with cultural representations of the Vietnamese struggle which proliferated across regions and genres. This remarkable intellectual profusion is crystallised in, for example, the following lines of the eminent poet Ram Basu:

> The warmth of rice
> Serenity of conscience
> Generosity of forests –
> Vietnam.
> We want your truth
> We want your sun
> We chant the incantation of purity:
> Vietnam.[21]

Similarly, poet and playwright Mohit Chattopadhyay would write:

> Blood from Vietnam,
> Spills onto Bengal,
> Ashes of Buddhist monks
> Float on Ganga's tides.
> Sorrows jostle together
> And cry from my heart
> Hanoi! Hanoi![22]

It is in consequence of such remarkable affective bonds that the streets of Kolkata would resonate with the cries of 'Tomar nam amar nam Vietnam Vietnam' ('Your name, my name, Vietnam, Vietnam') and thus reinforce the vision of Vietnam as an inspirational ideal marked by an egalitarian anti-imperialism for Bengal and the whole of India in general. Utpal Dutt's *Invincible Vietnam* was a product of this particular intellectual ferment and further contributed to his own programme of revolutionary theatre.

Utpal Dutt's revolutionary theatre and transnational imaginings

Dutt rigorously used his theatre not only to launch a scathing critique of the 'comprador bourgeoisie'[23] which made up India's ruling elite but also to inspire the masses with enactments of heroic mass-struggles of the past. To achieve this purpose he relied on something akin to Walter Benjamin's notion of revolutionary nostalgia[24] and presented through his plays some of the ignored or forgotten episodes of mass-struggle to both inspire the subaltern sections of the society and endow them with visions of alternative orders. This is exactly what he meant when he argued that a revolutionary play must advance a revolutionary ideology and further illustrated his methodology by insisting,

> It is ... our task to re-affirm the violent history of India, to re-affirm the martial traditions of its people, to recount again and again the heroic tales of armed rebels and martyrs ... It is imperative that we immediately begin re-asserting the heritage of revolutionary ideals, because the communists now struggling for the liberations of the masses are heirs to this heritage.[25]

Since, as Partha Chatterjee has illustrated, India only witnessed what Gramsci would define as a 'passive revolution',[26] where power changed hands without any radical alteration in hierarchies and production systems, the post-independence decades witnessed pervasive discontent and resultant dissidence.[27] Utpal Dutt's dramaturgy was the calculated response of a Marxist intellectual to this political context and he was unique in his advocacy of militant collective struggles through theatre. This is precisely why most of Dutt's plays excavated episodes of anti-colonial subaltern struggles which were largely ignored by an elitist historiography which primarily wove the narrative of the struggle for independence around the Gandhian movements and ignored most of the alternative strands. It is this political vision which makes Dutt's oeuvre, which runs to ten volumes, such a remarkable one, and yet it is perhaps for the same reason that he remains largely ignored in the annals of Indian drama. One of the significant features of this unexplored corpus is Dutt's firm belief, much like Guevara's, in the need for proletarian internationalism: this manifested itself through plays that not only dealt with the communist movements in Russia, China, Cuba and elsewhere but also focused on the French Revolution, Nazi Germany, Indonesia, Black Resistance in America and the liberation struggle in Bangladesh, for example. In an interview with Samik Bandyopadhyay he therefore declared:

> Communists are not sui generis. They inherit the legacy of all the revolutions and uprisings that have taken place in the past. Be it the French Revolution ... the October Revolution or the Chinese Revolution – all of these form our legacy. The communist movement in India is the consequence of all this ... all our attempts are designed to assimilate this legacy by citing international examples as only the communists know that even if a fighter, a freedom-fighter is killed in Nicaragua, then that too is our loss. Our duty is to bring these stories of struggle to our masses.[28]

Invincible Vietnam was part of this larger enterprise and used the political and cultural bond between Bengal and Vietnam to set up both an allegory of contemporary struggles and an ideal worth the struggle.

Analysing Invincible Vietnam

Invincible Vietnam focuses on one Vietnamese village's heroic resistance against American assault, with the centre of action being a makeshift military hospital looking after the wounded soldiers. It is based on an actual Vietnamese victory in the HoBo woods. The play revolves around a planned American assault on the HoBo village, the extremely well-organised resistance of the villagers whose courage and sacrifices are amply highlighted, and the eventual Vietnamese victory. Notably, the victory stems from the ingenuity of a female Vietnamese guerrilla warrior named Trac, who was actually part of the American operation as a mole. Through this plot Dutt foregrounds a paradigm of militant struggle by peasants which serves to connect Vietnam with contemporary Bengal. Dutt's fusion of two different struggles becomes evident when we read the repeated references to the Vietnamese as 'illiterate peasants' and learn that the American soldiers are benefiting from the help of Madame Tran Thi Lan Huu, 'the daughter of Neng, the dispossessed master of all the territory between Ben Suc and Ben Quat'(6), to hunt down Vietcong soldiers, many of whom worked as farmhands in her father's estate. It is this class identity that ensures her collaboration with the Americans as her father was dispossessed by the communists, who strengthened their rural base through the capturing and redistribution of huge portions of land that previously belonged to a minuscule elite. Notably, the same strategy was also employed by the communist political parties in contemporary Bengal, where they gained more and more popularity in the rural areas precisely because of their persistent campaigning about the redistribution of land through the removal of excess land from landlords. In such campaigns not only did the Bengali communists use the administration when they gained power but they also advocated independent vigilante actions by the peasantry as a mode of protecting their own rights. A play like *Invincible Vietnam* offers an artistic representation of these political policies as well as contributing to them by emphasising that element of class antagonism which was pivotal in ensuring united peasant action against landlords, usurers or colluding policemen and earning urban citizens' support for their struggles. Anal Gupta, Utpal Dutt's friend, contemporary and fellow playwright, significantly observed:

> *Krushobiddha Cuba* [*Crucified Cuba*], *Ajeya Vietnam* [*Invincible Vietnam*], *Jalianwalabagh* or *Leniner Daak* [*The Call of Lenin*] are not just documentary plays. They offer materialist explanations of the central conflict of an age. Conveying it in a comprehensible manner to the common people is an arduous enterprise ... Utpal Dutt had mastered it. Otherwise there would not have been surges of boundless spectators across rural Bengal.[29]

This popular surge was also perhaps made possible because of the inherent ability of theatre to communicate directly and passionately certain ideas and beliefs to the spectators in the manner of no other art form. Unlike poetry or a novel, which are primarily for personal individual consumption, theatre necessitates a world of collective participation and therefore fosters the possibility of such lines of solidarity and mobilisation which can only be paralleled by political processes. And it is precisely through such intervention that theatre retains its contemporary relevance. It is to emphasise these ideas that noted theatre activist Moloyashree Hashmi would remark that 'some larger connection to the real world, a world where people strive very hard to make ends meet, whether they are subjected to all sorts of violence and brutalization, a connection with this world is essential for our theatre to come alive'.[30] The reason why thousands flocked to Utpal Dutt's productions, in villages and in cities,[31] was his ability to establish such connections, making remote episodes of Indian or international history resonant with contemporary significations. This strategy is particularly relevant in *Invincible Vietnam* since the play implicitly creates a parallel between the Vietnamese struggle against the Americans and Bengali peasants' struggle against landlords and a colluding administration. It is these connections which made *Invincible Vietnam* and other such plays so popular among the people, both in cities and villages, as the spectators could identify with the Vietnamese and relate their crisis to the unfolding political scenario in Bengal. The international subaltern, without losing his or her own specificity, becomes the representation of the national subalterns and presents to them both a reflection of their struggles and the ideals towards which they must strive. As Dutt himself noted, 'not only does need produce an ideal but ideals also produce needs ... In consumption the products become objects of pleasure, objects of individual appropriation. Thus the creation of an ideal theatrical production also creates the need for it in society and its consumption is appropriated by individuals.'[32] The theatrical representation of Vietnam thus becomes both an allegorical representation of contemporary struggles and the projection of an ideal towards which one may aspire.

While similarity of political objective offered one mode of solidarity, another was offered by *Invincible Vietnam*'s emphasis on loss, suffering and agony. While the Vietnamese faced the wrath of American military monstrosity, their downtrodden Indian counterparts also continued to suffer as political movements demanding food or land were met with police reprisals or unchecked brutalities by landlords themselves. Instances of peasants being beaten or murdered by landlords, or women being raped or their crops being burnt were common enough in contemporary Bengal, and it is these facts which fostered the growing resentment of the rural peasantry which was effectively utilised by the Bengali leftists for their political ascent. It is this combination of loss and related anger which is crystallised in *Invincible Vietnam* through characters like Thuan, who is about to lose his child and has already lost his wife; Nurse Mao, who is raped to death; Dr Vinh, who is tortured and blinded for not revealing information about the guerrillas; or little Pupu, a child, who is shot dead.

This saga of sacrifice is evident too from the experience of Aunt Kim, Pupu's grandmother, who has also lost her son and daughter-in-law. She is a significant character within the transnational dimension of the play as she highlights that aspect of collective action which managed to transcend binaries of either gender or generation. Unlike many other authors, whose attempts to imagine the nation have often been circumscribed by patriarchal barriers, Dutt has always insisted on imagining an inclusive nation which treats women as equals. Accordingly, his plays repeatedly highlight the role of the gendered subaltern in resistance movements. Whether it is Waziran in *The Great Rebellion*, Indrani in *Hunting the Sun*, Laxmibai in *Kallol* or Shakuntala in *Delhi Chalo*, women in Dutt's plays have always performed the role of independent and active agents of rebellion and struggle, as opposed to the stereotype of the angel-in-the-house that nationalist discourses often promulgate. Aunt Kim is represented in the same way and is not only presented as the voice of reason within the play but is also an active revolutionary who successfully shoots down an American plane:

> *Duyet*: Listen, Comrades, two enemy planes have been shot down ... one by – (Kim desperately waves at him not to name her) by this seventy-five-year-old grandmother of Vietnam (He embraces her and lifts her off her feet. Another burst of cheering) ... She was cycling home. She sights the plane low over the fields, gets off the cycle, shoots it down, back on the cycle, and off home. What do you think of that! (12)

Duyet's passionate embrace symbolically represents the inclusion of women within the imagined community through an acknowledgement of their revolutionary agency. This is further emphasised later when Duyet represents Aunt Kim as an example to all of Vietnam's revolutionaries for her dedication and discipline:

> This lady touched a rifle for the first time in her life when she was seventy. Then she would go out into the fields at night, set up a little envelop with a burning candle behind it, and move back six hundred paces. What do you think the target looks like from that distance – a wee speck of light on a vast black canvas. And so she practiced shooting. (13)

Thus Aunt Kim, along with Nurse Mao and village schoolteacher Bui and others, represent to us the image of a struggling peasant community, beyond usual gendered hierarchies, where the subalterns refuse to linger in the shadows and literally come out, all guns blazing, as suggested by the final image of guerrilla leader Trac, disguised as Madame Lan Huu, leading a sudden raid against the Americans with a tommy gun slung across her chest. Such active participation of women in guerrilla combat was not at all uncommon in Vietnam and represents how, unlike with Spivak's Bhubaneshwari Bhaduri,[33] many female subalterns were able to make room for themselves within national communities during the course of their ascent to a non-subaltern space, even if such language flowed from the barrel of a gun. What is important to note is the way in which the gendered individual and the collective merge, without the individual voice being jeopardised in any way. Rather, all such voices voluntarily locate themselves within the village community, which is indisputably a peasant community. And this peasant community is seen to be the ideal which other oppressed peasant communities are supposed to replicate. Therefore Aunt Kim states:

> The people understand that Vietnam is fighting all of Asia's war of freedom ... They will also realize that Vietnam's way is Asia's way ... And the day will come when all oppressed people will have to take up arms and fight a people's war as we are doing now. The day is not far off. (36)

Through the representation of such heroic struggles from a militant peasantry, the village community of Vietnam's HoBo village is sublimated into a romantic ideal to inspire the Bengali peasantry who too would give birth to guerrillas willing to wage a people's war. It is not coincidental that within a year of *Invincible Vietnam*'s first production, the armed peasant insurrection originating in the village of Naxalbari would begin and be hailed by Radio Peking as 'Spring thunder over India'.[34] I obviously do not mean that such plays provoked the peasants into revolt, but it is undeniable that the plays contributed to the production of that revolutionary discourse which would shape such actions as the Naxalbari insurrection. A special correspondent of *Economic and Political Weekly* had observed in 1971, 'VIETNAMISATION of eastern India – including West Bengal, what was until recently East Pakistan, parts of Assam and Nagaland, and parts of Bihar, Orissa and Andhra Pradesh – is a political perspective that has been discernible to the expert eye ever since 1966.'[35] A play like Dutt's *Invincible Vietnam* was certainly a part of this 'Vietnamisation' process, especially since it was not just performed in urban auditoria but in fields, on makeshift proscenium stages, in front of large gatherings of peasants and labourers. Hence the significance of Trac's eventual arrival with a tommy gun and the consequent capture and destruction of American soldiers. Trac's successful leadership represents an ideal vision of revolutionary self-assertion, transcending gender hierarchies and highlights the role of the Vietnam War as both a representation of indigenous agrarian concerns as well as an ideal which Bengali peasants would need to emulate. The revolutionary wave triggered by the subsequent Naxalite Movement corroborated how well the lessons were learned and why the same special correspondent of *Economic and Political Weekly* would talk about the 'Vietnamisation of the Ganga delta' and declare: 'The soft clay of the Ganga-Padma-Meghna-Sunderbans delta is going to be burnt into the same hard metal of which have been made the soldiers of Algeria and Vietnam.'[36] The content and popularity of *Invincible Vietnam* is evidence of this on a cultural level.

However, Vietnamisation does not just operate, with regard to Dutt's play, as simply a signifier of political processes and guerrilla warfare – it also refers to a concerted effort at cultural development to negate the stereotype of peasants of a semi-colonial backward country. Most of the villagers are literate, they desperately try to save books and telescopes from American bombing, they read everything from the Bible to Shakespeare to Walt Whitman, and Dr Vinh even listens to Beethoven, Brahms and Chopin. Thus, through Dr Vinh and others, Dutt foregrounds the remarkable cultural development, along with political and military activities, of the Vietnamese people. This discourse further reaffirmed his own notion of the global nature of ideal proletarian culture. 'Vietnamisation' in the play therefore acted as an emblem of multifaceted plenitude which fostered the hope of a postcolonial utopia. It is in hope of this holistic ideal that Aunt Kim states: 'This nightmare will pass, little one, for the bandits' days are almost over throughout the world. The rice-fields shall be full again, the mother's womb will be heavy with child, and Ho Chi Minh's face, angry now, will once more be lit up with a smile.' (19)

Once again, what is important to note is that apart from the reference to Ho Chi Minh, all the other cultural markers are as applicable to Vietnam, as they are to India, and specifically Bengal, which is known for its lush green paddy fields. In the process, the play heralds not only a postcolonial utopia for Vietnam but a similar ideal for Bengal as well, provided, of course, that the people are able to endure as much torture and adversity as the Vietnamese.

Conclusion

Invincible Vietnam remains an important example of revolutionary theatre in terms of its glorification of subaltern self-assertion at a precise point in history when such struggles appeared to many across the global South to be the answer to a better world. Such transnational solidarity is also evident from the Tricontinental Conference of 1966 and the emergence of such organisations as the OSPAAL or the even earlier Bandung Conference. It is in recognition of this internationalism that *Invincible Vietnam* was performed in the erstwhile German Democratic Republic as *Unbesiegbares Vietnam* on 7 March 1967.[37] Such performances in communist countries further highlight how the cultures of decolonisation became tied up with the geopolitical concerns of the Cold War. What is ironic, of course, is the fact that many of the former communist regimes, which used the Vietnam struggle to consolidate anti-US propaganda, often utilised various undemocratic means for their own continuation, as would become evident a few years later. However, at that particular moment in time, for many of the left-leaning intellectuals in Third World countries, such ironies were less urgent and relevant than the hope that Vietnam had fostered. Like Fanon, whose words opened this chapter, they too were able to see in the Vietnamese resistance a projection of their hopes and aspirations. Utpal Dutt's *Invincible Vietnam* would remain an important artistic documentation of these hopes and aspirations which had been generated by the intersection of decolonisation and internationalism. The relevance of such intersections is experienced even today, to the extent that the organisers of the 2011 World Social Forum would claim,

> If in 1968 one was able to speak of a world revolution – as a convergence of the fights in the central countries, in the dependent countries and in the bureaucratized societies of Eastern Europe – now we are able to state that, if another world is possible, it will be built by the convergence of these apparently different actors, stimulating the encounter of these political subjects, favouring the creation of a common sense of purpose, identity and future visions ... And this encounter will be even richer if it is able to establish dialogue with the political experience of previous leftist generations, in the form of horizontal interaction, without prejudice and without impositions.[38]

Re-reading and re-exploring a play like *Invincible Vietnam* may serve as the opening turns of just such a dialogue which can fuse the legacy of the cultures of decolonisation with the anti-imperial struggles of today.

Notes

This paper grew out of a conference paper which I presented in London in 2012. My participation was sponsored by the Indian Council of Cultural Relations and I would like to thank them for their assistance. I would also like to thank Mrs Sova Sen Dutt for giving me a copy of *Invincible Vietnam* and opening her library to me for my research. The less familiar texts listed below can be found in the collections of the National Library of Kolkata and the internal library of *Ganashakti*, the organ of the Communist Party of India (Marxist) in Kolkata.

1 F. Fanon, *The Wretched of the Earth*, trans. C. Farrington (Harmondsworth: Penguin, 1967), p. 55.
2 R. Young, *Postcolonialism: A Very Short Introduction* (Oxford: Oxford University Press, 2003), pp. 121–8.
3 C. Guevara, 'Message to the Tricontinental' (1967), cited in Young, *Postcolonialism: A Very Short Introduction*, p. 18.

4 R. Young, *Postcolonialism: A Historical Introduction* (Oxford: Blackwell, 2001), p. 212.
5 A. Mukhopadhyay, *Utpal Dutt: Jibon o Srishti* (New Delhi: National Book Trust, 2008), pp. 1–74.
6 U. Dutt, *Towards a Revolutionary Theatre* (Kolkata: M.C. Sirkar and Sons, 1982), p. 63.
7 U. Dutt, 'Theatre as Weapon of Revolution', in N. Saha (ed.), *Utpal Dutt: A Comprehensive Observation* (Kolkata: Utpal Dutt Natyotsab 2005 Committee, 2005), p. 126.
8 Fanon, *The Wretched of the Earth*, p. 164.
9 P. Sarkar, 'Introduction', *Utpal Dutta Natya Samagra* (Kolkata: Mitra o Ghosh, 1993), p. 5.
10 U. Dutt, 'Invincible Vietnam', *Epic Theatre* (October 1967), 1–40. All subsequent textual references are from this edition and the page numbers are cited parenthetically.
11 A. Bera, 'Vietnam Dibosh, 1947', in Chhatra Sangram Editorial Board (ed.), *Vietnam Tomar Jonye: Probondho, Kobita, Golpo* (Kolkata: Chhatra Sangram Prokashonee, 2007), p. 48.
12 Bera, 'Vietnam Dibosh', p. 56.
13 S. Chakraborty, 'Shaater Doshoke Vietnaamer Songraamer Somorthone Chhatrosomaj', in *Chhatra Sangram* Editorial Board, *Vietnam Tomar Jonye*, pp. 37–40; *Ganashakti* (22 July 1968).
14 Chakraborty, 'Shaater Doshoke Vietnaamer Songraamer Somorthone Chhatrosomaj', p. 38.
15 *Chhatra Sangram* Editorial Board, *Vietnam Tomar Jonye*, pp. 142–4.
16 'Dokkhin Vietnamer Biplobi Sorkarer Swikritir Dabite Yuva Samabesh', *Ganashakti* (1 December 1969), p. 1 (my translation).
17 H. Konar, *Bharater Krishi Samasya* (Kolkata: National Book Agency, 1994), pp. 43–83.
18 'Vietnamer Mukti Songram', *Ganashakti* (21 December 1969), p. 1.
19 'Amra Joylabh Korboi – Nguen Van Tien', *Ganashakti* (22 December 1969), p. 3.
20 'Amra Joylabh Korboi – Nguen Van Tien', p. 3; 'Khardah-Titagrah Sromik Sommelon', advertisement, *Ganashakti* (22 December 1969), p. 3; 'Dokkhin Vietnamer Biplobi Sorkarer Sombordhona', *Ganashakti* (23 December 1969), p. 1; 'Mahajoni Shoshon Protirodher Ahvan', *Ganashakti* (20 November 1968), p. 1.
21 R. Basu, 'Vietnam', in P. Basu (ed.), *Vietnamer er Sopokkhe* (Kolkata: Seemanta, 1967), p. 19.
22 M. Chattapdhyay, 'Konomote Morbona Songkhyalaghu Bimaner Kachhe', in Basu, *Vietnamer er Sopokkhe*, p. 33.
23 Ngugi wa Thiong'o, *Decolonising the Mind: The Politics of Language in African Literature* (Heinemann: Portsmouth, 2003), p. 20.
24 F. Jameson, *Marxism and Form: Twentieth Century Dialectical Theories of Literature* (Princeton: Princeton University Press, 1971), p. 82.
25 Dutt, *Towards a Revolutionary Theatre*, pp. 57–8.
26 A. Gramsci, *Selections from the Prison Notebooks*, ed. and trans. Q. Hoare and G. Nowell Smith (Hyderabad: Orient BlackSwan, 2009), pp. 118–20.
27 P. Chatterjee, *Nationalist Thought and the Colonial World* (New Delhi: Oxford University Press, 1999), pp. 29–30.
28 U. Dutt, 'Interview with Samik Bandyopadhyay', *Shobdo*, special issue on 'Utpal Dutt' (2010), 366.
29 A. Gupta, 'Introduction', *Utpal Dutt Natya Samagra*, Vol. 3 (Kolkata: Mitra o Ghosh, 1994), p. 4 (my translation).
30 M. Hashmi, 'Response', in S. Deshpande, K.V. Akshara and S. Iyenger (eds), *Our Stage: Pleasures and Perils of Theatre Practice in India* (New Delhi: Tulika Books, 2009), p. 141.
31 S. Majumdar, 'Moharothi Mohanidrabrito', in Saha, *Utpal Dutt*, p. 154.
32 Dutt, *Towards a Revolutionary Theatre*, p. 25.

33 Bhubaneshwari Bhaduri was a young Bengali middle-class woman who was associated with an anti-colonial revolutionary group and had committed suicide. Spivak refers to her in the essay 'Can the Subaltern Speak?' and uses her example to assert the supposed unspeakability of subaltern subjects, especially the gendered subaltern. See G. Spivak, 'Can the Subaltern Speak?', in P. Williams and L. Chrisman (eds), *Colonial Discourse and Postcolonial Theory* (Hemel Hempstead: Harvester, 1993), pp. 66–111.
34 S. Sen Gupta, 'The Press and the People: Representing the Naxalite Movement, 1967–72', in P. Basu (ed.), *Discourses on Naxalite Movement* (Kolkata: Setu Prakashani, 2010), p. 80.
35 'Towards A Vietnam in the Ganges Delta', *Economic and Political Weekly*, 6:18 (1 May 1971), p. 905.
36 'Towards A Vietnam in the Ganges Delta', *Economic and Political Weekly*, 6:18 (1 May 1971), p. 906.
37 D. Chakraborty, 'Bishwa Natya Angane Utpal Dutt', in Saha, *Utpal Dutt*, pp. 434–6.
38 Group of Reflection and Support to the WSF Process, 'Let's Reinvent the World', October 2011, http://rio20.net/wp-content/uploads/2011/11/Vamos-reinventar-o-mundo_EN.pdf (accessed 21 April 2015).

CHAPTER SIX

Cultural heritage as performance: Re-enacting Angkorian grandeur in postcolonial Cambodia (1953–70)

Michael Falser

In 1964, a decade after the realisation of Cambodian independence, Robert Garry, the Canadian professor of Far Eastern geography, delivered his eulogy on Norodom Sihanouk's political and cultural action programme to the sixteenth International Congress of Orientalists in New Delhi. Norodom Sihanouk had been elected king of Cambodia by the French colonial rulers of Indochina in 1941, but in 1955 he abdicated in favour of his father Suramarit and named himself prime minister and leader of a new political movement, Sangkum Reastr Niyum (the People's Socialist Community). In 1960 Sihanouk became the autocratic head of state before he was deposed in March 1970 by a *coup d'état* sponsored by a pro-American military regime. Under his influence, Cambodia experienced what Garry described in his talk (and in the version published by the Départment de l'Information in Phnom Penh shortly afterwards) as a 'theatre of profound transformation': major developments occurred in the country's infrastructure, including in agriculture and industry, public instruction and public health, communication lines, urbanism and architecture. As Garry correctly surmised, Cambodia's 'renaissance from decadence' and its development towards an independent kingdom and modern 'Khmer nation' was also completely embedded in, and justified through, a social and political rhetoric of cultural heritage. This cultural heritage was founded upon a collective 'inheritance [*héritage*]' of the cultural 'grandeur' and oeuvre of the 'great kings as builders [*rois bâtisseurs*] of Angkor'.[1] Angkor, a temple site in the north-west of Cambodia dating from the ninth to the thirteenth century CE and the focus of this chapter, was the crux of much of this activity.

The topos of (legally) inheriting the built legacy of Angkor had been a vital element of the French colonial civilising mission (*mission civilisatrice*) in Cambodia from 1863 onwards; it was continually visualised through hybrid replicas of Angkorian temples during universal and colonial exhibitions in France between 1889 and 1937.[2] Yet this claim was subject to a novel ideological twist under Sihanouk's regime: the classic 'salvage paradigm' once practised by the European colonial power in order to 'rescue something authentic [and pure] out of destructive historical changes'[3] was now appropriated by the newly independent nation and its commentators. Particular attention was paid to a proclaimed direct continuity between Sihanouk's regime and the historical tradition of Angkor's ancient kings. In his article, 'La Renaissance du Cambodge de Jayavarman VII roi d'Angkor à Norodom Sihanouk Varman', Garry displayed an uncritical readiness to celebrate a seemingly unbroken link between Angkor's Buddhist king Jayavarman VII (who reigned around 1200 CE) and Norodom Sihanouk as the princely leader of independent Cambodia. In doing so, he effortlessly effaced five hundred years of intermediate post-Angkorian and colonial history.

This cultural-political construction surrounding Sihanouk and Angkor was unique in Asia's postcolonial history: not only did one of the smallest new nations on the decolonising planet of the 1950s inherit the world's largest temple site for use in the construction of its new identity, but it also instrumentalised a direct genealogical and religious continuity from ancient times by way of its simultaneously Buddhist, royal and secular charismatic leader.[4] Certainly, comparable postcolonial nations like India and Indonesia also incorporated their former colonial masters' research on the ancient histories, kingly genealogies and art historical classifications of their countries into their new cultural self-understandings.[5] However, in the case of Cambodia, Sihanouk – a renowned Francophile – displayed a particular discipleship to France which actually intensified during his reign: throughout his premiership he continued to delegate the high-tech restoration and presentation of the Archaeological Park of Angkor[6] (institutionalised in 1925–30) to the École française d'Extrême-Orient (established under the French around 1900), and he disseminated virtually all of his cultural-political visions in a series of newly founded journals that were published in French (or English) rather than in the Cambodian language.

Yet it would be too reductive to conclude that Cambodia's decolonising effort was a simple 'copy and paste' affair of the French colonial prescription of an Angkorian past. Investigated from an art historical viewpoint, Sihanouk's engagement with Cambodia's heritage will be shown to be a creative process of adaptation, appropriation and reinterpretation. Further, the self-inflicted task of inheriting a past Angkorian *grandeur* – or as Milton Osbourne described it, this aim to 'extol the virtues of the Angkorian age as a guide for modern actions'[7] – would result in a conflict-laden inferiority/superiority 'temple complex'[8] for the new nation-state. Indeed, it would prove to be an insurmountable burden. As Charles Meyer, Sihanouk's long-time adviser, claimed: 'With their mania of scientific research the Occidentals let arise the demons of history and helped impose on Cambodia a heritage [héritage] which was much too heavy for this state.'[9]

How, we might ask, was Angkorian cultural heritage conceptualised, materialised and performed during Cambodia's decolonisation? To answer this question, this chapter will focus on three specific forms of heritagisation which emerged in the creative recycling of the colonial topoi of grandeur, purity and origin(ality) of a glorious past for the postcolonial mindset. First, the religious and political reincarnation of Jayavarman VII in the name of Norodom Sihanouk will be examined; second, the revival of the built Angkorian legacy in a modern-day architectural interpretation will be investigated, and finally the various cultural performances à la Angkorienne within Sihanouk's strategies of cultural diplomacy[10] will be unpacked.

We will conceptualise these performative genres as highly creative, but also – in line with Elin Diamond's definition – as 'contested spaces where meanings and desires are generated, occluded, or multiply interpreted'.[11] In cultural studies, performances have been defined as socially relevant 'in the midst of profound disturbance and/or transformation',[12] and – even more relevant to our specific Cambodian context – as 'precarious liminal moments of a profound transition from a colonial to postcolonial state configuration'.[13] Here, we will also understand heritage performances in terms of their 'unity of kinaesthetic imagination and the affirmation of cultural memory'.[14] When performances take the form of historical re-enactments, they often use the latest multimedia instruments to compress space and time, restore ancient history or 'socially relevant events' and make living history directly palpable.[15] As will become evident in our case of Angkor, 'historical re-enactments' also employ supposedly authentic actors with historical apparatus, and often take place on credible, original cultural heritage sites.[16] As with heritage performances and historical re-enactments more broadly, in Cambodia the boundaries between fact and fiction were blurred in order to progress a global heritage industry; here, French-colonial research data were used to produce historical imaginaries on the one hand and postcolonial narratives of cultural rebirth on the other, with Angkor being one of the most prominent attractions.[17]

In the following pages, we will consider these practices and examine the colonial source material of a reimagined past, the media used to exploit such material, the events of representation and their audiences, the spatial strategies used to connect specific sites of decolonisation, the temporalities employed and the concrete agency of the patron and the actors behind these scenarios.

Norodom Sihanouk as the new Jayavarman VII: Khmer socialism à la Angkorienne

When the Cambodian Ministère de l'Information published the booklet *Considérations sur le socialisme khmer* in 1961, the Non-Aligned-Movement had just been founded in Belgrade by some of Sihanouk's most important political partners in the worldwide project of decolonisation. India's prime minister Jawaharlal Nehru, Indonesia's president Sukarno, Egypt's president Gamal Abdel Nasser and Yugoslavia's president Josip Broz Tito were all involved. Yet while Cambodia joined this global movement of internationalist, partly secular-Marxist socialism and anti-colonialism, Sihanouk nevertheless tried to provincialise this contemporary concept by tying it back to ancient Angkor. He emphasised both the 'morale of Buddhism ... as a precious guide [in] fighting social injustice' and the tradition of Angkorian kingship as the cornerstones of a socialism for a 'Khmer society which had [supposedly] never seen class struggles of a feudal regime or colonialist exploitation system (except from the outside)'. Furthermore, he characterised the Khmer kings 'not only as great temple builders' but also, in their socialist function to 'protect the soil', as 'realisers of great works of economic and social interest'.[18] In particular, Sihanouk underlined the benevolence of Jayavarman VII by quoting one of the king's twelfth-century steles at Say-Fong which reported on the king's creation of hospitals and pilgrims' inns (notably translated by the French in 1903). Finally, he subtly merged the claim of state control, collectivism in the name of 'Khmer socialism' and Buddhist principles in order to develop, as the French *Le Monde* journalist Jean Lacouture termed it, 'a tacit monopoly of power and an immediate monocracy'[19] of an enlightened dictator.

Two questions arise: what sources did Sihanouk have available for this bricolage of historical facts and cultural myths of Angkor and its kingly rulers? How was his creative reinterpretation of Angkorian royal religious leadership made visible and staged?

Concerning the first, it is safe to quote one crucial French colonial figure behind this modern myth-making process: the French archaeology-focused epigraphist Georges Coedès (1886–1969), who directed the Ecole française d'Extrême-Orient (EFEO) between 1929 and 1946. With his 1935 booklet *Un grand roi du Cambodge, Jayavarman VII*, published in French and Cambodian by the Phnom Penh-based Éditions de la Bibliothèque Royale, he disseminated for the first time the image of the glorious Angkorian king Jayavarman VII. The eloquent, if scientifically low-key choice of wording and the essentialising topoi employed made this publication a unique source for all following treatises on this king's historical relevance, and for Sihanouk's contemporary self-identification. Curiously, Coedès himself confessed that 'almost nothing had been known' about Jayavarman VII around 1900, but in 1935 he was already 'considered the greatest Cambodian sovereign who had pushed his country to the extreme limits, and covered the capital [Angkor] with the most prestigious monuments a monarch had ever planned'.[20] Here, Sihanouk's enormous building programme in the new-old capital Phnom Penh and the provinces would almost sound anticipated. A few years later, in his book *Pour mieux comprendre Angkor* and the chapter 'Le Dernier grand roi d'Angkor – Jayavarman VII', Coedès inflated his findings of 1935 to 'restitute for the descendants of the ancient Khmer the sentiment of a past grandeur'.[21] The characterisation of Jayavarman VII as a powerful and megalomaniac god-king, yet with a down-to-earth, humanist affection for his subjects, was essentially influenced by French colonial art historical research. Just recently, in 1927, the Parisian art historian Philippe Stern had reprovenanced Jayavarman VII's architectural masterpiece, the Bayon temple with its famous bas-reliefs, from its previous, early dating point to the end of the stylistic development of the Angkorian temples.[22] Only this chronological correction in the genealogy of the Khmer kings made Javayarman VII instantly relevant for the personification of Angkor's cultural apogee around 1200 CE.

Certainly the most inspiring source on Angkor for Sihanouk was the book *Angkor, hommes et pierres* of 1956, written by the historian and Conservateur des Monuments d'Angkor between 1960 and 1973, Bernard Philippe Groslier (1926–86). Groslier not only made 'archaeology a branch of history'[23] so as to situate Angkor prominently in a universal history of civilisation, he was also a close friend of Sihanouk and served as what we can call a cultural broker between postcolonial Cambodia and the former, yet still active, French colonial regime.[24] The book was unctuously formulated through a blend of scientific knowledge, hypothetical imaginings of Angkor, and impressive black and white illustrations of temple sites and sculptures; the section on 'L'apothéose d'Angkor'[25] that painted Jayavarman VII as Angkor's greatest, charitable, empathetic and, in modern parlance, socialist king and patron of the arts[26] served as a perfect script for Sihanouk's own desire to revive the notion of Angkorian kingship. In 1962, Cambodia's Ministry of Information published a further 300-page book, *Cambodge*, where the French colonial epigraphic, archaeological and art historical findings and imaginations of Angkor were now poured into the first large-scale master narrative of Cambodia's postcolonial efforts.[27]

If the 1961 publication *Considerations sur le socialisme khmer* had introduced the ancient *and* actual kings of Cambodia as 'protectors of the soil', then this role had also to be re-activated and visualised in public. In its English issue of May 1967, the journal *Kambuja* published the richly illustrated article 'At Angkor Thom, a Thousand Year Old Rite: "Chrat Preah Nongkol"' (with *chrat preah nongkol* translated as 'ploughing of the sacred furrow'). As the reader was told, from 1963 onwards, Sihanouk had decided to reintroduce (re-enact) this abolished rite at different places in Cambodia. In the specific year of 1967, 'on Thursday, the fourth day of the declining Pisak moon, in the year of the Goat, 2510 in the Buddhist calendar (27th April 1967)',[28] this re-enactment seemingly tried to decolonise the Archaeological Park of Angkor from its French secular, touristic connotations and, for a short moment, bring the ancient temple site back to its former authentic, religious and kingly context. In order to do this, a sacred rice field was symbolically delimited by four small canvas pavilions housing four Brahman divinities, and by a fifth central structure with a Buddhist statuette dominated by a 'traditionally roofed pavilion' for sheltering high officials and the diplomatic corps. A temporary exhibition structure was placed along the top of the ancient palace walls. An article and a double-page photograph (Figure 6.1) described the event: 'King Samdech Norodom Sihanouk, Head of State', in his old brocade-clad garments, had initially 'listened to the invocations made to the supernatural powers by a monk, which asked for peace and prosperity for the Kingdom. The Victory verses, called "Chayanto", had then been recited by a group of 38 monks' on the upper palace grounds. Then, the king was carried in a palanquin to the sacred paddy, where he took the sacred plough, drawn by two decorated grey oxen (see insert in Figure 6.1), to cross the field three times. He was accompanied by high officials and a traditional orchestra and followed by his daughter 'Princess Norodom Bophani [who acted as] the sower'. After 'taking a bath' in the enthusiastic crowd, Sihanouk entered the ancient Elephants' Terrace (archaeologically restored by the EFEO) to guide his high guests through the exhibition on Sangkum's achievements, and finally – bringing the mythical achievements of Angkor to an overlap with those of Cambodia as a modern nation-state – watched

Figure 6.1 The 'Ploughing of the Sacred Furrow', performed by Norodom Sihanouk on 27 April 1967 on Angkor Thom's Royal Square inside the Archaeological Park of Angkor, as depicted in Kambuja 26 (May 1967)

'the procession of mechanical harvesters (tractors)' pass by. After this, sports teams demonstrated ancient games and exercises. By staging ancient ritual practices and emphasising the actual ruler's royal links to ancient Angkor, Khmer kingship had, for a short moment in Cambodia's decolonising phase, found its re-enacted modern double in Norodom Sihanouk.

New Khmer architecture – in the name of Angkor

When Vann Molyvann (born in 1926 in Ream, Kampot Province) was an architecture student at Paris's prestigious École National Supérieur des Beaux-Arts in the 1940s, his mother country was still occupied by the French. Returning to Cambodia with his diploma in 1956, he was almost instantly chosen by Sihanouk as state and star architect for the new country's era of independence.[29] Contrary to the French colonial essentialising paradigm of cultural purity, Vann voted to fuse Western, in this case, US-European architectural and technological trends, with a modern interpretation of Angkor's built legacy. What he termed *La nouvelle architecture khmère*[30] was stylistically and structurally situated somewhere between the Angkorian spiritual, symbolic and monumental legacy, inspiration drawn from wooden pagoda and vernacular traditional house architecture, and the fruits of 'modern, Occidental civilisation'.[31] By this last phrase Vann was referring to the International Style of streamlined, rationalist buildings and the building technology of reinforced concrete.[32]

Besides these new visions as they were realised in Vann's many astonishing buildings, connecting ancestral traditions with a postcolonial claim of national continuity through the re-presentation of Angkorian style became especially relevant when King Suramarit (Sihanouk's father) died in April 1960. In this context, the gifted master builder Tan Veut from Battambang was commissioned to design Suramarit's funerary *stupa* (originally a mound-like or hemispherical structure containing Buddhist relics) after the examples of those for King Norodom (who died in 1904) and his wife on the same palace grounds. The stupas of Norodom and his wife were themselves based – as Vann Molyvann explained in the journal *Kambuja*[33] – on the tradition of the stupas in the post-Angkorian capital of Oudong. During King Suramarit's funerary ceremony in January 1961, before all kinds of family, state, military and ethnic representatives, the Royal Khmer Socialist Youth and the Corps de Ballet Royal, the reliquary of Sihanouk's daughter, Princess Kantha Bopha (1948–52), was also placed in a smaller stupa by Tan Veut 'in the style of the [ninth-century] tower of Banteay Srei' near Angkor.[34]

If these stupas were on private palace grounds, then another structure stood out in the public centre of the new-old capital Phnom Penh as Cambodia's most important modern-day interpretation of Angkor's stylistic grandeur: the Independence Memorial, built by Vann Molyvann, Tan Veut and others, was inaugurated on Independence Day, 9 November 1962. The delayed delivery of the memorial – nine long years after Cambodia's independence in 1953 – was most probably due to problems with the complicated subsoil structure of the site.[35] Ironically, just as French colonial strategies of simulating Angkor's stone temples in temporary exhibitions had utilised ephemeral hybrids or replicas made out of inner wooden scaffoldings and external lightweight fibre mouldings,[36] the long-term version for Phnom Penh was not made of solid stone either. The rampiled, internally reinforced concrete structure as a stepped platform was clad with external panels of grey Chinese marble with 'decorative patterns (Khmer: *kbach*) from [the tenth-century temple of] Banteay Srei',[37] as were the open lower walls and the five stepped tiers with their decorative *naga* (snakes). Finally, the project was finished with crushed marble to give the monument the dark-red colour of Banteay Srei. Vann Molyvann himself explained that the whole symmetric composition in the centre of a roundabout with radiating streets had been inspired by the Arc de Triomphe in Paris.[38]

In the following years, the Independence Memorial à la Angkorienne would become the annual central stage for Sihanouk's political theatre. For example, in 1964, 'delegations from all provinces of the kingdom'[39] drove past it in their honorary parade, and the monument was regularly depicted on the covers of Sihanouk's numerous self-glorifying journals, including *Le Sangkum* in September 1967. In November 1969, Sihanouk himself, in an elegant white suit – already strangely absent in his role as god-king-politician in front of the Buddhist monks present – lit the commemorative flame of Cambodia's independence for the last time before the 1970 *coup d'état*, and balloons in the colours of the national flag (itself depicting Angkor Wat) ascended towards the sky (Figure 6.2).

Cultural diplomacy: From cultural performance to on-site re-enactment of Angkor

In 1953, Sihanouk had visited the United States during his so-called 'crusade for independence'. In 1958, he returned as leader of a free Cambodge to speak at the thirteenth session of the UN Assembly in New York. Additionally, he brought with him a new tool of cultural diplomacy to foster Cambodia's decolonising cultural image of pure,

Figure 6.2 Norodom Sihanouk and the Independence Monument during the sixteenth anniversary of Cambodia's National Independence on 9 November 1969, as depicted in *Kambuja* (December 1969).

tradition-bound and peaceful (politically neutral) Khmerness. As *Cambodge d'Aujourd'hui* reported, his 1958 diplomatic mission was highlighted with a series of dance performances by the Ballet Royal, who were accompanied by two of Sihanouk's children, Princess Bopha Devi and Prince Chakrapong. The first performance took place during a reception at the New York Waldorf Astoria hotel on 19 September, where it was part of a 'discreet exhibition on the Khmer civilisation with traditional art objects, plaster casts of Angkorian statues and photographs [of Cambodian temples]' to help a 'particularly unstressed atmosphere [in which] political personalities of the two rivalling [Cold War] blocs came together'; the second came after the presentation of an original Khmer sculpture to President Eisenhower in the White House on 30 September, when the high-ranking dinner party at Cambodia's embassy watched 'a classical Khmer dance in all its purity'. A third took place on 16 October, after a reception conference in the Sheraton Hotel in San Francisco (Figure 6.3a). As Sihanouk himself explained to the readers of the journal, 'The Khmer royal dances have a very old origin which is hard to date with precision, but they attained their highest perfection during the apogee of Khmer grandeur. ... if one judges them on the basis of the bas-reliefs of the temples of Angkor, their gestures and the attitudes of the dancers have hardly changed until today [and] conserved their highest purity.'[40]

At this point, Sihanouk's Corps du Ballet was a fixed part of his diplomatic missions – some called them a charming '*Cirque Sihanouk* [with] acrobatic, illusionist and imitating diplomatic acts'.[41] Regular visits were conducted to China, Indonesia and India, and missions followed to the United Arab Republic and Yugoslavia in 1959, and, in 1960, to Czechoslovakia and the Soviet Union. In 1962, with stops in Malaysia, Singapore and Sri Lanka, Sihanouk was received by the Indonesian president Sukarno. Again, his daughter, Bopha Devi, was on the spot to perform her Khmer repertoire and also to 'interpret a classical Indonesian dance'; after all, as the journal text reconfirmed to diplomatic benefit, 'between the Indonesian and the Khmer dance [there had] existed very close links for about one thousand years'.[42] Again in 1962, Sihanouk's Ministère de l'Information contributed to the essentialisation of a '*danse classique*' in the voluminous publication *Cambodge*: 'The Corps de Ballet, *véritable conservatoire* of the Khmer classical dance, is the oldest choreographic formation of the world. Thanks to the personal care of Her Majesty the Queen [Kossamak] it came back with an incomparable éclat through the rigorous preservation of its traditions and thousand-year-old techniques.'[43] The Royal Khmer Ballet's biggest success, however, took place during Sihanouk's state visit to France in 1964: Bopha Devi's

Figure 6.3 3a/left: The Khmer Ballet performing in San Francisco's Sheraton Hotel on 16 October 1958. 3b/right: Princess Bopha Devi as dancing Apsara in front of the bas-reliefs of Angkor Wat, as depicted in *Cambodge d'aujourd'hui* (July/August 1962).

troupe had 'a triumphal success' on 26 June in the Opera of Paris for a *soirée de gala Franco-khmère*, competed with the Paris Ballet de l'Opéra, and repeated its repertoire in the Théâtre des Nations. As a result, the visit helped to deepen the mutual diplomatic relations with President Charles de Gaulle who hosted the event.[44] What was staged in 1964 almost 10,000 km from Cambodia in the Paris Opera House as a mobile commodity of authentic Khmerness corresponded exactly to what Sihanouk's journal *Cambodge d'Aujourd'hui* (or in this case its English version, *Cambodia Today*) had propagated as the founding myth of pure Khmer dance: 'the 12th-century bas-reliefs' of Angkor Wat, as brought back to life by 'Princess Bopha Devi' (Figure 6.3b).[45] Here, the carefully arranged propaganda photograph of Bopha Devi mirroring the goddesses of Angkor perfectly aligned with Sihanouk's myth-making ideology and even hinted at some feminist (albeit still conservative) undertones by highlighting the apparently important role of 'Women in Angkoran history'.

Again: where did these topoi of purity and originality in the Khmer dance and Angkor Wat's bas-reliefs initially come from? And how did Sihanouk's decolonising regime use them for its own performative strategies around the globe and at original temple sites in Cambodia?

An examination of French colonial history again provides the most important lead. Besides a traditional dance troupe which, in fact, existed inside the Royal Palace of Phnom Penh for the king's private entertainment, the first dance performances for a European public were organised by the French authorities in Phnom Penh, and staged as 'imaginative representations of the exotic "East"' in front of the fantastic Khmer-styled pavilions in Universal and Colonial Exhibitions in Paris and Marseille in 1889, 1900 and 1906.[46] In a second step, under French direction, the dancers were stereotyped as 'direct descendants of the Apsaras [celestial nymphs] on the bas-reliefs of Angkor Wat'[47] and gradually trained to help in re-enactments centred on the scale replicas of Angkor Wat built in 1922 at Marseille and in 1931 in Paris. In 1922, the same ballet troupe also performed at the Parisian Opera and was praised for its authenticity, purity and timelessness.[48] Nine years later, the Parisian International Colonial Exhibition of 1931 topped all earlier undertakings of exotic representations in scale, variety and performance: the 'illuminated apotheosis of Angkor [Wat]'[49] was a full-size replica of its Cambodian source temple, and its central causeway was used for cultural performances. These half-faked versions of the royal Khmer dance already contained characteristics of cultural performances as cultural theorists define them today; and these characteristics were exactly exploited by Sihanouk for his diplomatic Corps du Ballet Royal decades later during Cambodia's short period of independence: they were made for a specific occasion with a structured programme, and used real actors to satisfy the gaze of a defined audience.[50]

In 1907 the temples of Angkor became part of the French protectorate of Cambodia and, following this constitutional shift and as part of their consolidation of the region, the new political French owners wished to reconnect (i.e. salvage and re-establish) ancient Angkor – as an apparently authentic marker of ancient, unspoilt glory – to the wider contemporary canon of Cambodian culture. However, recreating the present within a supposedly *pure* Angkorian past tradition without *any* foreign influences was a delicate task. In reality, Angkor had been captured (indeed colonised) by the Siamese in the fifteenth century, and the royal court dance – like some of the Cambodian kings themselves – had only survived until the nineteenth century as a result of its 'Siamisation' at the royal court in Bangkok. These cultural influences from Siam were still considerable around 1900 when, in Phnom Penh, a 're-Khmerising' process[51] was initiated by the new occupants. As French authority increased, the entire system of art education in Cambodia was systematically grouped within the colonial 'salvage paradigm' of rescuing traditional Cambodian art forms from supposed degeneration, agony and impurity; the (re)writing of the history of Cambodia's traditional dance was no exception.

The central figure in this project was George Groslier (1887–1945), the first French citizen born in Cambodia, a Parisian École des Beaux-Arts graduate, gifted artist and writer, and director of the École des Arts Cambodgiens in Phnom Penh. Observing a contemporary crisis of religious beliefs, traditional morals and performing arts, his 1913 book *Danseuses cambodgiennes anciennes et modernes* was the first modern, in-depth study on the 'indigenous origins' of the Khmer dance. Here, Angkor Wat again seemed to provide the most authentic source material for his thesis. In his sketches, Groslier let the ballet dancers emerge – or be reborn in their purest reincarnation – from the celestial maidens on the temple's bas-reliefs, despite the fact that, from an iconographical standpoint, they had never been conceived of as earthly dancers *per se*, but as celestial guardian figures for the entertainment of a dead king after apotheosis. Concluding his study, Groslier reimagined a *'spectacle grandiose'* of an ancient procession at Angkor Wat,[52] depicting a virtual re-enactment of the past which included reinvented elements of contemporary dance performance. After Groslier, in 1927, Sappho Marchal, the daughter of the General Angkor Conservator, Henri Marchal, published a detailed study on the costumes and hairstyles of the '1700 devatas' of the Angkor Wat temple.⁵³ Both Groslier's and Marchal's publications served as perfect catalogues and pattern books with which to re-Khmerise and purify the Royal Ballet *à la angkorienne*.⁵⁴

As Groslier and Marchal were compiling their publications, the French authorities in Phnom Penh were simultaneously trying in vain to gain complete control over the real Royal Ballet in order to save it from 'decadence' and 'agony'.⁵⁵ Circumventing the ruling king's resistance to relinquishing authority over his real ballet, the French chose Say Sangvann, the wife of a member of the royal family who had already organised performances for the Résident Superieur in Phnom Penh, to create a privatised substitute which was equipped with costumes and masks from Groslier's art school.⁵⁶ With this essential shift from 'authentic' court dance to commercialised performance a dividing line was irreversibly crossed, even though the show was still sold as 'original' Khmer and 'of the greatest purity even from the viewpoint of Siamese *connoisseurs*'.⁵⁷ The reinvented performances for the exhibitions in the French metropole had, from a transcultural viewpoint⁵⁸ on Euro-Asian exchange processes, considerable consequences back in Cambodia: the aesthetics of these (more folkloric than historical) dance spectacles once shown in front of fabricated temple skylines by torchlight and later by government-sponsored electric floodlights in France, were now reimported back to the real site.⁵⁹ Say Sangvann's private troupe had gained 'the monopoly to perform the dance for tourists at Angkor Vat'⁶⁰ and her dancers produced a kind of 'staged authenticity'⁶¹ in gestures and costumes even more perfect than the depictions on the ancient bas-reliefs behind them.

The fight for the monopoly over the authentic Khmer ballet continued during the early 1940s as Princess Kossamak, the mother of Norodom Sihanouk, came to play a crucial role in decolonising the Khmer Ballet and in reloading it with new significance. She certainly took advantage of the detailed studies on the Khmer ballet by Groslier and Marchal which had re-established the ballet's purified link to the bas-reliefs of Angkor Wat, and she capitalised on the dance's international popularity in France and back home. Feeding the movement of an (anti-colonial) cultural nationalism, Kossamak changed the choreography to form a group precision dance, added entertaining effects by incorporating scenes from well-known stories and popular tales, and shortened the previous day-long private royal dance ritual into a publicly suitable two-hour programme. Outwardly, the result was meant to underline the new cultural self-confidence of the Khmer nation on the occasion of international state visits, and inwardly it symbolically demonstrated the authority of the new king (her son Norodom Sihanouk), who was rooted in a continued Angkorian antiquity traceable to his direct ancient royal ancestors. With this shift in format, the status of the Khmer dance now changed from its mere spectacular, almost folkloristic, effect at former French exhibitions to a deeper political meaning back in Cambodia. Between the late French colonial 1940s and Cambodia's decolonising phase in the 1950s the royal dance with its (ostensibly) apolitical ritual-like appearance beyond a specific time, space and direction was in fact the perfect performative medium with which to minimise tensions that opened up in Cambodia's 'liminal phase'[62] or ambiguous in-between stage between the end of French rule and the installation of a re-indigenised Khmer nation-state.

After Cambodia's independence in 1953, Kossamak succeeded (once again after the efforts of the French) in re-Khmerising, and now politicising, the royal dance with a new central element as part of what she called a national 'reconstruction and revival programme'.[63] She invented the *Apsara Dance* or *roban Apsara* which perfectly served the new Khmer national ideology. Ironically, in ideal fulfilment of Groslier's 1913 colonial study, the postcolonial choreography led five Apsaras to materialise out of the bas-reliefs of Angkor Wat, only to perform a dance of salutation before disappearing again into the stone surface.[64] To add density to the ideological message of an unbroken link between the ancient Khmer dance and Sihanouk's current political power, Kossamak made the Apsara dance with light and portable stage sets à la Angkorienne the showpiece for Bopha Devi, King Sihanouk's daughter. Cultural performance, cultural nationalism and cultural diplomacy were now, as elements of Cambodia's decolonising period, merged into one amalgam. The results of Kossamak's efforts were finally summarised by the Cambodian Information Agency in the comprehensive English publication *Royal Cambodian Ballet* in 1963.

In this context, another performative strategy had been invented: a diplomatic tour from Cambodia's new capital to its old centre and back, planned by Sihanouk's regime as a thematic itinerary and performative *parcours* with predefined spots of ideological indoctrination.[65] The tour included not only an obligatory showcasing of Phnom Penh's architectural modern highlights such as the Independence Memorial, the State Palace or the National Stadium (see below), but also side trips to new state projects in the countryside. The highlight, however, was certainly a visit to the Archaeological Park of Angkor, where Sihanouk himself and his friend and chief conservator Bernard Philippe Groslier acted as private guides through the ruins along the French colonial Grand and Petit Circuits, only to conclude the stay with a Khmer ballet performance and – a new invention – a *son et lumière* show in front of, and a firework show above, Angkor Wat.

One of the most detailed of these diplomatic *parcours* was elaborated for the eleventh anniversary of Cambodia's independence in 1964 and the inauguration of the National Sports Complex in Phnom Penh in the *Programme de visite pour toutes les délégations gouvernementales des puissances amies* from 7 to 18 November.[66] In three groups, from 7 to 13 November, the 'governmental delegations of the friendly powers' (non-aligned countries, but also other major investor countries in Cambodia) were guided through optional blocks of activities with official audiences at the Royal and State Palaces: they could choose from a visit to the royal tombs at Oudong with a picnic and folkloric representations; a military parade on Independence Day; a visit to the hill station of Kirirom with lunch at the Chalet Royal; a visit to a nearby handicraft village; a tour of the artistic representations in Phnom Penh's Chadomukh Hall; a visit to the building of the royal flotilla and to the community development centre at Along-Romeat; a folkloric representation and the inauguration of the Permanent Exhibition of the Realisations of the Sangkum Reastr Niyum at the Bassac river front; the inauguration of the National Sports Complex (12 November); and a visit to the National Museum Jayavarman VII (today known as the National Museum). On 14 November the departure for Siem Reap by aeroplane was scheduled with military honours, followed by visits to the temples, tea at the Angkor's Srah Srang (water reservoir) with the folkloric representation of the *Trott dance*, and an official dinner at the Grand Hotel. At 10 p.m. the artistic representation by the Corps du Ballet Royal took place on the *parvis* (esplanade) in front of Angkor Wat with the 'Dance of Welcome and Good Wishes' and a fragment of the Ramayana epos, and finally a visit of Angkor Wat in full illumination, before a return to Phnom Penh the next day.

If the above-mentioned 1964 celebration may easily count as the largest effort of Sihanouk's regime to merge past Angkorian glory with the present cultural-political ambitions of the new Cambodian nation-state in front of an international diplomatic audience, then one event in 1966 was no doubt the most important international event during Cambodia's independence: the visit of Charles de Gaulle. On his way from Ethiopia and continuing to Oceania to observe a French nuclear bombing experiment in the Pacific, the president of the French Fifth Republic – Sihanouk's greatest political reference – arrived on 30 August at Phnom Penh. On almost ninety pages, Sihanouk's journal *Kambuja* reported on the stay with its series of receptions and visiting tours in Phnom Penh. On 1 September, in the National Stadium, de

Gaulle gave a *discours de Phnom Penh* as a homage to the mutual French–Cambodian friendship and neutralist Cambodia, and as a warning against American aggression in Vietnam.[67] Reportedly, 'one hundred thousand people' greeted him with a mass performance of varying collective cardboard images. The 'final climax' of Charles de Gaulle's visit was a *son et lumière* show at Angkor Wat which was billed as 'the most perfect of all Asian monuments pay[ing] homage to the most famous of all Western Heads of State'.[68] At this show, the Khmer Ballet as a cultural performance became part of a large-scale historical re-enactment as, in line with Vanessa Agnew's definition, 'collapsing temporalities' and the recreation of a 'historical continuity [were] exploited for ideological ends'.[69] If re-enactments are predicated on their 'credible setting'[70] and their ability to narrow the 'mimetic gap' between fact and fiction,[71] then this was very much the case in Cambodia. Here, the king of a postcolonial nation let the pre-colonial, 'authentic past' of his direct ancestors be theatrically re-enacted in front of the head of the former colonial power at the original setting: in a *'reconstitution historique grandiose'*, 900 laymen and 600 monks in historical and religious costumes participated in the re-enactment of a historical coronation ceremony and procession of an Angkorian king in which the children of the real King Sihanouk, Prince Naradipo, and his daughter, Princess Botum Bopha, were cast as the historical royal couple (Figure 6.4). Never before or since in Cambodia's decolonising history were performative cultural elements, the original historical temple setting of Angkor Wat and hundreds of real and faked actors merged into a more impressive spectacle to evoke a newly born nation-state in the name of its ancient glory.

The gigantic illumination of Angkor Wat had been designed by Vann Molyvann and made possible by the electrification system by Siemens Germany. The acting Angkor general conservator, and George Groslier's son, Bernard-Philippe Groslier, wrote the script *The Voices of One Night in Angkor* for this performed journey into Angkor's re-staged past (although, notably, in a later paper he would explicitly correct his father's inventions regarding the 'dancing maidens emerging from the bas-reliefs of Angkor Wat'[72]). If Bernard-Philippe Groslier's approach tried to situate the Angkorian Empire in the all-encompassing grid of entangled world civilisations, then his poetic text for this event in 1966 counts as one of the most astonishing, myth-making documents to foster Cambodia's revived postcolonial notion of cultural *grandeur*. The first phrase of the text was all telling: 'Mon Général, La grandeur seule sied à la grandeur' (My General, only grandeur befits grandeur).[73] It was a classic example of the political role of re-enactments in the form of 'pageantry'[74] and concluded with

Figure 6.4 Illustrations of the *son et lumière* show at Angkor Wat during the visit of Charles de Gaulle on 1 September 1969

a rather decolonising and 'affirmative address' to the French president and the Cambodian king alike: tellingly, Angkor Wat was described as the symbol of a 'conjoint caring effort of both nations'. At this final point, King Sihanouk used the staging of the Khmer emergence myth to subliminally communicate (paradoxically through the voice of a French archaeologist) a new political self-confidence to his former colonial master.

However unique this *son et lumière* of 1966 might have seemed, it was repeated two years later for a political guest at the other end of the ideological spectrum. Josip Broz Tito, president of the Socialist Federal Republic of Yugoslavia, visited his non-aligned brother country with quite a similar *parcours* through Phnom Penh from 17 to 22 January 1968,[75] and a reduced de Gaulle-style sound and light show was performed on 19 January at Angkor Wat. Groslier's text from 1966 was only perfunctorally modified to give it socialist undertones: now, the 'Monsieur le Président de la République' and 'Maréchal' was addressed, but in this later version the Romans did not conquer the Gauls, instead 'Trajan and Hadrian brought the *pax romana* to the Dacians' (today a territory in Eastern Europe), and both the Cambodian and the Yugoslav nations were 'united in a common history of battles' against imperial politics.[76]

On 9 November 1968 Cambodia celebrated its fifteenth anniversary of national independence in the newly built National Sports Complex designed by Vann Molyvann and other international specialists (Figure 6.5). The stadium was the largest architectural complex of postcolonial Cambodia which itself had been promoted as a project of Angkorian scale and reference.[77] Vann's collaborator Vladimir Bodiansky (a Russian-French architect, colleague of Le Corbusier and CIAM member, teacher at the École des Beaux-Arts during Vann's formation in Paris and UN construction expert at Cambodia's Ministry of Public Works) focused on the political and social aspect of this 'Forum of the city of Phnom Penh'. In his description of the complex, Bodiansky noted that the stadium was

> not only assigned to national and international sport competitions, but also to all kinds of popular manifestations and reunions, national and religious festivities, processions and military parades, ... conferences, exhibitions and the reception of foreign guests ... in order to primarily assure direct audio-visual contact between the head of state, his adjuncts and the Khmer people.[78]

A critical article in the journal *Études Cambodgiennes* written by Alain Daniel found the perfect title for the Independence Day celebrations held there and supposedly organised by the Jeunesse

Figure 6.5 Illustrations of Phnom Penh's National Stadium during the celebrations of Cambodia's fifteenth anniversary

Socialiste Royale Khmère in honour of Sihanouk, the father of independence: *une expérience de théatre total*. According to Daniel, the aim of this veritable mass spectacle was to demonstrate that history would ratify that public support of the throne had enabled the Cambodian nation to preserve its imperilled national independence: 'The lesson was clear: Let us unite and "the nation will never die".'[79] The didactic aspect of the event was mass instruction in the name of history, making the people aware of their country's past. Yet Daniel was disapproving: 'But exactly here lies the danger. The evocative power of such a spectacle is enormous, and draws much more upon sensibility than on intelligence. This power somehow chokes any critical spirit, and requires a particular rigor on the content of the message.' As Daniel continued, the two-hour show programme reached a scale unprecedented in Cambodia's modern history, including the Royal Ballet, folkloric dance troupes, 500 actors, singers, musicians and dancers with the whole personnel of the École des Beaux-Arts, 200 schoolchildren, university students and, above all, 80,000 spectators on the tiers participating, a few guests attending from abroad, and Sihanouk's whole diplomatic corps. As Daniel could quote from the official descriptions of the event, Sihanouk's 'total theatre' merged mythical history and postcolonial imaginations of past, present and future grandeur into one 'magical dream world':

> The action takes place at the end of the twelfth century. Faithfully reconstituted after the bas-reliefs of Angkor Wat, drawn by six people on his chariot and protected by royal umbrellas, King Jayavarman VII enters the stage, followed by a long cortege. On the vast field of the stadium he decides to build a temple to the honour of Lord Buddha. Thus, coming from all four directions a crowd of workers runs together, carrying enormous cubic stone blocks. In few moments, the familiar silhouette of the Angkorian Bayon temple with its four-sided Buddha faces is reconstituted from plywood in the middle of the stadium. ... The Royal Ballet dances around the temple for its consecration, and crowds from the neighbouring villages come to see the new construction: peasants with their tools, dancers, men and women, as on the bas-reliefs on the real Bayon temple. ... But there are also wounded and disabled people, and loiterers. Full of compassion, the king approaches and heals them, as a stele of Jayavarman VII indicates ... But Buddha announced that the life of man brings war after peace ... and the stadium becomes full of fighting warriors. ... Finally there is victory, and songs of thanks are sung for the gods. ...

> The second part of the spectacle takes place in the modern epoch, the Sangkum era. After Jayavarman VII, Norodom Sihanouk in

1953 brings back again the light of independence. To illustrate the modern politics and the realisations of the regime, humour and poetry were chosen. Statistics of the results are shown in animated form: ... the politics of water, agriculture, industry, transport ... But the nation must constantly remain awake and needs collective orderliness: peasants, workers, railwaymen, sailors, dockworkers etc. ... become soldiers. And all the figures execute movements of a paramilitary ensemble. Night has fallen, all is dark apart from the very centre in shadows: the illuminated bust of the head of state. From here comes a light to illuminate the country and the whole kingdom, following the five principles of Pancha Sila: independence, neutrality, territorial integrity, Buddhist socialism and nationalism. With this image, the tiers become illuminated by innumerable fire flies, and the spectacle finishes in a magical dream world.[80]

If Garry had praised in 1964 Sihanouk's postcolonial regime as a 'theatre of profound transformation', Daniel's use of the term 'total spectacle' to describe the 1968 event was not only a thoughtful critique about the all-encompassing evocation of Angkor, but it also expressed his awe at this 'mass manifestation in the sign of the great [emerging] socialist countries of Asia'.

Indeed, in Daniel's description we may find a neat summary of each of the cultural tropes discussed in this chapter and used to re-enact Angkorian grandeur in Cambodia's decolonising period: first, the reimagined ancient kingship of the historical king Jayavarman VII in the person of Norodom Sihanouk in his new/old mission to bring (a new kind of socialist) Buddhism to the reborn Cambodian nation-state; second, the re-presented grandeur of Angkor's iconic temples as the ancient reference points for Cambodia's new Khmer architectural modernism, complete with its reworking of traditional spatial qualities and decorative patterns; and third, cultural performances combined with historical re-enactments à la Angkorienne used as a tool to foster – both in the domestic arena and on the external, international and diplomatic stage – Cambodia's image as a neutral and peace-loving nation of traditional vernacular culture in modern disguise.

Two themes appear in each of these tropes and deserve further emphasis and explanation here: first, the eminent and continuing role of cultural heritage from a colonial to a postcolonial state. The term 'cultural heritage' hints at a contested process of 'inheriting culture'. In Cambodia, this modern process had been initiated by the French colonial regime through its self-inflicted *mission civilisatrice* (or 'white man's burden' as Rudyard Kipling had it in his famous 1899 poem for the US colonial context in the Phillipines) to salvage and revive – and therefore legally and morally 'inherit' – Cambodia's colonised cultural heritage.[81] Typical Western tools of scientific data production (or, in our case the tools of art history: comparative taxonomies, inventories and museum collections) and scientific restoration methods (in our case archaeology)[82] helped to produce historical imaginings of Angkor's ancient glory. These imaginations were, in the decolonising phase, directly incorporated and continued as supposedly true, pure and original elements into Cambodia's Hobsbawmian,[83] and highly creative, self-reinvention process as a neo-Angkorian nation-state built upon a revived, pure and authentic antiquity.

Second, throughout this chapter we have seen the continued use of the temple site of Angkor Wat as a crucial and valuable source of inspiration. Here, the world's largest religious stone monument and the unquestioned architectural masterpiece of the ancient capital of the Angkorian Empire had gradually been turned by French colonial archaeology into a picture-perfect, ageless and anti-ageing heritage icon. In the form of a three-tower silhouette, it even became the central emblem of both the colonial and national flags of Cambodia. It is striking that (ex-colonial) French on-site restoration work continued until 1972, far into Cambodia's independence, as if no political change had occurred. If the discipline of art history had helped to reinvent Cambodia's self-esteem of national and civilisational grandeur as embedded in Khmer antiquity, then applied archaeology proved vital in terms of its 'function in building nation-states'.[84] Politics and archaeology alike transformed the 'real' site into a unique cultural heritage site. As a central nationalist reference point, Angkor Wat became – and still is in today's global cultural mass tourism – the performative stage for Cambodia's newly 'imagined [decolonised] community'.[85]

Yet the link between politics and culture was to take a fatalistic turn away from the glory of Cambodia's decolonisation. As independent Cambodia approached its financial and social abyss with the escalation of the war in neighbouring Vietnam, the US bombing of Cambodian territory, and the internally rising concern, both on the left and the right, about the misguided politics of Sihanouk's monocratic regime, the princely leader himself gradually left the real Cambodian stage and delved into one last refuge with which to realise his great vision of a reborn Angkorian nation-state: film-making.[86] After a long series of films with telling titles such as *Apsara, The Enchanted Forest, Le Petit Prince du peuple*, and

Shadow over Angkor, his final film *Crépuscule* (*Twilight*) staged him and his wife Monique in the main roles. In no other fiction of Sihanouk did all of the above-mentioned French colonial scientific and myth-making topoi of Angkor's *grandeur* shine more clearly through his historical *'re-imaginaire'* of ancient glory. However, the film, with its telling title and the symbolic characterisation of its protagonists, also gave melancholic, fatalistic – and visionary – undertones to the imminent downfall of the whole country and its leader.

In the short film/documentary *Cortège Royal* – with a poetical commentary unctuously spoken in French – Sihanouk drew his inspiration directly (again) from the scenic bas-reliefs of Angkor Wat. In more than twenty minutes, a long series of personnel from the Royal Palace, disguised in colourful dresses and ethnic distinctions, staged Cambodia's imperial past in a seemingly documentary way. In reality, however, it may count as Sihanouk's final artistic attempt to re-enact Angkor's kingly glory as a reflection of what by this time he had already lost in real political authority. For a last time, Sihanouk's extraordinary decolonising vision of a 'new Angkorian state', merging 'the real and suggested' and 'the present and [cultural] memory', came back to life. Here the staged procession walked into the night, as the real Cambodia approached a republican civil war and Khmer Rouge auto-genocide:

> The golden gates slowly close and here is the victory drum which starts the celestial ballet of the Apsaras, messengers of goodwill, for their danced offering of golden and silver flowers. On this day, oh how full of pomp, of Victory, the Angels of celestial Paradise dance so that your life will be long and your reign will be long. And the Bakous put their shells to their mouths at the end of this wonderful night, is this then the prelude? *At the shell's last sound, all the instruments send their allegories echo heavenwards. And then the cortege drawn up again resumes its majestic march towards the many-coloured and many-shaped night, of time and space, of real and suggested, of the present and memory.*[87]

Notes

This contribution is part of a larger research project entitled 'Cultural Heritage as a Transcultural Concept: Angkor Wat from an Object of Colonial Archaeology to a Contemporary Global Icon' which the author has conducted between 2009 and 2014 at the chair of Global Art History within the 'Cluster of Excellence: Asia and Europe in a Global Context – The Dynamics of Transculturality' at the University of Heidelberg. The results of this project will be presented in M. Falser, *Angkor Wat: From Jungle Find to Global Icon: A Transcultural History of Heritage* (Berlin: De Gruyter, 2016).

CULTURAL HERITAGE AS PERFORMANCE

1. R. Garry, *La Renaissance du Cambodge de Jayavarman VII, roi d'Angkor à Norodom Sihanouk Varman* (Phnom Penh: Imprimérie du Ministère de l'Information, 1964), pp. 9, 10, 1. Unless otherwise stated, all translations are mine.
2. M. Falser, 'Krishna and the Plaster Cast: Translating the Cambodian Temple of Angkor Wat in the French Colonial Period', *Transcultural Studies*, 2 (2011), 6–50. In more specific investigations, see M. Falser, 'The First Plaster Casts of Angkor for the French *Métropole*: From the Mekong Mission 1866–68, and the Universal Exhibition of 1867, to the *Musée Khmer* of 1874', *Bulletin de l'Ecole Française d'Extrême-Orient*, 99 (2012–13), 49–92; M. Falser, 'La Porte d'Entrée — Angkor at the Universal Exhibition of 1878 in Paris', *Zeitschrift für Kunstgeschichte*, 76 (2013), 191–216; M. Falser, 'From Gaillon to Sanchi, from Vézelay to Angkor Wat: The *Musée Indo-chinois* in Paris: A Transcultural Perspective on Architectural Museums', *RIHA Journal*, 71 (19 June 2013), n.p.; M. Falser, 'Colonial Appropriation, Physical Substitution and the Metonymics of Translation: Plaster Casts of Angkor Wat for the Museum Collections in Paris and Berlin', in G.U. Großmann and P. Krutisch (eds), *The Challenge of the Object*, CIHA Congress Proceedings 2 (Nuremberg: Germanisches Nationalmuseum, 2013), pp. 528–32.
3. J. Clifford, 'The Others: Beyond the "Salvage" Paradigm', *Third Text*, 6 (1989), 73.
4. In India, a whole postcolonial subcontinent was to deal with a more balanced correlation of territorial size and ancient built heritage; and independent Indonesia became a primarily Muslim state under President Sukarno, who claimed no direct ancestry from the country's ancient stone-built temple heritage of primarily Buddhist or Hindu origin.
5. On India see T. Guha-Thakurta, *Monuments, Objects, Histories: Institutions of Art in Colonial and Postcolonial India* (New York: Columbia University Press, 2004). On Indonesia see M. Bloembergen and M. Eickhof, 'Save Borobudur! The Moral Dynamics of Heritage Formation in Indonesia across Orders and Borders, 1930s–1980s', in M. Falser (ed.), *Cultural Heritage as Civilising Mission: From Decay to Recovery* (Heidelberg and New York: Springer, 2015), pp. 83–119.
6. M. Falser, 'Colonial Gaze and Tourist Guide: The Making of the Archaeological Park of Angkor in the French Protectorate of Cambodia', in M. Falser and M. Juneja (eds), *'Archaeologising' Angkor? Heritage between Local Social Practices and Global Virtual Realities* (Heidelberg and New York: Springer, 2013), pp. 81–106.
7. M. Osborne, 'History and Kingship in Contemporary Cambodia', *Journal of Southeast Asian History*, 7:1 (March 1966), 1. See also M. Osborne, *Politics and Power in Cambodia: The Sihanouk Years* (Victoria: Longman, 1973) and M. Osborne, *Sihanouk: Prince of Light, Prince of Darkness* (St Leonards: Allen & Unwin, 1994).
8. P. Edwards, *Cambodge: The Cultivation of a Nation, 1860–1945* (Honolulu: Hawaii University Press, 2007), p. 242.
9. C. Meyer, *Derrière le sourire khmer* (Paris: Plon, 1971), p. 44.
10. See also M. Falser, 'From a Colonial Reinvention to a Postcolonial Heritage and Global Commodity: Performing and Re-enacting Angkor Wat and the "Royal Khmer Ballet"', *International Journal of Heritage Studies*, special issue on 'Reenacting the Past', 20:7–8 (2014), 702–23.
11. E. Diamond, 'Performance and Cultural Politics', in L. Goodman and D. de Gay (eds), *The Routledge Reader in Politics and Performance* (London: Routledge, 1989), p. 69.
12. R. Schechner and W. Appel (eds), *By Means of Performance: Intercultural Studies of Theatre and Ritual* (Cambridge: Cambridge University Press, 1990), p. 2.
13. D. Bachmann-Medick, *Cultural Turns: Neuorientierungen in den Kulturwissenschaften* (Reinbeck bei Hamburg: Rowohlt, 2009), p. 130.
14. M. Carlson, 'Performing the Past: Living History and Cultural Memory', *Paragrana*, 9:2 (2000), 247.

15 I. Arns, 'Strategies of Re-enactment in Contemporary (Media) Art and Performance', in I. Arns and G. Horn (eds), *History Will Repeat Itself: Strategien des Reenactment in der zeitgenössischen (Medien-)Kunst und Performance* (Frankfurt am Main: Revolver, 2007), pp. 37–63.
16 See V. Agnew, 'What is Re-enactment?', *Criticism*, 46:3 (2004), 327–39; V. Agnew, 'History's Affective Turn: Historical Re-enactment and its Work in the Present', *Rethinking History*, 11:3 (2007), 299–312; A. Cook, 'The Use and Abuse of Historical Re-enactment', *Criticism*, 46:3 (2004), 487–96.
17 See, amongst others, K. Miura, *Contested Heritage: People of Angkor* (PhD dissertation: SOAS London, 2004); T. Winter, *Post-conflict Heritage, Postcolonial Tourism: Culture, Politics and Development at Angkor* (London: Routledge, 2007).
18 Ministère de l'Information (ed.), *Considerations sur le socialisme khmer* (Phnom Penh: Imprimerie du Ministère de l'Information, n.d. [1961]), pp. 3–7.
19 J. Lacouture, 'Norodom Sihanouk ou le prince d'effervescence', in J. Lacouture, *Quatre hommes et leurs peuples: sur-pouvoir et sous-développement* (Paris: Seuil, 1969), p. 208.
20 G. Coedès, *Un grand roi du Cambodge, Jayavarman VII* (Phnom Penh: Éditions de la Bibliothèque Royale, 1935), p. 3.
21 G. Coedès, *Pour mieux comprendre Angkor: cultes personnels et culte royal, monuments funéraires, symbolisme architectural, les grands souverains d'Angkor* (Paris: Adrien-Maisonneuve, 1947; first published in Saigon, 1943), pp. 176–210.
22 See P. Stern, *Art khmer. Le Bayon d'Angkor et l'évolution de l'art khmer: étude et discussion de la chronologie des monuments khmers* (Paris: Annales du Musée Guimet and Bibliothèque de Vulgarisation, 1927).
23 G. Condominas (ed.), *Disciplines croisées: hommage à Bernard Philippe Groslier* (Paris: Éditions de l'École des Hautes Études en Sciences Sociales, 1992), p. 24.
24 M. Prodromidès, 'Bernard-Philippe Groslier et la cité hydraulique khmère', in M. Prodromidès, *Angkor: chronique d'une renaissance* (Paris: Kailash, 1997), pp. 240–62.
25 B.P. Groslier, *Angkor: hommes et pierres* (Paris: Arthaud, 1956), pp. 153–93.
26 J. Boisselier, 'Reflexions sur l'art de Jayavarman VII', *Bulletin de la Société des Etudes Indochinoises*, 27:3 (1952), 261–73.
27 Ministère de l'Information (ed.), *Cambodge* (Phnom Penh: Continental Printing, 1962).
28 'At Angkor Thom, a Thousand Year Old Rite: "Chrat Preah Nongkol"', *Kambuja*, 26 (15 May 1967), 60–70.
29 H. Grant Ross and D. Collins, *Building Cambodia: New Khmer Architecture, 1953–1970* (Bangkok: The Key Publisher, 2006), pp. 200–33; D. Ly and I. Muan (eds), *Cultures of Independence: An Introduction to Cambodian Arts and Culture in the 1950s and 1960s* (Phnom Penh: Reyum, 2001), pp. 3–29. See also H. Grant Ross, 'The Civilizing Vision of an Enlightened Dictator: Norodom Sihanouk and the Cambodian Post-independence Experiment (1953–1970)', in Falser, *Cultural Heritage as Civilising Mission*, pp. 149–78.
30 M. Vann, 'La nouvelle architecture khmère – le complexe sportif national (A l'école des maîtres angkoriens)', *Nokor Khmer*, 1 (Octobre-December 1969), 34–47.
31 M. Vann, *Essai sur la culture Khmère – Enquête sur les rélations entre les cultures*, typescript, signed 'Paris, 18 August 1949', UNESDOC database online, file UNESCO/PHS/CE/7, http://unesdoc.unesco.org/images/0015/001550/155069fb.pdf p. 11 (accessed 27 May 2015).
32 Similarly, independent India staged its new national identity in a hybrid mix of modern and traditional vernacular art forms. See R. Brown, *Art for a Modern India, 1947–1980* (Durham: Duke University Press, 2009).
33 M. Vann, 'Art et culture – le renouveau des arts Khmers', *Kambuja*, 2 (15 May 1965), 68–73.

34 'L'enfouissement des cendres royales', *Cambodge d'Aujourd'hui*, 1 (January 1961), 14–15.
35 Grant Ross and Collins, *New Khmer Architecture*, pp. 88–9.
36 For the whole history of Angkor being represented in French colonial and universal exhibitions (1867–1937), see M. Falser, *Angkor Wat* (see introductory paragraph at start of notes).
37 M. Vann, 'A Conversation with Vann Molyvann, Phnom Penh, 24 August 2001', in Ly and Muan, *Cultures of Independence*, p. 22.
38 Vann Molyvann was interviewed by the author in March 2010 in his house in Phnom Penh.
39 'Célébration du XIe anniversaire de l'Independence', *Cambodge d'Aujourd'hui*, 72 (November–December 1964), 10–12.
40 'Le Prince Norodom Sihanouk aux U.S.A.', *Cambodge d'Aujourd'hui*, 10–11 (October–November 1958), 4, 6, 14, 15.
41 Meyer, *Derrière le sourire Khmer*, p. 236.
42 'Le Prince Norodom Sihanouk visite le Sud-Est Asiatique', *Cambodge d'Aujourd'hui*, 48–51 (September–December 1962), 5.
43 Ministère de l'Information, *Cambodge*, p. 270.
44 'La Visite officielle du chef de l'état à Paris', *Cambodge d'Aujourd'hui*, 67 (May–June 1964), 24. Also: C.M. [Charles Meyer], 'Le Ballet Royal à Paris', *Cambodge d'Aujourd'hui*, supplement, 2 (April–June 1964), 35.
45 'Cambodian Women', *Cambodia Today*, 46–7 (July–August 1962), 22.
46 M.I. Cohen, *Performing Otherness: Java and Bali on International Stages, 1905–1952* (Basingstoke: Palgrave Macmillan, 2010), p. 4; see also G. Bois, *Les Danseuses cambodgiennes en France* (Hanoi and Haiphong: Imprimerie d'Extrême-Orient, 1913).
47 A. Artaud (ed.), *Exposition National Coloniale de Marseille* (Marseille: Sémaphore, 1923), p. 207.
48 F. de Miomandre, 'Rêveries sur les danseuses cambdgiennes', *La danse*, 38 (1923), n.p.
49 R. de Beauplan, 'La Nuit merveilleuse', *L'Illustration*, 89:4616 (22 August 1931), n.p.
50 For performances in this general context, see E. Fischer-Lichte, C. Horn, S. Umathum and M. Warstat (eds), *Performativität und Ereignis* (Tübingen and Basel: Franke, 2003), pp. 11–37. For Cambodia, see C. Diamond, 'Emptying the Sea by the Bucketful: A Difficult Phase in Cambodian Theatre or the Creation of a Culture of Independence', in R. Chaturvedi and B. Singleton (eds), *Ethnicity and Identity: Global Performance* (New Delhi: Rawat, 2005), pp. 389–96.
51 C. Meyer, 'Le Corps de Ballet Royal', *Nokor Khmer*, 1 (October–December 1969), 4 and 5.
52 G. Groslier, *Danseuses cambodgiennes anciennes et modernes* (Paris: Challamel, 1913), p. 173, translated and republished in K. Davis (ed.), *Cambodian Dancers: Ancient and Modern* (Holmes Beach: DatASIA, 2010).
53 H. Marchal, *Costumes et parures khmèrs d'après les Devatâ d'Angkor-Vat* (Paris: G. van Oest, 1927), p. 2.
54 See Falser, 'From a Colonial Reinvention'.
55 G. Groslier, 'L'Agonie de l'art cambodgien', *Revue Indochinoise* (1918), 547–60.
56 Cambodian Information Agency, *Royal Cambodian Ballet* (Phnom Penh: Ministry of Information Press, 1963), p. 19; compare Edwards, *Cambodge*, pp. 171–3.
57 S.C. Thiounn, *Danses cambodgiennes* (Hanoi, 1930, reprinted Phnom Penh: Institut Bouddhique, 1956), pp. 31, 58.
58 On the concept of 'transculturality' in critical heritage studies see the introduction in M. Falser and M. Juneja (eds), *Kulturerbe und Denkmalpflege transkulturell: Grenzgänge zwischen Theorie und Praxis* (Bielefeld: Transcript, 2013), pp. 17–34.

59 P. Cravath, *Earth in Flower: The Divine Mystery of the Cambodian Dance Drama* (Holmes Beach: DatASIA, 2007), p. 143.
60 H. Sasagawa, 'Post/colonial Discourse on the Cambodian Court Dance', *Tonan Ajia Kenkyu (Southeast Asian Studies)*, 42:4 (2005), 429.
61 An expression from D. MacCannell, 'Staged Authenticity: Arrangements of Social Space in Tourist Settings', *American Journal of Sociology*, 79:3 (1973), 589–603. See also J. Tivers, 'Performing Heritage: The Use of Live "Actors" in Heritage Presentations', *Leisure Studies*, 21:3–4 (2002), 187–200.
62 On this term, see V. Turner, *From Ritual to Theatre: The Human Seriousness of Play* (New York: Performing Arts Journal Publications, 1982), pp. 28–94.
63 S. Burridge and F. Frumberg (eds), *Beyond the Apsara: Celebrating Dance in Cambodia* (London: Routledge, 2010); see also T. Shapiro-Phim and A. Thompson, *Dance in Cambodia* (Kuala Lumpur: Oxford University Press, 2001).
64 D. Heywood, *Cambodian Dance: Celebration of the Gods* (Bangkok: River, 2008), p. 76.
65 M. de Certeau, *The Practice of Everyday Life* (Berkeley: Berkeley University Press, 1988), pp. 119–20. In his 1980 publication *L'Invention du quotidien*, Michel de Certeau reflected on '*parcours*' which the user follows to see specific scenes (*tableaux*) and to execute different actions. In our ideologically loaded case study, the diplomatic tour through the country was painstakingly 'produced' by Sihanouk's agents in order to provide his guests – within a limited time frame – a fine-tuned mix of picture-perfect impressions of cultural rootedness of and modern progress in Cambodia.
66 National Archives, Phnom Penh, printed programme, Royaume du Cambodge (ed.), *Programme de visite pour toutes les delegations (gouvernementales des puissances amies) du 7 au 18 novembre 1964*.
67 N. Sihanouk, *Souvenirs doux et amers* (Paris: Hachette, 1981), pp. 317–20.
68 'General de Gaulle's State Visit to Cambodia', *Kambuja*, 18 (15 September 1966), 64; see also *Photo-souvenirs du Cambodge: Sangkum Reastr Niyum, 1955–1969, Vol. 7: Le Prestige au plan international du Cambodge* (Phnom Penh: Ramat Print, 1993), pp. 128–67.
69 Agnew, 'History's Affective Turn', 309.
70 S. Gapps, 'Mobile Monuments: A View of Historical Re-enactment and Authenticity from Inside the Costume Cupboard of History', *Rethinking History*, 13:3 (2009), 395–409, here 403.
71 Agnew, 'What is Re-enactment', 332.
72 As Bernard-Philippe Groslier stated: 'At Angkor Wat, the god-serving enchantresses are multiplied ad infinitum, *however, they do everything but dance*' (emphasis added), see B.P. Groslier, 'La Musique et la danse sous les rois d'Angkor [1969]', in J. Dumarcay (ed.), *Mélanges sur l'archéologie du Cambodge (1949–1986), Bernard-Philippe Groslier* (Paris: Ecole Française d'Extrême-Orient, 1998), p. 91.
73 B.P. Groslier, 'Les Voix d'une nuit d'Angkor: Texte de spectacle "son et lumière" offert au Général de Gaulle, sur le parvis d'Angkor Vat, par le Royaume du Cambodge, le 1er septembre 1966', in Dumarcay, *Mélanges*, p. 79.
74 J. Lamb, 'Historical Re-enactment, Extremity, and Passion', *Eighteenth Century*, 49:3 (2008), 243.
75 'La Visite d'état du Maréchal Tito', *Études Cambodgiennes*, 13 (January–March 1968), 6–7; see also 'Le Cambodge accueile le Président Tito (17–22 January 1968)', in *Photo-souvenirs*, Vol. 7, pp. 256–303, 332.
76 N. Sihanouk, *The Glory of Angkor – Son et Lumière: After the Idea of Samdech Norodom Sihanouk, Chef d'Etat. In Honor of His Excellency Mr. Josip Boroz Tito, President of the Socialist Federal Republic of Yugoslavia* (title translated from Serbo-Croatian), printed programme (Phnom Penh: National Archives, 1968); compare *Photo-souvenirs*, Vol. 7, pp. 305–14.
77 As Vann Molyvann explained in 1969, never before or since was such a close relationship established between the Angkorian architectural legacy and the new

Khmer architecture as that founded during Cambodia's independence (Vann, 'La Nouvelle architecture khmère').

78 Équipe du Complexe Olympique de Phnom-Penh, 'Forum de la ville de Phnom-Penh, Cambodge. Complexe olympique du Sud-Est asiatique', *Cahiers du Centre Scientifique et Technique du Bâtiment*, April 65 (1964), livraison no. 73, 2.

79 A. Daniel, 'XVe anniversaire de l'Indépendance. Une expérience de théatre total', *Études Cambodgiennes*, 16 (October–December 1968), 5.

80 Daniel, 'XVe anniversaire', 6, 7.

81 For the interrelation between cultural heritage and civilising missions, see Falser, *Cultural Heritage as Civilising Mission*.

82 In the colonial context, we may find these specific 'historiographical, observational, surveying/mapping, enumerative/collection-oriented, museological, surveillance-based, and investigative/classificatory and investigative modalities'. See B. Cohn, *Colonialism and its Forms of Knowledge: The British in India* (Princeton: Princeton University Press, 1996), pp. 6–14.

83 After E. Hobsbawm and T. Ranger, *The Invention of Tradition* (Cambridge: Cambridge University Press, 1983).

84 I.C. Glover, 'Some National, Regional, and Political Uses of Archaeology in East and Southeast Asia', in M. Stark (ed.), *Archaeology of Asia* (New York: Wiley, 2006), pp. 17–36.

85 B. Anderson, *Imagined Communities: Reflections on the Origins and Spread of Nationalism* (London: Verso, 1983). See also B. Anderson, *The Spectre of Comparisons: Nationalism, Southeast Asia and the World* (London: Verso, 1998).

86 See O. de Bernon and P. Geneste (eds), *Les Archives de Norodom Sihanouk, roi du Cambodge: données à l'Ecole française d'Extrême-Orient et déposées aux Archives Nationales (1970–2007)* (Paris: Somogy, 2010).

87 Last scene of *Cortège Royal* (1969) (emphasis added), transcribed from: N. Sihanouk, *La Cinématographie de N. Sihanouk (Décennie 1960), Site officiel de SM le Roi-Père Norodom Sihanouk du Cambodge*, at http://norodomsihanouk.info/media/film_3.html (accessed 27 May 2015).

CHAPTER SEVEN

'I still don't have a country': The southern African settler diaspora after decolonisation

Jean Smith

This chapter traces the impact of decolonisation on the trajectories and sense of identity of British migrants to southern Africa in the second half of the twentieth century. Based on oral history interviews, it explores the disorienting effects of decolonisation and the serial migrations to which it often led. Focusing on South Africa and Rhodesia, nations which declared independence from Britain to preserve minority rule rather than to end it, this chapter interrogates multiple layers of decolonisation. Those who settled in southern Africa experienced a double dislocation, both when South Africa declared itself a republic and left the Commonwealth in 1961, and Rhodesia declared independence from Britain in 1965, and again when these white minority regimes ended with the advent of the 'new' South Africa in 1994 and independent Zimbabwe in 1980. The first instance called into question ideas of 'Britishness' or 'Englishness', with new emphasis on Rhodesian or South African identities, though some, especially in South Africa, asserted a British identity, often in criticism of their government's actions. At the onset of majority rule, when Rhodesia and apartheid South Africa no longer existed, these Rhodesian or South African identities were also called into question.

Like recent scholarship on 'orphans of empire', this chapter broadens the work on French and Portuguese imperial 'repatriates' to include the British experience, focusing attention on southern Africa and, importantly, on those who did not return to Britain.[1] Close attention to these alternative sites demonstrates that, although British South Africans and ex-Rhodesians are far more scattered, they have much in common with other 'colonials' after the end of empire, including a sense of exile, exclusion and a loss of status.

With the exception of Australia, colonial migration from the United Kingdom is most often associated with the nineteenth and early twentieth centuries; however, post-Second World War migrants to southern Africa made up a large group. Close to half a million British-born immigrants arrived in South Africa between 1945 and 1994, and though the Rhodesian government did not keep statistics based on birthplace, Britons made up the majority of the 366,214 immigrants classified as European who arrived there from the Second World War until independence in 1980.[2] Even accounting for repeat migration and those who moved between these nations, this is a substantial number. Many stayed on in Africa after independence, while others relocated within the wider Commonwealth or beyond it. Though some did return to Britain, they did not do so as a large and visible group.

The experience of these migrants is similar to their counterparts earlier in the history of the British Empire in many ways, though the added complication of decolonisation meant that not only did they have to adapt to the settler colonial nations to which they moved, but they also had to adapt again when these nations severed ties with the United Kingdom and then again at the onset of majority rule. David Lambert and Alan Lester's examination of nineteenth-century imperial migrations found that such travels could leave migrants with a feeling of 'double exile' from both their place of origin and another previous location where they had lived.[3] Lambert and Lester also consider the 'reformulations of identities' and 'changes in personhood that came from dwelling in different spaces'.[4] Post-war British migrants underwent similar experiences as they changed physical location and also as the changing political circumstances of decolonisation transformed the nations in which they lived. Like Britons who returned to the United Kingdom from India after decolonisation, these migrants often felt like exiles and struggled to feel at home in British society.[5] Looking beyond the British case, there are parallels with migrants in other European empires, who, as Andrea L. Smith argues, formed 'diasporas of decolonisation' focused on more than one homeland including one that no longer exists.[6] Like the *retornados* from Portuguese colonies and *pieds noirs* from Algeria, ex-Rhodesians and other British migrants form part of a diaspora with multiple homelands, including both the settler colonial society in which they lived but which no longer exists, and the United Kingdom or some imagined version of it.

This chapter's analysis of individual accounts provides a way to explore the impact of multiple instances of decolonisation on British migrants through specific cultural practices and performances of identity and nationalism, such as accent, self-presentation, interior design, dress, outdoor leisure in the 'bush', support of a national sports team and attendance at a Rhodesian reunion in Las Vegas. This attention to the micro-levels of decolonisation shows it to be a process uncontained by the realm of high politics or the timeline of flag independence. Through focusing on individual narratives, this account highlights the complex and varied impact of decolonisation on the ways in which British migrants understand themselves. To this end, the chapter is based on close readings of self-narrations of six migrants in the form of oral history interviews conducted in the United Kingdom, South Africa and the United States between 2009 and 2011.

Oral history is used here as a unique means to gain insight into subjectivity, to better understand how migrants present their stories and what meanings they attribute to decolonisation in the larger narrative of their lives. As Alessandro Portelli has argued, whether the oral histories are precise recollections is less important than the meaning the narrator attributes to particular events.[7] Because these interviews were undertaken decades after many of the events under consideration and in a very different political context, this is likely to have shaped their content and therefore it is this retrospective appraisal that is the subject of analysis. To convey the often-complex ways that these migrants made sense of their experiences, I have relied on extended quotations.[8]

The first section describes the way in which the identity and self-presentation of post-war British migrants evolved through the sequential decolonisations of South Africa and Rhodesia and the serial migrations these provoked. The second describes the way in which nostalgia for the landscape and the wildlife of southern Africa both formed part of the material culture of decolonisation and became a seemingly apolitical way to express the loss of the status and way of life accorded to members of the ruling white minority in South Africa and Rhodesia.

Serial migration and dislocation

A primary theme threading through the oral histories of British migrants is that of dislocation, of not really belonging to any specific nation or group. As others have commented in different geographic contexts, for those who have lived in more than one country, their primary identity often becomes that of a migrant.[9] In the case of British migrants to southern Africa this dislocation was intensified by the turmoil of decolonisation and the serial migrations spurred by the end of empire. Although there was nothing like the mass migration from Algeria, Mozambique and Angola at independence, many left Rhodesia in the 1970s and 1980s, often going to South Africa and other destinations including the United Kingdom, Australia and the United States in the 1980s and 1990s. Such multiple migrations, combined with the redefinition of postcolonial nations, meant that many post-war migrants did not feel that they belonged fully in any of the places where they had lived and their self-presentation often shifted in response to their changing circumstances.[10]

Andrew Smith moved from England to what was then Northern Rhodesia (now Zambia) as a child, went to school in Southern Rhodesia (now Zimbabwe), and subsequently migrated to South Africa and later to the UK. His movements loosely followed the progress of decolonisation, from Zambian independence in 1964 to majority rule in South Africa in 1994. His account illustrates this complicated trajectory of migration, corresponding changes in his perception of his own identity and the resulting sense of not really belonging anywhere:

> And, the first time I came [to the United Kingdom] in 1969, the guy said, 'Welcome home sir.' I thought okay well I s'pose I'm English. You have a kind of, well ... a crisis of identity. I actually still don't have a country. One of the reasons I want to go back to Zambia is I want to see if that's my country. I don't feel at home anywhere. I feel at home with people and I like being with people of many races. And I guess I am a citizen of the world or whatever but I don't have a country. When I was growing up in what was then Northern Rhodesia, I said to my Dad, 'We're Rhodesian.' He said, 'No you're not, you're English.' I said, 'We're Rhodesian.' He said, 'No you're English.' ... I thought I was Rhodesian. That was the only country I knew, I had been there since I was a baby so I thought this was what I am. Then of course it became Zambia and we had a choice, you could either give up your British passport, you weren't allowed to have dual nationality. I was advised not to give up my British passport so I couldn't become a Zambian. So I wasn't a Zambian. And by that stage anyway, I then moved to South Africa. When I got to South Africa I found out I was an Englishman, or an Engelsman, not an Afrikaner so I was not a South African. And, then of course when independence came I was white not black, so I, you know, I wasn't really the real thing either ... So I have never had a country. So I always used to, perhaps to the disappointment of my sons particularly, I always used to support English sports teams. So I said, 'Well, I'm English, I must be English. I was born in England. I'm English. I'll support the English sports teams.' But then I came to England and I've been here for eight years and I'm not English and I don't mind living here. I enjoy what I do. I enjoy being with all kinds of people but I am not English.[11]

Multiple instances of decolonisation shaped both the physical trajectory of Smith's life and his perceptions of himself. Decolonisation meant that Smith could no longer be Rhodesian or Zambian and he did not feel that he was really a South African either. In what became a recurring theme in my interviews, this sense of not belonging led

Smith to define himself as English, but only while he remained in southern Africa. For example, supporting English sports teams provided a way to signify an English identity in South Africa, but the instability of this affiliation became evident on his return to the United Kingdom, when it became clear that he was not considered to be English in England. Not feeling that he was really South African or English, while being considered by others to be English in South Africa and South African in England, Smith describes himself as both a 'citizen of the world' and a man without a country.

A series of migrations and the end of Rhodesia also meant shifts in the identity of William Jervois. Jervois moved to Southern Rhodesia in the late 1940s on the Fairbridge Memorial College child migration scheme.[12] Unhappy at school, he joined the Rhodesian Air Force in his teens and although he travelled to England for training in his twenties, he returned to Rhodesia and remained there, continuing to work for the newly independent government in Zimbabwe until the mid-1980s. Though initially hopeful about the new Zimbabwe, he later become disillusioned and he and his wife moved to South Africa in the 1980s, eventually settling in Grahamstown. When asked about his identity, Jervois replied,

> I have always thought of myself as British. Because now I can't claim ... I did feel quite strongly that I was a Rhodesian, certainly ... But, when Rhodesia ceased to exist, then I just think of myself as British. I am not a South African citizen. I took an oath of loyalty to the queen when I joined the Air Force.[13]

For Jervois, the end of Rhodesia meant the end of that identification. His phrasing that after the end of Rhodesia 'I just think of myself as British' and his mention of the oath of loyalty to the queen suggests that even before 1980 he had thought of himself as both Rhodesian and British.

This is borne out in his discussion of his childhood and young adulthood. Jervois described a sense of being stuck between two identities, as he moved between southern Africa and the United Kingdom. In a sense this perception was also heightened by the ideology of the institution he was raised in, the Fairbridge Memorial College, which brought British children to Rhodesia to supplement the settler colony's white British population. Jervois mentioned that the reason that Fairbridge Memorial College, like many other imperial immigration schemes, focused on children was that they were 'considered to be more adaptable and more malleable'. He went onto say that generally speaking this was true, although not entirely, as many Fairbridge students 'maintained our sense of British identity very strongly' and were 'very slow to adopt Rhodesian mannerisms or southern African mannerisms and dialect.' This idea of being caught between two nationalities, belonging fully to neither, is also evident in his reflection of how he was perceived by others, which shifted depending on the context. As he explained, 'when I go to England now I am regarded as some sort of colonial just by the way I speak and coming back here I am regarded as some sort of Englishman.' Accent here serves as a marker of identity and contributed to how Jervois was perceived by others. The fact that in England he was considered to be a 'colonial' rather than an Englishman may also have contributed to his self-described identity as British, rather than English, and his mention of his oath of loyalty to the queen was also more abstract than a specific geographically based identity.

It follows that Jervois would feel a connection to the United Kingdom: he was born there, spent his early childhood there, returned several times as an adult and grew up in an institution with a very British and indeed imperial ethos. However, it was also related to the nature of settler culture in Rhodesia, which had only been settled relatively recently (in the 1890s) and still had close cultural affiliations with the United Kingdom.[14] As he describes:

> Everybody in Rhodesia in those years, even the ones whose grandparents had immigrated there in the 1890s, we all still talked about Britain as 'home'. There was a very strong sense of identity with the Empire, right up ... to UDI in fact. There was still this very strong loyalty to the crown and to the British way of life, generally. Remember of course, most Rhodesians were totally unaware of the rapid social changes that were taking place in Britain and uh, all sorts of things, people came out to visit Rhodesia, often said it was like stepping back fifty years. The clothing that we wore, the suits that men wore were maybe twenty years out of fashion, with what was happening overseas or more. From here, when Helen and I first got married, I would wear a suit to go to town. Helen would wear a hat and gloves. It was the done thing. I remember in the tiny little town of Gwelo, when I first went there, people going to the cinema; a lot of them would wear evening dress. Black coat and bow tie and all the rest of it, simply to go the pictures. It was a social occasion and there were things like Mrs Antoniadus's musical evenings and the schools would put on Gilbert and Sullivan as a standard thing. So it was a very, very, imperial mindset that a lot of people had. In fact, one of the only really socialist people we had were a small bundle of people who came out from Britain to join our Air Force and uh, that was the first time that I ever heard any hostility expressed towards the queen and I was absolutely staggered by this chap.[15]

This quote illustrates not only the 'Britishness' of Rhodesian settler culture, but more specifically the particular conservative version of 'Britishness' that it upheld: allegiance to the empire, to the monarchy and even to social conventions in things such as dress that were increasingly outdated in the United Kingdom itself. This idea of Rhodesia as an outpost of imperial values in a rapidly changing world became stronger after the Rhodesian government declared itself independent in 1965. Jervois mentions UDI, the Unilateral Declaration of Independence, as a potential rupture for this affiliation with Britain, a moment of decolonisation addressed in more detail below.

The way that identities might shift over time in response to the politics of decolonisation and the personal moves they often led to is also clear in Brien Bonnynge's story. Born in South Africa to Irish parents who came out after the war, Bonnynge moved as a young child to what was then Southern Rhodesia. After serving in the British South Africa Police, including during the war for independence, Bonnynge, who had married a woman he met on a trip to England in the 1970s, moved back to South Africa, where he lived until 2012, when he and his wife moved to Liverpool to be closer to her family.

Bonnynge described a strong sense of being Rhodesian as a child and young adult, heightened by the experience of the Unilateral Declaration of Independence in 1965. When asked about his identity growing up, Bonnynge described the coexistence of distinctive national identities within an overriding sense of being Rhodesian. He reflected on his childhood in Southern Rhodesia when everyone would attend various events hosted by patriotic societies:

> Well everybody there had this Rhodesian sense, okay, everyone was in it together. Okay? ... You had the Mashonaland Irish Association, you had the Greek Association, you had all these different associations ... everybody just got together, you just happened to be of Irish descent but the overriding feeling was [pause] Rhodesia was all important. But we would be Irish within that and be very good friends with the Scots and the Welsh and a few of the English, you know ... My parents actually ended up being on the committee ... of the Mashonaland Irish Association ... they used to have St Patrick's nights, but everyone came to them and the Scots would have Burns nights and everyone would go to them. So it was just an excuse for a party ... So the Irish made a party and then the Scots made a party and the English made a party and whatever ...
>
> *Jean Smith*: So ... you have more than one identity, more than one affiliation?
>
> *Brien Bonnynge*: Yes, definitely, yes the overriding one was the country you were in, but within that you had your own because you

had to cling to something. Because it was all so new, you couldn't be, there's no history so you tend to go back to your roots to be what you are, well ... I don't have an Irish accent and I have never lived there but I have an Irish passport so I suppose that makes me Irish. But I have never lived there.[16]

Here Bonnynge describes a sense of needing another identity, beyond that of being Rhodesian, attributing this to the idea of Rhodesia as a country without history. While this could be interpreted as the stereotypical colonial view of African history beginning only with the arrival of Europeans, it also reflects Bonnynge's own personal sense that his roots lay outside of Rhodesia. Yet although he does come to the eventual conclusion that he must be Irish based on his passport and his family, he does so with ambivalence, with numerous caveats about how he has never lived there and does not speak with an Irish accent. These multiple national affiliations, subsumed by the umbrella identity of Rhodesian, would also provide a possible alternative form of belonging, especially after the collapse of Rhodesia.

Before that and especially after UDI, the sense of community Bonnynge describes is one of a *white* Rhodesia, which in reflected in his assertion that everyone, regardless of national origin, would attend the events of the various patriotic societies and that 'Rhodesia was all important'. His discussion of UDI in 1965 highlights this and illustrates the way that political events could crystallise a sense of identity, even if it might change again later. On the 11 November 1965, the Rhodesian cabinet announced that Rhodesia, which had been a British colony with internal self-government since 1923, now considered itself to be a sovereign nation. This unilateral declaration, the first in the British Empire since the 1776 United States Declaration of Independence, was prompted by the British government's refusal to grant Rhodesia independence without the ruling white minority's acceptance of majority rule. UDI, like the South African declaration of republic in 1961, was a moment of decolonisation in that it resulted in the severing of ties between metropole and colony. Both were distinctive moments of decolonisation because they were undertaken to preserve settler colonial rule rather than to end colonialism. UDI therefore was a moment of decolonisation that promoted and strengthened settler colonial identity and culture.

Bonnynge describes watching television coverage of the announcement of UDI at Plumtree, the boarding school he attended, and the way that it reinforced his Rhodesian identity:

I remember seeing it on TV. Everyone told me this was important. Look, I was, I was, about fifteen, sixteen so *ja*, you know, it was going to affect me. I knew it was going to affect me. Of course we were all imbibed with the spirit of [holds up his middle finger] 'Up yours!' okay. Because that's how we all felt about UDI. So we thought, yeah, bring it on. You know what I mean? Not understanding the full, impact ... Because you don't know. I had no clue about politics, or politicians. But I knew that something momentous had happened. For the next two years of school nothing really changed. Nothing in my life really changed. Because Rhodesia still maintained. They were still doing the politics with the UDI and everything else. So, there was a bit of bravado because I was a youngster and ... *Ja* come here, I thought, We'll go and sort out these pommie bastards. *Ja*.

For Bonnynge as a schoolboy, UDI cemented a strong sense of Rhodesian unity and identity.[17] His memory of aggression against 'pommie bastards' shows a clear division between himself and the 'English', which may also have been informed by his Irish ancestry. His strong sense of being Rhodesian was also further cemented by his service in one of the most Rhodesian of all institutions, the British South Africa Police, including during the war against anti-colonial nationalists in the 1970s, a period of his life that he was not willing to speak about in the interview.

Despite this strong affiliation with Rhodesia, another moment of decolonisation, Zimbabwean independence and Bonnynge's move to South Africa in the 1980s, meant another shift in identity presentation. In a similar way to Smith's recollection of not being a South African because he was not an Afrikaner, Bonnynge described a return to a more British identity in the South African context. He was hired by the cigarette company Rothmans of Pall Mall to drive a Rolls Royce as their sales representative, with the persona of 'Mr Dunhill'. He believed that he got the job in part because of his Rhodesian accent, which meant that he fitted better with Dunhill's image:

> So here I was going around in two- or three-piece suits, oooh, with little fob pockets and everything. Yes, from all accounts I did it very well. Well, you see the accent is good too. They wanted people who didn't have a, [puts on an Afrikaans accent] '*Ja sommer*, you know I am from Dunhill,' I mean it would never have worked you understand. You had to have someone who had an English feeling to it. And the colonial accent was considered quite English, so okay ... So yes, I ended up being Mr Dunhill.

Though the display of Englishness was in part the gimmick of being 'Mr Dunhill' and perhaps connected to his marriage to a woman from England, it also became a way of differentiating himself from Afrikaners. Bonnynge describes a party he threw in Durban to celebrate Prince Andrew and Sarah Ferguson's wedding in 1986:

We got a meal with silver service from the Royal Hotel, which is, I mean really top-notch. It was a five-star hotel. So silver service laid out there with everything. All the different glasses in ascending and descending order. And you get confused because of all the knives and forks you have. We all took the day off and we got the British embassy to give us a flag. And we got a flag pole and we put up the flag and saluted the flag and pulled it up and pulled it down at night. And all the rest. And everyone came and had a party with us. It was ... it was a good reason for a party. But it was also, that was what Dunhill was all about, it was very British, very English. Wonderful time. Yes.[18]

Holding a party to celebrate the royal wedding and saluting the Union Jack in the Republic of South Africa made a definite statement, just as expressing the desire to get 'the pommie bastards' after UDI did. Taken together, they illustrate the complexity of cultures of decolonisation and the way in which presentation of national identity shifted and changed in relation to the politics of decolonisation and personal circumstances.

As Bonnynge's discussion of 'Mr Dunhill' illustrates, accent acted as an important marker of identity. Aside from how he perceived his own national identity, Jervois's accent marked him as an outsider both in South Africa and in the United Kingdom. Bonnynge specifically mentions his lack of an Irish accent when discussing his claim to an Irish identity and how his Rhodesian accent in South Africa allowed him to play the role of the English 'Mr Dunhill'. The writer Alexandra Fuller also notes the importance of accent in her memoir. Her British-born mother, Nicola Fuller, returned from Kenya to London for secretarial school in the 1960s. She describes how her mother turned down the offer of a coming-out ball with characteristic flair, 'the sort of Englishman who went to those balls would have sneered at me because I was a colonial ... They'd all have been terribly snobbish and listened like hawks for a slip in my accent; if I made the slightest mistake with my pronunciation, they would have pounced.' Despite her criticism of English snobbery, Fuller also describes her mother's attempts to teach her children received pronunciation, to bring down the pitch of their voices and avoid Rhodesian slang, illustrating her keen awareness of the importance of accent as a marker of identity and social standing.[19]

Smith, Bonnynge and Jervois all moved to South Africa from Zambia and Southern Rhodesia as those countries gained or were close to gaining independence. Despite differences in their experience, they illustrate the compounding sense of dislocation engendered by the repeated migrations undertaken by many Britons who came to southern Africa in the decades after the Second World War. As they describe, because of family influence – or in the case of Jervois the institution that he grew up in – this idea that they were not Rhodesian or not only Rhodesian but also English or British or Irish was reinforced. But, because their formative experiences were spent away from the United Kingdom, this identity was not secure. They might consider themselves English or British and then find that they were not accepted as such when they visited the British Isles. This was a common experience for those who travelled to the United Kingdom from the settler empire, as Angela Woollacott in her study of Australian women travelling to Britain in an earlier period has shown.[20] Here the dislocating effects of migration were compounded by decolonisation.

Nostalgia and the southern African landscape

As well as dislocation, the theme of loss and nostalgia came through quite strongly in many of the interviews. Those who had left after independence often expressed a strong sense of loss. Many specifically mentioned the houses and gardens that they had left behind when leaving Rhodesia or South Africa. Another expression of nostalgia came in the form of memories about spending time in the outdoors and the freedom and adventure it connoted.[21] The 'bush' was a common feature in the oral history of migrants. It served as a seemingly neutral way to explain the attraction of moving to and living in the minority settler colonial regimes of southern Africa without condoning or even addressing the racial policies of those states. As David Hughes has argued, an important locus of a distinctive white Rhodesian identity was the landscape and wildlife of southern Africa and a similar trend is evident among many white South Africans.[22]

Thelma and Harold Robson, currently living in the United States, had both moved to Southern Rhodesia from England in the 1940s, Thelma as a child and Harold as a young adult. They moved to the United States first in the 1970s and later returned for a time to Rhodesia before permanently settling in California. Though they were convinced that they had made the right decision in leaving, especially for their sons' future prospects, their discussion of their time in Rhodesia was tinged with a sense of loss. After gaining the green card that would allow them entry to the United States, they had to leave Rhodesia within three months and consequently abandoned their house in Harare:

> *Harold Robson*: So imagine, three months, we got to get rid of this, get rid of that ... We still have a house sitting there. Can't do

> nothing about it. Sitting in Harare. Still got a house. Don't get no money from it. Nothing. But it's sitting there ...
> *Thelma Robson*: Fully furnished.
> *Harold Robson*: Got the title deeds. Everything.
> *Thelma Robson*: But there's an African woman in there with her daughter.
> *Harold Robson*: And the house is as good as this ... [points to the wall of their current home]
> *Thelma Robson*: It's brick.
> *Harold Robson*: Yes it's brick and it has got a nice garden, everything. In a nice area within the view of Salisbury or Harare. So. Anyway that was ... [trails off] Then we got here and we got back on our feet again. So, it's been a battle. So, that's twice I left a country with nothing ...[23]

This house, made of permanent brick with a 'nice garden' and in a 'nice area' represented the standard of living that they had achieved in Rhodesia. The loss of the house without compensation was the direct consequence of decolonisation. Though they still had the title deeds, their house was now occupied by an African family, a microcosm of the collapse of minority rule in Rhodesia and the displacement of white Rhodesians by Africans.

William Jervois also described his house in Harare, explaining that it was part of his reluctance to leave after independence. As he put it: 'we had a very comfortable house with three acres of balancing rocks and bushmen paintings and such like and a very pleasant way of life, living in Salisbury.'[24] This large property with 'balancing rocks' and rock paintings strongly evokes not only the lifestyle available to white Rhodesians but also distinctive features of the southern African landscape, again illustrating the connection between nostalgia for the landscape and the way of life it signified.

This comes through even more clearly in the Robsons' reminiscences about Rhodesia. These were largely focused on the 'bush':

> *Thelma Robson*: And I do miss the bush. You could turn the clock back and you could live just like an African and I was quite happy with that ... I love the bush. He really loved the bush. In fact I introduced him to the bush. When we got to Rhodesia, my dad met this electrician ... Man, he was three generation Rhodesian, whoa! Did he show us the bush! Did he show us the bush. Man, oh, man, oh when we used to go and sleep next to a river. All you had was one blanket and a pillow if you were lucky and we dug the sand out.
> *Harold Robson*: With crocodiles, with lions roaring.[25]

This discussion of 'living like an African' in the bush, though it was discussed positively as a exciting adventure, reflects the common imperial trope of Africans as primitive, as stuck in the past, living outside of civilisation. It also provided a way to express a sense of belonging in Africa. Sleeping under the stars undeterred by the threat of crocodiles and lions was a way of claiming and mastering the landscape. Professing a love for the outdoors and camping also provided a way to express the sense of loss entailed by leaving Rhodesia without explicitly addressing racial politics or the economic and social privileges of belonging to the ruling white minority.

The interior decor of the Robsons' home in the United States also reflected this nostalgia and formed a material representation of their Rhodesian identity.[26] The house, filled with depictions of African wildlife and scenes, demonstrated their love of the African landscape. As well as hammered-copper art showing lions and elephants, they displayed African leatherwork, wood carvings and other curios. This self-presentation and their impressive collection of Rhodesian memorabilia, including back issues of Rhodesian magazines, suggest a deep-rooted nostalgia for their time in southern Africa, despite decades of living in the United States. The Newsams' identification with Rhodesia and nostalgia about their time there is also connected to their sense of loss, having abandoned their home in Harare to start a new life in the United States. The way they decorated their house illustrates that their time in Africa remains an important part of their identity.

Another indication of this ongoing affiliation was the Robsons' involvement with the Rhodesian Association of the USA, which holds an annual reunion, usually in Las Vegas. The themes of these events also often focused on the landscape. In recent years these included Jacaranda Days, with decorations resembling the distinctive purple of the jacaranda tree, and Kariba, focused on the Kariba Dam and complete with inflatable crocodiles in the pool.[27] Here representations of the Rhodesian landscape stand in for a vanished homeland and become the material culture of decolonisation. More than just decorative features, inflatable crocodiles are a way to recreate the bush and the leisure and outdoor lifestyle that it represented and so to deal with the consequences of decolonisation, especially the resulting geographical displacement from southern Africa.

An affinity for the landscape and animals of southern Africa could also be a justification for moving to southern Africa, especially in the 1960s and afterwards, when Rhodesia and South Africa were coming under more international criticism. It is a seemingly apolitical reason, which eludes the question of whether by moving to South Africa or Rhodesia in the 1960s and 1970s, often as part of government-sponsored schemes to increase the white population, migrants were complicit in supporting the systems of racial discrimination and dispossession in these countries. Ian Jones, for instance, mentioned his interest in African animals based on watching nature programmes on television when explaining his decision to move in the late 1960s and continued to express a strong affiliation with the South African landscape and the lifestyle that it represented.[28] He moved as a young adult in the late 1960s from England to South Africa on one of the migration schemes set up by the South African government to increase the white population. Though his children, grandchildren and ex-wife had all moved to Australia, he remained in South Africa and was the only oral history interviewee to state clearly that he felt he was South African.[29] When asked whether he considered himself British he replied:

> No, I don't. Now I have my English accent, which was being mentioned by some friends last night. They say, 'Ian is never getting rid of his accent. He has always got an English accent.' But that of course isn't what they say when I used to go back to England ... Then I would have a South African accent. So, no, I am happy to say, I'm not proud but I am happy to say I am South African. That's what I feel like. I couldn't go back to England. In fact I won't dare do that in case somehow I get trapped there and my nightmare comes true.

Here again accent acts as a signifier of identity and the influence of migration means that Jones's accent is neither English nor South African. Though Jones noted a similar phenomenon to Jervois – that in England he is considered South African and in South Africa he is considered English – he is clear in his own self-identification as South African. In part, this was because he was so much happier in South Africa than in England, but it also seems that his age at migration was also a factor. Having made the decision to move to a new country as an adult, for Jones it was a conscious rejection of his home country and a wholesale adoption of his adopted one.

His strong identification with South Africa and consequent rejection of England were explicitly tied to the landscape and climate of these countries and the different lifestyles that they engendered. The nightmare that he refers to above dates from a time when his English-born wife was pressuring him to return to the United Kingdom. His refusal to return was a large part of the reason for their subsequent divorce:

> I used to have a nightmare, when Janice was putting the pressure on me to go back. I was in, I was an old, I mean a doddery, shaky old

> man and I was sitting in, like a bath chair sitting in a little room, with a washroom and a sink in the corner, in front of the window, with the curtain drawn. The window was covered in rain and you couldn't see anything anyway because a couple of metres beyond the window was a brick wall. At which point I would wake up in hot sweats. [laughs] And I had that recurring for a long, long time. But it finally stopped. So, *ja*, I suppose I buried my roots fairly deeply. The only thing was that I didn't marry a South African. I should have married a South African.

Here he mentions not only the rainy English climate as part of his nightmare but also the cramped living conditions he might expect if he returned, signifying the different lifestyle available to him there.

For Jones, England was crowded and congested in contrast to the wide open spaces of South Africa. He described the traffic in Guildford, where he lived, and the long commute into central London when he would leave home at seven o'clock in the morning and return at half past six in the evening. For him:

> Years and years of that was just too much. Too much out of one's life. All that travelling. I suppose that was also a bit of a factor. Because Johannesburg was drivable in those days. Not like now when virtually the whole city is gridlocked all day long. But you could drive and *ja*, it was different. Much more free. And just beyond Johannesburg, there wasn't much for miles and miles. You could go out there, I think it's completely surrounded by suburbia now, there was the Lion Park. The famous Lion Park, a favourite place ... you could drive the little hill and just over the hill there was buck and lots of birds and you could go and play with the little baby lions. It was a great adventure for us. You can't do that in England. So, *ja*. *Ja* [sighs] ... I remember my mother sort of saying to me when I had to visit back because my father was ill, 'Well you have had your trip and seen Africa now. When are you back?' 'I am not coming back!' ... Perhaps it isn't about the place being so different but it's about getting out and being an individual on your own. Doing your own sort of thing .... [pause] It was easier to come here than it was to, sort of, move to another town or city in London. That would have been, 'Why do you want to leave home? What's wrong with us? With our home? Here in Guildford?' If you were going to emigrate, you can't ask that because of course, because of course you are going to get so much more by going to a complete and total new country. New job. New people. New scenery. New everything.

His mention of the hills, the animals in the Lion Park and the birds echo the affinity with the landscape and wildlife of southern Africa in the Robsons' narrative. The sense of freedom and adventure that the African landscape signifies in these accounts functions in two primary ways. One is to serve as a claim-making device. In a twist to the way Bill Schwarz shows that the 'incessant claim' to 'know the native' reflected the self-justified authority of settlers to rule during the colonial period, to state that you could live 'like an African' is to say that you possess a deep understanding of Africa and its wildlife and that you belong there even after the colonial order has collapsed.[30] The other is to express nostalgia for Rhodesia and apartheid South Africa in a way that elides the racial politics and exploitation that enabled the privileged lifestyle of the ruling minority in those states.[31]

Conclusion

British post-war migrants are more scattered around the globe and more likely to have remained in Africa than other 'orphans of empire', even if not necessarily in the place to which they originally moved. But it is clear that British people who moved to Africa in the mid-twentieth century, though less visible than the *retornados* or other groups such as the *pieds noirs* of Algeria, share much in common with them. As these oral histories reflect, many felt displaced and unmoored. Their sense of identity is fluid, influenced by both large-scale political events such as UDI and personal ones such as a move from Rhodesia to South Africa or the United States. Many expressed nostalgia for the landscape and wildlife of southern Africa, which became a way to discuss the losses entailed by decolonisation and to mourn the end of the privileged lifestyle of the white minority without addressing race or politics explicitly. The material culture of decolonisation often focused on signifiers of 'the bush', whether the inflatable crocodiles in the Las Vegas pool at the Rhodesian reunion or paintings of elephants and lions and baobab trees. While much of the ambivalence and fluidity in identity described above comes from the individual experience of migration, it was also shaped, though often in unexpected ways, by the end first of British and then finally of white rule.

Examining the experiences of white settlers in southern Africa illustrates the complex consequences of political decolonisation which, in South Africa and Zimbabwe, occurred twice, with very different implications for the populations of these countries: first, reinforcing white settler identities, and then diminishing them. This layered process of decolonisation and especially the first stage, which served to disassociate British migrants in southern Africa from the United Kingdom, has served to obscure their experience of decolonisation. That many moved multiple times means that their experience of and contribution to shaping cultures of decolonisation is difficult to perceive without attention to the individual stories and reflections provided by oral history. The material presented here highlights decolonisation as an identity-making process, in which some people and practices are included in the new order and others rejected. Identities are performed through cultures of association, sociability, ceremony, accent and interior decoration; therefore, oral history evidence can help us to understand the ways in which decolonisation was experienced, negotiated and contested, by different communities and individuals caught up in the political transitions that marked the end of empire.

Notes

This chapter is based on research funded by the Institute for Historical Research, the University of California and the American Historical Association.

1 See R. Bickers (ed.), *Settlers and Expatriates: Britons over the Seas* (Oxford: Oxford University Press, 2010), especially the chapters by Elizabeth Buettner and John Darwin. For work on French and Portuguese 'repatriates' see A.L. Smith (ed.), *Europe's Invisible Migrants* (Amsterdam: Amsterdam University Press, 2003).
2 Between 1945 and 1994, 481,434 migrants arrived in South Africa listing their previous country of residence as Britain: figures for 1939 to 1948 from Union of South Africa, *Statistics of Migration 1948* (Pretoria: The Government Printer, 1950), p. 43; figure for 1949 calculated based on specific data for the years 1945 to 1948 as above and a figure for the period 1945–49 presented in Republic of South Africa, *Report No. 286: Statistics of Immigrants and Emigrants 1924–1964* (Pretoria: Government Printer, 1964), p. 3; figures for 1950 to 1960 from Republic of South Africa, *Report No. 286*, p. 4; figures for 1961 to 1969 taken from Republic of South Africa Department of Statistics, *Report No. 19-01-01, Migration Statistics: Immigrants and Emigrants, 1966 to 1969* (Pretoria: Government Printer, 1969), p. 1; figures for 1970 to 2004 taken from S. Peberdy, *Selecting Immigrants: National Identity and South Africa's Immigration Policies, 1910–2008* (Johannesburg: Wits University Press, 2009), pp. 276–90. Immigration statistics were not collected systematically for country of previous residence, citizenship or birth for Southern Rhodesia/Rhodesia. Figures for 1946 to 1953 taken from Cory Library, Rhodes University, Grahamstown, Ian Smith Papers, Deposit 1/78/002, Southern Rhodesia Cabinet Memoranda 1953, 'Memorandum on Immigration'. Figure for 1954 is an estimate from A.S. Mlambo, *White Immigration into Rhodesia from Occupation to Federation* (Harare: University of Zimbabwe Publications, 2002), p. 8. Figures for 1955 to 1970 taken from *Monthly Migration and Tourist Statistics for March, 1970* (Salisbury: Central Statistics Office, 1970), p. 1. Figures from 1971 to 1979 taken from J. Brownell, *The Collapse of Rhodesia: Population Demographics and the Politics of Race* (London: I.B. Tauris, 2011), p. 125.
3 D. Lambert and A. Lester, 'Introduction: Imperial Spaces, Imperial Subjects', in D. Lambert and A. Lester (eds), *Colonial Lives Across the British Empire: Imperial Careering in the Long Nineteenth Century* (Cambridge: Cambridge University Press, 2006), p. 27.
4 Lambert and Lester, 'Introduction', p. 26.

5   E. Buettner, *Empire Families: Britons and Late Imperial India* (Oxford: Oxford University Press, 2004), pp. 188–251.
6   A.L. Smith, 'Introduction', in Smith, *Europe's Invisible Migrants*, p. 25. See also S.C. Lubkemann, 'Race, Class and Kin in the Negotiation of "Internal Strangerhood" Among Portuguese Retornados, 1975–2000', in Smith, *Europe's Invisible Migrants*, pp. 75–94; S.C. Lubkemann, 'Unsettling the Metropole: Race and Settler Reincorporation in Postcolonial Portugal', in C. Elkins and S. Pederson (eds), *Settler Colonialism in the Twentieth Century* (New York: Routledge, 2005), pp. 257–70; K. Middlemas, 'Twentieth Century White Society in Mozambique', *Tarikh*, 6:2 (1979), 44; R.E. Ovalle-Bahamón, 'The Wrinkles of Decolonization and Nationness: White Angolans as Retornados in Portugal', in Smith, *Europe's Invisible Migrants*, pp. 147–68.
7   A. Portelli, 'What Makes Oral History Different', in A. Thomson (ed.), *The Oral History Reader* (New York: Routledge, 2006), pp. 32–42; S.F. Miescher, *Making Men in Ghana* (Bloomington and Indianapolis: Indiana University Press, 2003), p. 14.
8   I left the decision about whether to use a pseudonym up to the individual interviewee; where this is the case I have noted it.
9   A.J. Hammerton and A. Thomson, *Ten Pound Poms: Australia's Invisible Migrants* (Manchester: Manchester University Press, 2005), p. 341.
10 Ellen Boucher described a similar sense of dislocation in relation to child migrants to Rhodesia, E. Boucher, *Empire's Children: Child Emigration, Welfare, and the Decline of the British World, 1869–1967* (Cambridge: Cambridge University Press, 2014), pp. 236–41, 249–58.
11 Interview with A. Smith, London, UK, 22 July 2009.
12 Boucher, *Empire's Children*; G. Sherington and C. Jeffery, *Fairbridge: Empire and Child Migration* (London: Woburn Press, 1998).
13 Interview with William Jervois, Grahamstown, South Africa, 20 April 2011.
14 Alois Mlambo attributes this to the proximity of Afrikanerdom, that in Rhodesia settler nationalism took on a distinctly British character in opposition to an expansionist South Africa. Mlambo, *White Immigration into Rhodesia from Occupation to Federation*, p. 51.
15 Interview with William Jervois, Grahamstown, South Africa, 20 April 2011.
16 Interview with Brien Bonnynge, Randburg, South Africa, 3 April 2011.
17 On the coalescence of white Rhodesian national identity after UDI see Brownell, *The Collapse of Rhodesia*, p. 16.
18 Interview with Brien Bonnynge, Randburg, South Africa, 3 April 2011.
19 A. Fuller, *Cocktail Hour Under the Tree of Forgetfulness* (London: Simon and Schuster, 2011), p. 159.
20 A. Woollacott, *To Try her Fortune in London: Australian Women, Colonialism and Modernity* (Oxford: Oxford University Press, 2001), p. 14.
21 Ellen Boucher found a similar trend in the memoirs of child migrants to Rhodesia (Boucher, *Empire's Children*, pp. 228–9).
22 D. McDermott Hughes, *Whiteness in Zimbabwe: Race, Landscape and the Problem of Belonging* (New York: Palgrave Macmillan, 2010).
23 Interview with Harold and Thelma Robson, California, 3 October 2009. At the interviewees' request, these names are pseudonyms.
24 Interview with William Jervois, Grahamstown, South Africa, 20 April 2011.
25 Interview with Harold and Thelma Robson, California, 3 October 2009.
26 For more on the connection between domestic decoration and display and self-presentation and identity see C. Wintle, 'Career Development: Domestic Display as Imperial, Anthropological and Social Trophy', *Victorian Studies*, 50:2 (2008), 279–88; D. Cohen, *Household Gods: The British and their Possessions* (New Haven: Yale University Press, 2006).
27 See reports of these events for 2011 and 2009 respectively in the newsletters: 'The 31st Annual Reunion in Las Vegas – Report', *Rhodesian Association of North America Newsletter* (2011); M. Kondourajian, 'The 2009 Annual Rhodesian

Reunion in Las Vegas Revisited', *Rhodesian Association of North America Newsletter* (2009).
28 At the interviewee's request, this name is a pseudonym.
29 Interview with Ian Jones, Grahamstown, South Africa, 16 April 2011.
30 B. Schwarz, *The White Man's World* (Oxford: Oxford University Press, 2011), p. 22.
31 Will Jackson has identified a similar phenomenon in relation to nostalgia for colonial Kenya (W. Jackson, 'White Man's Country: Kenya Colony and the Making of a Myth', *Journal of East African Studies*, 5:2 (2011), 344–68).

PART III

Decolonising expertise

CHAPTER EIGHT

Managing the cultural past in the newly independent states of Mali and Ghana

Sophie Mew

The transition from colonial- to self-rule in West Africa generated new interpretations of public culture that were shaped according to the innovative agendas and approaches of shifting governments. In Mali and Ghana in the 1950s and 1960s, national museums were viewed by some as vehicles of the state, prized for their potential ability to serve the nation and to reach and shape its citizens. They were, however, ambiguously received. This chapter analyses the role of public cultures of display in nation-building, providing a historical account of the processes of decolonisation through the lens of museum practice in West Africa. The National Museum of Ghana and the Musée National du Mali are discussed as central case studies, with the trajectories of these institutions contextualised within the relatively short but crucially important decade surrounding independence. Both museums' relative marginalisation by local audiences at the time is considered in light of a final case study – the Semaines de la Jeunesse (or *semaines culturelles*) – a series of week-long festivals launched in Mali shortly after independence. Simultaneously celebrating the nation's material heritage as well as promoting its modernisation projects, these festivals enjoyed huge success, attracting significant audience participation. The study of these events and cultural institutions in Mali and Ghana informs the study of cultures of decolonisation: through a focus on their design and reception we can question how the cultural past was negotiated, remembered and forgotten during the construction of new nation-states in West Africa.

All museums necessarily edit and sanitise the past and, through the dissemination of their constructed narratives, can be effective in shaping particular communal memories and identities.[1] They can be used as powerful instruments with which to legitimise and promote specific interests in the present, including the construction of the postcolonial nation – yet, despite this power, they can also be ignored.

Audiences can choose to read their own curatorial narratives into particular displays, or they can remain absent from such sites entirely. Yet even where cultural institutions are dismissed by their potential audiences, they remain significant as indicators of popular sentiment. Museums have often been seen as powerful symbols of the nation and its modern history: the rejection of these sites is therefore a strong ideological statement. This chapter examines some of the reasons why the museums of Ghana and Mali did not play a more prominent role in the processes of decolonisation, when they might well have been expected to. As such, the museum itself is considered here as 'an artifact'[2] that provides a fascinating window on public perceptions. It also enables a reflexive interpretation of the making of communities and societies within the contexts of decolonisation.

This chapter draws on semi-structured interviews with two professionals involved in the construction of cultural heritage in Mali shortly after independence. Abdoulaye Sylla was an employee at the Musée National du Mali in the 1960s and 1970s, and eventually became deputy director of the institution before his recent retirement. Over several interviews, Sylla provided insight into what it was like to work for the museum at the time and was particularly vocal in his recollections of its reputation. Sada Samake, a retired youth inspector, was also interviewed at length at his home in 2010. Samake had participated in the first ever *semaine culturelle* and had helped to coordinate all of the festivals thereafter until their conclusion in 1968. He provided a fascinating oral testimony on the subject, describing in detail how it felt to be part of such a large movement at the time and to participate directly in these events. He shared his own and his friends' excitement for the future of the Malian nation as well as their strong anti-colonial sentiments. While providing revealing insights, both Sylla and Samake's oral testimonies also raise certain challenges in terms of historical accuracy. These accounts are personal memories of events that happened over fifty years earlier and represent the perspectives of those who worked to promote the museum and the festivals as successful ventures. This chapter therefore combines interviews with contemporary newspaper reports and the political speeches of presidents Kwame Nkrumah and Modibo Keïta, drawing on a range of (albeit still partial) perspectives to contextualise their words.

Historical trajectories of decolonisation in West Africa

Before discussing these cultural sites, this chapter offers an overview of the years preceding and immediately following the dates of independence of 6 March 1957 for Ghana and 22 September 1960 for Mali, in order to provide an understanding of the 'social contexts'[3] within which cultural practitioners operated. Despite the continued extraction of Ghanaian resources for metropolitan reconstruction by Europeans, the post-Second World War period in the Gold Coast, as Ghana was then known, was notable for its relatively conciliatory policies. Investment in infrastructure led to improved paved roads, extended railways, more housing projects and greater access to potable water in rural areas. There was a surplus of goods on the market, production rose, training schools multiplied and primary school education was made free and compulsory for those aged six to twelve years. Increased opportunities developed for the intellectual elite to reassert themselves and to promote their visions for an independent future. However, in 1947 a campaign was launched against the large Lebanese-owned firms based in the Gold Coast, leading to an embargo in January 1948 and serious riots taking place. An economic depression set off more strikes and protests when crop prices soared; regular boycotts were staged against expatriate trading companies and against imported goods. The cocoa swollen-shoot virus in the late 1940s triggered a slump in production, resulting in mass inflation, and discontented farmers sided with the expanding local intelligentsia who highlighted the farmers' predicaments. With unemployment high, and the return of soldiers from Burma and the Middle East, the situation provided a fertile ground for nationalist agitation.[4]

Students returning from overseas after the war were also influenced by the radical activities and ideas that were circulating abroad. Kwame Nkrumah (prime minister, 1952–60; president, 1960–66) himself returned from the US, where he had encountered Civil Rights and nascent Black Power philosophies, and the UK, where he had been involved in the militant West African Students Union.[5] Supported by the frustration of the masses and by an emergent class of individuals seeking emancipation and change, the students highlighted the cause for nationalism and promoted independence. The rise in national political consciousness took shape across all of West Africa throughout the 1950s. African intellectuals Léopold Senghor (in Senegal and co-founder of the *négritude* movement with Aimé Césaire), Houphouët-Boigny (in the Ivory Coast), Sekou Touré (in Guinea) and Kwame Nkrumah sought, albeit in different ways, to gain autonomy in West African relations with their colonial governments. Kwame Nkrumah and his party (the United Gold Coast Convention, from which he split to form the Convention People's Party – CPP) were instrumental in providing political freedom and the British with a means of transferring power. During the elections of 1956 the CPP gained victory, allowing Nkrumah to call for independence from Britain. The date for the inauguration of the independent state of Ghana was set for 6 March 1957.

Mali, or the French Sudan as it was then known, gained independence three years after Ghana and followed a similar trajectory with regards to the impact of an emergent elite, discontent from large sections of the population and disillusionment following the return of the *tirailleurs sénégalais* (West African soldiers) from the war. Opposition to continued French governance came from bureaucratic classes and traders who organised themselves into syndicates.[6] Mobilisation also came from a range of groupings, ethnicised in part by French colonial occupation, that included Bamana speakers in the south, Tuareg speakers in the north and the Muslim sect known as the Hamallists in the west. From the 1930s onwards, elite constituencies in urban centres formed voluntary organisations that were promoted under the guise of sporting or cultural organisations. They strategically provided a forum for discussing political affairs and formed the basis for political parties that negotiated the eventual break from French rule.

In 1937 Mamadou Konate established the first trade union – for teachers – in the Sudan. He became head of the Union Soudanaise political party in 1945 whilst, Fily Dabo Sissoko founded the Parti Progressiste Soudanais (PPS). The Union Soudanaise stood firmly against French colonial rule and affiliated itself with the Pan-African Rassemblement Démocratique Africain (RDA) set up by Modibo Keïta, mayor of Bamako in 1956.[7] General elections were held across the Sudan in 1956 and won by the RDA and the Union Soudanaise. The PPS joined the Union Soudanaise and RDA in 1959. Following Konate's death that year, Modibo Keïta took up the leadership and guided the nation towards independence. In 1958 the French had offered all its West African colonies a referendum for independence, an option that only Sékou Toure in Guinea claimed, but for two years the Sudan was semi-autonomous. Following a three-month union with Senegal, on 22 September 1960 the Sudan renamed itself 'Mali' and gained its complete independence, with Keïta ruling as president via a single-party system.

After independence, Nkrumah in Ghana and Keïta in Mali sought to consolidate their countries as autonomous nation-states through the development of vital infrastructure, economic regeneration (through cash crops and mining) and improving access to education for all. There was a huge rise in population and extensive migration within Ghana to the wealthier southern and coastal areas and from rural to urban settings. There were severe economic disparities as the divide between the wealthy and the poor widened and discontent rose from both the urban and rural masses. This became a particular concern for Nkrumah, who initially placed unity and unifying the nation-state as one of his main priorities. Mali, on the other hand, remained an overwhelmingly rural economy. The French had left a limited industrial legacy and, after its split with Senegal, Mali became a landlocked nation with seven borders and suffered from a series of related economic consequences in terms of possibilities for export.

Following Malian independence in 1960, Keïta invested heavily in infrastructure and factories in order to intensify agriculture, stimulate mining research and build up a state-controlled economy. Just as in Ghana, in order to appeal to a sense of unity across the nation, the colonial regime and the commercial model of capitalism were actively rejected in favour of a socialist approach. Culture arenas were a crucial part of this dynamic rejuvenation. In an interview in February 2010, Abdoulaye Sylla explained how he and his friends and colleagues 'were proud of being independent and we wanted to follow in the footsteps of the great [pre-colonial] figures'.[8] Yet the museum – as we shall now see – formed only a limited component of this cultural framework.

The formation of the National Museum of Ghana

The National Museum of Ghana opened to the public on Barnes Road in Adabraka, Accra, on the eve of independence and was inaugurated by HRH the Duchess of Kent. The museum building was designed by Denys Lasdun, a British architect with Fry, Drew, Drake & Lasdun, the firm that had received commissions for public buildings such as schools, banks, department stores, new houses and even villages across the Gold Coast, the Punjab, Togo and Nigeria throughout the 1950s. The museum's structure was centred upon a striking dome that recalled the similar structure in London designed for the Festival of Britain in 1951; highly uncharacteristic of architecture in Ghana at the time, it introduced an alien and Eurocentric construction to the local landscape.[9] Within the museum, the exhibits of archaeological specimens and Ashanti regalia, stools, *kente* cloth, swords and drums were displayed inside glass cases that had been imported from Europe. They were set out in sequential order in a circular exhibition gallery that was described as 'inflexible' by an exhibition curator who had travelled from London's Guildhall Museum and 'cumbersome' by Richard Nunoo, the museum's African first director.[10]

Although the museum was not inaugurated until 1957, over thirty years of earlier efforts, discussions and debates from a myriad of British teachers, educators, anthropologists, archaeologists, colonial officers and curators, and a range of disciplinary and institutional perspectives, would contribute to the formulation of the National Museum. The European parties involved were convinced of their duty to conserve Ghanaian cultural heritage in the face of perceived rapid acculturation, and the displays thus reflected specific historical values that were influenced by the 'salvage' paradigm[11] practised by some European collectors in the 1930s. They promoted a particular indigenous material culture that tended to valorise the preservation of distant cultural pasts.[12] The five thousand objects that made up the original museum collection founded at Achimota College (a co-ed school and the Gold Coast's first university) in 1929 were mainly archaeological specimens that had been dug up during the construction of the college and ethnographic donations contributed by colonial administrators and their their widows, missionaries, British firms with a presence in Ghana (such as Cadbury's) and local community leaders whose offerings were solicited by European organisers.[13]

Drawing on this legacy, the National Museum, when it eventually opened, was conceptualised as a space to restore pride and dignity by looking 'back' towards the achievements of the pre-colonial past. Yet the often arbitrary boundaries separating communities across West Africa, defined and emphasised by British colonial officials, were also incorporated as an ideological element into the museum in a system of 'separating things',[14] of classifying and constructing social boundaries and of playing social units off against each other. This, of course, was part of a wider trend of delineating and imagining 'an Africa' according to colonial conceptualisations of unitary 'tribes' and 'traditions' that had long helped to produce static and essentialised categories across the continent.[15] The National Museum of Ghana's first public exhibition at independence, 'Man in Africa', for example, assembled collections according to European-style classifications and traced the origins of the Gold Coast people beyond national boundaries. Notably, in doing so, it moved beyond the new state borders inaugurated at independence, stressing the complex ethnicities contained by the Gold Coast (such as the peoples of the Ashanti region and the Northern Territories, and the Ewe people, whose land was split by the Gold Coast–Togo border). How processes of reflection and nostalgia were integrated into the contemporary political ideologies of the new government and thus, by implication, how the cultural past was managed alongside Ghana's emerging modern identity during the decolonisation period, remain key considerations throughout this chapter.

The constitutional and cultural changes that occurred in Ghana at the time of independence were gradual processes that had begun well before 1957 and continued thereafter, yet the moment of independence saw a decisive shift in identity politics that was fundamentally rooted in cultural infrastructure. It was now all the more necessary for Nkrumah to redefine colonial interpretations and to consolidate the diversity of emergent ethnic identities – both collective and individual – within a wider sense of national identity that could be governable and economically sustainable. Based on his perceived need for centralisation, there was a focus on constructing a collective sense of belonging across linguistic and cultural differences. The National Museum, however, remained divisive due to its cumbersome colonial legacy. As suggested, it continued to display peoples and their artefacts according to an origin and 'type' delineated by colonial anthropology. These ideas were communicated to visitors through display areas which demarcated specific social units, and individual cases which were allocated to groupings framed by anthropologists of the colonial era. Further challenges arose as the museum was confronted by a sudden lack of funding and trained personnel, and was unable to provide adequate public services such as acquiring artefacts, developing exhibitions or carrying out valuable research. There was uncertainty over the institution's purpose and how to redefine it according to the new contexts of nation-building; as David Aradeon has explained, all across West Africa, museum professionals inherited such institutions from their colonial predecessors whose missions were not sufficiently understood.[16] Despite the ideology of decolonisation, it became evident that there was a lack of clear strategy for the museum from the new government. Representing and preserving a people's history through material culture in a national museum would be a highly sensitive, complex and political challenge.[17] The National Museum of Ghana could have been a key site for shaping collective identities – regional, national and/or pan-African – but in the end, it struggled to fulfil the difficult task of mediating state policy, negotiating the complex nature of 'national identity' and appealing to multiple identities on different levels.

Ghanaian artist Kojo Fosu has since emphasised the utility of the arts during the twentieth century in 'consolidat[ing] the identifying bonds of kinship and nationalism among the varying ethnic compositions of ... new nations'.[18] However, the exclusion of arts specialists within Nkrumah's government administration suggests a more complex political interpretation of the role of culture in Ghana at this time.[19] During his presidency, Nkrumah expressed enthusiasm for arts and cultural institutions and, according to Y.A. Nyameh, a journalist reflecting on the period in 1989, firmly believed in the potential of national museums.[20] In 1963 the Museum of Science and Technology (MST) opened in Accra and, in his review of the renovations, Richard Nunoo, the National Museum's director from 1961, stated that Nkrumah was 'personally interested' in designing and building extensions for the institution.[21] There is little doubt of Nkrumah's vision and support for cultural institutions: he founded a number that celebrated the arts and cultures of Ghana and used them to promote a sense of nationalist pride, and, later, emphasise his ideas surrounding pan-Africanism. These new organisations included the Arts Council of Ghana (established in 1957), the Research Library on African Affairs which opened in 1961 and the Institute of Arts and Culture, formed in 1962. Similarly, the Institute of African Studies was inaugurated at the University of Ghana in 1963, followed by the Ghana Film Corporation in 1964 and the Ministry of Arts and Culture in 1965. However, the museum did not receive comparable support.

Nkrumah's desire to promote national unity through culture (for example, through his wearing of *kente* cloth and the northern smock, the *batakari*) may have helped to serve the museums in Ghana, yet the relationship between material culture and the political tensions imbued in the ethnic makeup of a postcolonial Ghana discouraged him and his party from becoming directly involved in the National Museum or from establishing firm policies in this field.[22] The highly controversial Avoidance of Discrimination Act of 1957, for example, sought to ban political parties where they were based on divisive religious, regional or ethnic foundations; regional flags[23] and emblems – many of which were represented in the museum's collections – were also proscribed. Later, as Nkrumah encountered difficulties in consolidating his socialist visions for the nation against his country's more reactionary groupings – including those which he identified as 'traditional' chiefs – the display of these communities' material cultures in the museum clashed with his desire to rid his new nation of these 'interfering' factions. Another source of divisive tension emerged from the cocoa-rich Ashanti region, again, richly represented by the museum's collections. Not only did these ethnic groups, and by extension their material culture, challenge Nkrumah's political authority, but they also hindered attempts to draw upon the cultural past in order to project a united future collective. Evidence of these various political difficulties was thus prominent in the galleries of the National Museum: visible in the collections, the style of display and labels, and orientation in the galleries. In neglecting to revisit its collections and displays following independence, the museum provided little opportunity for expunging the elements of Ghana's cultural history that were incompatible with Nkrumah's vision for the new nation-state.

This raises the question of whether and how, given the political complexities and social realities involved, the museum could possibly conceptually (re-)position itself at this stage. George Hagan has effectively summarised a broader dilemma that applies in this context, stating that 'Nkrumah would have liked to abolish tribalism; but how does one root out tribal identity without erasing the culture that gives the African his cultural identity and awareness?'[24] Mark Crinson has also highlighted the difficulties that Nkrumahist political ideologies faced with regard to celebrating the wealth and the diversity of indigenous cultures.[25] As both Hagan and Cati Coe have inferred for other cultural forms, despite concerted efforts to cultivate a renewed sense of cultural identity across Ghana through education, public display and the establishment of cultural institutions, Nkrumah generated a *philosophy* of an African personality but no official *policies*.[26] Further, Hagan has concluded that 'historical evidence shows that many of these institutions had come into being before [Nkrumah] had formulated any cultural policies to guide their operations' and this continued throughout his presidency.[27] It was not, for example, until 1975, three years after Nkrumah had died, that the first official government document outlining cultural policies in Ghana was produced.[28] This lack of clear direction seriously affected the management of cultural heritage, the development and the ensuing marginalisation of the National Museum during the processes of decolonisation.

The formation of the National Museum of Mali

The Musée Ethnologique et Archéologique du Soudan was founded in Bamako, Mali, in 1951 and renamed the Musée National du Mali at independence in 1960. Its implementation drew direction from the model of the Institut Fondamental d'Afrique Noire (IFAN), a research institution that was established in Dakar, Senegal, in the late 1930s. The collections and exhibitionary practices at the museum thus – like the National Museum of Ghana – pre-dated its inauguration by over thirty years, and this next section details some of the expeditions and institutions that were influential in shaping the future Musée National in Bamako.

As in Ghana, early twentieth-century French administrators and ethnographers in Mali were swayed by a strong sense of urgency to preserve cultural artefacts before they disappeared. Such artefacts still form the core collections of many cultural institutions both in France and in current-day Mali, and include wood carvings of doors, house posts, ancestral figures and religious masks. Throughout the colonial period, collections were assembled for export to the museums and colleges in France, but objects began to remain in the territories and were kept for safeguarding *in situ* from the inter-war period onwards. By the late 1920s with the rise of collecting missions, the methods of acquisition became increasingly methodological and, as the discipline of ethnography matured, collectors employed collections as a coherent mode of representation, drawing on them as *'pièces à conviction'*.[29] Vast amounts of works were reinterpreted according to ethnographic testimonies to 'native' ways of life. They were reproduced in journals and, once they found their way into museums, were given labels that again, as in Ghana, denoted identities and boundaries that corresponded to neat colonial categories, or 'types'. Mary Jo Arnoldi has reflected that the 'bounded entities' presented in the Musée National du Mali 'masks the complexity of people's lived experience in both historical and contemporary Mali'.[30] Indeed, after independence, the museum continued to adhere to fixed delineations of identities rooted in colonial interpretations, which failed to adhere to the changing notions of identities and belonging in the postcolonial nation-state.

Arguably the most significant event to shape French ethnography in relation to West African collections was the major fieldwork expedition, the Dakar-Djibouti mission carried out by ethnographer Marcel Griaule and his team following the opening of the colonial exhibition in Paris in 1931. IFAN was launched in Dakar seven years after the mission, with Theodore Monod, the celebrated naturalist and former employee of the Muséum d'Histoire Naturelle in Paris, appointed as the institute's first director. The Benin-born Alexandre Adandé was employed in the museum section. Collecting began in 1941 and Monod rapidly conceived that IFAN should act as a centralised institution for satellite offices with small museums attached across all the capital cities of the territories of French West Africa. They were subsequently created throughout the 1940s and 1950s, from Saint Louis in Senegal to Niamey in Niger.

The IFAN branch of Bamako was set up in 1951 and two years later a small embryo museum opened to the public at the Ecole des Travaux Publics on 14 February 1953. It was inaugurated by the French high commissioner, Bernard Cornut-Gentille, and named the Musée Soudanais de Bamako.[31] The first appointed director was Polish archaeologist George Szumowski and the collections were heavily biased towards his own archaeological (and some ethnographic) finds from the region (approximately 2,500 in total, with 2,350 archaeological pieces).[32] According to a report in the daily newspaper,[33] geological and ornithological items were later added in an attempt to entice local audiences, as archaeological collections were perceived as being quite difficult to access for the untrained general public. Despite this, while few records exist in newspaper archives on how the museum was received in its early years, visitor figures were probably low. In 1955, the French geographer, Gerard Brasseur, became director and was able to enrich the collections due to a stricter regime for export licences at the time. The institution relocated to a small gallery space in Bamako's zoological gardens in 1958 and at independence was renamed the Musée National du Mali and associated with the Institut des Sciences Humaines. In its final move in 1977, the collections were transferred nearby, to the museum's current location north of the city near the government administrative offices.

The museum suffered during the decolonisation period in part due to a lack of interest from the public, poorly trained museum personnel, a lack of appropriate facilities and funding and declining collections.[34] The museum was not used as a public space for the display of material culture, but rather it gained the reputation as a storehouse or as a necessary site required of all nations. It was not until the directorship of the Malian historian Kléna Sanogo began in 1973 that the museum started to receive its due attention. Indeed, a later director, Claude Ardouin, argued that it was the intervention of A.O. Konaré, the archaeologist and future president of Mali, three years later that allowed the public dimension of the museum to be fully addressed.[35] At a seminar on museums and cultural heritage in Mali in May 1976, participants advocated the construction of a new national museum and the creation of regional institutions to promote 'the democratisation and decentralisation of the museum'.[36] A newspaper reporter who attended the seminar declared that much remained to be done to improve the situation and described the Musée National as a 'mouldy depository'.[37] Notably, he concluded by advocating its restoration and associating the fight for the museum with the fight for national dignity. This view of the role of the museum as the guardian of cultural heritage for the nation and its duty to promote the unity of the nation-state was not, however, made apparent at an earlier stage, during decolonisation.

Throughout his presidency, following independence, Modibo Keïta appealed strongly to a sense of unity of the nation, and the colonial regime was actively rejected. As the economy declined and riots erupted in 1962, many of Keïta's unification projects fell through; there were problems with the newly introduced national currency, and the Tuareg in the north of the country also expressed resistance to the over-centralised system of power in the capital. However, while the movement towards one-party state control had dire consequences for the economy and led to a military bloodless coup six years later (in 1968), this period had great influence on state-sponsored social and cultural movements. The role of the state was paramount in orchestrating celebrations of nationalist excitement, though, tellingly, museums continued to remain marginal to this. The Stade Omnisport Modibo Keïta, with capacity for 25,000 people, was completed in 1965, the Institut National des Arts was inaugurated in 1966, and the national theatre troupe of Mali was set up in 1959, with the national theatre completed in 1969. Keïta invested extensively in the promotion of youth, education and sport, and, according to an interview with Samake encouraged Malians to 'take what we have ... tools et cetera, and construct the nation'.[38] While these efforts led to a plethora of youth organisations and activities, this cultural revolution did not include the Musée National, the situation of which remained sluggish.

Keïta believed that his 'ethnically unifying' policies and strong national identity were attainable due, in part, to Mali's long-standing reputation as a 'melting pot' of African, Berber and Arab cultures.[39] He appealed to the common historically distant as well as recent, regional and ethnic heritage of the nation, drawing on historical figures from Soundiata Keïta (Bamana), el Hadj Oumar (Tukulor from Senegal), Amadou Tall (Peuhl), to Samoury Touré (from Guinea), to cite just a few shared heroes. Keïta focused heavily on the liberated African and his position in relation to his former 'colonial masters'. His political theory of 'the decolonisation of our mentality'[40] drawn from the ideologies of *négritude* carried important legacies that focused on inclusive and heterogeneous roots for the Malian state.[41] During this period the new regime in Mali actively sought to reintegrate its pre-colonial heroes into the collective psyche and to reorganise its rich past by looking towards the future.[42] Ultimately, this was something that the museum did not do.

The museum instead served as a reminder of the old regime and failed to partake in the remaking of the colonial past through what Richard Werbner has referred to as 'anti-memory', or a politics of forgetting.[43] Elsewhere, the red, gold and green flag for the Sudan was reappropriated with the political slogan 'One people, one goal, one faith', and the celebrated author Seydou Badian Kouyate composed a new national anthem; streets and squares were renamed and statues were removed or rebuilt according to the resurrected memories of past indigenous figures. Yet when the 1933 statue of Borgnis-Desbordes, the former French *commandant-supérieur*, was pulled down, such was the perception of the museum that it was deemed appropriate to relocate the statue to its grounds.[44] In his work *Vestiges of the Colonial Empire in France*, Robert Aldrich tackles the ways in which the colonial past was actively forgotten in museums and art galleries across France; he describes how colonial works were 'packed away in storerooms', 'treated with shame', artists were forgotten, collections 'mothball[ed]' and vestiges were 'banished in an effort to forget the colonial past'.[45] These were important active and collective means of dealing with the colonial past in museums in France, and similar processes were reflected in the Malian state's endeavours towards 'anti-memory' – through the adaptation of history schoolbooks in order to cultivate nationalist pride and to help counteract previous interpretations, for example. Keïta increased the education budget and in 1968 implemented a national language (Bamanan) as a written language for the first time. However, in contrast to Aldrich's claims for France, in Mali the museum remained on the margins of these processes, in part because of its inability to redefine its role or incorporate new displays. Instead it retained outmoded representations of identities that conflicted with the new social environment.

Rather than playing an active role in unifying the nation and joining in the processes of constructing the state, overall, according to Sylla, during Modibo Keïta's presidency, the conservation of material culture in Mali, including at the museum, was severely neglected: there simply was no significant local interest in the collection itself nor in the display of material culture in museums, and the authorities remained indifferent to what happened to the institution.[46] Sylla decried, 'they didn't give a damn, it had become a place for storing presents [for visiting VIPs to the country]!'[47] The situation continued well into the mid-1970s, with artefacts badly preserved and frequently lost or stolen. The collections dwindled from an estimated 15,000 items to 1,500 between 1964 and 1975.[48] There were extraordinary accounts of widespread and blatant looting and, by 1975, the collections were split up and distributed across four venues in Bamako, including the National Engineering School, the Institut National des Arts and even a private home in Korofina. Through its lack of imagination the museum did not support the wider colonial past and the celebration of modernisation projects; it did not participate in rewriting its singular version of history to welcome the new heroes of independence, nor did it engage with the exciting youth movements that were happening outside of its space. The Musée National did not utilise its limited resources to participate and enhance the processes of decolonisation.

The Semaines de la Jeunesse and the national museums of Mali and Ghana

The national museums in Mali and Ghana seemed to have missed their opportunity to contribute to rebuilding identities in the new nation states. Having examined the ways in which museums did and did not partake in the processes of decolonisation in the previous sections, it is worth considering a cultural phenomenon that did succeed and that was incredibly popular in the years immediately following decolonisation in Mali. The Semaines de la Jeunesse (1962–68) were weeklong festivals of arts, cultures and sport that celebrated the developments of the new state and its modernisation projects as well as championing the regions' material culture and the diversity which made up the new nation. The *semaines* allowed for wide participation by the public; as such, they were inclusive and dynamic events that came into direct contrast with the static position of the Musée National at the time.

The Semaines de la Jeunesse were organised by the Pioneer Youth Movement, an organisation established in 1959 by students across the French Sudan. Young people played a significant role in promoting both nationalism and decolonisation during the middle years of the twentieth century in both Mali and Ghana. In Ghana, for example, in 1960 Nkrumah set up the Young Pioneers,[49] which were instrumental to the development of his political party. In Mali, the Pioneer Youth Movement rivalled the much less popular French-introduced Scouts organisation. The latter had been expressly forbidden to Muslims, and, like the museum, was perceived as a foreign and imported institution and rejected according to the spirit of the new nation. In 1962 the Pioneer Youth Movement organised the first festival; it was attended by over a thousand students. The festivals were always held at the end of the school year and united students from across the nation's ethnic and regional groups, bringing together secondary and primary school pupils to celebrate and promote a unified and national sense of identity and belonging to the Malian state.[50] Wearing a uniform with red berets, singing the national anthem and meeting the president, the students came from rural villages, towns and cities to perform regional songs, dances, music and plays. The state sponsored the orchestras, but otherwise the events were organised and financed by the students themselves.

The *semaines* provided opportunity for young people, rather than museum curators, for example, to act as mediators between the state and the general public and between the urban and the rural areas. Recalling the events, Samake believed that the displays of *boubous* (Malian dress) and plaits, for example, contributed towards providing a positive national outlook. These items could be found displayed in vitrines in the museum, but became animated within the context of the *semaines*, where they formed part of a collective celebration of cultural values that instilled pride in Malian cultural heritage among urban youths. Another integral aspect of the festivals was the staged performances to promote state enterprises. Via these shows, students publicised state products and factories and their merchandise, including tobacco, matchboxes and canned foods.[51] Accordingly, they boosted the nation's economy (and, by comparison, rendered the museum even more redundant). By 1968, there were a staggering 25,000 participants with over 5,000 staged performers.[52]

During the *semaines*, the Musée National exhibited a series of artefacts, including chiefs' staffs that had been brought to the capital by the Young Pioneers with permission from their elders. Museum staff prepared accompanying labels for display and, at the opening events, trained guides explained the exhibits to the visiting heads of state and other members of the government. On the whole, however, these exhibitions did not generate a great deal of local interest: according to Sylla, who was already employed by the museum, the Pioneers' artefacts rarely attracted much enthusiasm and, while the museum had various opportunities to acquire these works through sale, sadly staff did not take up these offers. Indeed, there seems to have been very little consideration given to the role the Musée National could play at the time. The material culture on display continued to refer to distant pasts that left no room for the collective voices of the 'liberated' African.

In his speech entitled 'Cultural Problems of the New Mali',[53] Keïta championed the adaptability of oral and written traditions and music as 'striking and vibrant manifestations of our culture'. His description of these cultural forms recalls the cultural celebrations performed by the youths at the *semaines* and other similar movements, including the plethora of regional orchestras sponsored by the state that gave rise to 'Manding swing' with Cuban and/or jazz beats.[54] In contrast, Keïta cautioned against 'negative elements' of culture that he claimed held a nation back and prevented it from growing. He argued for the rebuilding of Malian national culture, seeking to 'free it from foreign influences that ... hinder its development', and used his article to consider which dynamic 'cultural assets' to integrate in modernisation processes, and which to leave behind. Writing more recently, Adame Bâ Konaré has argued that '[t]he perpetual agitation of the past and its heroes does not permit us to move forward; rather, it leads to the hardening of positions around values that are undoubtedly shared but which belong to another era. Too much remembering can become an obstacle.'[55]

The museums in Mali and Ghana – perhaps in part due to the physical permanence of their buildings, their permanent collections, their inflexible displays and their inherited 'foreign' legacies – were unable to eschew (or to 'forget') the new nations' colonial heritages. Historically, museums have been used in Europe as powerful symbols of the nation and as a means of shaping national identities; case studies abound of their reformatory nature.[56] Yet the narratives from Mali and Ghana presented in this chapter come into conflict with these ideas because wider publics ignored them due to the fact that these institutions did not, or, could not, negotiate the past and contend with the changing society around them. Both practical and ideological challenges confronted the first presidents of Mali and Ghana with regards to integrating their nations' museums – and their institutional pasts – into the construction of the nation. This chapter has contrasted the histories of the national museums of Ghana and Mali with a series of cultural festivals in Mali to further our understanding of why the national museums' roles were ambiguously received during the period of decolonisation. That the *semaines* were so popular but the museums' contents and sites were seen by many as irrelevant, gives great insight into the forms of culture that were required to enact independence. Ultimately, of all the cultures of decolonisation, those events that appeared to eschew colonial references, that remained flexible and provided opportunity for mass participation and active involvement in their planning and delivery, were in great demand. Yet for the historian, the museum remains important as a 'culture of decolonisation' too: it is in the act of rejection that these perceptions are revealed.

Notes

The research for this chapter is part of my PhD fieldwork (2005; 2006–7; 2010), which received support from the funding bodies Central Research Fund; SOAS Additional Fieldwork Research Fund and the Radcliffe-Brown and Firth Fund (RAI).

1. See A. Coombes, *Reinventing Africa: Museums, Material Culture and Popular Imagination in Late Victorian and Edwardian England* (New Haven: Yale University Press, 1994).
2. Jeanne Cannizzo, cited in M.N. Philip, *Frontiers: Selected Essays and Writings on Racism and Culture, 1984–1992* (Stratford: Mercury, 1992), p. 104.

3   'The "social context" in which archaeologists operate' is borrowed and adapted from Bruce Trigger's analysis of nationalist, colonialist and imperialist archaeology. B.G. Trigger, 'Alternative Archaeologies: Nationalist, Colonialist, Imperialist', *Man*, 19:3 (1984), 357.
4   K. Nkrumah, *The Autobiography of Kwame Nkrumah* [with portraits] (Edinburgh: Thomas Nelson & Sons, 1957), p. 74.
5   K. Botwe-Asamoah, *Kwame Nkrumah's Politico-cultural Thought and Policies: An African-centered Paradigm for the Second Phase of the African Revolution* (New York: Routledge, 2005), p. 8.
6   D.T. Niane and J. Suret-Canale, *Histoire de l'Afrique occidentale* (Conakry: Ministère de l'Education Nationale de la République de Guinée, 1960), pp. 134–6.
7   A.R. Blanchet, *L'Itinéraire des parties Africains depuis Bamako* (Paris: Librarie Plon, 1958), p. 202.
8   Author's interview with Abdoulaye Sylla, private address, Bamako, Mali, 12 February 2010.
9   M. Crinson, 'Nation-building, Collecting and the Politics of Display: The National Museum, Ghana', *Journal of the History of Collections*, 13:2 (2001), 233.
10 'In a round building such as this Museum it is not easy to display specimens in any effective systematic order nor is it easy for the visitor to know where to start ...', R. Nunoo, *National Museum of Ghana Handbook: Ethnographical, Historical and Art Collections* (Tema: published for Ghana Museums and Monuments by Ghana Publishing Corporation, 1970), p. 6.
11 J. Clifford, 'On Ethnographic Allegory', in J. Clifford and G.E. Marcus (eds), *Writing Culture: The Poetics and Politics of Ethnography* (Berkeley: University of California Press, 1986), p. 112.
12 See J. Fabian, *Time and the Other: How Anthropology Makes its Object* (New York: Columbia University Press, 1983).
13 F. Agbodeka, *Achimota in the National Setting: A Unique Educational Experiment in West Africa* (Ghana: Afram Publications, 1977), p. 109. By 1951 funds were made available to transfer the collections to the University of Ghana, Legon, but the collection was split three years later between non-Ghanaian and non-African works (staying at the university for pedagogical purposes) and the remaining core collections were transferred to the site at Adabraka, where they remained.
14 R. Goldwater, 'Judgements of Primitive Art, 1905–1965', in D.P. Biebuyck (ed.), *Tradition and Creativity in Tribal Art* (Berkeley: University of California Press, 1969), p. 37.
15 See W. Fagg, 'The African Artist', in Biebuyck, *Tradition and Creativity in Tribal Art*, p. 45; and P. Ravenhill, 'The Passive Object and the Tribal Paradigm: Colonial Museography in French West Africa', in M.J. Arnoldi, C.M. Geary and K.L. Hardin (eds), *African Material Culture* (Bloomington: Indiana University Press, 1996), p. 267.
16 D.E. Aradeon, 'Museums in West Africa: The Impact on Urban Cultures', in A. Adande and E.N. Arinze (eds), *Museums and Urban Culture in West Africa* (Oxford: James Currey, 2002), p. 135.
17 Crinson, 'Nation-building, Collecting and the Politics of Display'.
18 K. Fosu, *Twentieth Century Art of Africa* (Zaria: Gaskiya Corporation, 1986), p. 12.
19 J. Hess, 'Exhibiting Ghana: Display, Documentary and "National" Art in the Nkrumah Era', *African Studies Review*, 44:1 (2001), 63.
20 Y.A. Nyameh, 'Importance of a Museum', *People's Daily Graphic* (18 January 1989), p. 56.
21 R. Nunoo, 'The National Museum of Ghana, Accra', *Museum*, 18:3 (1965), 156.
22 Mark Crinson suggests that Nkrumah may have also regarded the museum with equivocation due to the involvement of his major opponent, Kofi Busia, who was close to the archaeologist A.W. Lawrence, the director of the museum in the late

1950s. See Crinson, 'Nation-building, Collecting and the Politics of Display', 240.
23 Not a reference to Asafo (warrior group) flags.
24 G.P. Hagan, 'Nkrumah's Cultural Policy', in K. Arhin (ed.), *The Life and Work of Kwame Nkrumah: Papers of a Symposium Organised by the Institute of African Studies, University of Ghana, Legon* (Trenton: Africa World Press, 1993), p. 13.
25 Crinson, 'Nation-building, Collecting and the Politics of Display', 240.
26 Hagan, 'Nkrumah's Cultural Policy', p. 8; C. Coe, *Dilemmas of Culture in African Schools: Youth, Nationalism, and the Transformation of Knowledge* (Chicago: University of Chicago Press, 2005), p. 61.
27 Hagan, 'Nkrumah's Cultural Policy', p. 22.
28 *Cultural Policy in Ghana* (Paris: UNESCO Press, 1975).
29 Mission Dakar-Djibouti, *Instructions sommaires pour les collecteurs d'objets ethnographiques* (Paris: Musée d'Ethnographie, 1931), p. 8.
30 M.J. Arnoldi, 'Overcoming a Colonial Legacy: The New National Museum in Mali, 1976 to the Present', *Museum Anthropology*, 22:3 (1999), 34.
31 S. Sidibe, 'L'Exposition au Musée National du Mali', in E. Bassani and G. Speranza (eds), *Arte in Africa 2* (Florence and Milan: Centro Studi di Storia delle Arti Africane Firenze Associazione 'poro' Milano, 1991), p. 174.
32 Musée National du Mali, 'Histoire du Musée', from a site archived in 2009, available at www.oocities.org/infomali/Musee/collecti.htm (accessed 21 April 2015).
33 V. Lescot, 'Du musée soudanais au musée national', *L'Essor* (6 November 2002), p. 4.
34 Arnoldi, 'Overcoming a Colonial Legacy', 28.
35 Author's interview with Claude Ardouin, British Museum, London, UK, 18 February 2010.
36 Arnoldi, 'Overcoming a Colonial Legacy', 28.
37 K. Dembélé, 'Le Rôle des musées dans le développement', *Sunjata* (10 April 1979), p. 11.
38 Author's interview with Sada Samake, private address, Bamako, Mali, 10 February 2010.
39 M. Keïta, 'Speech at the National Assembly 20 January 1961', in M. Keïta, *A Collection of Speeches September 22, 1960–August 27, 1964* (Moscow: n.p., 1965), p. 34.
40 Keïta, 'Speech at the National Assembly 20 January 1961', p. 21.
41 See R. de Jorio, 'Politics of Remembering and Forgetting: The Struggle over Colonial Monuments in Mali', *Africa Today*, 52:4 (2006), 83.
42 V.Y. Mudimbe and B. Jewsiewicki, 'Africans' Memories and Contemporary History of Africa', *History and Theory: Studies in the Philosophy of History*, 32:4 (1993), 2.
43 R.P. Werbner, *Memory and the Postcolony: African Anthropology and the Critique of Power* (London: Zed Books, 1998), p. 74.
44 De Jorio, 'Politics of Remembering and Forgetting', 91.
45 R. Aldrich, *Vestiges of the Colonial Empire in France: Monuments, Museums, and Colonial Memories* (Basingstoke: Palgrave Macmillan, 2004), pp. 211–12, 322
46 Author's interview with Abdoulaye Sylla, private address, Bamako, Mali, 12 February 2010.
47 Author's interview with Abdoulaye Sylla, private address, Bamako, Mali, 12 February 2010.
48 S. Malé, 'La Présentation des objets de cultures vivantes: le cas du Musée national du Mali', *Journal des Africanistes*, 69:1 (1999), 30.
49 The Young Pioneers later, however, became a major source of contention among the general population.
50 M.J. Arnoldi, 'Youth Festivals and Museums: The Cultural Politics of Public Memory in Postcolonial Mali', *Africa Today*, 52:4 (2006), 58.

51 *Les boîtes de Baguinda* referred to vegetable products canned at a state-sponsored factory that opened in Mali on 21 February 1964.
52 Author's interview with Sada Samake, private address, Bamako, Mali, 10 February 2010. See also R. de Jorio, 'Narratives of the Nation and Democracy in Mali: A View from Modibo Keïta's Memorial', *Cahiers d'Études Africaines*, 172 (2003), 832, footnote 10, and de Jorio, 'Politics of Remembering and Forgetting'.
53 Keïta, 'Speech at the National Assembly 20 January 1961', p. 33.
54 See L. Duran, 'Stars and Songbirds: Mande Female Singers in Urban Music, Mali, 1980–99 (PhD dissertation, University of London, 1999).
55 A.B. Konaré, 'Perspectives on History and Culture: The Case of Mali', in R.J. Bingen, D. Roinson and J.M. Staatz (eds), *Democracy and Development in Mali* (East Lansing: Michigan State University Press, 2000), p. 22.
56 E.g. B. Taylor, *Art for the Nation: Exhibitions and the London Public, 1747–2001* (Manchester: Manchester University Press, 1999); C. Duncan, *Civilizing Rituals: Inside Public Art Museums* (London: Routledge, 1995); T. Bennett, *The Birth of the Museum: History, Theory, Politics* (London: Routledge, 1995).

CHAPTER NINE

More than tropical? Modern housing, expatriate practitioners and the Volta River Project in decolonising Ghana

Viviana d'Auria

The endurance of material cultures of colonialism through the built environment beyond the moment of liberation has been an important insight of much postcolonial research. However, since 2000, readings of postcolonial architecture and urban projects as the mere continuation of colonial power relations have also been critiqued and nuanced. These debates have contributed to the recent reappraisal of 'matter' itself, and its ambivalent role in decolonisation.[1] No longer an 'undifferentiated externality standing apart from the social or cultural', the materiality of things has increasingly been included in equations considering the agency of both human and non-human associations.[2] As an actant itself, the designed environment is not only the concrete embodiment of negotiated physical space, but should also be understood as a repository for culturally situated and socially constructed knowledge prone to constant reappropriations over time.[3]

Researchers drawing on these reappraisals are now acknowledging that the colonised were key contributors to the colonial production of space in ways that did not originate in the metropolis. If building technology, housing design and urban planning under colonialism are increasingly assessed as outcomes of transculturation, how does the 'material turn' help one (re)consider architectural production during decolonisation? At least part of the answer resides in understanding architecture as a practised process, where human mattering – including inhabiting, redesigning and feeling – significantly contributes to the material matter of artefacts. Design professionals are increasingly placed amidst a dynamic web of encounters underscoring the multitude of architecture's makers. Rethinking the architect's prominence contributes significantly to our understandings of the built environment's role in decolonisation. First, it highlights various forms of redesign, from everyday adjustments to political re-signification.

Second, it allows for a consideration of the levels of agency available to professionals involved with modernising the built environment in the context of broader processes of (geo)political struggles and economic globalisation. Inquiring into the performative capacity of modern architecture can therefore help to unpack the relationship between decolonisation, transculturation and globalisation. This is even more crucial when exploring mid-century built environment, designed while the project of worldwide modernity responded both to the 'promise of cosmopolitan inclusiveness' and that of globalisation's 'unclear logic of the hegemonic'.[4]

These issues are explored here in relation to decolonising Ghana, and specifically to the role of expatriate experts in housing design related to the Volta River Project (VRP) from 1951 to 1966. In placing emphasis on cultural dimensions, this chapter reflects a more complex definition of decolonisation itself, which is not of political liberation alone (which took place in 1957). Rather, Ghana, as modern Africa's 'first self-directed attempt at nation-building' allows for a consideration of efforts to construct viable independent political geographies and identities through urban design.[5] This exploration muddles the timeline of official independence by focusing on the tensions between colonial and neo-colonial pressure, Africanising institutions and professional bodies, international policy and private capital. The first part of the chapter introduces the VRP and discusses the contested place of modernism and architectural expertise in the colonial and postcolonial world. Following this, discussion turns to the different phases of planning in the VRP, working chronologically, and highlighting the shifting terms of engagement of a range of international experts involved in the project from the late colonial to the postcolonial period. The planners involved ranged from town planners advising colonial government, to consultants for aluminium companies, state corporations, public utility authorities and commissions, as well as to global players such as the United Nations Technical Assistance Administration (UNTAA) delivering technical assistance. All were preoccupied with the challenging task of planning resettlement towns and new industrial settlements in a context of modernisation, industrialisation and socio-political 'transition'. The chapter concludes by highlighting the role and valorisation of internationalism and local culture in architecture, and architecture's role in building the nation, in the era of decolonisation.

The Volta River Project: Development, international expertise and modern architecture

Straddling both sides of official independence, the VRP's lifecycle has accompanied the most salient steps of Ghana's emergence as a nation-state. At its most embryonic stage, it was the brainchild of Australian geologist E.A. Kitson, who first associated the opportunities of bauxite reservoirs in the Gold Coast with the generation of electrical power by means of spanning the tortuous Volta River with a dam. In 1945, the entrepreneurial drive of Duncan Rose and Christopher St John Bird established the West African Aluminium Company, bringing Kitson's proposal close to implementation. Several documents evaluating the VRP's feasibility were released by the Gold Coast and UK governments before the fear of another Aswan Dam (where Soviet funding of this Egyptian scheme had strong implications for the Cold War power balance) finally confirmed North American support for the scheme in the early 1960s.[6] By then its main ingredients included the planned resettlement of 80,000 Ghanaians, the electrification of major cities, mineral resource extraction, industrialisation and economic diversification, as well as the mechanisation of agriculture. Figure 9.1 illustrates the scheme's main components, from Kitson's proposal to final plans, including both unrealised and constructed works and showing the increasing size of Lake Volta known as the 'world's largest man-made lake'.[7]

Throughout the years the VRP was under consideration, uneven promises of financial and political support from the UK government, the World Bank and British and North American aluminium companies were inherently bound to the worldwide scramble for bauxite.[8] The rapid succession of VRP assessment reports from 1940 to 1960 mirrored the struggle between conflicting objectives: securing access to mineral deposits was an important aim for the British and American governments and companies involved; for liberation leader Kwame Nkrumah local redistribution of resources, through electricity, irrigation and other infrastructure, was key. The fact that ultimately the Volta Aluminium Company (Valco) was the main utiliser of cheap electricity produced by damming the Volta River supports the argument of post-development scholars who, like Arturo Escobar, have condemned river basin development schemes as an epitome of neo-colonial developmentalism and its ideology of unequal growth.[9]

As an extension of such critiques, large-scale projects such as the VRP have recently earned the appellation of 'reservoirs of imperial power' due to their capacity to maintain 'spatial orders' through time

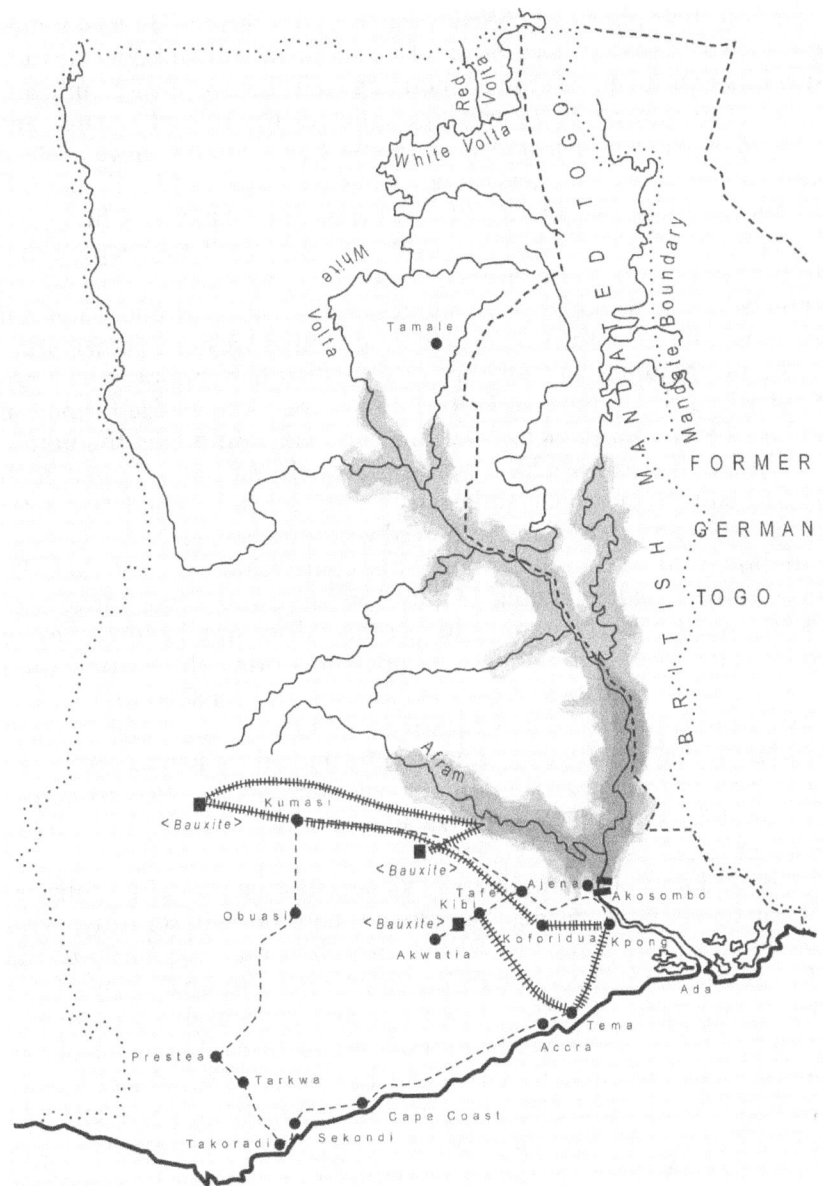

Figure 9.1 Map of the Volta River Project, 1966, drawing by author.

based on their physically fixed infrastructural form.[10] Understanding the VRP as a spatial inscription of neo-colonialism and globalisation suggests that it can be seen as inducing enduring socio-economic and political asymmetries. However, studies of the role of science and technology in colonial and postcolonial development have yielded more nuanced accounts, acknowledging the impact of local contexts on the assumptions of external experts. For example, Christophe Bonneuil has illustrated how science and the social engineering that accompanied its 'experiments' constituted a particular mode of crafting knowledge about indigenous societies, thus creating preconditions for growing interest in the values of local as well as Western knowledge.[11] A recent environmental history of Canadian dam-building has also emphasised the iterative relationship between knowledge formation and its dissemination across various contexts, reinforcing the notion that travelling knowledge implies transculturation; state-led high modernism is informed and transformed by 'local' and 'situated' expertise, rather than being imported without change.[12]

Building on such scholarship, this contribution argues that the predominant understanding of physical things as mere mirrors of social norms and economic interests has discounted the agency of professional architect-planners, besides neglecting the participation of particular indigenous constituencies and the consideration of the actual built form as situated knowledge. While the imposing physical presence of the power-generating scheme upon the Ghanaian territory is undeniable, the spatial conflicts generated by the VRP are rarely discussed in terms of their physical negotiation on a daily basis by designers and dwellers alike.[13]

The undoing of colonialism in Ghana through specific political acts and popular struggles has already come under scrutiny, with particular attention paid to Nkrumah.[14] Referring frequently to the VRP as his 'baby', Nkrumah provided unconditional support for the hydroelectric scheme, viewing it as indispensable to Ghana's emancipation from previous colonial inequalities. But what of the professionals solicited to formulate the plan? What designs were proposed by the international consultants asked to house Ghana's common man, the liberated wage earner increasingly expected in cities as a result of the VRP's agenda of modernisation and industrialisation? Experts with an explicitly international pedigree and rarely from Britain were summoned to shape the VRP's components, their work running in parallel with the Africanisation of public authorities and state administration. Through their personal histories (they were frequently displaced émigrés) and their professional profiles often involving work in other decolonising territories, these practitioners represented the benevolently internationalist nature of development and legitimised emerging nations' claims to modernity and its physical manifestations. Frequently summoned by international players such as the United Nations or the World Bank, these professionals referred to technical assistance as their prime realm of intervention; they were intentionally global in their scope and declaredly benign in their intent.

Mark Crinson and Vikramaditya Prakash have recently underscored the profound need to re-politicise modernist architecture and urbanism, and to highlight the 'combination of anti-colonialism, anti-nationalism and anti-globalism' its enactment implied.[15] Reflecting on modernism's ethical aspiration towards internationalism, Crinson (re)presents modernism as a form of criticism against nationalism, (neo-)colonialism and globalisation. He reminds us of the inherently 'critically internationalist' sentiments behind the realisation of modernist buildings during late colonial and post-independence times. Extending the idea of modernism as a counter-national and counter-colonial expression, Prakash highlights its truly postcolonial stance that ironically made it so effective for independent nation-building. Using Chandigarh as a main site to discuss these themes, Prakash concludes that modernism's self-construction as a counter-colonial expression made it ideally expressive of the aspirations of the newly constituted secular nation-state.[16] It was precisely the anti-colonial political stance that most appealed to emerging nations' leaders such as Jawaharlal Nehru and Nkrumah, a guarantee for accelerating decolonisation and effectively joining the list of independent nation-states.

This understanding of modernism's potential to be critically internationalist allows for a further examination of specific projects, their link to development, and the position of architecture as professional practice within this. Architects working during decolonisation were often involved in multiple renegotiations of their terms of reference in a rapidly changing environment. Frequently rooted in a developmentalist confidence in worldwide progress, designers' endeavours illustrate how their approaches to 'development' were subject to change, running in parallel with a re-evaluation of modern urbanism's potential contribution to the dismantling of the colonial enterprise. While decolonisation was underway, architectural and planning expertise shifted from a trans-colonial setting to multiple transnational networks of technical assistance.[17] Conceptual and technical apparatus expanded beyond the confines of former empires, significantly aided in its diffusion by the creation of global players like the UN and the Breton Woods institutions.[18] Bilateral technical cooperation agencies and re-articulated colonial bureaux were no longer the only active engines of dissemination, though many former colonial officers found room for their know-how in the course of UN missions and the like.[19]

Professional mobility and trans-cultural knowledge production encouraged by the prominence of internationalism and UN-induced development can therefore hardly be understood as merely old colonial relations living on in post-colonial linkages.[20] The heterogeneous nature of architectural and urban production during decolonisation can be witnessed in the diverse practices of emerging transnational groups of practitioners whose presence did not always conform to broader geopolitical logics.[21] Moreover, high levels of professional mobility increased the international nature of development projects, and built wide coalitions of solidarity. Ghana and the VRP confirm this trend: by the mid-1960s Hungarian architects, East German academics, British engineers, Italian contractors, Russian advisers, Indian experts, Canadian specialists, Australian consultants and US 'housers' grouped and regrouped themselves into professional constellations working towards the implementation of the multipurpose river basin development scheme. The resulting genealogy is one that speaks of globalisation in-the-making as multiple technical assistance networks coexisted (and conflicted) on the open terrain of a newly forming nation.

Architecture and urbanism were therefore influential tools in the muddled scene of Ghanaian decolonisation, marked by the complex cohabitation of political spheres within the diarchy, the joint rule of the British colonial state with Nkrumah's nationalist Convention People's Party. Symptomatic of the conflicting political objectives of deferring or accelerating the dismantlement of colonial presence was the struggle of the Ghana Institute of Architects (GIA) against the Gold Coast Society of Architects' (GCSA) 'monopoly in the acquisition of Government as well as private projects'.[22] The latter was founded in 1954 and was depicted as an 'exclusive Club of expatriates-only who worked in most of the various branches of the Public Works Department'.[23] This domination only ended, at least in institutional terms, in December 1964, when the GIA, composed of 'indigenes ... trained abroad' acquired official recognition amidst highlife tunes played by the Ghana Police Band in the Commonwealth Hall of the University of Ghana in Legon (Accra).[24] Within the context of such problematic cohabitation, appeals to expertise from outside colonial circles led first to the engagement of the Dutch firm Schokbeton and later, in November 1954, to the solicitation of a UN expert team on housing.[25] The UN Technical Assistance Administration (TAA) mission provided an ideal mechanism to avoid contentious issues of political sovereignty.[26] As the next section illustrates, housing and city design under the diarchy struggled between attention on climatic conditions, supposedly extending beyond Ghana's specific context to the 'Tropics' more generally, and the integration of local dwelling cultures, largely more 'particular' in their requirements.

The diarchy's architecture: Between tropical climate and Ga dwelling culture (1951–57)

By 1954 when the UN team was engaged, work on a major VRP component, the port city of Tema, had already begun. British architects and planners working for the Tema Development Corporation (TDC) had largely conducted the new town's planning, including the village of Tema Manhean for the forcibly relocated fishermen formerly occupying the site where Tema would rise. The succession of blueprints produced between 1951 and 1958 show a clear adherence to the principles of neighbourhood-unit planning – a major planning tool in the post-war period that was meant to provide a non-alienating environment for newly urbanised populations.[27] It was conceived as a self-sufficient module articulating housing around a central space with collective amenities. This travelling model was localised through the introduction of 'African markets' and 'palaver grounds'.[28] Housing advisers Maxwell Fry and Jane Drew, in West Africa since 1945, would help the TDC team define some of the thirty-two housing types in Tema's neighbourhoods, spreading 'Tropical Architecture' from Ghana's main cities to the new port settlement. The British husband-and-wife partnership would not only focus on high-income housing design for Tema's 'cosmopolitans', as shown in Figure 9.2, but would also plan the resettlement village of Tema Manhean.[29]

Fry and Drew's work has come under intense scrutiny in recent studies focusing on the ambivalent position of late colonial architecture and town planning in contexts such as Ghana, Nigeria and India. Paladins of Tropical Architecture since the mid-1940s, their work has been held up as emblematic of a modernism amended to the conditions of 'underdevelopment', where very specific (and paternalistic) interpretations of local climates and cultures helped coin what Fry termed 'a "dialect of internationalism," namely an approach to modernism which proved its contextual capacities'.[30] This found its best materialisation in the schools and universities Fry and Drew designed in West Africa from the mid-1940s onwards.[31] In the field of dwelling conception, Fry and Drew would lament the lack of

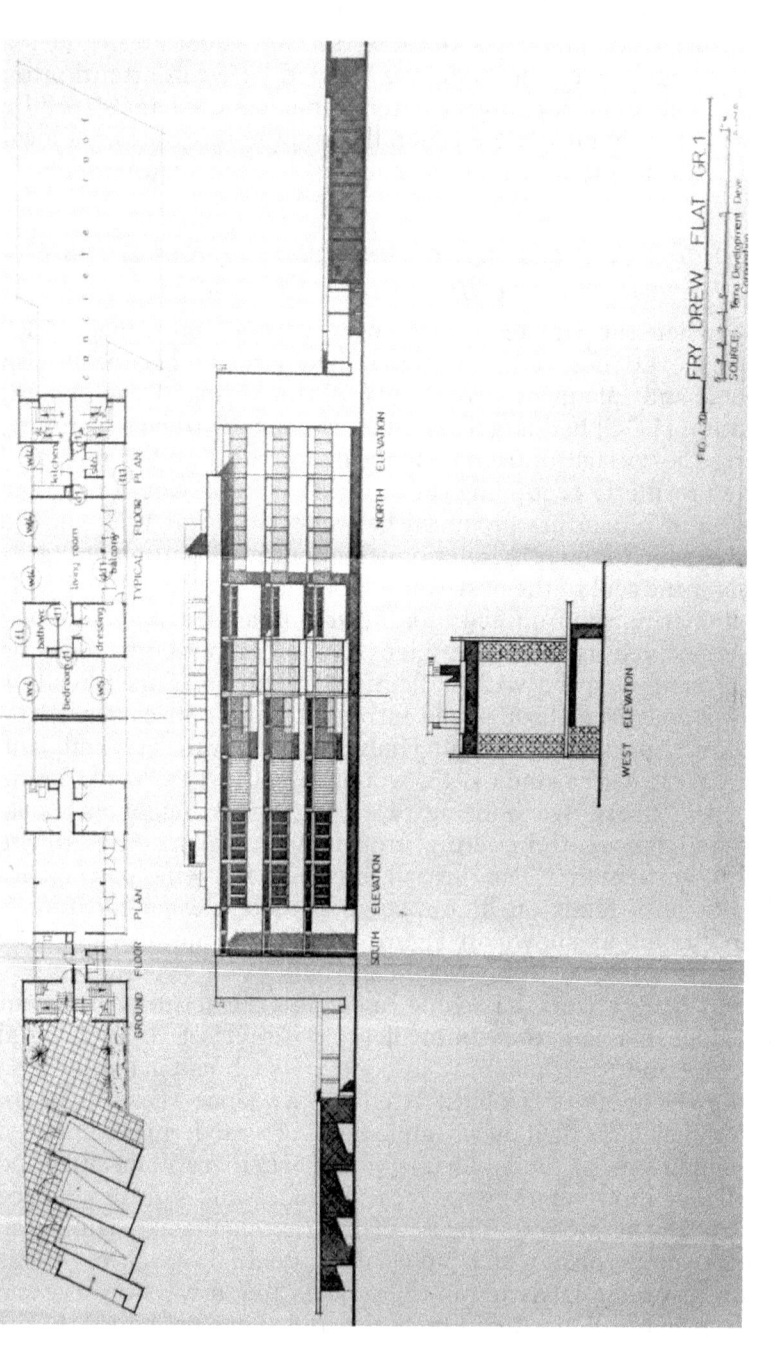

Figure 9.2 Maxwell Fry and Jane Drew, drawing for 'Fry Drew Flat' (four-storey flat for high-income 'cosmopolitan' residents), 1954-59.

interdisciplinary work with social anthropologists for the elaboration of housing types that could transcend the mimicry of earlier colonial efforts, but also surpass the supposed obsolescence of indigenous compound houses. While not overtly anti-colonial in writing, their West African work seems to imply indigenous emancipation along Fabian socialist lines where 'education' in town planning and improved low-cost housing is espoused with the encouragement of communal activities.[32]

These ideals would quickly dissolve when Fry, Drew, Drake and Lasdun's first plan for Tema Manhean met with extensive local resistance from 1951 to 1959.[33] Though contestation mainly revolved around the resettlement process *tout court*, the devil was also in the detail. Old Tema's inhabitants felt that 'intermediate' housing types devised by the architects left no room for extension, a crucial requirement for extended families of the Ga people.[34] In local vernacular building, social structures and spatial practices came together to produce a compound house with rooms accumulating incrementally around a courtyard in proportion to expanding households. Furthermore, as fishermen and farmers, Old Tema's inhabitants were considered ineligible for life in a multicultural modern township with full amenities, where industrial livelihoods prevailed. Ultimately, they would be fully excluded from the new port city located on their former settlement: access to serviced housing, wage labour and urban amenities was only for modern dwellers yet to come. Tropical modernism had thus proved abortive at least twice: first, the compromise it offered by means of a midway typology was rejected by its intended users, however climate-responsive its design might have been. Second, the scheme produced forced resettlement, the considerable disruption of livelihoods and the segregation of the least wealthy. Maintaining 'tradition' as a counter-figure to the new architecture, the social modernity to be fabricated in the new town was constructed as coming from outside a 'native' village. The next section shows how the desire for 'growing dwellings', which Old Tema's inhabitants had made explicit, was incorporated into national plans in order to meet the priorities of international housing policy. Shifting the focus from British Tropical Modernist architects, it illustrates the fundamental role played by UN technical assistance during Ghana's decolonisation.

Decolonising Tropical Architecture: The economy of self-help housing and unfinished dwellings (1954–64)

The decolonisation of architecture and urbanism picked up pace as professionals working internationally were able to carve space for their work from the one left (partially) void by the end of late colonial enterprise. A major symptom of this shift was the decreasing tension between the dichotomy of 'modern' and 'traditional' lifestyles, as the 'transition' of populations towards an improved future became the aim of housing experts.[35] As independence moved closer, tradition was no longer understood as an artificial point in time where autochthonous populations should remain in order to be preserved; rather, indigenous dwelling practices became a wealth of experience designers could selectively choose to revisit to encourage 'development'. In Ghana this reorientation would be advanced by US 'houser' Charles Abrams, head of the UNTAA housing mission which also involved Otto Koenigsberger and Vladimir Bodiansky. The threesome surveyed the Gold Coast colony, the Ashanti Protectorate, the Northern Territories and British Togoland shortly before these territories were brought together as the independent nation of Ghana in 1957. Their task took in the VRP as the UNTAA was expected to advise on national housing policy at a moment when the hydroelectric scheme (which included much housing) was under question due to the excessive investment it required.[36]

The UN 'missionaries' promoted significant shifts in housing provision discourses based not only on their findings from visits to Ghanaian settlements, but also on an appreciation for the work completed by the Gold Coast's Department of Social Welfare and Community Development.[37] The latter was responsible for the mass education offensive of the late 1940s and early 1950s, when improvement boiled down to equipping the territory with a welfare web composed of self-constructed feeder roads, dispensaries, village wells and civic buildings. Colonial officers who strived for betterment through durable building materials, improved sanitation and type-layouts (standard plans), heavily condemned 'traditional' housing's 'inadequacy' and 'impermanency'.[38] Abrams and his colleagues reversed the order of terms: the provision of housing should come before the installation of commons such as schools, sewage lines, latrine blocks and compost collectors.[39] Facilitating home ownership, protecting private property and promoting individual entrepreneurialism were prime ingredients to include in a revised agenda for housing the nation. In other words, the redistributive welfare of colonial planning was being replaced by market-oriented self-help, where individual participation and responsibility were deemed crucial for terminating corrective government-led programmes in the long run. Not incidentally, housing was increasingly being recognised as a prime locale for economic development.[40] Reports from Ghana's Ministry of Housing followed a similar line of argument, reflecting the emphasis on home ownership.[41]

For the consolidation of self-help to occur, the notion of the inadequacy of traditional building was inverted, and the 'communal spirit' of the 'great builders' of Ghana praised. UNTAA's concluding report leaves little doubt on the issue:

> The Mission was impressed by the high standards of building in most rural districts of the Gold Coast ... Even more important than the high quality of workmanship in most of the peasant houses, is the fact that, in the villages, practically everybody is a builder and knows how to construct a house.[42]

On a similar note, in the same report the experts would enthusiastically insist: 'All building in the rural areas of the Gold Coast is "self-help" building and as such it is almost perfect ... Any change in the self-help traditions of the villagers would result in a deterioration of quality standards.'[43] Ultimately such appraisal would materialise in the form of core housing and self-help schemes for relocated villagers in the fifty-two new settlements following Lake Volta's banks. Figure 9.3 embodies this shift in planning ideas: both houses and future residents are 'in progress' as views of buildings in the making provide the backdrop for women and men industriously building their dwellings.

Abrams's views would be further shaped by an encounter with the Ghanaian practice of the 'unfinished house' depicted by the Ministry of Housing as a fundamental feature of the Gold Coast. Consisting of an incomplete dwelling flanked by a long-standing deposit of building materials (especially blocks and bricks) awaiting employment, it embodied both a specific temporal dilation and the incremental nature of dwelling culture. The house's completion was indefinitely postponed to what could either be a near future or a remote point in time. Similarly, the blocks were also an indication of the incremental self-build capacity of extended families. Though it clearly pertained to the praiseworthy 'self-help traditions of the villagers', the practice of the unfinished house sparked little sympathy among the UNTAA members.[44] It seemed to be simultaneously demon and angel: on the one hand it was an incarnation of the inertia of community's capital, on the other it was the epitome of local knowledge propagated through mutual solidarity. The experts' statements would be indicative of the mixed feelings for the contradictory components the incomplete dwelling embodied: it was praised for its spontaneous construction and self-regulated teamwork, disapproved of for the squandering of

Figure 9.3 Women and men at work in the resettlement town of Ajena, c. 1962.

resources. The next section traces the ways in which these efforts to both accommodate the cultural practice of a self-built expanding house and foster the capitalistic entrepreneurialism of urbanising dwellers resonated with the work of other professionals in Ghana.

Transitional neighbourhoods, flexible housing standards and contextualised typologies in the smelter towns of Kpong and Tema (1955–64)

Following the 1952 White Paper on the Volta River Aluminium Scheme, discussions on the VRP's implementation as an integrated development had indeed picked up pace. While reservations about feasibility gave way to an augmented confidence in the integrated bauxite and aluminium scheme due to the involvement of Canadian and British aluminium companies (Alcan and BACo), plans were drafted for the next step in the project, the smelter township of Kpong. Nine months after the UNTAA mission's end in January 1955, the VRP's construction seemed certain. At this point the VRP's five major components – bauxite mines, railway lines, a dam and power station, a deepwater port and an aluminium smelter – were to be delivered by a promising partnership between the UK and Gold Coast governments with Alcan and BACo.

As a result of networking by the new head of the VRP's Preparatory Commission, Robert Jackson, the Commission's working team on housing and planning gained new advisers in 1955. Otto Koenigsberger was appointed as consultant to the Commission itself, whilst the North American practice of Albert Mayer and Julian Whittlesey were appointed to a key consultancy role with Alcan. Mayer & Whittlesey, with a common background as US Corps of Engineers in Asia, would deal with the conception of a new smelter town drawing on significant experience: they had already planned Kitimat in Canada for Alcan. Both Alcan's involvement and Mayer & Whittlesey's appointment show how remote regions of the world were in the process of being tied together not only in terms of a global chain of production, but also in terms of professional expertise. However, unlike the steel towns of Nehruvian India, Kpong could not be a government-led creation even though Ghanaian independence was imminent and African politicians had become participants in the VRP well before 1957. Rather, the space of the new town of Kpong remained caught between conflicting expectations: foreign financing and private interests encouraged the inclusion of new corporate spaces of production (and access to cheap electricity) while the patronage of colonial government funds meant paternalist welfare provision could be continued (and with it control over mineral resources). As a result, emerging nationhood was caught between the lingering of colonial planning and the entrepreneurial reframing of these practices as technical assistance by transatlantic private capital. Emblematic of these divergences was the discussion between the aluminium companies and the Ministry of Housing staff, with the latter contesting the minimum standards proposed by the private companies for the lowest-income employees as non-compliant with the requirements of the time, especially in light of the territory's expected progress. 'Flexibility' in planning and housing was the panacea for securing an agreement.

Mayer & Whittlesey seemed considerably preoccupied by the 'sociological pattern of the town' and the laying out of a multiracial, multiclass entity unmarked by segregation. As Sanjeev Vidyarthi has discussed when examining Mayer and Koenigsberger's collaboration for the design of various Indian cities, the neighbourhood unit principle was invested with ideals of liberation and site-specificity.[45] In Kpong the same goal of designing urban sectors as a 'cross-section of society' would be played out along the lines of tribe and race rather than class. Main objectives included the 'free mixing of overseas and African people', to the point that 'nothing should be included in the plan which would make such free intercourse more difficult'.[46] The synopsis by Mayer & Whittlesey also stated, 'there should not be segregation as between Africans coming straight from rural backgrounds and those that had already some experience of living in urban communities.'[47] For this reason, the proposals for town layout would provide 'a certain intermingling of these two classes in order to assist adjustment of rural people to city environment and to ease their transition to a different mode of life'.[48] Finally, another potential producer of segregation, that of difference between workers in the aluminium industry and other forms of employment was also to be prevented; by mixing these categories freely in the various neighbourhoods proposed, the planners hoped to eliminate an eventual lack of integration.

Taking the transition to a life where 'greater reliance is placed on wage earning and the individual family' as their basic assumption, the US firm considered the physical design of the town, the neighbourhood, the house and its relationship to other dwellings as components which 'can assist in this transition'.[49] Their arrangement, shown in Figure 9.4, was thus laid out in order to encourage smooth societal change. The town layout was regarded as having a 'flexible' configuration, which essentially meant that the three broad types of neighbourhoods (and related housing types, density values and school

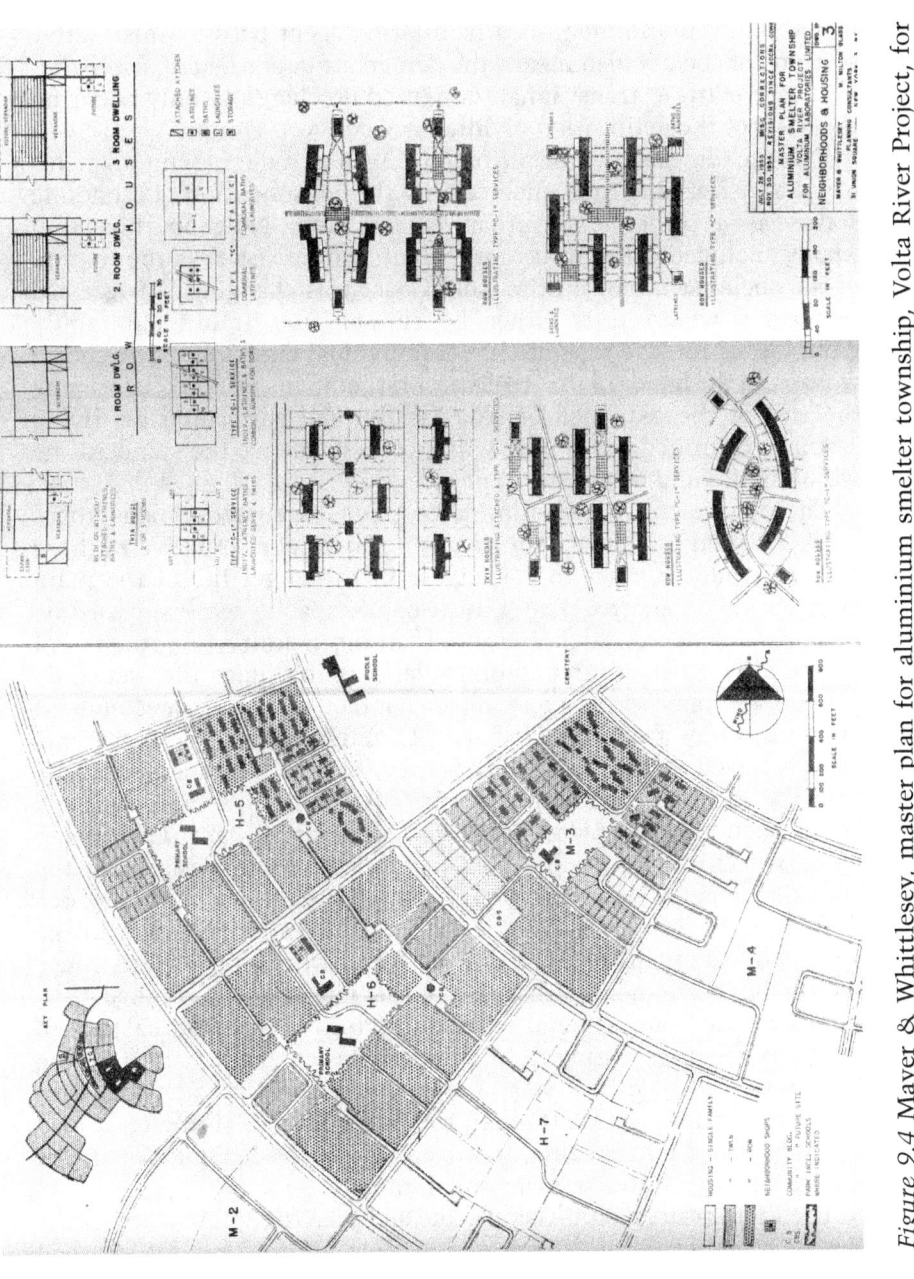

Figure 9.4 Mayer & Whittlesey, master plan for aluminium smelter township, Volta River Project, for Aluminium Laboratories Limited, 1955-56.

provision) could be added or subtracted if modification was required, without impairing the plan's main structure. However, the notion of the built environment as a facilitating agent between distinctive sections of society also meant the demarcation of separate categories from the start; a 'transitional' design could therefore only occur on the basis of the delineation of difference between groups.

Transcending race would ultimately mean introducing employment-based divisions and thus underscoring the consolidation of economic status as a principle of urban organisation. Neighbourhoods in Kpong included housing layouts which recognised that the 'nature of the social structure in the Gold Coast was changing'.[50] Suggested typologies would thus either be suitable for 'traditional family grouping' or for 'the separate life of individual families'.[51] The choice was left in the hands of the African (or rather in his pocket): 'Loosening the ties of the extended or clan family, and patterning his living around his immediate family, will greatly influence the standards he will embrace and be *willing to pay for*.'[52]

These preoccupations culminated in 'sub-neighbourhood groupings', foreseen as a device for proposing 'a social alternative to those not yet ready or eager to participate in the larger life of the main neighbourhood centre'. The 'transitional' capacity was expressed by their assemblages, which presented 'an opportunity for grouping of extended families around common land as in village life, yet ... do not impose any excessively close contact if social development proceeds away from this trend'.[53] Different cluster arrangements were believed to afford not only 'variety in site planning' but also a 'familiar intimacy of living pattern'.[54] Twin and row housing could be subsequently upgraded by the attachment of bath, latrine and laundry facilities. Both the plea for 'flexibility' in design and the encouragement of suppleness in social mobility presented tremendous challenges for Mayer & Whittlesey. From overall city design to the outline of verandahs, the North American partnership tried to infuse the smelter settlement with a system that encouraged the move away from extended families and tribal gatherings. The historical role of company towns as testing grounds for the design of affordable housing for low-income workers was complicated in the decolonising sub-Saharan African context through the issue of race. However, it also provided space for resisting improved standards of living because of the transitional status of many inhabitants.

The Preparatory Commission's role had been to explore whether the Volta River aluminium scheme was feasible, and by March 1956 it had achieved its end when the Secretary of State for the Colonies released a dispatch stating the scheme was 'technically sound' and 'could be carried out successfully'.[55] However, the design for Kpong would never reach beyond the blueprints included in the Preparatory Commission's report, as the global interest in aluminium plummeted in the late 1950s. The knotty tie between foreign investment, decolonisation and nation-building was made manifest by the failure of the 'Rubicon Talks', which Nkrumah had hoped would officially launch the VRP. Though the British government had hoped to manage decolonisation by developing the VRP and fostering the active role of a public corporation, it was still dependent on Alcan to carry the risk of the project and make the integrated scheme commercially viable. With the aluminium company's withdrawal, the British government postponed work on the development, leaving Nkrumah and his entourage as the only believers in the benefits of the VRP. For Nkrumah however, the vision for the integrated scheme shone brighter still, with the glow of a plan not-yet-achieved. It would take several more years and a considerable amount of negotiations before work on the VRP would be confirmed. The questions raised by the shelved plans for Kpong – in terms of racial segregation and social transition – remained high on the agenda as the VRP entered a new phase.

Due to the deep suspicion of 'colonial chicanery' in the country, Jackson singled out the United States' technical assistance programme, known as the Point Four programme, as ideal funding alternative for the VRP. As the 'American century' was reaching its post-war height, it was to US involvement that independent Ghana turned when searching for interested new partners. By 1960, the office of the governor-general was abolished, signalling a further shift away from colonial rule, and the *Kaiser Reassessment Report* commissioned by Kaiser Inc., one of the most important US corporations, had been approved. This led to the resuscitation of the VRP, albeit under the conditions set by the US company. Though initially positioned as technical adviser, Kaiser Inc. was soon to present proposals for several initiatives besides the dam project itself, as part of its broader global expansion. Among the changes requested was the relocation of the dam from Kpong to Akosombo and that of the aluminium smelter to Tema.

Revisiting Tema's urban configuration to include large-scale industrial activities required the solicitation of a new planning team, and the Athens-based firm of Doxiadis Associates was entrusted with the new town's (re)development on 1 May 1961. By then, Valco, the aluminium company in charge of the smelter's operation, was 90 per cent owned by Kaiser Aluminum. Meanwhile, Nkrumah's statements on Ghana's orientation as an avowedly socialist state were becoming more explicit: socialist economic development and African communitarian legacy were presented as the result of a harmonious marriage inherent in Ghanaian culture.[56] The involvement of Doxiadis's firm, therefore, conveniently matched the challenge to negotiate fresh terms of reference for Ghana's development in the midst of the muddled Cold War contraposition: on the one hand Doxiadis Associates' scientific neutrality was in tune with Nkrumah's position amongst the non-aligned leaders; on the other hand the firm's almost unconditional support of international development strategies could conceal the geopolitical motives of those investing.

Bounded by the harbour, the industrial area and the lagoons, the new town imagined by Doxiadis' Associates was a productive city dynamically expanding northwards, its growth supported by a grid of high-speed infrastructure that included the Accra–Tema motorway. Yet another variant of the neighbourhood unit occupied the space between the main arteries and formed a recurring pattern of identical Community Class sectors. Developed by Doxiadis, these were both units of social engineering and of spatial programming. Despite working in a variety of geopolitical settings, the practice would employ the interlocking system of Community Class sectors in most of its interventions across the globe. Doxiadis's efforts to elaborate a non-locational, generic model of social organisation were made manifest in a system that had, in the consultant's view, the potential of 'creating optimum conditions for social intercourse, human growth and organization'.[57] However, there was a contradiction inherent in the unit's conception: the self-contained sectors and prearranged socio-spatial components within it neither met the ambition of dynamic development, nor fostered real social interplay.

Given Doxiadis's declared objective of social mixing and aggregation, income-based separation was a highly questionable device designed to foster 'appropriate intermingling' within residential communities.[58] Pairing different incomes never more than one step apart within the same neighbourhood was meant to facilitate social 'transition', albeit following a more regimented system than the one proposed for Kpong. In Doxiadis's view, social mobility should culminate in modern communities living in multistorey dwellings, examples of which already existed in Tema, courtesy of earlier work by Fry and Drew. The practice revisited the generic type of middle-rise walk-up flats and included culturally specific socio-spatial features. This same attentiveness towards (a particular version of) Ghanaian dwelling culture was replicated at every level of design, from the housing unit to the urban fabric.

These efforts were part of a long-standing debate within modern architecture itself, whereby repetition and standardisation were equated with an egalitarian social order, even as vibrancy and variety became the ideal. The avoidance of monotonous urban landscapes which Doxiadis felt would inevitably derive from the unrestricted use of mass-housing solutions was combated by typological assortment and regional details incorporated in universal models. Diversity was cultivated to circumvent dullness. As noted in Doxiadis's diaries, the experience of Brasilia and Chandigarh triggered his sensitivity to the difficulties of providing shelter to a massive, urbanising working base. Thus Tema's residential sectors were infused with the necessary variety and site-specificity, particularly in the low-income areas, where 'transition' was most delicate and urgent. Indeed, the 1962 housing study prepared by the Athens-based consultants as part of the *Immediate Needs and Programme of Priorities* focused on the construction of an experimental low-cost scheme for Tema's least wealthy sectors.[59]

In this study, Ghana's vernacular building was analysed schematically, revealing the conceptualisations inherent in Doxiadis Associates' housing and urban design strategies and highlighting the limitations of the firm's approach in bridging the local and global scale. Doxiadis's starting point was an evaluation of the compound house. As a 'traditional' dwelling type, it ultimately reflected the relatively simpler mode of living of the rural dweller; its scope served the needs of the extended family and it also clearly expressed kinship ties. Basically, it belonged to those elements of the urban environment considered 'passé'.[60] Other elements of traditional Ghanaian society were included. For example, the verandah became essentialised as a component of traditional culture, understood as an element which would not 'change easily with the passage of time or progress of culture' and was included in a number of variants in housing schemes of different kinds, including multistorey blocks (see Figure 9.5).[61]

Doxiadis's drawings expose his fondness for historical and vernacular forms and produced a fascinating universal database from which designers could draw to attune modern urbanism to specific contexts. The verandah was part of a repertoire that was, above all, the keeper of a culture and the guarantee that no shift from rural to urban conditions would be incurably abrupt. Though the verandah was soundly espoused in colonial building (and within the colonial gaze), this legacy did not prevent Doxiadis from electing it as the main cultural trait to localise modern dwelling typologies. The assumption that Ghanaians recognised this cultural component as overarching revealed an essentialist interpretation of identity that not even the presence of Ghanaian and other African architects in the office could adjust.[62] Nonetheless, Doxiadis' over-reliance on the more formal

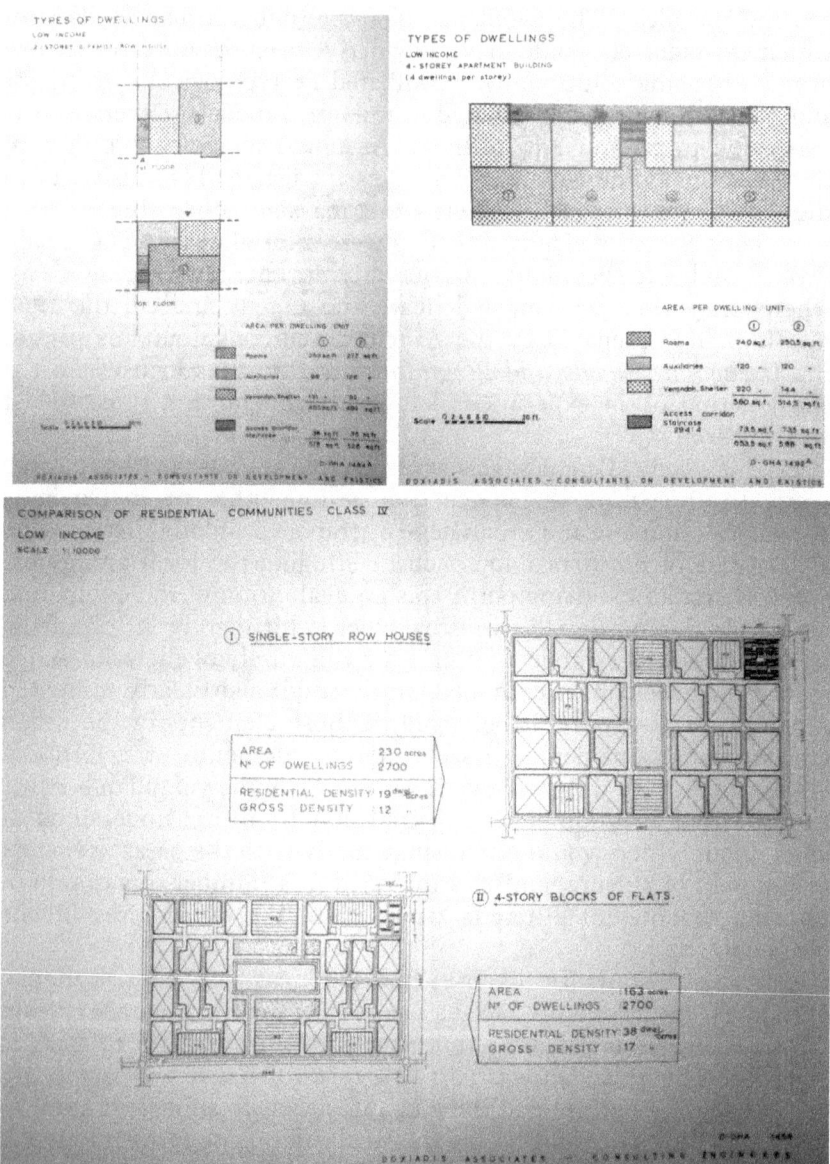

Figure 9.5 Doxiadis Associates, density studies of verandah-equipped row-housing and multistorey blocks in Tema's Community Class Sector, 1964.

aspects of vernacular urbanism and confidence in the city's gradual layering ultimately highlighted a view of the importance of design disciplines and their capacity to re-interpret the urban form.

Conclusion

This chapter has explored the ways in which expatriate professionals consulting on VRP-related policy and urbanism contributed to the cultural and material performance of decolonisation in sub-Saharan Africa's first independent country. In this context, the significance of a 'material turn' to reconsider architectural production has been posited. Well beyond the case of decolonising Ghana, the consideration of 'practised' architecture opens inspiring avenues for comparable inquiries that recognise the contested and trans-cultural process of producing artefacts, which includes apprehending architecture as an ongoing process rather than a finalised product. An emphasis on the materiality of architecture is also crucial to understanding decolonisation: it supports explorations of the tensions and synergies between planners' visions of urban spaces and residents' experiences of them as a long-term exchange rather than solely occurring at the time of a building's construction.

In decolonising Ghana, new town planning, housing developments and resettlement villages followed – though not always coherently – the transformation of the VRP from a colonial development project to a postcolonial hybrid rooted in private business ideas and rampant concessions. The shifting role of African politicians and aluminium companies within and outside the Commonwealth further intensified these changes in the conception and design of the built environment. Expatriate architects were appointed by a variety of different players, from the state corporation of the Tema Development Organisation to companies such as Alcan and Kaiser Inc., as well as ministries established during the diarchy. Though priorities varied (from industrial development to access to cheap electricity), this did not keep professionals from aspiring to a pluralist urban environment and encouraging a genuine decolonisation. As part of their anti-colonial stance, any reference to racial discrimination was avoided, a process that obscured other forms of segregation that entered the scene, with income and employment status becoming main drivers for socially engineering the city. As part of their internationalism, other design experiences from abroad were a prerequisite, with partners of Mayer & Whittlesey having worked in India, Israel and Canada, and with Doxiadis Associates' substantial involvement in Iraq and Pakistan. When their internationalism strived to become 'critical' (in Crinson's sense), specific references to the project's locale were employed to nuance the intensive development of large-scale urban neighbourhoods. The use of 'local' and 'contextual' features as refining devices of a worldwide applicable urbanism implied an extreme faith in the trans-cultural design of the physical environment, and in the design of a fully decolonised nation-state capable of expressing itself by its own means.

Policies, plans and projects proposed by the UNTAA housing mission, the US firm of Mayer & Whittlesey and the Athens-based practice of Doxiadis Associates also illustrate how interpretations of 'local culture' were used differently to reshape housing and planning agendas during decolonisation. Whether in the name of aided self-help policy or in support of collective housing types, ignoring existing indigenous dwelling was no longer an option.[63] From their work we can recognise the formation of two major fronts of housing policy which would go head-to-head for several decades on the global arena: on the one hand, the market-oriented aided self-help which privileged home ownership and proclaimed the virtues of individual entrepreneurialism; on the other, the extension of the developmental state in the form of government-led neighbourhood design. The former revisited the self-help initiatives of village improvement schemes, the latter extended colonial welfare housing delivery. Both approaches viewed indigenous dwelling cultures as a dynamic legacy with which to reinvigorate urban policies and design for 'new' African cities. They could thus avoid the rigid socio-spatial division that the dismal tale of Tema Manhean, through resettlement, resistance and project refusal, embodied. However, they could not escape the major paradox of decolonisation, namely the contradictory cohabitation of nation-building with internationalism. If nationalism, as Immanuel Wallerstein has suggested, is an alternative which, once taken, can only be followed to the very end, the balancing act of a critically internationalist modernism was destined to fall short of its promises.[64] As other experimental and trans-cultural city-making experiences such as Ciudad Guayana remind us, internationalism was much more effective when it came to the mobility of corporate capital than in the shared aspirations of 'one world' free from difference and inequality.[65]

Notes

1 J.M. Jacobs and P. Merriman, 'Practising Architectures', *Social & Cultural Geography*, 12:3 (2011), 211–22; B. Anderson and D. Tolia-Kelly, 'Matter(s) in Social and Cultural Geography', *Geoforum*, 35 (2004), 669–74; A. Latham and D. McCormack, 'Moving Cities: Rethinking the Materialities of Urban Geographies',

MORE THAN TROPICAL?

Progress in Human Geography, 28:6 (2005), 701–24; D. Miller (ed.), *Material Cultures: Why Some Things Matter* (Chicago: University of Chicago Press, 1998).
2   Anderson and Tolia-Kelly, 'Matter(s) in Social and Cultural Geography', 672.
3   D. Haraway, 'Situated Knowledges: The Science Question in Feminism and the Privilege of Partial Perspective', *Feminist Studies*, 14:3 (1988), 575–99; B. Latour, *Science in Action: How to Follow Scientists and Engineers through Society* (Cambridge: Harvard University Press, 1987); B. Latour, *Reassembling the Social: An Introduction to Actor-Network-Theory* (Oxford: Oxford University Press, 2005).
4   S. Osha, 'Appraising Africa: Modernity, Decolonisation and Globalisation', in L. Keita (ed.), *Philosophy and African Development: Theory and Practice* (Dakar: CODESRIA, 2011), p. 172.
5   Osha, 'Appraising Africa', p. 172.
6   D. Hart, *The Volta River Project: A Case Study in Politics and Technology* (Edinburgh: Edinburgh University Press, 1980).
7   J. Moxon, *Volta: Man's Largest Lake* (London: André Deutsch, 1969).
8   R.S. Gendron, M. Ingulstad and E. Storli (eds), *Aluminum Ore: The Political Economy of the Global Bauxite Industry* (Vancouver: UBC Press, 2013).
9   A. Escobar, *Encountering Development: The Making and Unmaking of the Third World* (Princeton: Princeton University Press, 1995).
10 See the panel convened by Birte Förster and Julia Tischler, 'Large-scale Infrastructure Projects in Sub-Saharan Africa: Spatial Inscriptions of Imperialism and Globalisation?', at the conference Embattled Spaces, Contested Orders, Cologne University, 30 May–2 June 2012.
11 C. Bonneuil, 'Development as Experiment: Science and State Building in Late Colonial and Postcolonial Africa, 1930–1970', *Osiris*, special issue on 'Nature and Empire: Science and the Colonial Enterprise', 15 (2000), 258–81.
12 T. Loo and M. Stanley, 'An Environmental History of Progress: Damming the Peace and Columbia Rivers', *Canadian Historical Review*, 92:3 (2011), 399–427.
13 A notable exception is S.F. Miescher, 'Building the City of the Future: Visions and Experiences of Modernity in Ghana's Akosombo Township', *Journal of African History*, 53 (2012), 367–90.
14 See, among others, C.A. Boateng, *Nkrumah's Consciencism: An Ideology for Decolonization and Development* (Dubuque: Kendall/Hunt, 2005; first published 1995).
15 M. Crinson, 'Modernism Across Hemispheres, or, Taking Internationalism Seriously', in W. Lim and J. Chang (eds), *Non West Modernist Past: On Architecture & Modernities* (Singapore: World Scientific Publishing, 2012), pp. 37–46.
16 V. Prakash, 'Third World Modernism, or Just Modernism: Towards a Cosmopolitan Reading of Modernism', in D. Lu (ed.), *Third World Modernism: Architecture, Development and Identity* (London and New York: Routledge, 2011), pp. 255–70.
17 J. Chang, 'Building a Colonial Technoscientific Network: Tropical Architecture, Building Science and the Politics of Decolonisation', in Lu, *Third World Modernism*, pp. 211–35.
18 V. Baweja, *A Pre-history of Green Architecture: Otto Koenigsberger and Tropical Architecture, from Princely Mysore to Post-colonial London* (PhD dissertation, University of Michigan, 2008), pp. 115–28.
19 R. Home, 'From Colonial Housing to Planning for Disasters: The Career of David Oakley (1927–2003)', *Papers in Land Management*, 8 (2007), 5–17; U. Kothari, 'Spatial Practices and Imaginaries: Experiences of Colonial Officers and Development Professionals', *Singapore Journal of Tropical Geography*, 27:3 (2006), 235–53.
20 See also M. Casciato and T. Avermaete, *Chandigarh Casablanca: A Report on Modernization* (Zurich: Park Books, 2014).
21 H. Le Roux, 'Modern Architecture in Postcolonial Ghana and Nigeria', *Architectural History*, 47 (2004), 361–92; L. Stanek, 'PRL™ Export Architecture and Urbanism from Socialist Poland', *Piktogram*, 15 (2010–11), 95–148.

22 History of GIA supplied by past GIA President Kojo Gyinaye Kyei (Nana Ankoanna Apoma Kyekyeku), formerly available on the institute's website at www.arcghana.org/gia_history.htm (accessed 27 May 2014).
23 History of GIA supplied by Kojo Gyinaye Kyei.
24 History of GIA supplied by Kojo Gyinaye Kyei.
25 K. Konadu-Agyemang, *The Political Economy of Housing and Urban Development in Africa* (Westport: Praeger, 2001), pp. 142–4.
26 Cornell University Library, Charles Abrams Papers (hereafter CAP), Box 82, Folder 3, E.O. Asafu-Adjaye, 'Talk on Housing in the Gold Coast', 1 November 1954; CAP, Box 35, basic agreement between the UN and the Gold Coast Government, 25 June 1951.
27 D.L. Johnson, 'Origin of the Neighbourhood Unit', *Planning Perspectives*, 17 (2002), 227–45.
28 A.E.S. Alcock, 'A New Town in the Gold Coast', *Town and Country Planning*, 23 (1955), 51–5.
29 I. Jackson and R. Oppong, 'The Planning of Late Colonial Village Housing in the Tropics: Tema Manhean, Ghana', *Planning Perspectives* (2014), 1–25.
30 M. Crinson, *Modern Architecture and the End of Empire* (Aldershot: Ashgate, 2003), p. 137.
31 R. Windsor-Liscombe, 'Modernism in Late Imperial British West Africa: The Work of Maxwell Fry and Jane Drew, 1946–56', *Journal of the Society of Architectural Historians*, 65:2 (2006), 188–215; T. Livsey, '"Suitable Lodgings for Students": Modern Space, Colonial Development and Decolonization in Nigeria', *Urban History*, 41:4 (2014), 664–85.
32 T.R. Batten, *Problems of African Development, Part II: Government and People* (Oxford: Oxford University Press, 1948); R. Hinden (ed.), *Fabian Colonial Essays* (London: George Allen & Unwin, 1944); M. Perham, *Education for Self-Government* (London: Foreign Affairs, 1945). See also the following memorandums: *The Education of African Communities*, Colonial No. 103 (London: HMSO, 1935); *Mass Education in African Society*, Colonial No. 186 (London: HMSO, 1944).
33 G.W. Amarteifio, D.A.P. Butcher and D. Whitham, *Tema Manhean: A Study of Resettlement* (Accra: Ghana Universities Press, 1966).
34 Integrating Ga dwelling cultures in modern housing became a key challenge for colonial architects and planners during 'transition' and decolonisation. For more on this experience in Greater Accra, see V. d'Auria, 'In the Laboratory and in the Field: Hybrid Housing Design for the African City in Late-Colonial and Decolonising Ghana (1945–57)', *Journal of Architecture*, 19:3 (2014), 329–56.
35 Crucial here is Muzaffar's analysis of refugees and 'transition': M.I. Muzaffar, 'Boundary Games: Ecochard, Doxiadis, and the Refugee Housing Projects Under Military Rule in Pakistan, 1953–1959', in Aggregate (ed.), *Governing by Design: Architecture, Economy and Politics in the 20th Century* (Pittsburgh: University of Pittsburgh Press, 2012), pp.142–98.
36 D. Seers and C.R. Ross, *Report on Financial and Physical Problems of Development in the Gold Coast* (Accra: Office of the Government Statistician, 1952); IBRD, *Report on the Gold Coast* (Washington: IBRD, 1953).
37 Gold Coast Government, *Report of the Department of Social Welfare and Community Development 1946–1951* (Accra and London: Government Printer, 1953).
38 Colonial Office, *Memorandum on Housing in British African Territories* (London: HMSO, 1954).
39 C. Abrams, V. Bodiansky and O. Koenigsberger, *Housing in the Gold Coast* (New York: UNTAA, 1956).
40 E.g. G. Arku, 'The Economics of Housing Programmes in Ghana, 1929–66', *Planning Perspectives*, 24:3 (2009), 281–300.

41 CAP, Box 35, letter from E.O. Asafu-Adjaye to Charles Abrams conveying the terms of reference as regards to the UNTAA Mission to the Gold Coast in 1954, 5 November 1954.
42 CAP, Box 35, United Nations Technical Assistance Administration Housing Mission, *Draft Report on Technical Education* (New York: UNTAA, 1955), pp. 3–4.
43 United Nations Technical Assistance Administration Housing Mission, *Draft Report on Technical Education* (1955), pp. 3–4.
44 United Nations Technical Assistance Administration Housing Mission, *Draft Report on Technical Education* (1955), pp. 3–4.
45 S. Vidyarthi, 'Reimagining the American Neighborhood for India', in P. Healey and G. Upton (eds), *Crossing Borders: International Exchange and Planning Practices* (London: Routledge, 2010), pp. 73–94.
46 CAP, Box 82, Folder 2, Volta River Project Working Group 'C', minutes of 2nd meeting held on 4 October 1954, p. 2.
47 Volta River Project Working Group 'C', minutes of 2nd meeting held on 4 October 1954, p. 2.
48 Volta River Project Working Group 'C', minutes of 2nd meeting held on 4 October 1954, p. 2.
49 Mayer and Whittlesey's report was included in Appendix XII in addition to Koenigsberger's general recommendations: Preparatory Commission, *The Volta River Project, Vol. 2: Appendices to the Report of the Preparatory Commission* (London: HMSO, 1956), p. 302.
50 Preparatory Commission, *The Volta River Project*, p. 302.
51 Preparatory Commission, *The Volta River Project*, p. 302.
52 Preparatory Commission, *The Volta River Project*, p. 302 (emphasis added).
53 Preparatory Commission, *The Volta River Project*, p. 306.
54 Preparatory Commission, *The Volta River Project*, p. 306.
55 J. Moxon, *Volta: Man's Greatest Lake – The Story of Ghana's Akosombo Dam* (London: Andre Deutsch, 1969), p. 84.
56 As a statement of the time see M. Dei-Anang, *Ghana Resurgent* (Accra: Waterville, 1964), pp. 171–2.
57 Constantinos Doxiadis Archives (hereafter CDA), DOX-GHA 16-22, Vol. 9, Doxiadis Associates, 'Master Programme and Plan: Preliminary Report', July–December 1961, p. 138.
58 CDA, DOX-GHA 16-22, Vol. 9, Doxiadis Associates, 'Tema – The Immediate Needs: A Programme of Priorities', 1961, p. 44.
59 Doxiadis Associates, 'Tema – The Immediate Needs', p. 44.
60 CDA, DOX-GHA 37-41, Vol. 20, Doxiadis Associates, 'Tema – Types of Dwelling', 1962, p. 350.
61 Doxiadis Associates, 'Tema – Types of Dwelling', p. 350.
62 Interview with Palmer Ofori-Nyako, trained at the Athens Centre of Ekistics and part of Doxiadis Associates' local team, August 2009.
63 See d'Auria, 'In the Laboratory and in the Field'.
64 I. Wallerstein, *The Road to Independence: Ghana and the Ivory Coast* (Paris: La Haye Mouton, 1964), pp. 132–3.
65 E.g. D. Appleyard, *Planning a Pluralist City: Conflicting Realities in Ciudad Guayana* (Cambridge: MIT Press, 1976); L. Peattie, *The View from the Barrio* (Ann Arbor: University of Michigan Press, 1968).

CHAPTER TEN

Designing change: Coins and the creation of new national identities

Catherine Eagleton

As the former British colonies in Africa moved towards independence, their new governments faced a complex set of decisions about money. In the colonial period currencies had been issued and managed by currency boards which were either headquartered in London or led by expatriates based in the colonies. This made the establishment of central banks and new national currencies an important statement of independence and of sovereignty.[1] For example, in the case of Ghana, the first of the British colonies in sub-Saharan Africa to gain independence, decolonisation was marked by the establishment of a new central bank and a new currency which featured the image of the prime minister, Kwame Nkrumah, on the coinage. Nkrumah himself argued that with such visual imagery his people could be 'shown that they are now really independent' through signs as well as words.[2] In the process of decolonisation, new currencies were imagined as visible signs of sovereignty that could rival the significance of a new national flag – a point explicitly made at the time.[3]

However, economic and political interests in Ghana and in the UK meant that the disentanglement of the former colony from colonial monetary institutions was complex.[4] The new central banks often operated, at least initially, in very similar ways to the currency boards which they replaced. This was because the economic realities of a turbulent period required that newly independent countries establish their credibility and the trustworthiness of the currency, but also because many countries maintained strong business links with Britain and the sterling area.[5] Moreover, although many have interpreted Nkrumah's actions in putting himself on the new coins as evidence of resistance and redefinition, and as showing Ghana's separation from Britain and from colonial rule, there was also opposition within Ghana – more than in Britain or elsewhere – to these new images appearing on the country's coins.[6] Although there have been a number of country studies exploring the relationship between currency imagery and national identity in an African context,[7] much of this literature pays insufficient attention to the process of the creation of that imagery, and to the non-state institutions, including commercial organisations, that were involved. To analyse the symbolic content of money without studying the processes through which it was created risks assuming too much state control over the images produced.[8] Studying not only the images but also the individuals, institutions and companies that were involved in the process of their production gives a more complete picture and allows insight into the ways the relationships between these state and non-state actors changed in the years immediately following decolonisation.

This chapter focuses on the issue of new currencies for newly independent countries in East Africa, considering Uganda, Tanzania and Kenya – three countries that had shared their colonial monetary histories and institutions. Many studies of decolonisation consider the relationship between the former coloniser and a newly independent country, but regional tensions and alliances were also often important as countries strove to differentiate themselves not only from the former colonial power but also from other new nation-states, as well as to create a sense of the nation that could be shared by all its citizens. By taking a regional approach, and examining the period immediately after independence in Uganda, Tanzania, and Kenya, it is possible to consider the similarities and differences between these three countries' currency designs during the tentative early period of decolonisation, and through this to understand how international, regional and national circumstances intersected.

More tangibly than economic policy, or political debates, coins and banknotes become part of everyday life, and their acceptability is crucial. Currency is issued by the state, and carries images into circulation to be used by people – coins and banknotes are among the few types of object that clearly link a nation and its citizens, and as such they can provide insights into the changing relationship between them. This chapter considers the process of designing coins in particular, both because their imagery tends to be simpler, using a more distilled visual language than the more complex images on banknotes, but also because of the easier availability of the papers relating to the details of the process of production for coins.[9] Unravelling the complexities of the processes involved in designing currency helps us understand more clearly the creation and circulation of these images – artists, committees, production contractors and politicians were all involved in the process of designing and minting coins – and the ways in which the designs that resulted were created at the intersection between politics, economics, emerging national identities, international relations, aesthetics and pragmatism. Political choices and ideals may have shaped the imagery that was chosen for currencies, but the requirement that new coins be widely accepted meant that the designs had to be relatively uncontroversial. In the end, I will argue, the choice of imagery on currency was limited by domestic, regional and international political realities in much the same way that the newly independent countries' broader economic policies were conditioned by global economic forces.

The end of the East African Currency Board and new coins for Uganda

British East Africa had, since 1919, used coins and notes issued and managed by the East African Currency Board.[10] The coins for East Africa were struck at the Royal Mint in London or at the private Birmingham Mint, while notes were printed by commercial contractors, including Thomas de la Rue, and currency was shipped out to East Africa through the Crown Agents for circulation.[11] As was the case for other colonies, the pre-independence designs for East African coins were relatively simple: the image of the ruling monarch featured on the obverse of the coins, and, depending on the denomination of the coin, the reverse featured either a pair of elephant tusks either side of a central hole, or an image of a lion in front of Kilimanjaro.[12]

In 1962, as Uganda, Kenya, Tanganyika and Zanzibar prepared to become independent from British rule, the East African Currency Board prepared new designs for the banknotes in use across the four countries in East Africa. Prompted by a request from the government of Tanganyika, the new notes were no longer to feature the portrait of the queen, but instead depict designs relating to local places or crops, with wording in English, Swahili, Arabic and Gujarati.[13] However, this change in imagery was not enough, and a decision soon came from Tanzania to issue its own national currency. Paul Bomani, the Tanzanian finance minister, confirmed widespread rumours of a new currency and central bank in April 1965.[14] It is possible that this decision was influenced by Kwame Nkrumah, with whom Julius Nyerere, president of Tanzania, was in close contact as a result of both men's commitment to the Organisation of African Unity and shared socialist political ideals. Nyerere explained the decision to break up the East African Currency Board by saying that his government could not plan effectively for economic development if it was not in control of its own currency.[15] However, the Kenyan finance minister blamed

Nkrumah for influencing the Tanzanian authorities, and causing this split between the East African countries. He had, he explained, tried to persuade Uganda and Tanzania not to issue their own currencies.[16]

Once Tanzania had broken away from the East African Currency Board, discussions about a single currency for East Africa quickly unravelled, and all three countries began to make plans for setting up central banks and issuing new currencies, placing orders with the Mint for the new coins to be designed and struck. For the Uganda coinage, staff at the Mint commissioned the London-based medallist and sculptor Cecil Thomas to work on designs.[17] Thomas was one of a group of artists who had a long association with the Mint, and who were regularly commissioned to design coins or medals for it. Indeed, the Mint saw the artistic quality of its coins as a significant selling point. By demonstrating its artists' skill and high design standards it hoped to win business for export orders – although the Mint was a government department, it was also a business, and its directors were keen to secure orders for overseas coinages. Thus, as internal documents in the National Archives describe, it announced the names of the artists who had designed specific coins to the press:

> [The Royal Mint] does considerable export trade to countries both inside and outside the British Commonwealth and I have taken the view that we should seize such opportunities [to name artists in press announcements about new coins] as may arise of getting a little publicity for our activities in the hope that both new and old customers may be kept aware of our existence.[18]

The briefing note that Thomas received as he began his work on the designs explained, 'Uganda are apparently undecided whether to use their Coat of Arms or a portrait of the Premier. I think it would be an advantage to offer sketches of both.'[19] Considerable artistic freedom on the reverse designs was offered, with the instructions simply suggesting that the produce of Uganda could feature, but also suggesting an image of a crested crane.[20] Within a month, Thomas sent photographs of his designs to the Mint – they featured reverse designs of the Uganda kob, crested crane, the coffee plant and the cotton plant, and three possible obverse designs, including portraits of the president, the prime minister, and the coat of arms.[21] Writing to the Crown Agents, the Mint suggested that using one of the portraits might be better, since the reverse designs were, in fact, all elements from the coat of arms.[22]

Within Uganda, however, this choice was much more politically complex. The prime minister, Milton Obote, held most of the executive power, and the president had a ceremonial role. However, the first president of independent Uganda was the Kabaka of Buganda, Mutesa II, and although Obote's Uganda People's Congress had been in coalition with the Buganda royalist party, Kabaka Yekka, during the independence elections, by 1964 this coalition had collapsed. Had a portrait of one of the two leaders of Uganda been chosen for the coinage, it would have been unacceptable to other political groups, and therefore the more neutral symbol of the coat of arms was preferred.[23]

For the reverse designs, the initial instructions given to the artist were that he could think freely about the images, but the Ugandan authorities changed their requirements and instead asked that they should be as similar as possible to the old coins of the East African Currency Board, with only minor changes.[24] The inscription was to be changed to 'BANK OF UGANDA', and on the lower-denomination coins the design of two elephant tusks was to be retained, while on the higher-denomination coins the same design as had appeared on the colonial coins was to be kept, with minor modifications: the mountains were changed to represent the Muhavura Volcano in south-west Uganda, and the lion was replaced by the Ugandan national symbol of the crested crane.[25]

Replacing the mountains with volcanoes, and the lion with the crane, were less visual statements of independence from British colonial rule than they were representations of separation from Kenya and Tanzania, since the mountain on the colonial coins was Kilimanjaro in Tanzania, and the lion standing in the foreground was the symbol of Kenya. These coin designs, then, point to the regional context for decolonisation, and to the importance of creating a national identity distinct from

Figure 10.1 Shilling coin, Uganda, 1966.

neighbouring countries. By replacing details while keeping the overall reverse design the same, and replacing the queen's image on the obverse with the Ugandan coat of arms (see Figure 10.1), the coins show change and independence, in terms of Uganda's relationship with Britain as well as the other countries in East Africa. At the same time, however, by drawing visual comparisons with the East African Currency Board coinage that they replaced, the new coins acted to reassure people of the stability of the currency and promoted trust. This concern with stability and acceptability was made explicit by the Ministry of Finance in Entebbe when discussing the designs with the Mint, and it was a regular theme in the correspondence of new finance ministers and central bank officials in the period of decolonisation.[26] During a period of turbulence and uncertainty, the images on currency had to be carefully balanced to give impressions not only of independence but also of continuity, for both Ugandan and international audiences.

Tanzania

The government of Tanzania, whose action sparked the break-up of the East African Currency Board, had already signed a contract with the commercial banknote-printing company Thomas de la Rue when Finance Minister Bomani announced further plans to establish a new central bank and national currency in June 1965. De la Rue had printed the banknotes for newly independent Ghana, and was in the 1960s pushing to expand its business in Africa. Indeed, since at least the 1940s, de la Rue had been working with the Mint in order to help it secure export orders for the production of coinage, which were often managed through non-government channels, through local agents or representatives.[27] This arrangement had, by the early 1960s, been formalised into a three-way non-competition agreement between de la Rue, the Royal Mint and the Birmingham Mint in relation to the production of coinage.[28] Not only does this agreement blur the lines between government and commercial organisations in the production of currency, and therefore in our understanding of the processes of decolonisation, it also demonstrates that the Mint's own motivations for undertaking export coinage orders were commercial, despite its being a government department. As the deputy master of the Mint explained to his Treasury contact in relation to the production of the coins for newly independent Ghana, orders for coinage for overseas countries helped to keep the cost of minting UK coinage low, by 'filling up troughs in the United Kingdom demand' and keeping the factory busy year-round, as well as by bringing in revenue to subsidise the operations of the Mint.[29]

In line with their agreement, Thomas de la Rue approached the Mint about the production of new coins for Tanzania, passing on to it the specific instructions it had received for the designs. If in the case of Uganda the concern of the government was to show the changes at independence while maintaining a sense of stability and trust in the currency as well as marking the country's separation not only from the UK but from the other East African countries, the Tanzanian authorities wanted to make a bolder claim through the imagery on their coins. On the obverse, the coins were to feature a portrait of Tanzania's president, Julius Nyerere, and a picture of him was sent from Tanzania, with a note to the artist asking that his frown be removed. Nyerere was to be surrounded by the inscription in Swahili, 'Rais mwalimu J E Nyerere' ('President teacher J.E. Nyerere'), or the Swahili slogan that appeared on the new national coat of arms, 'Uhuru na umoja' ('Freedom and unity').[30] In the end, however, another inscription was suggested, which simply read 'Rais wa kwanza' ('First president') without naming Nyerere at all.[31] The language choice of the coin inscription links to Nyerere's promotion of Swahili as the language of the nation, and its association with the anti-colonial struggles leading up to independence. Lutz Marten and Nancy Kula suggest that in this context, the colonial currency denomination of the shilling was retained to ensure continuity with the East African community countries, but changed to the Swahili 'shilingi' in line with broader Tanzanian nationalist policies.[32]

The reverse designs were to feature a tuna fish, an ostrich, an elephant and Kilimanjaro 'from the Tanzania side ... with a giraffe in the foreground', the giraffe being the national symbol of Tanzania.[33] As on the Uganda coins, the lion of Kenya was to be replaced with a different national symbol, but a degree of continuity in the coins' designs would be maintained. However, almost as soon as sculptor and theatre designer Christopher Ironside was asked to prepare these designs, the choice of images was changed, and the 50-cent coin was now to feature a rabbit – a striking choice, in light of the fact that from the 1970s, Nyerere was known as 'Sungura', or 'the Rabbit'. However, it is not clear whether this lay behind this choice of coin design in 1965, and it could equally have been that the lower denominations simply featured a fish, a bird and an animal that provided food.[34] Carrying a much clearer political message, the largest-denomination coin, of 1 shilingi, was to have a 'torch of freedom leaning forward with hand and flame blowing back', to show movement forward.[35] This represented the freedom torch (the 'Uhuru Torch') that had been lit atop Kilimanjaro in 1961 to mark the coming independence of Tanzania, a symbol that resonates today. Ironside prepared sketches to send to the Tanzanian government, presenting them first to officials at the Mint, who suggested some modifications to the design of the torch, and a 'beefier-looking arm'.[36] These modifications made, the Mint sent Ironside's designs (Figure 10.2) to the Tanzanian government for its comments.

The designs were sent to Finance Minister Bomani along with a letter explaining that the Mint preferred one of the two designs for the torch of freedom (design A), which they thought was 'a much stronger and more satisfactory design'.[37] Ironside's opinion was that although smaller, the torch and arm in option A gave a 'more energetic feeling'.[38] Despite this strong steer from both artist and Mint, the Tanzanian authorities responded that they nonetheless preferred design B for the torch.[39]

This should, then, have been the final word on the issue. However, one further stage in the design process remained before the coins could go into production, which was the approval of the designs by the Royal Mint Advisory Committee on the Design of Coins, Medals, Seals and Decorations.[40] This committee, reporting to the Treasury in London, had been established in 1922 with the aim of improving the quality of the design of coins and medals, and to advise the Mint on its production. Their input usually took place at three key stages: in the selection of subject matter and the commissioning of artists, in the consideration of initial sketches of designs, and in the details of the final designs and plaster models of the coins.[41] They approved all designs before striking began. Since its inception the Advisory Committee had always included a senior representative of the monarch, and from 1952 the president of the committee was the Duke of Edinburgh, Prince Philip.[42]

Designs for coins and medals for the British Empire had, since 1922, been considered by the committee, but transition to independence in Africa (and elsewhere) challenged this procedure. What role should the committee have in criticising or approving coin designs for sovereign nations that were no longer part of the British Empire? More specifically, how could a committee chaired by Prince Philip provide this advice when Commonwealth countries were replacing the image of the queen – his wife – on their coins? Later, by the early 1970s, the Advisory Committee began to review its own role in relation to the design of coins, concluding that its remit was to advise on the design of United Kingdom coins, medals and seals, and that it would only consider, 'when asked, designs prepared for the Royal Mint's export customers'.[43] Yet it is clear from the minutes of Advisory Committee meetings in the 1960s that while it was concerned primarily with designs that featured the image of the

Item 8　　　　　　　　COINAGE FOR TANZANIA

Alternative obverse designs

Alternative reverse designs

Figure 10.2 Christopher Ironside, design options for the Tanzanian coinage, 1965, as shown to the Royal Mint Advisory Committee.

queen, and less concerned with designs for other Commonwealth countries who had chosen not to have the image of the sovereign on their coins, it was still usual for all coin designs to be seen by the committee at this time.

However, the Advisory Committee usually met only two or three times a year, and in many cases, including in that of the Tanzanian coins, the designs had been sketched out, designed and approved before the committee had met. Informed that the designs 'have virtually been dictated by Tanzania, [and] have already been submitted to Tanzania', the Advisory Committee gave no criticisms of the Tanzanian designs, noting only that they 'make a very handsome set', and that they were about to enter production (for the final design, see Figure 10.3).[44] Indeed, one member of the Advisory Committee, the poet and broadcaster John Betjeman, was so impressed with the designs that he bought the whole set of drawings from Christopher Ironside in exchange for a signed copy of his collected poems, as he could not bear to think of them 'just being filed away in an office'.[45]

In cases like this one, the decision of the client took precedence over the opinions of the committee and the designer. Yet it is clear from his notebooks that Ironside found himself uncertain about the role of the Advisory Committee in relation to orders for coinage:

> Committee
> Some think they're designers
> Some think they're clients
> Some think they're art masters
> Difficult to know their function
> ...
> Difficult on export – no means of knowing local political
>   acceptability. Client comes first
> Export – Tanzania
> Design can be important
> Clients requirements
> Presentation
> Involvement of designer early on[46]

Ironside's comment about the political acceptability of designs was perceptive, since it was clear that in relation to the torch of freedom, the Mint and the Tanzanian government were applying different criteria. The British artist and officials considered the design only from an aesthetic perspective, primarily taking into account the balance and visual appeal of the design. For the Tanzanian government, however, it was more important to show energy, vigour and forward movement, and for the flaming torch to be more prominent.

Figure 10.3 Final version of the one-shilingi coin, Tanzania, 1966.

Gradually, towards the end of the 1960s, the Advisory Committee became less involved in the process of designing coins for the former British colonies, although it was always willing to be involved should the customer request it. The minutes for the committee for 1969 record that 'for reasons of urgency or because designs were finalised by the customer', several designs for overseas customers were not shown to the committee.[47] In the same year, despite describing the committee as still having 'considerable influence' in a letter to the sculptor and Royal Academician David McFall, the deputy master of the Mint, went on to note that 'in many cases the wishes of the Government concerned to feature particular animals or devices had to be overriding and the results less satisfactory than the Committee might have wished'.[48] Perhaps a lament over diminishing influence, this comment illustrates the Mint, its Advisory Committee and its artists adjusting to the new realities of decolonisation and the demands of newly independent governments.

Within Tanzania, the symbol of the torch of freedom was very recognisable, and so the Tanzanian coins made a bolder statement about independence than those designed for Uganda, although different audiences were targeted. In line with Nyerere's developing policy of 'Ujamaa', or self-reliance, the focus for the Tanzanian coins was domestic – and the language and imagery on them aimed primarily at local audiences, although they maintained the link to the other East African shilling currencies in name. The banknotes, too, promoted these messages, with images including sisal drying and cattle herding, and of course the portrait of Nyerere, who was by now becoming increasingly personally associated with the nation as well as with his political principles of self-reliance.

Kenya and Kenyatta

During 1965 the Mint was also asked to produce designs for the new currency for Kenya. These were to feature a portrait of President Jomo Kenyatta and the inscription 'Republic of Kenya'. London-based sculptor Norman Sillman was commissioned to prepare the designs, and the Mint requested detailed information from the Kenyan authorities about how Kenyatta was to be depicted, including whether he should face to the right or the left (each of his ears looked rather different to the other), whether he was to be wearing a hat, and whether he should be wearing European or African dress. Mint officials also suggested potential titles, stressing that a phrase such as 'Jomo Kenyatta President of Kenya' would be the longest that could fit on the obverse around the portrait,[49] but in their reply a week later the Crown Agents confirmed that there would be no inscription on the obverse.[50] In passing this and other information on to Sillman, the unusual nature of this request was noted, with one Mint official saying, 'I can't think of any coin which shows just a portrait and nothing else,' before adding, 'if you felt ... that a portrait alone would result in an unsatisfactory design please feel at liberty to submit alternative designs with the same wording as before, i.e. "PRESIDENT JOMO KENYATTA" or "MZEE JOMO KENYATTA"'.[51] Designs, both with and without titles for Kenyatta, were considered by the Advisory Committee, which made suggestions for their improvement. Revised designs were sent to Kenya for comment, and approved for production: in the end, no inscriptions featured on the obverse side, and the Kenyan coat of arms featured on the reverse side of the one-shilling coin (Figure 10.4).[52]

It is striking that despite suggestions for a more complex design from Mint officials, the Kenyan authorities were firm in their insistence that there were to be no inscriptions on the obverse side. However, the simplicity of these designs makes sense in the context of Kenyan politics in the mid-1960s. Kenyatta had been elected president in 1964, and would begin later in the 1960s to amend the constitution to extend his powers, leading to Kenya being a single-party state by the end of the 1960s. However, in 1965 this process was still somewhat tentative. Kenyatta was pursuing a policy of the Africanisation of the institutions of Kenya, replacing European and Asian holders of key government and business posts with Africans, so the image of an

Figure 10.4 One-shilling coin, Kenya, 1966.

African leader on the coinage would have sent an important message. However, at this point, it might not have been wise to press a stronger nationalist or political message through the designs on Kenyan coins.

Evidently, Kenyatta liked his image on the new coins, and the Mint soon received enquiries about the possibility of making a series of gold coins to commemorate his seventy-fifth birthday in 1966 – to be sold as collector coins rather than for circulation. The request for these coins came not through the Crown Agents or through Thomas de la Rue, but from an import-export company called Metalimport, and the Mint queried whether the coin issue would 'have official blessing and not be a private venture on the part of the President'.[53] The necessary assurances were provided from Kenyatta himself, and the agent acting on his behalf then also wrote to discuss the wording of the inscriptions on the coins:

> I mentioned the question of politics involved in the Royal Mint production where such words as 'Father of the New Africa' were used. The wording should cause no stumbling block, though personally I would like the wording to be as laudatory of His Excellency's achievements within Kenya and the 'New Africa' as possible.[54]

The concern expressed about the wording of the inscriptions related to the strong political statements that they made – Kenyatta had suggested 'Mzee Jomo Kenyatta', 'Leader or Father of the Kenyan Nation' or 'Mzee Leader of New Africa'.[55] The Commonwealth Relations Office of the British Government feared that 'Mzee Leader of New Africa' might sound 'presumptuous in other capitals' and suggested that this option could 'conveniently be omitted from sample proofs'.⁵⁶

Kenyatta suggested that the coins could have reverse designs including Mount Kenya, a flywhisk, a cockerel, a map of Kenya and perhaps also a map of Kenya in relation to Africa. These were all political symbols linked to Kenyatta himself or to the political party he led, the Kenya African National Union (KANU): Kenyatta usually carried a flywhisk, and the cockerel was the symbol of KANU. The images chosen, then, linked Kenyatta, his party, the nation of Kenya and the continent of Africa, and, with their overt political symbolism were different from those that had recently been adopted for the circulating coinage. It seems, however, that the Mint officials may not have been fully aware of the significance of Kenyatta's choices of images, since notes made by officials at the time described the cockerel with an axe as a local image for a prosperous future, making no mention of its political connotations.⁵⁷ The images suggested by Kenyatta were developed into coin designs, but given their concern at the proposed inscriptions, the Mint, and the Commonwealth Relations Office, exerted some influence, toning down the inscriptions that would appear on them.

The Mint was keen to take on the order, as Kenya was an important customer, and by this point business from overseas clients had become significant and profitable for them. These gold coins were to be minted in relatively small quantities, to be sold to coin collectors around the world. However, at the same time, there were restrictions on the circulation of gold coins in sterling-area countries owing to the sterling crisis of 1964–67 and the efforts of the Bank of England to manage the pound and avoid devaluation. This meant that, although the gold coins were not intended for circulation in Kenya, they would technically have been legal tender there, and so the Mint had to seek permission to produce them from the Bank of England.⁵⁸ One Bank official was particularly unimpressed with the proposal, replying:

> I would hope that Kenya could be dissuaded from proceeding with this application: President Kenyatta's 75th birthday hardly seems a sufficient reason for an issue of commemorative gold coins. If this application were allowed, we should be plagued from all quarters of the Commonwealth with requests to commemorate almost any sort of anniversary, and it would make nonsense of some of the reasons we have advanced when rejecting other requests.⁵⁹

Notable here is the assumption by Bank officials that, despite the political independence of Kenya from Britain, the stability of the

Figure 10.5 Gold coins celebrating Jomo Kenyatta's seventy-fifth birthday, 1966.

sterling zone was still sufficient reason to exert influence over whether these coins should be issued. However, there were disagreements between government departments, and the Commonwealth Relations Office took a more balanced view, pointing out that Kenyatta Day was celebrated in Kenya each 20 October, and that it was likely to be popular if a coin was issued to make a special occasion of his seventy-fifth birthday. Given the good relationship between the UK and Kenyatta, they hoped it would be possible to meet his request, and, in the end, the benefits of allowing the issue to go ahead overrode the concerns expressed. The Treasury approved the minting of these commemorative gold coins for Kenya in April 1966, on the proviso that it was stressed to the Kenyan authorities that this was an exceptional occasion.[60] The designs were prepared, with the same portrait as had been used on the circulating coinage, but with the new reverse designs. The potentially problematic inscription was split into two, with 'Mzee Jomo Kenyatta' around the portrait of the obverse, and 'Father of the Kenyan Nation' around the design on the reverse of each denomination (Figure 10.5).[61]

The contrast between the designs chosen for the circulation coins and these gold collector coins minted in the name of Kenya is conspicuous. Produced in the same year, only months apart, they indicate the different ways in which Kenyatta was presenting himself and his country to different audiences. Within Kenya the greater need was to present himself as the leader of the country in a more understated and less political or factional way, while in the designs for the gold coins we perhaps see the way that Kenyatta presented himself when freed from those domestic political concerns, to an audience of collectors around the world.[62] The comparison between these two cases shows that the choice of images on coinage for newly independent nations might be constrained not only by the need to maintain the impression of trust and stability, but also by the domestic, as well as international, political realities of decolonisation.

Conclusion

Fifty years later, it is still possible to trace the influence of these early representations of African leaders who appeared on the coins and banknotes issued in the immediate post-independence period. In 2000, the Bank of Tanzania announced that a new 1000-shilling note would feature the portrait of Nyerere, who had died the year before, to recognise his 'immense contribution to Tanzania, Africa and the world'. In Kenya, Kenyatta's portrait remained on coins and notes until his death in 1978. In 2003, however, Kenya's Central Bank issued a batch of old notes from 1978, once again featuring Kenyatta's portrait, as an interim measure. These old notes were greeted with nostalgia by many Kenyans, as they dated from a period of economic prosperity, and from 2005 new coins and notes were issued that once again featured Kenyatta, as 'a historical figure who would be a unifying force of the country'.[63] However, following ethnic violence, a new constitution was adopted in 2010 which included the provision that notes and coins issued in Kenya should have no images of individuals on them – only images that represent the country of Kenya.[64] Even the commemorative coin for the celebration of the fiftieth anniversary of Kenyan independence, it was announced in December 2013 by President Uhuru Kenyatta (Jomo Kenyatta's son), would not bear any individual's portrait.[65]

Examining closely the years immediately following independence, the three case studies in this chapter show the roots of these contemporary debates. Decolonisation brought changes in many areas, and, as nation-states established themselves, there was a concern – often explicit – with the need to create a new national currency as a mark of independence. The new currencies bore images and inscriptions that showed a new national identity, but these images and inscriptions were chosen and developed through a complex set of relationships with individuals, companies and governments, and thus were often not the product of a single, coherent, vision for a new national identity.

In the cases of Kenya, Uganda and Tanzania, the three countries had been inaugurated as republics by the time of their coins' designs, and each therefore chose to issue new currencies without the image of HRH Queen Elizabeth II on them. Ugandan authorities decided on designs based on the old East African Currency Board coins, to ensure continuity and acceptance of the new currency, while the Tanzanian government took the opportunity to depict political symbols like the flaming torch on the coins, and to change the language of their inscriptions to Swahili. In the case of Kenya, the issue of circulating coinage and a collector coin set at almost the same time point to the restrictions that might be placed on images for coinage by the need to ensure acceptance by those whose politics diverged from the leader depicted on the coin. Clearly, then, in thinking about coin design in the period of decolonisation, it is important to understand this phenomenon not only as a method of circulating images relating to the new nation and making statements about independence and national identity, but also as a process and a set of design decisions that were as constrained as they were free. Central banks, ministers of finance, prime ministers and presidents of newly independent countries still had to ensure the acceptability of their currencies, and to ensure belief in their value, at home as well as overseas.

Looking at the design process is also instructive, since it allows insight into the gradual process of decolonisation in the institutions, organisations, committees and officials in London. The Mint had previously been able to rely on securing the contracts for producing coins for the British Empire, but now faced increasing competition from other government mints, as well as from commercial companies. The influence of the Advisory Committee over export orders declined gradually over a period of several years, although it still saw itself as upholding the high design standards of the Mint, something that was important for securing new business. The artists working on coin design, mostly based in London, worked to a more or less well-defined brief, and within a set of aesthetic norms that were encouraged by the Advisory Committee, but occasionally found it frustrating when, despite their best efforts, what they considered to be their better designs were not selected. There was occasional direct influence from government officials in London as well: suggested images might be altered, titles might be reworded, and, as in the case of the Kenya example, influence brought to bear in the interests of avoiding unnecessary difficulties in other African capital cities.

The process of decolonisation as seen through coin design and the imagery on currency also shows a more gradual change than might be supposed from the existing literature, which tends to describe a significant and sudden political and cultural rupture. By looking closely at the process of making money, the politics implicit in this process and the artistic and business concerns that were involved, the process of decolonisation appears in a different frame. Uncertain, often, of how to proceed, or how far to push their influence, officials at the Mint and in government offices in London gradually worked out their new relationship with African governments and central banks, and they did this in part through the details of small and apparently insignificant objects like coins.

African governments, for their part, presented images on the new currencies that would not only mark the constitutional change that independence represented, but also ensure the necessary trust in their currencies within and beyond their borders, and prove acceptable across domestic political divides. Taking a comparative approach to this subject, and looking at Uganda, Tanzania and Kenya, shows the process of decolonisation as more than just a redefinition of the relationship between Britain and its former colonies. The three countries had shared a single currency, and there had been the expectation that they would continue to use a single East African currency after independence. However, the political and economic tensions between African countries and their leaders meant that each instead issued its own national currencies. Each of the three countries had its own distinctive domestic political concerns and took a slightly different approach to the process of designing and issuing coins and notes. Common to all three countries, however, was a concern to differentiate themselves from each other, as well as from Britain. Through this we can see decolonisation and the construction of new national identities as a process that had to work at several levels: national, regional and international. More broadly, it points to the insights that might be gained from studying other aspects of decolonisation in a comparative way, to understand not only the relationship between colonised and coloniser, but also to consider how newly independent countries negotiated their relationships with each other.

Notes

This research was made possible thanks to generous support from the Leverhulme Trust, as part of the Money in Africa research project (research project grant F/000 52/D, 2010–13).

1 One of the only unquestioned powers involved in sovereignty is the right to mint currency: J. Herbst, *States and Power in Africa: Comparative Lessons in Authority and Control* (Princeton: Princeton University Press, 2000), p. 201.
2 K. Nkrumah, 'Why the Queen's Head is Coming Off our Coins', *Daily Sketch* (20 June 1957), p. 12.
3 E. Helleiner, *The Making of National Money: Territorial Currencies in Historical Perspective* (Ithaca: Cornell University Press, 2003), p. 205. See also D. Hammett and P. Nugent, *Making Nations, Creating Strangers: States and Citizenship in Africa* (Leiden: Brill, 2007), p. 248. See also E. Gilbert and E. Helleiner, 'Introduction: Nation-States and Money: Historical Contexts, Interdisciplinary Perspectives', in E. Gilbert and E. Helleiner (eds), *Nation-States and Money: The Past, Present and Future of National Currencies* (London: Routledge, 1999).
4 C. Schenk, in 'Monetary Institutions in Newly Independent Countries: The Experience of Malaya, Ghana and Nigeria in the 1950s', *Financial History Review*, 4:2 (1997), 181–98, argues that the economic realities of the time explain the essential continuity between the colonial currency boards and the new central banks in Ghana, Nigeria and Malaya. Sarah Stockwell, in 'Instilling the "Sterling Tradition": Decolonisation and the Creation of a Central Bank in Ghana', *Journal of Imperial and Commonwealth History*, 26:2 (1998), 100–19, considers the case of Ghana to explore the combination of political and economic interests in the foundation of the Bank of Ghana and the new national currency.
5 On the political motivations for the establishment of central banks, see Schenk, 'Monetary Institutions in Newly Independent Countries'. On central banks in West Africa, see C.U. Uche, 'J.B. Loynes and Central Banking Development in British West Africa', *South African Journal of Economic History*, 15:1–2 (2000), 112–33. On economic decolonisation and business interests, see, for example, D.K. Fieldhouse, *Merchant Capital and Economic Decolonization: The United Africa Company, 1929–1987* (Oxford: Clarendon Press, 1994) and R.L. Tignor, *Capitalism and Nationalism at the End of Empire: State and Business in Decolonizing Egypt, Nigeria, and Kenya, 1945–1963* (Princeton: Princeton University Press, 1997).

6 H. Fuller, 'Civitatis Ghaniensis Conditor: Kwame Nkrumah, Symbolic Nationalism and the Iconography of Ghanaian Money 1957 – the Golden Jubilee', Nations and Nationalism, 14:3 (2008), 537, and J. Penrose, 'Designing the Nation: Banknotes, Banal Nationalism and Alternative Conceptions of the State', Political Geography, 30 (2011), 433. On other representations of Nkrumah in the construction of national identity, see J. Hess, 'Exhibiting Ghana: Display, Documentary, and "National" Art in the Nkrumah Era', African Studies Review, 44:1 (2001), 59–77.
7 See, for example, V. Hewitt, 'A Distant View: Imagery and Imagination in the Paper Currency of the British Empire, 1800–1960', in Gilbert and Helleiner, Nation-States and Money; J.M. Galloy, 'Symbols of Identity and Nationalism in Mexican and Central-American Currency', Applied Semiotics, 4:9 (2000), 15–34; T. Unwin and V. Hewitt, 'Banknotes and National Identity in Central and Eastern Europe', Political Geography, 20:6 (2001), 1005–28; W. Mwangi, 'The Lion, the Native and the Coffee Plant: Political Imagery and the Ambiguous Art of Currency Design in Colonial Kenya', Geopolitics, 7:1 (2002), 31–62; J. Hymans, 'The Changing Colour of Money: European Currency Iconography and Collective Identity', European Journal of International Relations, 10:1 (2004), 5–31; A.E. Tschoegl, 'Change the Regime – Change the Money: Bulgarian Banknotes, 1885–2003', Balkanologie, 8:2 (2004), 7–31; I. Cusack, 'Tiny Transmitters of Nationalist and Colonial Ideology: The Postage Stamps of Portugal and its Empire', Nations and Nationalism, 11:4 (2005), 591–612; J. Lauer, 'Money as Mass Communication: US Paper Currency and the Iconography of Nationalism', Communication Review, 11:2 (2008), 109–32; K. Strassler, 'The Face of Money: Currency, Crisis, and Remediation in Post-Suharto Indonesia', Cultural Anthropology, 24:1 (2009), 68–103; J. Penrose and C. Cumming, 'Money Talks: Banknote Iconography and Symbolic Constructions of Scotland', Nations and Nationalism, 17:4 (2011), 821–42; and Y. Wallach, 'Creating a Country through Currency and Stamps: State Symbols and Nation-building in British-ruled Palestine', Nations and Nationalism, 17:1 (2011), 129–47.
8 Penrose, 'Designing the Nation', notes some exceptions to this general point, including Unwin and Hewitt, 'Banknotes and National Identity in Central and Eastern Europe'.
9 The series MINT 20 is held at The National Archives, London (hereafter TNA) and consists of files relating to the production of coins for export to other countries. The Royal Mint Museum also arranged for access to the designs and other materials held in its corporate archive.
10 On currency boards, see, for example, A.J. Schwartz, 'Currency Boards: Their Past, Present and Possible Future Role', Carnegie-Rochester Conference Series on Public Policy, 39 (1993), 147–87; on the establishment of the East African Currency Board, see W. Mwangi, 'Of Coins and Conquest: The East African Currency Board, the Rupee Crisis, and the Problem of Colonialism in the East African Protectorate', Comparative Studies in Society and History, 43:4 (2001), 763–87.
11 The Royal Mint (hereafter 'Mint') was the government department responsible for producing British coin, and also for supplying coin for British colonies. When completing orders for coins for British colonies, it often contracted out production of the smaller denominations to privately owned mints, including the Birmingham Mint, but the Royal Mint would in all such cases be responsible for the negotiation of the contract, and for the design of the coins.
12 Mwangi, 'Of Coins and Conquest', and Mwangi, 'The Lion, the Native and the Coffee Plant'.
13 TNA, FCO 141/7049, secret memo by Minister of Finance, Nairobi, 14 July 1962.
14 TNA, T 317/757, secret Treasury memo, 9 April 1965.
15 Helleiner, The Making of National Money, p. 206.

16 'Sharp Attacks in Nairobi on Dr Nkrumah and Mr Chou', *The Times*, London (12 June 1965), p. 17.
17 F. Simmons, 'Thomas, Cecil Walter (1885–1976)', in *Dictionary of National Biography*, first published 2004; online edn, 2007.
18 TNA, MINT 20/2052, Mint to Treasury, 17 and 24 November 1955.
19 TNA, MINT 20/3084, unsigned letter from Mint official to Cecil Thomas, 26 June 1965. The reference here, and in correspondence relating to other countries, to the coat of arms of a country as an alternative symbol to an image of the leader of the country, is interesting. In African countries, of course, European-style heraldry was itself a colonial-era import, but one which endured after independence, with new coats of arms being designed for newly independent countries. See, for example: B. Smith, J.D. Lewis-Williams, G. Blundell and C. Chippindale, 'Archaeology and Symbolism in the New South African Coat of Arms', *Antiquity*, 74 (2000), 467–8, and A. Barnard, 'Coat of Arms and the Body Politic: Khoisan Imagery and South African National Identity', *Ethnos*, 69:1 (2004), 5–22; and D.H. Ross, 'The Heraldic Lion in Akan Art: A Study of Motif Assimilation in Southern Ghana', *Metropolitan Museum Journal*, 16 (January 1981), 165–80, on how the European heraldic symbol of the lion became a 'traditional' element of Akan art.
20 TNA, MINT 20/3084, letter from Mint to Cecil Thomas, 26 June 1965.
21 TNA, MINT 20/3084, letter from Cecil Thomas to Mint, 19 July 1965.
22 TNA, MINT 20/3084, letter from Mint to Crown Agents, 20 July 1965. This file also includes photographs of the original designs, which were not in the end adopted.
23 TNA, MINT 20/3084, letter from Ministry of Finance, Uganda, to Crown Agents, 1 December 1965.
24 As Cecil Thomas was on holiday, these revised reverse designs were prepared by another artist, William Newman: TNA, MINT 20/3084, letter from Mint to William Newman, 21 December 1965.
25 One of the most striking of Uganda's birds, the crested crane had been adopted as the national emblem by Sir Frederick Jackson in 1893. There was some discussion about whether the bird would stand in front of the volcano, or in front of an image of the new Central Bank building: see TNA, MINT 20/3084, letter from Crown Agents to Mint, 14 March 1966, enclosing photographs for the artist's reference.
26 TNA, MINT 20/3084, letter from Ministry of Finance, Uganda, to Crown Agents, and clarifying letter from Mint to Crown Agents, both 20 December 1965.
27 TNA, MINT 20/2158, letter from Mint to Foreign Office clarifying the relationship with Thomas de la Rue, 15 May 1951, and explaining that this relationship sometimes entailed sharing confidential information with de la Rue.
28 TNA, MINT 20/3501, 20/3502 and 20/4294, and TNA, T 326/1475.
29 TNA, MINT 20/2563 part 2, letter from Mint to Treasury, 11 July 1955.
30 Nyerere was often given the title 'mwalimu': see A.H.M. Kirk-Greene, 'His Eternity, His Eccentricity, or His Exemplarity? A Further Contribution to the Study of H. E. the African Head of State', *African Affairs*, 90:359 (1991), 177–8.
31 TNA, MINT 20/3075, letter from Mint to Christopher Ironside, 8 March 1965.
32 L. Marten and N. Kula, 'Meanings of Money: National Identity and the Semantics of Currency in Zambia and Tanzania', *African Cultural Studies*, 20:2 (2008), 191–2.
33 TNA, MINT 20/3075, letter from Thomas de la Rue to Mint, 1 March 1965.
34 On the reassessment of Nyerere's legacy after his death, see M. Fouéré, 'JK Nyerere entre mythe et histoire: analyse de la production d'une mémoire publique officielle en Tanzanie post-socialiste', *Cahiers d'Afrique de l'Est*, 41 (2009), 197–224.
35 TNA, MINT 20/3075, letters from Mint to Christopher Ironside, 5 and 8 March 1965.
36 TNA, MINT 20/3075, letter from Mint to Christopher Ironside, 19 March 1965.

37 TNA, MINT 20/3075, letter from Thomas de la Rue to Minister of Finance, Tanzania, 7 April 1965.
38 TNA, MINT 20/3075, note by Christopher Ironside in minutes of Advisory Committee, 29 April 1965.
39 TNA, MINT 20/3075, letter from Treasury, Tanzania, to Thomas de la Rue, 21 April 1965.
40 Henceforth, 'Advisory Committee'.
41 TNA, MINT 20/3931, letter from Mint to Design Centre, London, 14 August 1974.
42 C. Frayling, 'Continuity through Change: The Royal Mint Advisory Committee', in K. Clancy (ed.), *Designing Change* (Llantrisant: Royal Mint, 2008), pp. 39–50. See also J. Porteous, 'Speech by John Porteous at the Farewell Lunch for His Royal Highness, the Prince Philip, Duke of Edinburgh, at St James's Palace, 24 November 1999', *British Numismatic Journal*, 70 (2000), 178–9.
43 TNA, MINT 20/3929, undated 1972 note in preparation for the Chancellor of the Exchequer's lunch with the Advisory Committee on 30 November.
44 TNA, MINT 20/3075, extract of minutes of Advisory Committee, 29 April 1965.
45 British Museum, Department of Coins and Medals, Christopher Ironside Archive, letter from John Betjeman to Christopher Ironside, 29 April 1965, unnumbered item.
46 British Museum, Department of Coins and Medals, Christopher Ironside Archive, notebook 2006,0601.475.
47 TNA, MINT 20/3927, note relating to Advisory Committee meeting, 22 October 1969.
48 TNA, MINT 20/3934, letter from Mint to David McFall, 10 December 1969.
49 TNA, MINT 20/3036, Mint to Crown Agents, 30 September 1965.
50 TNA, MINT 20/3036, Crown Agents to Mint, 7 October 1965.
51 TNA, MINT 20/3036, Mint to Norman Sillman, 15 October 1965. On the title 'Mzee' as part of Kenyatta's construction of the image of himself as the leader of Kenya, see Kirk-Greene, 'His Eternity, His Eccentricity, or His Exemplarity?', 177–8.
52 Designs and reference material for these commemorative coins are in an unnumbered envelope titled 'Kenya' in Royal Mint Museum.
53 TNA, MINT 20/3037, letter from Mint to Commonwealth Relations Office, 23 February 1966.
54 TNA, MINT 20/3037, letter from Metalimport to Mint, 16 February 1966.
55 TNA, MINT 20/3037, letter from Jomo Kenyatta to Metalimport, 12 February 1966.
56 TNA, MINT 20/3037, letter from Commonwealth Relations Office to Treasury, 24 March 1966.
57 Royal Mint Museum, unnumbered envelope 'Kenya' (1966).
58 On the Bank of England and the sterling crisis, see F. Capie, *The Bank of England: 1950s to 1979* (Cambridge: Cambridge University Press, 2010), especially chapter 5. On the sterling zone, see C.R. Schenk, *The Decline of Sterling: Managing the Retreat of an International Currency, 1945–1992* (Cambridge: Cambridge University Press, 2010).
59 TNA, MINT 20/3037, letter from Bank of England to Treasury, 22 February 1966.
60 TNA, MINT 20/3037, letter from Treasury to Mint, 7 April 1966.
61 See drawings and correspondence in TNA, MINT 20/3037. V.T. Le Vine, 'Changing Leadership Styles and Political Images: Some Preliminary Notes', *Journal of Modern African Studies*, 15:4 (1977), 633, discusses the transformation of the image of Kenyatta from a leader associated with Kikuyu nationalism to a leader above all factional conflict.
62 In the end, however, these messages were seen by only a few people, since the gold coin sets did not sell well, and the coin dealers Spink, in London, wrote to the Mint in 1967 to request permission to melt down their remaining stock: see

TNA, MINT 20/3037, note of telephone call from Spink & Son, London, 4 April 1967.
63 W. Thuku, 'Kenyatta Currency Back in Circulation', *The Nation* (Nairobi, 6 May 2003); C. Riungu, 'Kenya: Sh2.9b in Kenyatta Currency for Circulation After 24-Year Absence', *The Nation*, Nairobi (11 May 2003); and O. Orlale, 'Kenyatta Image Coins Back', Nairobi, *The Nation* (22 May 2005).
64 J. Nyabiage, 'Kenya: Draft Constitution – Currency to Exclude Portraits', Nairobi, *Daily Nation* (18 November 2009); and 'Kenya: Work Starts On Notes And Coins Without President's Portrait', *Daily Nation*, Nairobi (22 April 2011).
65 'Kenya: "Legacy Projects" Are the Hallmarks of Kenya@50 Celebrations', *Catholic Information Service for Africa* (11 December 2013), available at http://allafrica.com/stories/201312170495.html (accessed 21 April 2015).

CHAPTER ELEVEN

What colonial legacy? The Dewan Bahasa dan Pustaka (House of Language) and Malaysia's cultural decolonisation

Rachel Leow

What exactly is a colonial legacy? Simple examples can be produced, the most salient being the way the political territory of many colonial states have mapped irrationally onto the boundaries of the postcolonial state, often with devastating diplomatic after-effects; one might think, for example, of Zimbabwe, or Sudan. A second example could be how, as a consequence of the systematic restructuring of colonial society for European economic benefit, there are undoubtedly colonial origins to the inequalities of the postcolonial political economy. At its most inclusive, or vaguest, the term 'colonial legacy' is used as criticism, to trace some undesirable features of the contemporary world, such as ethnic conflict and genocide, corruption and authoritarian regimes, racism and restrictive immigration policies in Europe, to their alleged colonial roots. Legacies of violence in particular are sometimes accompanied by claims to recompense for past colonial atrocities, as with the furore surrounding the declassification of documents pertaining to the Kenyan and Malayan Emergencies.[1]

We can identify two shortcomings of these conventional treatments of colonial legacies. The first has to do with the relative neglect of the cultural effects of colonialism in favour of its political or economic impact. 'Culture' has been harder to trace quantitatively, though in many ways it has generated the most impassioned and vitriolic responses. A given country's experience of being colonised, it is charged here, had effects beyond merely those relating to economic exploitation or military force. Colonialism altered entire peoples' mentalities; alien cultural values became internalised, or in Fanon's word 'epidermalised', into native consciousness.[2] Fanon and others inveighed against these subtler but perhaps more devastating acts of violence: the 'cultural bomb' of colonialism, which annihilates people's beliefs in their names, their languages, themselves, which moves them to revile their own histories as a 'wasteland of non-achievement'.³ Such effects may have been in part unintended; there could have been no systematic colonial programme for the psychological devaluing of the colonised. And yet, of course, colonial officials were not entirely innocent. Snouck Hurgronje (1857–1936), colonial adviser in the Netherlands East Indies, was quite direct in his advice to the Dutch to involve themselves more deeply in Indies primary education. 'Our inheritance', he wrote, 'consists of the beautiful rich tributary regions held by us by force. But if this claim is to withstand the stormy pressures of the times, we must now follow the material annexation by a spiritual one.'⁴

The second shortcoming is that discussions of colonial legacies often produce more accusations of *effects* than acounts of *process*. How exactly, as Jean-François Bayart and Romain Bertrand have asked, is a colonial legacy transmitted? What are the processes by which aspects of the colonial experience are 'handed down' across the uncertain boundary of independence? Any discussion of generic 'colonial legacies', Bayart and Bertrand suggest, will be unsatisfactory; each colonial situation is so different that generalities about what effects colonial rule 'cause' will risk being too abstract to be useful. Causal factors are 'valid only in distinctive configurations of given historical situations'. What is needed, according to them, is not some global interpretation of what a colonial legacy is, but rather a way to define and implement an analytical approach: a 'game of scales' adapted according to what specific effects of colonial rule one is looking for. More than an assertion of a causal chain between colonial factors and their postcolonial effects, they call for a contextual understanding of how the remit of postcolonial action is configured by that of its colonial past: following Foucault, they seek not linear origins (*Ursprung*) but the emergence (*Entstehung*) of postcolonial social practices and phenomena from their colonial pasts.⁵

The extent to which these legacies are merely 'handed down', too, requires unpacking. The emotional registers of discussions surrounding cultural imperialism tend to result in an understanding of colonial legacies as static, violent impositions: of alien cultural values upon local moral systems, for example, or of the coloniser's language upon native tongues and minds. Language has often been written about in this way, particularly in African and Indian contexts. For postcolonial African intellectuals, language was no merely neutral vessel for communication: it was a conduit for deep psychological alienation. 'To speak', Frantz Fanon wrote, 'means above all to assume a culture, to support the weight of a civilization'; but while speaking French may have turned one's mind French, one's skin colour forever foreclosed the possibility of total assimilation.⁶ Learning in English, for Ngugi wa Thiong'o, altered one's thought processes forever and produced a profound disassociation between formal colonial education and the natural-language world of daily life: the former insisting, even predicated, on the inferiority of the latter.[7] These assertions are born from a sense of grievance against the affliction or imposition of colonial effects onto native victims: but even if they are used to call for resistance, a project which both Fanon and Ngugi were invested in, they also suggest a kind of submissiveness on the side of the colonised, implicitly placing postcolonial subjects in a position of 'passive receivers of a legacy from the past'.[8]

Are the cultural effects of colonialism simply bequeathed to a passive recipient population? Many analyses of the colonial roots of ethnic tension in Malaysia certainly give this impression. Contemporary Malaysia suffers from an intractable 'race problem', in which frictions between Chinese, Malay and Indian communities in the post-independence period have continued to shape as well as utterly stymie politics.[9] The British are often, understandably, held accountable. Malaysia's ethnic tensions have been widely interpreted as a 'byproduct' of British colonialism: some argue that British colonialism created an unstable demographic balance through restrictive and self-serving immigration policies; others argue that there was a more deliberate 'divide and rule' policy that sought to sow mutual distrust between ethnic populations in order to undermine any broad basis for anti-colonial resistance; still others point to the lasting effects of European race ideologies in the late nineteenth century, which transformed the potential for natural interethnic acculturation into the more divisive model of 'race relations'.[10] All these narratives contain important truths. But they transform postcolonial Malaysians into victims of the colonial experience and, in doing so, leave little room for understanding how these tensions continue to be perpetuated in the postcolonial era long after the departure of the British.

If colonial legacies are not simply bequeathed and imposed, then, how may we uncover some processes by which they come to inflect postcolonial experience? This chapter is an account of a 'colonial legacy' in the realm of culture – specifically, language – which tries to recover the historical processes by which undesirable aspects of the colonial past are produced and reproduced through the actions of the colonised (and indeed, the decolonised) into the postcolonial present. It focuses on the Dewan Bahasa dan Pustaka (DBP), or House of Language and Literature, a state-sponsored agency established in Malaya on the eve of independence in 1956, tasked with fashioning Malay into a modern national language. The first decade of the DBP's cultural work, from the beginning of formal independence in 1957 to the passage of the National Language Act in 1967, coincided with a critical and formative period for Malaya. The 1950s to the mid-1970s were a time of immense possibilities for alternative political, social and intellectual configurations of the postcolonial state: a period of political dynamism and pluralism, of a multitude of 'paths not taken', which were eventually collapsed into the authoritarian and fundamentally ethnocratic state forms which characterise Malaysia today.[11] In focusing on the actions and agency of the DBP during this crucial period, I offer a different account of the 'colonial legacy' of ethnic tensions in Malaysia – one which highlights the problematic agency of postcolonial subjects in the making and breaking of the liberal postcolonial nation-state – as well as of the cultural dimensions of Malaysia's decolonisation.

The first section gives a brief history of the DBP. The following sections identify three possible answers to the question of what a national language ought to be in a polyglot society. Each of these three critical positions – English, multilingualism and linguistic hybridity – represented, I argue, one possible configuration of postcolonial national language policy; each offered, as a national language arguably ought to in a deeply multi-ethnic country like Malaysia, a genuinely interethnic mode of communication. Yet the DBP regarded these alternative configurations as anathema to the national project it conceived. As I will also suggest, its battles against each of them were shaped in complex ways by preceding British attitudes towards language and race in colonial society. What the DBP sponsored instead were the roots of a rigid, hegemonic monoculture which persists today in wilful defiance, and at the great expense, of Malaysia's multi-ethnic reality.

The House of Language

On 22 June 1956, a year before Malaya gained its independence, the Balai Pustaka (House of Language) was founded in Johor, the southernmost state of the peninsula. At this time, it was little more than a glorified book-purchasing agency, its name a ghostly echo of a much earlier Indonesian predecessor.[12] But it was the realisation of a decade-old ethnonationalist dream by a Malay literary front known as the Angkatan Sasterawan '50 (ASAS 50). Members of this 'Generation of Writers of the 1950s' were, intellectually as well as in name, deeply influenced by earlier generations of Indonesian writers – the Angkatan '30 and Angkatan 1945 among them – and, by the time of independence, had arrived at the same conclusion as their literary brothers across the Malaccan Straits: there was no art and literature worth making but that which was in the service of society.[13] ASAS 50 was thus fundamentally socially oriented at precisely the moment of decolonisation, when possibilities for cultural autonomy had seemed uniquely available. Activist in nature and intent, ASAS 50 united Malay-language activism as never before, consolidating about fifty literary groups from all over the peninsula, and assembling a membership body comprising some of the most illustrious figures of the Malay literary scene at the time. The founding manifesto of the DBP was read at the Third Congress of Malay Language and Literature, held in Singapore in September 1956, outlining a vision for an agency of letters supported by the newly independent state, whose sole purpose would be to advance, develop and protect the Malay language.

In the first decade of its existence, between 1957 and 1967, the DBP canonised literature, translated textbooks for primary and secondary education and literature from other languages into Malay, invested in adult education and undertook to flesh out the lexicon with new terminologies. Importantly, it created a large cultural bureaucracy that opened new careers for citizens in writing, publishing and policy-making: positions which had previously been scanty or non-existent, at least for the colonised. In 1960 the DBP inaugurated a National Language Week, which in 1961 expanded into a National Language Month, held annually until 1966. These were designed to stimulate interest in the Malay language, and more particularly, 'to arouse ... in the hearts of the non-Malays ... a desire to learn and use the national language in their daily communications'.[14] The DBP held literary and language competitions, cultural performances, writers' seminars, book fairs and language courses, exhortatory speeches and receptions, reinforced with a colossal assault of promotional materials. In 1962 alone, for example, National Language Month activities generated 60,000 posters, 270,000 bumper stickers, 105,000 campaign buttons, 24 highway banners, 50,000 ribbons, 30,000 pledge forms, 6 billboards and a rousing anthem commissioned for the occasion. By the end of 1966, the DBP had published 475 school textbooks and coined over 70,000 words.[15]

The DBP's slogan, *'Bahasa Jiwa Bangsa'* (Language is the Soul of the Nation), stands in for its mission: to support the creation of a national language that would unite its citizens. But what language, and what nation? In claiming and asserting control over the former, the DBP, I suggest below, was in a position to set the shape and discursive limits of the latter in ways which have contributed significantly to the continuation of ethnic tensions in postcolonial Malaysia today.

Fighting English and multilingualism

The fight against former colonial languages is of course shared widely across the decolonising world. The extent to which it was possible to claim an effective anticolonial critique while writing in the language of the oppressor was of central concern to Third World writers and intellectuals. Like the Gikuyu language for Ngugi and his sympathisers, the Malay language was held up by Malay intellectuals as a means of empowerment, of full decolonisation and release from the shackles of British colonial rule, embodied above all by the English language.

English had been an exclusive language in Malaya, intended to serve only a small elite. In the inter-war years, although free education was extended to more children in Malaya, colonial officials disagreed over the extent to which this education should be in English or Malay. The prevailing view, supported by colonial philologists R.J. Wilkinson and R.O. Winstedt, was the 'orientalist' rather than 'anglicist' one, which preferred that ethnic groups be taught in their respective 'mother tongues'.[16] Andrew Caldecott, the Straits Settlements colonial secretary between 1933 and 1935, believed that English possessed a dangerous 'rarity value', for it was associated in the public eye with 'the idea of an open sesame to sweatless livelihood'. An indiscriminate provision of English-language education would produce more students with ambitions beyond their 'station' (that is to say, work befitting the unlettered) than could be absorbed by a native civil service or any white-collar labour economy. This, Caldecott concluded, could only end in mass discontent. 'To unstopper the phial now,' he wrote with characteristic affectation, 'while its contents are still precious, and to drench the body politic with the froth of a careless spilling, would be the abrogation of statesmanship.'[17] English education was also more expensive, estimated to cost the colonial state nearly five times as much per child per year than vernacular education, because it required more highly qualified, expensive, teachers.[18] The colonial government thus threw its support behind Malay-language education; English education remained highly commodified and restricted to elites, while education in other languages, particularly in Chinese languages, was devolved to private initiative.[19]

In the post-war years, it became clear that this system of education had bred a generation of Anglophone elites who often had more in common with each other than with their original language communities. As Singapore's Minister of Culture between 1959 and 1965, S. Rajaratnam, remarked, 'The English language acted as a kind of cement for a new kind of community which was not completely

Chinese or completely Malay.'[20] This community was being nurtured in the University of Malaya (UM), the 'crucible of the Malayan nation', envisioned as a place where a truly non-communal nation would be fostered by the English language.[21] The UM, established in 1949 in Singapore (at the time still part of the Federation of Malaya), was an explicit corollary of the British post-war objectives of eventual self-government, part of broader post-war imperial designs for a colonial university education 'designed to imbue elites of emerging nations with a British view of the world and to prepare them for postcolonial membership of the Commonwealth'.[22] The UM was a colonial success story – by 1952, it was the largest university in the colonial empire, with an intake of 875 students.[23] Its English department nurtured an eager literary movement in an effort to produce a language and a literature fit for this non-communal nation.[24]

English thus offered an opportunity for forming a genuinely 'national' community across ethnic and sectarian lines. But it was dogged by its elitist nature; worse, its speakers were vulnerable to charges of colonial subservience. It was this colonial orientation which freighted English with the disagreeable burden of being 'a symbol of the humiliation of the Malay nation'.[25] When UM undergraduates claimed to speak for the polyglot Malayan nation in the language of the colonisers, and to dedicate themselves to the creation of a national literature in it, this laid bare the familiar tensions of postcolonial literature in many colonised countries whose tongues and minds were shaped by a language irrevocably foreign. One is reminded of Ngugi's bitter reaction to the claim by many African writers that English held an 'unassailable position in [African] literature'. 'It is the final triumph of a system of domination,' Ngugi remarked dryly, 'when the dominated start singing its virtues.'[26]

The DBP certainly did not sing odes to English. In the eyes of the national language movement, English was in direct competition with Malay; it was the antithesis of the linguistic autonomy the DBP sought. Under the tireless directorship of Syed Nasir, the DBP sought to fight against 'the tide of English', and the *nujum sangkamara* (prophets of doom) who said that Malay was *tidak lengkap* (incomplete). Such naysayers, Syed Nasir fumed, broke the spirit of the people, causing them to ask for English as the more complete, more perfect language of unity. However important English was as a world language, he insisted, in the Federation its functions were confined to just three areas: high-level administrative affairs of government, technical and scientific vocations, and higher education.[27]

In the spirit of pragmatism, the constitution had outlined a grace period for the continued use of English in official capacities, stipulating that 'for a period of ten years after Merdeka day, *and thereafter until Parliament otherwise provides*, the English language may be used' in all official purposes.[28] But Syed Nasir had no intention of allowing parliament to provide for any use of English which continued past 1967, and it is in this context that his energies in the first decade of the DBP's existence should be understood: as he saw it, he had ten years to prove that the Malay language would be modern, rich and stable enough as a language to serve as the sole national language of postcolonial Malaysia, without recourse to English. Much of the DBP's early language planning activities were oriented towards this; the creation of terminologies of administration, science, politics and government remained high on its agenda throughout this crucial decade.[29]

Thus 1967 was a key year in Malaysia's cultural decolonisation. As required by the constitution, a National Language Bill was passed by Parliament in March, by an effortless 95 votes to 11, effectively rejecting official-language status for all languages other than Malay and requiring all official texts at state and federal levels to be solely in Malay. But it hedged the question of English. The final bill outlined exceptional cases in which it could and would continue to be used in official capacities. Nearly all of them pertained to matters of law. The bill also hedged the question of multilingualism: it allowed for Malay translations of communications or documents from any other language community, which meant that the government, not unreasonably, was willing to continue to communicate with non-Malay speakers on matters pertaining to governance and the public interest.[30] The first prime minister of Malaya, Tunku Abdul Rahman, issued a speech on the implementation of the bill as a plea for tolerance. 'I have chosen the peaceful way,' he said.[31]

The passage of the act sparked a distinctly unpeaceful range of reactions. The National Language Action Front (NLAF), formed in 1964 from a coterie of Malay teachers and intellectuals to champion the cause of Malay, were outraged, accusing the Tunku of 'having sold the Malays down the drain'.[32] On 3 March 1967, a day after the debates on the act began in the lower house, the NLAF organised a demonstration to oppose the act. Over 2,000 people from 129 Malay-language organisations assembled at the DBP to protest the bill for its provision of English use, as well as for signalling that the government was still willing to accept communications from Chinese and Tamil, thus, as one party suggested, granting them a 'semi-official' status and thus allegedly regressing the national language struggle.[33] On the other hand, Chinese-language activists were equally alienated by the bill, since it did not actually grant Chinese official language status.[34] The whole thing was, as one academic observer remarked, a 'non-solution'.[35]

At the DBP itself, Syed Nasir was dismayed at the extension. In a speech several months afterwards, he continued to insist that there should no longer be any doubt that Malay could take its place as the national language. He sent a strident memorandum to the Tunku and heads of state, charging them with failing to stand firm in the quest to replace English with Malay as the official language. The DBP's labours over the past decade, he insisted, had borne fruit; Malay, he insisted, was undoubtedly the equal of English.[36]

But despite their opposition to it, English, with all its colonial baggage, was deeply implicated in the DBP's language project, at least in the form it took under the leadership of trenchant ethno-nationalists such as Syed Nasir.[37] It is perhaps no coincidence that some of the most successfully English-educated Malays – those who had the greatest facility in English – were also the most vocal about the need for a national language, and insisted on Malay achieving absolute parity with English. The two first directors of the DBP, Ungku Aziz and Syed Nasir, were bilingual successes of the elite Anglo-Malay education system; they were also natives of the state of Johor, a historic centre for literary activity as well as a sultanate with a long tradition of adaptation under British tutelage.[38] Deep insecurities about the Malay language certainly stemmed in part from a cognisance of literary and linguistic standards instilled by their English education: a standard grammar and orthography, an authoritative dictionary, a literary canon, a modern vocabulary and a rigourous pedagogy. While imbued with the spirit of young Malay nationalism, then, the task of the DBP was at the same time conceived in a spirit of derivative comparison, one in which the Malay language was found lacking by transplanted standards.[39]

But even if English could not be championed as a national language, why the rabid insistence on a *monolingual* national language policy? In Malaya's polyglot environment, the sole use of Malay as a national language would challenge not only English, but other languages spoken widely in Malaya as well: most prominently, Chinese and Indian languages. The question, in the Malayan context, was thus not only one of replacing the coloniser's language; it was also one of exclusivity, which went right to the heart of the formation of the postcolonial nation: to what extent ought Malay to be the *sole* national language of Malaya? In the profoundly multilingual context of Malaya, could a single national language unite communities, or was the attempt doomed to elevate one tongue over the others in an act of unavoidable cultural imperialism?

For the DBP this was never a question at all. Its rhetoric was that of the former – the national language as a route towards the unity of all races – but in practice, it sought the latter: to replace one cultural imperialism (that of English) with another (that of Malay). This meant that rather than any one particular language, such as Mandarin or Tamil, it was the plurality of languages itself that posed a threat to Malay monoculture. As Syed Nasir said ominously in 1964, at the height of the National Language Month campaigns: 'I am of the opinion that those people who advocate the principle of multilingualism are treading on dangerous ground and are adopting a very unhealthy attitude which is very dangerous for the people of this country.'[40] The DBP was founded on the same premises; after all, the constitution had in 1957 set out, in the endlessly controversial Article 153, the legal foundations for Malay cultural imperialism by providing for the 'special position' of the *bumiputras* ('sons of the soil', i.e. Malays) above all other communities in Malaya, often referred to as Malaysia's 'social contract'.[41] There is no space to recount the political furore over multilingualism here, save to note that the possibility for a plural language policy was mostly raised, then killed, in the battles over education policy. It should be made clear that few, if any, were denying that Malay should be the national language; those who advocated multilingualism were rather saying that citizens could speak Malay as well as other languages without being subject to accusations of national disloyalty. Scholars who have examined these events closely have observed that this more inclusive position, in favour of multilingualism in schools, ended up being promulgated principally by non-Malays; thus, an agenda of cultural equality and plurality became susceptible, in a bizarre discursive twist, to charges of ethnic chauvinism.[42]

The DBP also refused to concede the possibility that a national literature could be written in multiple languages. In 1962, the first Malayan Writers' Conference was convened in Singapore to discuss this very question.[43] All streams of language were represented in a range of sessions over three days. Attended by writers and literary organisations from both the Federation and Singapore, it was the Federation delegates, mostly DBP representatives, who staged a disgruntled walkout on the final day of the conference, unwilling to countenance propositions from Malay, Chinese and Tamil writers in Singapore that literature in any language other than Malay could be accepted as Malayan or national.[44] This minor fracas symbolised an early discursive battle between alternative configurations of state language policy: on the one hand, the Federation's monocultural imperative (a Malay-language Malaysia), and on the other, Singapore's willingness to conceive of a culturally plural state (a multilingual Malaysia). It was an ominous foreshadowing of what would become of the political merger between Singapore and Malaysia the following year: a union which was, of course, practically stillborn, ending in 1965 with the expulsion of Singapore from the Federation.[45] The positions which the DBP took over multilingualism helped to close down alternative configurations of the postcolonial nation itself: language, truly, was the beleaguered soul of the nation.

Fighting hybridity

The DBP fought a third battle against linguistic hybridity, even though, as I suggest here, hybrid or creolised tongues offered yet another possible route to genuinely interethnic communication. Rather, the DBP sought to propagate a *bahasa Melayu tulen* (unadulterated Malay) or *Melayu halus* (refined Malay) as the national language, to be scrupulously distinguished from what it called an impure, *kacukan* (mixed) Malay: *bahasa pasar* or 'bazaar Malay'.[46] This search for linguistic purism is arguably one of the most abiding legacies of colonialism in Malaya. For the DBP, Malay was to be the common tongue, but it should not be 'common' in the sense of 'debased'; it should stand firm and pure against the ever-present danger of contamination by other languages. Its flagship periodical, the *Dewan Bahasa*, established itself in the early years of independence as the central source for all questions regarding the Malay language, and, in its pages, DBP writers and language enthusiasts set about the task of language purification in remedial terms, seeking to correct the 'problem' (*masalah*) of language hybridity by imposing and fixing standards of *Melayu betul* (correct Malay).

It is worth recalling at this point that *bahasa pasar* was a register of the Malay language long denigrated by colonial officials as the 'grossly degenerate patois' of the Straits.[47] Yet that patois is arguably a good indicator of how Malay culture as it evolved over the last century should be understood; it is, as Joel Kahn has called it, 'the ultimate *peranakan* (hybrid) culture'.[48] Often touted as the historic *lingua franca* of an extremely diverse region arguably stretching from Madagascar to Papua New Guinea,[49] Malay's hybridity and its openness to change and adaptation were seen by some as virtues, not vices. Malay writers from an earlier period, in the 1930s, did not lament *kacukan*: 'We may not have intended for Malay to become *kacukan*,' a writer for the *Majallah Guru* said, 'but what can we do? It seems to be our fate.' For this writer, Malay's *kacukan* lent it an enormous flexibility that would ensure its survival:

Malay is so hybrid that it cannot possibly be lost, for how do you lose a hybrid? Surely it would merely change into a new hybrid?... O! If we take a foreign language and let the sound of it shift to correspond to the sound and style of Malay, don't you good readers fight! The Malay tongue itself will alter without having to be told. *London* will be sounded as 'Landan' and *Inspector* will be pronounced 'Sepitir' and *Go Astern* will turn into 'Gostan' and *Puncture* will be pronounced 'Pancit'. And so on. Without any instruction from anyone.[50]

The DBP, however, undertook to be that source of 'instruction' for Malay, a voice of authority which not only lamented but abhorred *kacukan* Malay. It was a position which certainly has colonial roots: an 1894 dictionary of Malay by two British philologists, for example, breezily asserted that 'all authorities are agreed that the purest Malay is spoken ... by the natives of the Peninsula, especially in the States of Pĕrak, Kĕdah, Jŏhor and Păhang, and it is here that the student should look for specimens of the language in its highest and most elegant forms.'[51] The sentiment may be easily found elsewhere, and earlier; take, for example, William Marsden's 1812 dictionary, which inveighs against *'bhāsa kachūk-an'* as 'the basest and most corrupt style ... the mixed jargon of the bazaars of great sea-port towns'.[52]

Crucially, a reading of the *Dewan Bahasa* reveals a strong perception of a relationship between *bahasa pasar* and Chinese speakers of Malay.[53] The following excerpt, taken from the *Dewan Bahasa*'s column 'Questions and Answers Regarding Language', is indicative of the hierarchy of Malay speakers which the DBP articulated through its guardianship of the language. In it, Zainal Abidin, today widely regarded as the 'grandfather of Malay letters', fields enquiries about the proper use of language, in this case, from one Tuan Abdullah bin Haji Abdul Rauf concerning the Johor-Riau pronunciation of Malay. The principal difference between the Johor-Riau pronunciation and Tuan Abdullah's own dialect lay in the articulation of the schwa. This is a phonemic vowel sound (ə) found in many languages (in English, for example, it is heard in the second syllable of the word 'sofa') and is especially common in the Malay language, in which a large proportion of words end with the vowel 'a'. Johor-Riau pronunciation dictated that the 'a' at the ends of Malay words, such as *lada* (pepper) and *ada* (have), should always be pronounced with a final schwa (as in 'ladə'), rather than with a final 'ah' sound (as in 'lad-ah'). Tuan Abdullah wished to ascertain the implications of DBP's standardised pronunciation for northern Malays, who tended to pronounce the 'ah' rather than the schwa. Zainal Abidin's reply was as follows:

The final 'a' sound pronounced as an elongated 'ĕ' [i.e., the schwa] follows the Riau-Johor dialect or accent (which includes Melaka, Selangor, Pahang, Perak and Terengganu). In the Negeri Sembilan accent it is pronounced 'o'. In the Kelantan accent it is pronounced somewhere between an 'a' and an 'o'. But whatsoever the pronunciation, its spelling will be 'a'. In all languages there are sure to be various accents (*pelat*), and the accent most admissible as the 'standard', the most correct ... is determined by those who are more educated or who became civilised (*mendapat cara tamaddun*) in the sense of refinement of upbringing and manners (*kehalusan didikan dan budi pekerti*). For most Malays, the 'ĕ' sound is considered more educated and correct. Those who pronounce the final 'a' as 'a' [i.e., 'ah'] are only those who speak *bahasa pasar* (Chinese, Indians, Arabs and others who are not Malay) or Malays who are influenced by those races.[54]

Under the DBP, the charge that *bahasa pasar* was a Chinese, Indian or Arab creole of Malay assumed national significance. It was a 'problem' which attracted much heated debate in the pages of the *Dewan Bahasa*. Contributors denounced it as an abomination resulting from the tendency of 'non-native' speakers of Malay to translate Chinese or Tamil sentence structures directly into Malay; or from overlaying Malay with Chinese or Tamil phonetics. These read like charges of contamination, and they held for both grammar and pronunciation. Grammar purists inveighed against misuses of pronouns and tenses thought to be bastardisations wrought upon Malay by mistranslations from Chinese: for example, the use of *nanti* (wait/afterwards) instead of *akan* (will) to denote the future tense, or the liberal use of the proprietary pronoun *punya*.[55] *Bahasa pasar* was also attacked on the oral front, which in many ways seemed a more indelible charge, for it implied a physical incapacity. Contributors compiled lists of words that had been 'bastardised' in foreign mouths. In these, Chinese speakers of Malay came under the most fire. Chinese speakers of Malay (so the criticisms ran) regularly mispronounced *r* and *d* sounds as *l* sounds and turned hard *g* sounds into the softer *ng* sounds; they confused glottal stops with hard consonants, and hard consonants with sibilants. These were unsalvageable defects: those whose tongues and mouths had been shaped by Chinese vowels and consonants were simply not capable of speaking 'proper' Malay. *Goyang* (shake) was regularly distorted in Chinese mouths into 'ngoyang'; *tujuh* (seven) into 'tiuchu', *roti* (bread) into 'loti', and *atas* (up) into 'atat'. The list of deficiencies among Tamil Malay-speakers was smaller: 'saya' was pronounced 'chaya', and they occasionally slipped on vowels. English speakers of Malay tended to be lampooned rather than castigated: they pronounced schwas with a risible nasal twang.[56]

In its hypersensitivity to prescribing correct Malay speech, the DBP thus preserved strong and seemingly insurmountable distinctions between speakers of what ought to have been a national language from different ethnicities. It was not enough for non-Malay speakers to learn Malay as a marker of national loyalty. Indeed, in a flush of national enthusiasm in the early 1960s, many did, encouraged by the DBP's energetic language campaigns.[57] Rather, in a sense, non-Malay speakers of Malay could *never* truly speak the national language, as defined by the DBP. *Bahasa pasar*'s 'deviations' from DBP's standard Malay were established, and then maintained, as unassailable indices of ethnic difference. This, as well as the extreme suspicion of hybridity, continues today in all respects. The contemporary incarnation of *bahasa pasar*, now called *bahasa rojak*, is characterised above all by hybridity. A truly unifying *lingua franca*, its speakers codeswitch with breathtaking ease and creativity between all manner of languages in popular use in Malaysia; in lexicon, register and prosodics, it is understood and used daily by Malaysians of all racial backgrounds. Yet *bahasa rojak* has been spectacularly banned in national media outlets as a threat to and contamination of the monocultural national identity espoused and championed by the DBP.[58] Recent ethnographic research has shown that Malaysian national language planning is fundamentally at variance with language use: far from a single national language, there are instead many Malaysian languages, which dissolve under the rigid structures of planned Malay into a sea of language shifts between Malay, English, Portuguese, Malayalee, Tamil, Javanese, Hokkien and more besides. This language use is undergirded not by the DBP and its plans and monolingual standards, but by utterly normative practices of multilingualism and codeswitching.[59]

The DBP's obsession with monolingual purity may be suggestively read alongside accounts of colonial race and the dangers that hybridity and *métissage* – interracial unions – posed to the 'colonial order of things'.[60] Such studies, focusing on colonial governance of bodies and sexualities, have shown how nineteenth-century European discourses of race allowed the colonial state to delineate categories of European from native and civilised from uncivilised; to identify 'not primarily its external foes, but its enemies within'; and pertinently, how mixed-race unions challenged the colonial state's ability to maintain imperial distinctions.[61] Language in postcolonial Malaya, I suggest, offered a similar discursive tool, used for the purpose of maintaining racial boundaries in a consociational state whose political claims to power and hegemony still depended on them.[62] The DBP sought to establish 'internal frontiers' which distinguished one set of language speakers from one another, along lines which mapped onto, and thus actively reinforced, boundaries of colonial-era ethnicities. Chinese-speakers were Chinese, Tamil-speakers were Indian, Malay-speakers were Malay, and never the three shall meet – certainly not if they spoke English; perhaps not even when they spoke the same 'national' language. And it was against the 'unruly', 'impure' but truly interethnic argot that emerged naturally out of the linguistic collision of cultures that the DBP raised its strongest and most indignant objections.[63] *Métissage* and mixed-blood bodies threatened the colonial order just as *kacukan*, hybrid tongues threatened (and continue to threaten) the postcolonial order. We might discern here too, in this strange and subtle transition that cannot be spoken of in terms of *Ursprung*, something like a colonial legacy.

Conclusion

This chapter has sought to reveal some of the historical processes out of which the 'colonial legacy' of ethnic tensions emerged in Malaysia. Furthermore, it has offered support to Benoit de L'Estoile's critique of mere passivity on the side of the colonised in this process. It should be clear from the discussion above that colonisers do not simply bequeath their politics, economics and structures and practices of governance to decolonising nations. The insights I offer here – from the perspective of culture and the complex processes of colonial inheritance – should find resonance in other studies of decolonisation. For the concept of decolonisation itself is a strange line in the sand: an epoch which by its very definition is to sit causally between 'the colonial' and 'the postcolonial', and thus, as Frederick Cooper has suggested, risks artificially dividing and reifing both.[64] The transition identified by the concept of decolonisation is said to have produced the normative, prolific world of nation-states in which we live. But it is not at all reducible to merely the colonial making of the 'postcolonial condition', despite the prevalence and often indiscriminate application of the notion of a 'colonial legacy'. Yet the difficulties of recognising other factors and agents in this important transition are compounded by the politics of disengagement between metropole and colony, which has tended to produce discursive belligerence. Particularly in the realms of economics and politics, it has often proven too easy to condemn the 'colonial legacy' for its sins of distortion and injustice

– and too difficult to acknowledge junctures of choice, of agency, of deep continuity – by postcolonial histories which are still invested in blame and indignation, still feeding on their memories of colonial oppression.

We are not, as Cooper observes, faced with a stark choice between a 'light-switch view of decolonization ... and a continuity approach [which suggests that] colonialism never really ended'. Rather, we ought to try to understand what, in the course of the struggles of political independence, became possible, impossible or reconfigured in the new polities which emerged from those struggles – and crucially, what structures of constraint persisted, and how.[65] It is thus perhaps especially in the realm of culture that we ought to try to excavate, as I have tried to do in this essay, a problematic agency in the perpetuation of certain structures of domination across this mid-twentieth-century conjuncture of multidimensional change which we call 'decolonisation'. For it is in the realm of culture that the claims of the colonised most frequently gained traction through a politics of overt disavowal in a bid for 'postcolonial' autonomy, and yet it is also the realm of culture which ought to be more resistant than, say, the realm of high politics, to any easy division between its reified 'colonial' and 'postcolonial' incarnations.

By scaling the analysis to place the DBP at the centre of the postcolonial transition, I have tried to show how colonial conceptions of ethnicity were not inflicted, but maintained through to the postcolonial present. In pitting itself against these alternative configurations of national language policy, the DBP pressed forward a monocultural definition of the nation which was profoundly at odds with Malaysia's multi-ethnic reality. More than that, it bound conceptions of ethnicity to language in a configuration which today seems unquestionably natural, but which is in fact one that requires constant maintenance. The idea that English, multilingualism and hybrid speech were illegitimate forms of national communication took a huge amount of discursive work precisely because they were, and continue to be, naturally occurring features of Malaysia's rich, multi-ethnic language ecology.[66] As Foucault wrote, 'Humanity does not gradually progress from combat to combat until ... the rule of law finally replaces warfare,' but rather 'installs each of its violences in a system of rules and thus proceeds from domination to domination'.[67] The DBP's monocultural discourse on language is part of an ideological structure of the postcolonial Malaysian state that seeks to control its citizens through the belief that what *is*, is natural. Ethnic tensions in Malaysia today are not merely an inheritance passively received from our colonial past, but a violent stasis we wreak upon ourselves.

WHAT COLONIAL LEGACY?

Notes

I wish to express my thanks to the many people who have shaped my thinking and offered insightful criticism at various stages in the drafting of this essay: in particular, Tim Harper, Sumit Mandal, Geoff Wade and the editors of this volume, Ruth Craggs and Claire Wintle. All shortcomings and errors remain my own.

1. B. de L'Estoile, 'The Past as it Lives Now: An Anthropology of Colonial Legacies', *Social Anthropology*, 16 (2008), 267–79; J.-F. Bayart and R. Bertrand, 'De quel "legs colonial" parle-t-on?', *Esprit* (2006), 134–60.
2. F. Fanon, *Black Skin, White Masks: The Experiences of a Black Man in a White World*, trans. C.L. Markmann (New York: Grove Press, 1967).
3. Ngugi Wa Thiong'o, *Decolonizing the Mind* (London: James Currey, 2008; first published 1986).
4. D. Jedamski, 'Balai Pustaka: A Colonial Wolf in Sheep's Clothing', *Archipel*, 44 (1992), 24.
5. Bayart and Bertrand, 'De quel "legs colonial" parle-t-on?'; on Enstehung see M. Foucault, 'Nietzsche, Genealogy, History', in M. Foucault, *Language, Counter-Memory, Practice: Selected Essays and Interviews*, trans. D.F. Bouchard and S. Simon (Ithaca: Cornell University Press, 1977).
6. Fanon, *Black Skin, White Masks*, pp. 17–18.
7. Ngugi, *Decolonizing the Mind*.
8. L'Estoile, 'The Past as it Lives Now'.
9. For a recent argument in this vein, see M.D. Barr and C.A. Trocki, *Paths Not Taken: Political Pluralism in Post-war Singapore* (Singapore: National University of Singapore Press, 2008).
10. Those inclined to political science tend to emphasise the demographic imbalance argument; see, for example, J. Liow, *The Politics of Indonesia–Malaysia Relations: One Kin, Two Nations* (London: Routledge, 2005). For British divide-and-rule policies, see, for example, W.Y. Hua, *Class and Communalism in Malaysia: Politics in a Dependent Capitalist State* (London: Zed Books, 1983); C. Abraham, 'Racial and Ethnic Manipulation in Colonial Malaya', *Ethnic and Racial Studies*, 6:1 (1983), 18–32. For colonial paradigms of race relations, see C. Hirschman, 'The Making of Race in Colonial Malaya: Political Economy and Racial Ideology', *Sociological Forum*, 1:2 (1986), 330–61.
11. For this argument, see Barr and Trocki, *Paths Not Taken*; for this argument from a purely political angle, B.K. Cheah, 'The Left-wing Movement in Malaya, Singapore and Borneo in the 1960s: "An Era of Hope or Devil's Decade?"', *Inter-Asia Cultural Studies*, 7:4 (2006), 634–49. For the characterisation of contemporary Malaysia as an 'ethnocracy', see G. Wade, 'The Origins and Evolution of Ethnocracy in Malaysia', Asia Research Institute Working Paper Series, 112 (2009), available at www.ari.nus.edu.sg/docs/wps/wps09_112.pdf (accessed 21 May 2015).
12. For the Indonesian origins of the Balai Pustaka, see G.W.J. Drewes, 'D.A. Rinkes: A Note on his Life and Work', *Bijdragen tot de Taal-, Land-en Volkenkunde*, 117 (1961), 417–35; Jedamski, 'Balai Pustaka'; see also A. Sanusi Ahmad, *Peranan Pejabat Karang Mengarang* (Kuala Lumpur: Dewan Bahasa dan Pustaka, 1966).
13. For historical background to the DBP, see T.N. Harper, *End of Empire and the Making of Malaya* (Cambridge: Cambridge University Press, 1999), pp. 296–307. On Malay writers and society, see V.M. Hooker, *Writing a New Society: Social Change Through the Novel in Malay* (Honolulu: University of Hawaii Press, 2000); on Indonesian writers and society, see K. Foulcher, *Social Commitment in Literature and the Arts: The Indonesian 'Institute of People's Culture', 1950–1965* (Clayton: Centre of Southeast Asian Studies, Monash University, 1986); on the close relationship between Malay and Indonesian literary traditions, see H. Maier, *We Are Playing Relatives: A Survey of Malay Writing* (Leiden: KITLV Press, 2004).

14 Syed Nasir, 'Menjelang dan sesudah minggu bahasa kebangsaan', in Syed Nasir, *Koleksi Ucapan Tun Syed Nasir* (Kuala Lumpur: Dewan Bahasa dan Pustaka, 1996), p. 107.
15 C.L. Mitchell, 'Language as an Instrument of National Policy: The Dewan Bahasa dan Pustaka of Malaysia' (PhD dissertation, University of Wisconsin-Madison, 1993).
16 P. Loh, *Seeds of Separatism: Educational Policy in Malaya, 1874–1940* (Oxford: Oxford University Press, 1975), pp. 2–4.
17 'Attack on Education Policy in the Colony', *Straits Times* (13 February 1932), p. 12.
18 H. Wilson, *Social Engineering in Singapore: Educational Policies and Social Change, 1819–1972* (Singapore: Singapore University Press, 1978), pp. 39–43.
19 Questions of language in Malaysia have been most frequently dealt with in terms of the education question, and will not be dealt with from this angle here; see L.E. Tan, *The Politics of Chinese Education in Malaya 1945–1961* (Kuala Lumpur: Oxford University Press, 1997).
20 A.L. Chua, 'Imperial Subjects, Straits Citizens: Anglophone Asians and the Struggle for Political Rights in Inter-War Singapore', in Barr and Trocki, *Paths Not Taken*, pp. 16–36.
21 A.J. Stockwell, '"The Crucible of the Malayan Nation": The University and the Making of a New Malaya, 1938–62', *Modern Asian Studies*, 43 (2009), 1149–87.
22 Stockwell, '"The Crucible of the Malayan Nation"', 1163.
23 A. Brewster, *Towards a Semiotic of Post-colonial Discourse: University Writing in Singapore and Malaysia, 1949–1965* (Singapore: Heinemann Asia, 1989).
24 T.A. Koh, 'Singapore Writing in English: The Literary Tradition and Cultural Identity', in S.C. Tham (ed.), *Essays on Literature and Society in Southeast Asia: Political and Sociological Perspectives* (Singapore: Singapore University Press, 1981), pp. 160–85.
25 Harper, *The End of Empire and the Making of Malaya*, 299.
26 Ngugi, *Decolonising the Mind*, 20.
27 Editorial, 'Kedudokan Bahasa Inggeris', *Dewan Bahasa* (June 1958).
28 See the Federal Constitution of Malaysia (1986), available at http://unmis.unmissions.org/Portals/UNMIS/Constitution-making%20Symposium/Federal%20Constitution%20of%20Malaysia.pdf (accessed 21 May 2015), p. 122; emphasis added.
29 Collections of these glossaries are held at the British Library. First glossary, 'Officials and Offices', was published in 1960, followed by (respectively) Administration, Economics, Education, Geography, Biology, Forestry, Agriculture, Physics, Mathematics, Chemistry, Engineering, Law, Linguistics, Literature, Postal, Business, History, Home Economics, Music, Visual Arts, Physical Education, Islam, Librarianship, Architecture and Printing/Publishing.
30 See the National Language Bill, 1967, subsequently enacted as National Language Act 1967, Act no. 7 of 1967, available at www.agc.gov.my/Akta/Vol.%201/Act%2032.pdf (accessed 21 May 2015).
31 Tunku Abdul Rahman, 'Language: I Have Chosen the Peaceful Way', *Straits Times* (3 March 1967), p. 8.
32 K.S. Kua, *Malaysian Cultural Policy and Democracy* (Kuala Lumpur: Resource and Research Center, 1990), p. 90.
33 'An All-Alliance Yes', *Straits Times* (4 March 1967), p. 1; Dewan Rakyat, 2nd Parliament, 3:45 (2 March 1967), p. 6022.
34 This conflagration has a longer history and cannot be covered here, but for a summary, see T.H. Lee, *Chinese Schools in Peninsular Malaysia: The Struggle for Survival* (Singapore: ISEAS, 2011).
35 C. Enloe, *Multi-Ethnic Politics: The Case of Malaysia*, Research Monograph Series (Berkeley: University of California Press, 1971), p. 101.
36 Syed Nasir, 'Speech to Majlis Perasmian Perayaan Sepuluh Tahun Dewan Bahasa dan Pustaka, 27 Jul 1967', in Nasir, *Koleksi Ucapan*.

37 The DBP, though, was more than Syed Nasir: during its lifetime it also employed and officially sponsored writers such as Usman Awang or Keris Mas, whose politics and cultural agendas were much more open than the DBP's official stances as they appeared under Syed Nasir's directorship. In a way, it is symptomatic of the openness of the time that even in its most trenchantly ideological state, the DBP was by no means a monolithic entity. My thanks to Sumit Mandal for pushing me to recall this point more firmly.
38 Syed Nasir was born in Batu Pahat, Johor in 1921 and was educated at the Royal English School in Batu Pahat, passing his Senior Cambridge in 1938, subsequently transferring to the Sultan Idris Training College, a Malay teacher training institution in Perak. See 'Biodata', in Nasir, *Koleksi Ucapan*, p. 303.
39 On this theme, P. Chatterjee, *Nationalist Thought and the Colonial World: A Derivative Discourse* (Minneapolis: Minneapolis University Press, 1993).
40 'Nasir: Role of National Language to Unite all Races', *Straits Times* (5 May 1964), p. 7.
41 See Article 153 of the Malaysian Constitution, still in existence, available at http://unmis.unmissions.org/Portals/UNMIS/Constitution-making%20 Symposium/Federal%20Constitution%20of%20Malaysia.pdf (accessed 21 May 2015).
42 See Tan, *The Politics of Chinese Education*; H.G. Lee, 'Ethnic Politics, National Development and Language Policy in Malaysia', in H.G. Lee and L. Suryadinata (eds), *Language, Nation and Development in Southeast Asia* (Singapore: ISEAS, 2008).
43 *Report of the Malayan Writers' Conference* (Singapore: DBKK, 1962).
44 'Fiery End to Writers' Talks', *Straits Times* (19 March 1962), p. 9.
45 On the merger, see A. Lau, *A Moment of Anguish: Singapore in Malaysia and the Politics of Disengagement* (Singapore: Times Academic Press, 1998).
46 For this distinction, see H. Maier, 'From Heteroglossia to Polyglossia: The Creation of Malay and Dutch in the Indies', *Indonesia*, 56 (1993), 37–65.
47 For this attitude see in particular H. Clifford and F. Swettenham, *A Dictionary of the Malay Language* (Taiping: Government Printing Office, 1894).
48 J. Kahn, *Other Malays: Nationalism and Cosmopolitanism in the Modern Malay World* (Singapore: National University of Singapore Press, 2006), p. 170.
49 See, for example, J. Collins, *Malay, World Language: A Short History* (Kuala Lumpur: Dewan Bahasa dan Pustaka, 1998).
50 'Peraturan Menulis Zaman Ini', *Majallah Guru* (January 1931), pp. 13–16.
51 Clifford and Swettenham, *Dictionary*.
52 W. Marsden, *A Grammar of the Malayan Language* (London: Cox & Baylis, 1812), p. xvii. On high/low diglossia in Malay see especially J. Errington, *Linguistics in a Colonial World: A Story of Language, Meaning, and Power* (Oxford: Oxford University Press, 2008).
53 A point strongly elaborated for Indonesian in J. Siegel, *Fetish, Recognition, Revolution* (Princeton: Princeton University Press, 1997) and H. Maier, 'Forms of Censorship in the Dutch Indies: The Marginalisation of Chinese-Malay Literature', *Indonesia*, 51 (1991), 67–81.
54 Za'ba, 'Soal Jawab Bahasa', *Dewan Bahasa* (June 1956), pp. 294–96; monthly columns run from 1956 to 1964.
55 For discussion of *'punya'* see A. Pakir, 'A Linguistic Investigation of Baba Malay' (PhD dissertation, University of Hawaii, 1986), pp. 147–62.
56 Ismail bin Haji Yusof, 'Mas'alah Bahasa Pasar dalam Pengajaran Bahasa Kebangsaan', *Dewan Bahasa* (October 1958), 495–505.
57 See, for example Q.Y. Yang, *Memoir Yang Quee Yee: Penyusun Kamus Anak Penoreh* (Bangi: Penerbit UKM, 2006).
58 'Gag Order on Bahasa Rojak', *Star* (2 April 2006), at www.thestar.com.my/story/?file=%2F2006%2F4%2F2%2Fnation%2F13849132&sec=nation (accessed 21 April 2015); also Husni Abu Bakar, 'Codeswitching in Kuala Lumpur Malay: The Rojak Phenomenon', *Explorations*, 9 (2009), 99–107.

59 D. Mukherjee and M.K. David (eds), *National Language Planning and Language Shifts in Malaysian Minority Communities: Speaking in Many Tongues* (Amsterdam: Amsterdam University Press, 2011).
60 On *métissage* and the 'colonial order of things', see A.L. Stoler, *Race and the Education of Desire: Foucault's History of Sexuality and the Colonial Order of Things* (Durham: Duke University Press, 1995).
61 Stoler, *Race and the Education of Desire*, especially pp. 26–32.
62 On the persistence of communalism in Malaysian political life, see B.K. Cheah, *The Challenge of Ethnicity: Building a Nation in Malaysia* (Kuala Lumpur: Marshall Cavendish Academic, 2004).
63 For an account of the greater normativity of such encounters than the existence of 'pure' monoglot language situations, see M. DeGraff, 'Linguists' Most Dangerous Myth: The Fallacy of Creole Exceptionalism', *Language in Society*, 34 (2005), 533–91.
64 F. Cooper, *Colonialism in Question: Theory, Knowledge, History* (Berkeley: University of California Press, 2005), p. 19.
65 See Cooper's comments on the 'epochal fallacy' of colonialism studies, in *Colonialism in Question*, pp. 19–22.
66 A point well elaborated by Mukherjee and David; see their conclusion in *National Language Planning*.
67 Foucault, 'Nietzsche, Genealogy, History'.

INDEX

Note: literary and artistic works can be found under the author or artist's name

Abidin, Zainal 256–7
Abrams, Charles 206
Accra (Ghana) 43, 181, 184, 202, 214
Achimota College (Gold Coast) 182
agency
   colonial/postcolonial 7, 14, 20, 120, 129, 197, 248, 260
   of culture 3, 9–11, 196
   of experts 196, 197, 200
Ajena (Ghana) 208
Akosombo (Ghana) 213
Alcan (Aluminium Company of Canada) 209, 213, 217
Aldrich, Robert 6, 189
Algeria 15, 31, 38, 41, 56–9, 61, 62, 109, 122, 157, 158, 171
All India Students' Federation 113
Allen, Chadwick 51
Alloway, Lawrence 97
Anderson, Benedict 91, 103
Angkor (Wat) 10, 19, 126–55
Angola 158
Ankatan Sasterawan '50 (ASAS 50) 248
Anthony, Michael 70
Aotearoa New Zealand 14, 51–66
Appadurai, Arjun 17
Aradeon, David 183
Araeen, Rasheed 54
architecture 1, 2, 3, 8, 9, 17, 19, 79, 126, 133–4, 181, 196–221
   see also modernism in architecture
Ardouin, Claude 187
Arnoldi, Mary Jo 186
Arts Council of Ghana 184
Arts Council (UK) 72

Aswan Dam (Egypt) 198
audiences 2, 3, 9, 17, 74, 81, 129, 142, 177, 178, 187, 227, 232, 237
Australia 52, 55, 63, 156, 158, 166, 169, 202

BACo (British Aluminium Company) 209
Bacon, Francis 93
Bailkin, Jordanna 6, 87
Baker, Kriselle 58, 61
Baker, Roy Ward 88
Baldwin, James 31, 40, 74, 76–7
Bamako (Mali) 180, 185, 186, 187, 189, 193, 194, 195
Bandung Conference of Asian and African States 42, 45
   see also Non-Aligned Movement
Bandyopadhyay, Samik 117
Bangladesh 117
Banham, Rayner 97
Bank of England (UK) 235
Barry Lett Galleries, Auckland (New Zealand) 61
Basu, Ram 115
Bayart, Jean-François 246
BBC see British Broadcasting Corporation
Belgium 6
Benjamin, Walter 116
Berger, John 93, 94
Bertrand, Romain 246
Betjeman, John 231
Bird, Christopher St John 198
Black Arts Movement 74, 78, 83 n26
Black Power 13, 15, 29, 67, 73–4, 76, 77, 78, 179

[265]

INDEX

Bodiansky, Vladimir 145, 206
Bomani, Paul 224, 227, 228
Bonneuil, Christophe 200
Bonnynge, Brien 162–5
Bophani, Princess Norodom 131
Bose, Subhash Chandra 109
Boswell, James 62
Bowen, Denis 62
Bowen, Donald 63
Bradley, Kenneth 1
Braque, Georges 97
Brasilia (Brazil) 215
Brasseur, Gerard 187
Bratby, John 86, 87, 92–6, 99
   Jean and Still Life in Front of Window 86, 95, 103
Brathwaite, Edward 70, 71–2, 79, 80
Breton Woods institutions 201
Britain *see* United Kingdom
  see also London
British Broadcasting Corporation (BBC) 6, 13, 18, 68–71
British colonialism 1, 2, 16, 29, 30, 31, 32, 36, 42, 43, 87, 88, 89, 90, 112, 113, 156, 157, 161, 163, 171, 182, 209, 210, 224, 226, 239, 247, 248, 250
British Council 72
Brown, Rebecca M. 54
Browne, Michael 63
Buettner, Elizabeth 6
Bullmore, Edward 57, 63
Burton, Gary 79–80
Butler, Reg 93

Caldecott, Andrew 250
Cambodia 10, 126–55
Camus, Albert 39
Canada 2–3, 52, 63, 198, 200, 202, 217
Carew, Jan 70
Caribbean 67
  intellectuals 33
Caribbean Artists Movement (CAM) 13, 17, 18, 67–85
Caribbean Voices 68–73

Carmichael, Stokely 74
Central School of Art (London, UK) 56
Césaire, Aimé 38–40, 179
Chandigarh 201, 215
Chandra, Avinash 92
Chatterjee, Partha 116
Chattopadhyay, Mohit 115
China 117, 136, 247, 251, 252, 257
Chinese language 251, 253, 247, 250, 252, 259, 254, 256, 257
Ciudad Guayana 218
Civil Rights movement 15, 16, 18, 29, 42, 61, 62, 67, 74, 100, 179
Coe, Cati 185
Coedès, Georges 129–30
coin design 10, 11, 16, 17, 19, 222–44
Cold War 4, 14, 40, 109–25, 136, 198, 214
Commonwealth 2, 13, 16, 52, 62, 63, 89, 156, 157, 217, 225, 251
  countries 1, 62, 229, 231
  see also New Commonwealth Internationalism
Commonwealth Institute (Imperial Institute) 1–3, 20, 55, 63
Commonwealth literary cultures *see* literary cultures, Commonwealth
Commonwealth Relations Office (CRO) 234, 235, 237
Communism 15, 41, 118, 122
Communist International 109
Communist Party 32, 34, 41, 111, 115
comparative
  character of decolonisation 3, 17
  research 7, 17–18, 239–40
Comrie, Locksley 75
Congress Party (India) 115
Convention People's Party (Ghana) 41, 179–80, 202
Cooper, Frederick 7, 259, 260
Craig, Karl 'Jerry' 73
Crinson, Mark 185, 201, 217–18

INDEX

Crow, Thomas 99
Crown Agents (UK) 224, 225, 234
Cuba 61, 112, 117
Culbert, William 62
cultural diplomacy 3, 128, 134–50
Cyprus 88
Czechoslovakia 136

Dabydeen, David 71
Dadi, Iftikar 54
Damas, Léon 38
dance 81, 134–42, 147, 150, 190
Daniel, Alain 145–6, 148
Darnton, Roger 68
Darwin, John 5
Day, Melvin 63
Deardon, Basil 86, 101–3
  Sapphire 86, 87, 101–3
de Beauvoir, Simone 37, 38
de Gaulle, Charles 138, 142–3, 145
development 11–13, 126, 180, 190, 196–221
Dewan Bahasa 255, 256, 257
Dewan Bahasa dan Pustaka (House of Language and Literature) (DBP) 13, 20, 245–64
Doxiades Associates 213–15, 216, 217, 218
Drawbridge, John 62
Drayton, Richard 67
dress 8, 68, 76, 91, 94, 134, 137, 139, 140, 143, 150, 157, 161, 162, 164, 190, 199, 233
Drew, Jane 11, 97
  see also Fry, Drew, Drake & Lasdun
DuBois, W.E.B. 40, 43
Dutt, Uptal 11, 15, 16, 17, 19, 109–25
  Invincible Vietnam 19, 109–25

East African Currency Board 16, 224, 225, 226, 227
East Germany 202
Egoni, Uzo 54
Eickhoff, Martijn 7

Eisenhower, Dwight D. 136
English language 13, 32, 250–5, 257
Escobar, Arturo 198
Ethiopia 142

Fabre, Michel 36, 38
Fairbridge Memorial College (Bulawayo, Rhodesia) 160
Fanon, Frantz 16, 31, 37, 39–40, 109, 112, 123, 245, 246
  Black Skin, White Masks 31, 37, 39
  Wretched of the Earth, The 37, 69, 109
Festival of Britain (1951) 97, 181
festivals 8, 9, 13, 177, 178, 190–2
film 10, 18, 86–105, 88–91, 101–3, 149–50
fine art 10, 15, 18, 51–66, 67, 72, 78, 79, 86–105
  see also Māori art; modernism in fine art; pop art
Fosu, Kojo 183
Foucault, Michel 10, 246, 260
France 6, 14, 16, 18, 31, 32, 33, 37, 40, 41, 56, 64, 110, 112, 113, 126–7, 136, 138–40, 142, 180–1, 185–6, 189
  see also Paris
Front de Libération Nationale (FLN, Algeria) 58
Fry, Drew, Drake & Lasdun 12, 181, 203–5, 204, 214
  see also Drew, Jane; Lasdun, Denys
Fuller, Alexandra 165
Fuller, Nicola 165

Gandhi, Mohandas Karamchand 30, 112, 116
Garlake, Margaret 94, 96
Garry, Robert 126, 148
gender 7, 10–11, 90, 121–2
Geoffrey, Iqbal 92
Germany 112, 122

INDEX

Ghana 1, 9, 12, 14, 16, 19, 35, 41, 42, 44, 177–85, 186, 190, 192, 196–221, 222, 227
   Ministry of Arts and Culture 184
   see also Gold Coast
Ghana Film Corporation 184
Ghana Institute of Architects (GIA) 202
Gilroy, Paul 32, 81–2
Gold Coast 30, 36, 42–4, 179, 181, 182, 196–221
   Department of Social Welfare and Community Development 206
   Ministry of Housing 207, 210
   see also Ghana
Gold Coast Society of Architects (GCSA) 202
Gramsci, Antonio 116
Grant, Kevin 15
Gregory, Dick 76, 77, 78
Griaule, Marcel 186
Groslier, Bernard Philippe 130, 141, 143, 145
Groslier, Georges 139–40, 141, 143
Guevara, Che 109, 110, 117
Guinea 179, 180, 188
Gupta, Anal 118

Hagan, George 185
Haiti 39–40
Hall, Stuart 70, 92
Hamilton, Richard 86, 87, 97–101
   Just What Is It That Makes Today's Homes So Different, So Appealing? 86, 97–101, 103
Hanley, Pat 57, 62
Harare (Zimbabwe) 166–7
Harrison, Martin 94
Hashmi, Moloyashree 118
Hebdige, Dick 99
Heidegger, Martin 38
heritage sites 10, 19, 126–55, 182, 185
Ho Chi Min 115, 122
Hopkins, A.G. 29–30, 52

Hotere, Ralph 18, 52–66
   Algérie series 56, 58, 59
   Black Painting 60
   Black Union Jack series 62
   Human Rights series 60, 61, 62
   Polaris paintings 56, 57
   Sangro paintings 56
housing 9, 12, 16, 19, 179, 196–221
   see also architecture
Hudson, R.S. 2
Hughes, David 166
Hungary 202
Hurgronje, Snouck 246
Hurst, Brian Desmond 86
   Simba 86, 87, 88–91, 103
Husserl, Edmund 38
Hyman, James 93

Illingworth, Michael 57
immigration 2, 6, 34, 67, 88, 91, 160, 245, 247
   see also migration
India 9, 15, 54, 109–25, 127, 136, 157, 202, 203, 209, 210, 217
Indian High Commission (UK) 2
Indian languages 246, 247, 253, 257, 259
Indian People's Theatre Association (IPTA) 111
Indonesia 117, 127, 136, 246, 248
Institute of African Studies, University of Ghana 184
Institute of Arts and Culture (Ghana) 184
Institute of Contemporary Arts (ICA, UK) 12, 61, 97
Institut Fondamental d'Afrique Noire (IFAN, Mali) 185, 186
Institut National des Arts (Mali) 188
interior design 19, 186
Iraq 217
Ireland 162–3, 164, 166
Ironside, Christopher 228, 229, 231
Israel 217
Italy 202

INDEX

Jackson, Robert 209, 213
Jamaica 14, 75, 77, 78, 79
James, C.L.R. 11, 16, 33–6, 39–40, 44, 74, 75
  Black Jacobins, The 33, 43
Jayavarman VII 129–30, 147
Jervois, William 160–1, 167, 169
Johannesburg (South Africa) 170
Johnson, Lyndon 114
Johor (Malaysia) 248
Jones, Ian 169–70
Jones, Le Roi (Amiri Baraka) 74

Kabake Yekka 226
Kahn, John 255
Kaiser Inc. 213, 217
Kambuja 131, 133, 142
Katz, Jonathan 99
Keïta, Modibo 178, 180, 187–8, 189, 191
Keïta, Soundiata 188
Kenya 14, 17, 19, 87, 88–91, 165, 223, 224, 226, 228, 233–7, 238, 239, 245
Kenya African National Union (KANU) 235
Kenyatta, Jomo 233, 234, 235, 236, 237, 238
Kenyatta, Uhuru 238
Kilimanjaro 224, 226, 227
King, Martin Luther 30
Kirk Smith, Rodney 61
Kitimat (Canada) 209
Kitson, E.A. 198
Klein, Yves 62
Koenigsberger, Otto 206, 209
Konaré, Adame Bâ 192
Konaré, Alpha Oumar 187
Konate, Mamadou 180
Kouyate, Seydou Badian 188
Kpong (Ghana) 209, 213, 214
Kula, Nancy 228
Kynaston, David 94–9

Lacouture, Jean 129
Lambert, David 15, 157

Lamming, George 37, 40, 42, 69–70
landscape 90, 158, 166–71
language policy 10, 13, 20, 245–64
La Rose, John 72, 73, 74, 78
Lasdun, Denys 181
  see also Fry, Drew, Drake & Lasdun
Las Vegas (United States) 157, 168, 171
Lefebvre, Henri 102
Legêne, Susan 7
Lester, Alan 15, 157
Lévi-Strauss, Claude 32
Levine, Philippa 7, 15
literary cultures 29–50, 67–85, 109–25
  African 39–40
  American 31, 33–4, 37, 38, 39
  Caribbean 33–4, 37, 40, 68–71, 81–2
  Commonwealth 68
  French 37–9
  Indian 111–13, 115, 117–23
  Malay 245–64
  see also non-fiction; novels; poetry; theatre
London (UK) 1–3, 15, 18, 54–5, 70–1, 78, 101–3, 165, 222, 239, 256
Louis, Wm Roger 29–30, 42
Low, Gail 68

McClintock, Anne 86
McFall, David 232
MacKenzie, John 5, 86
McNamara, Robert 114
Madagascar 255
Malay language 245–64
Malaya 29, 88, 245–64
  see also Malaysia
Malayan Writers' Conference 254
Malaysia 10, 14, 29, 88, 136, 245–64
  and Malay nationalism 13, 20, 245–64
  see also Malaya

[269]

Mali 9, 13, 14, 19, 177–81, 185–92
Mansfield, Edgar 63
Māori art 15, 18, 51–66
　see also fine art; modernism, in fine art; modernism, indigenous
Marchal, Henri 139
Marchal, Sappho 139–40
Marsdan, William 256
Marson, Una 70
Marten, Lutz 228
Marxism 35, 93, 109, 111, 112, 115, 116, 129
Massey, Anne 97
material culture 2, 8–10, 13–14, 20, 60–1, 86, 90, 94–7, 99–100, 120, 122, 127, 130–9, 141–7, 149, 150, 157, 163, 164, 165, 167, 168, 170, 171–2, 177, 181, 182, 183, 184, 185, 186, 187, 188, 189, 191, 192, 196, 197, 200, 206–9, 213, 215–16, 217–18, 223–4, 228–32, 235–6, 238
　see also architecture; coin design; dress; heritage sites; housing; interior design; landscape; museums
Maxwell, Marina 78–9, 80–1
Mayer & Whittlesey 209–12, 211, 217, 218
Mercer, Kobena 53, 55, 58
Metalimport 234
Michael Karolyi Memorial Foundation 56, 58
Middlesbrough Art Gallery (UK) 56
migration 2, 6, 15, 92, 156–74, 180
　see also immigration
Minton, John 93
Mittelholzer, Edgar 70
modernism
　in architecture 12, 133–4, 141, 146, 148, 181, 198–221
　in fine art 18, 51–66, 92–3, 97–8
　indigenous 42, 52, 53–4, 63–4
Monod, Theodore 186

Montreal (Canada) 75
Moody, Ronald 92
Mount Kenya 235
Mozambique 158
Muhammad, Elijah 74
Muhavaru Volcano 226
Musée National du Mali 19, 177, 178, 185–90
Muséum d'Histoire Naturelle (France) 186
museums 1–3, 12, 14, 19, 177–95
　see also individual museums
Musgrave, Victor 62
Mutesa II, Kabaka of Buganda 226

Naipaul, V.S. 70–1
Nasir, Syed 251, 252, 253, 254
Nasser, Gamal Abdel 129
National Language Action Front (NLAF, Malaysia) 252
National Museum of Ghana 19, 177, 181–5
National Stadium (Cambodia) 141, 142, 145, 146
National Theatre (Mali) 188
Nehru, Jawaharlal 129, 201
Netherlands 6, 202, 246
Netherlands East Indies 246
　see also Indonesia
New Commonwealth Internationalism 54–5, 62–4
new towns 12, 205, 209
New York (United States) 32, 36–7, 136
New Zealand see Aotearoa New Zealand
Ngugi wa Thiong'o 247, 250, 251
Niger 186
Nigeria 1, 54, 181, 203
Nkrumah, Kwame 16, 30, 34, 35, 41, 43, 44, 178, 179, 180, 181, 183–5, 198, 200, 213, 222, 224, 225
Non-Aligned Movement 16, 129, 142, 145, 214
non-fiction 6, 8, 35, 42–4, 130, 139

INDEX

Northern Rhodesia 1, 159
  Northern Rhodesia Chamber of Mines 1
  see also Zambia
Notting Hill (London, UK) 2, 81, 91
novels 6, 8, 31, 32, 38, 69, 70, 71, 72, 118, 249
Nunoo, Richard 181, 184
Nyerere, Julius 16, 224, 228, 237

O'Brien, Gregory 62
O'Sullivan, Vincent 58
Obote, Milton 225, 226
Oguibe, Olu 54
Organisation de l'Armée Secrète (OAS, Algeria) 58
Organisation of African Unity 16
Osbourne, Milton 127–8

Padmore, George 11, 33–6, 39, 41, 44
Pakistan 217
Pan-Africanism 15, 33, 38, 40, 109, 180, 184
Paolozzi, Eduardo 93, 97
Papua New Guinea 255
Paris (France) 15, 18, 30–1, 36–42, 134, 136–7, 186
Paris Noir 37
Parti Progressiste Soudanaise (PPS) 180
Parvez, Ahmed 92
Patterson, Orlando 72
performance 8, 17, 12, 19, 78, 80, 100, 102–3, 122, 126–55, 128–9, 138, 140–1, 143, 148, n. 50 153, 157–8, 164, 191, 249
Philip, HRH Prince, Duke of Edinburgh 229
Phnom Penh (Cambodia) 133–4, 146, 141–2, 145
Picasso, Pablo 92, 97
Pioneer Youth Movement (Mali) 190
Pizer, Dorothy 11, 33–6, 41–2, 43
poetry 8, 18, 35, 37, 38, 70, 71, 72, 81, 115, 118, 148, 149, 231

Pollock, Jackson 97
Pop Art 92, 97, 100–1
  see also fine art
Portelli, Alessandro 158
Portugal 6, 157
Potter, Simon 6
Pound, Francis 61
Powell, Enoch 6, 67
Prakash, Vikramaditya 201
Presénce Africaine 37–40, 41
Princess Kossamak 11

Queen Elizabeth II 224, 227, 229, 238

race 7, 29, 30, 32, 37, 42, 45, 67, 74, 75, 82, 87, 91, 92, 96–103, 159, 163, 166–71, 210, 212, 247, 248, 254, 257, 258–9
Rajaratnam, Sinnathamby 250–1
Raman, Tunku Abdul 252, 253
Ramchand, Kenneth 70
Rassemblement Démocratique Africain (RDA) 180
Reinhardt, Ad 60, 61
Research Library on African Affairs (Ghana) 184
Rhodesia 10, 14, 19, 156–174
  see also Zimbabwe
Rhodesian Association of the USA 168
Robert Matthew, Johnson-Marshall and Partners 1
Robeson, Paul 40
Robinson, Jenny 17
Robson, Harold and Thelma 166–9
Rodney, Walter 75, 76–7
Rose, Duncan 198
Royal College of Music (UK) 101–2
Royal Khmer Ballet 136–40, 137, 147
Royal Mint (UK) 11, 224–44
  Royal Mint Advisory Committee on the Design of Coins, Medals, Seals and Decorations 229, 231, 232, 233, 239

Russia 109, 110, 112, 117, 145, 202, 117, 202
  see also Union of Soviet Socialist Republics (USSR)

Said, Edward 4
Salkey, Andrew 70, 71–2, 76, 78, 80–1
'salvage' paradigm 127, 139, 182
Samake, Sada 178, 188, 191
Sanogo, Kléna 187
Sarkar, Pabitra 112
Sartre, Jean-Paul 37–8, 69
Schokbeton 202
Schwarz, Bill 5, 16, 87, 171
Second World War 56
Selvon, Sam 70–1
Semaines de la Jeunesse (Mali) 190–2
Senegal 179, 181, 186, 188
Senghor, Léopold 38–40, 179
settler societies 51–2, 63, 69, 89, 156–174
Sewell, Vernon 88
  Wind of Change 88
Sherman, Daniel J. 6
Shohat, Ella 17
Sickert, Walter 94
Sihanouk, Norodom 11, 12, 13, 126–55, 132, 135
Sillman, Norman 233
Singapore 136, 249, 250, 251, 254, 255
Sissoko, Fily Dabo 180
Small, Richard 75, 76
Smith, Andrea L. 157
Smith, Andrew 159
Smithson, Peter and Alison 97
Smuts, Jan 6
South Africa 10, 14, 19, 52, 62, 156–74
Souza, Francis Newton 54, 62
Soviet Union *see* Union of Soviet Socialist Republics (USSR)
Spalding, Francis 99
Spivak, Gayatri Chakravorty 120

sport 133, 157, 159, 160, 180, 190
Sri Lanka 136
Stade Omnisport Modibo Keïta 188
Stam, Robert 17
Stern, Philippe 130
Straits Settlements *see* Malaysia
Sudan 188, 245
Sukarno 29, 45, 129, 136
Sutherland, Graham 93
Swanzy, Henry 68–73
Sylla, Abdoulaye 178, 181, 189, 191
Sylvester, David 93
Szumowski, George 186

Tall, Amadou 188
Tanganyika 224
  see also Tanzania
Tanzania 14, 16, 17, 19, 223, 224, 225, 226, 227–33, 237, 238, 239
Tema (Ghana) 196–221
Tema Development Corporation (TDC) 203, 217
Temps Modernes, Les 37–9, 41
theatre 8, 9, 19, 78–81, 109–25, 147, 188, 228
Third Congress of Malay Language and Literature 249
Thomas, Cecil 225
Thomas de la Rue 224, 227, 228, 234
Tito, Josep Broz 129, 145
Togo 181
Touré, Samoury 188
Touré, Sekou 179, 180
transnationalism
  of cultures of decolonisation 3, 8, 12, 14–18, 19, 20, 30, 52, 53, 68, 109–10, 114, 116–17, 119, 122, 201, 202
Trentmann, Frank 15
Tricontinental Conference of Solidarity of the Peoples of Africa, Asia and Latin America 110, 122

INDEX

Trinidad 14, 39, 75,
Turnbull, William 56

Uganda 14, 20, 223, 224–7, 228, 237, 239
  Ministry of Finance 22
Uganda People's Congress 226
Union of Soviet Socialist Republics (USSR) 33, 41, 44, 136, 198
  see also Russia
Union Soudanaise 180
United Arab Republic 136
United Kingdom 2, 5, 6, 10, 11, 13, 14, 18, 20, 29, 30, 40, 52, 55, 56, 57, 60, 62, 63, 67, 68, 69, 70, 71, 72, 73, 74, 75, 76, 78, 79, 80, 81, 82, 86–105, 156, 157, 158, 159, 160, 161, 162, 163, 164, 165, 166, 169, 171, 179, 180, 181, 182, 198, 200, 202, 203, 205, 209, 213, 222, 224, 227, 229, 231, 232, 234, 235, 239, 240, 247, 251, 256
  Treasury 237
  see also British colonialism; London
United Nations (UN) 16, 201, 202
United Nations Technical Assistance Administration (UNTAA) 197, 202–3, 205–9, 218
United Negro Improvement Association 32
United States of America 4, 14, 18, 29–33, 38, 60, 62, 74–5, 93, 99–101, 110, 113–25, 134, 158, 166, 171, 198, 202
  Technical Assistance Programme (Four Point Programme) 213
University of Calcutta 113
University of Ghana 202
University of Malaya (UM) 251
US Corps of Engineers 209
USSR *see* Union of Soviet Socialist Republics

Vann Molyvann 133–4, 143, 145, 146
Vence (France) 56
Vietnam 9, 14, 15, 17, 19, 29, 109, 110, 112, 113–16
Volta Aluminium Company (Valco) 198
Volta River Project (VRP) 196–221, 199
von Eschen, Penny 32

Wainwright, Leon 64
Wallerstein, Emmanuel 218
Ward, Stuart 5, 86, 87
Watt, Harry 88, 91
Webb, Constance 11, 33–6
Webster, Wendy 6, 88–9
Werbner, Richard 188
West African Aluminium Company 198
West African Students Union (London, UK) 179
West Indian Students' Centre (London, UK) 72, 73, 74, 75–6, 77, 79
Whitechapel Art Gallery (London, UK) 62, 98
whiteness 30, 31, 90, 91, 92, 96, 100, 101, 102
Wilkinson, R.J. 250
Williams, Aubrey 54, 92
Williams, Eric 39, 42, 43, 75
Winstedt, R.O. 250
Woollacott, Angela 166
World Bank 114, 198, 201
Wright, Ellen 11, 33–6
Wright, Richard 9, 11, 16, 18, 29–50
  Black Boy 37, 39
  Black Power 42, 44
  Colour Curtain, The 9, 42
  Native Son 33, 39
  White Man, Listen! 31, 42

X, Malcolm 74

Young, Lola 88, 91
Young, Robert 110
Young Pioneers (Ghana) 190
Yugoslavia 136, 145

Zambia 159, 165

see also Northern Rhodesia
Zanzibar 224
Zimbabwe 14, 19, 156, 159, 160, 164, 171, 245
see also Rhodesia

EU authorised representative for GPSR:
Easy Access System Europe, Mustamäe tee 50,
10621 Tallinn, Estonia
gpsr.requests@easproject.com

www.ingramcontent.com/pod-product-compliance
Lightning Source LLC
Chambersburg PA
CBHW071404300426
44114CB00016B/2178